Substance Abuse Counseling

THEORY AND PRACTICE

PATRICIA STEVENS-SMITH
University of Colorado

ROBERT L. SMITH
University of Colorado

Merrill,
an imprint of Prentice Hall
Upper Saddle River, New Jersey   *Columbus, Ohio*

Library of Congress Cataloging-in-Publication Data

Smith, Robert L. (Robert Leonard)
    Substance abuse counseling/Robert L. Smith, Patricia Stevens-Smith.
       p.   cm.
    Includes bibliographical references and index.
    ISBN 0-02-412532-6
    1. Substance abuse—Treatment. 2. Substance abuse—Patients—Counseling of.   I.
Stevens-Smith, Patricia. II. Title.
  RC564.S624   1998
  362.29′186—dc21   97-5057
                                   CIP

Cover art: Dave Cutler Studio, Inc./SIS
Editor: Kevin M. Davis
Production Editor: Mary M. Irvin
Design Coordinator: Julia Zonneveld Van Hook
Text Designer: Mia Saunders
Cover Designer: Raymond Hummons
Production Manager: Pamela D. Bennett
Electronic Text Management: Marilyn Wilson Phelps, Matthew Williams, Karen L. Bretz,
    Tracey B. Ward
Director of Marketing: Kevin Flanagan
Advertising/Marketing Coordinator: Julie Shough

This book was set in Galliard by Prentice-Hall, Inc., and was printed and bound by R. R.
Donnelley & Sons Company. The cover was printed by Phoenix Color Corp.

Prentice-Hall International (UK) Limited, *London*
Prentice-Hall of Australia Pty. Limited, *Sydney*
Prentice-Hall of Canada, Inc., *Toronto*
Prentice-Hall Hispanoamericana, S. A., *Mexico*
Prentice-Hall of India Private Limited, *New Delhi*
Prentice-Hall of Japan, Inc., *Tokyo*
Simon & Schuster Asia Pte. Ltd., *Singapore*
Editora Prentice-Hall do Brasil, Ltda., *Rio de Janeiro*

Preface

Substance abuse ranks as one of the major public health issues in today's society. The use and abuse of substances cross gender, socioeconomic levels, ethnicity, age, religion, profession, geography, and most dimensions of human existence and background. Only recently have comprehensive programs at undergraduate and graduate levels been developed to systematically study substance abuse and subsequent treatment modalities. This book was written out of a personal and professional need to educate clinicians about substance abuse. The authors believe that everyone during their lifetime will be touched by substance abuse or addiction. We further agree that clinicians should be adequately trained to recognize the enormity of this problem, how to assess it, and ultimately how to treat the individuals and families who come to them for assistance. This text helps both the beginning general clinician as well as the beginning substance abuse counselor. It is meant to serve as the major text for substance abuse classes. It is not intended to replace basic counseling theory and techniques texts and coursework.

Contributors to this text have extensive backgrounds in substance abuse work as well as a special knowledge in a particular segment of the field. Space and time limitations prevented us from examining all of the issues in the field—for example, public policy, working in a school setting, substance abuse in the workplace, and a more in-depth study of the dual diagnosis issues of mental illness and substance abuse.

This textbook takes the reader through the process of working with substance-abusing clients. Chapters build on each other but could also be used independently as resource information. Chapter One provides the foundation for the text by providing a history of drug use, basic terminology, references to subsequent chapters, and case studies that are used throughout the text. Understanding the etiology and theories is necessary for all professionals working in this field. Chapter Two provides this foundation and brings theory into reality through the case applications. Chapter Three examines major drugs and their addictive properties and provides essential knowledge for anyone entering this field. The beginning of treatment starts with Chapter Four by emphasizing assessment and diagnosis, again using cases from earlier chapters to understand assessment and diagnosis on a more applied basis.

Treatment is emphasized in Chapters Five and Six. First treatment settings are discussed, followed by a closer look at treatment modalities most often used alone or with other methods in treating substance abuse clients. Relapse is seen as an element of the treatment process and is the focus for Chapter Seven, again using case examples. Chapters Eight and Nine provide an in-depth analysis of substance abuse prevention and intervention with selected cultures and specific groups: men, women, adolescents, African Americans, American Indians, Asian Americans, Hispanics, and the elderly. Chapter Ten presents a synopsis of research findings as well as contemporary issues in the field that are currently being studied.

Because it was impossible to portray a "real" client, three case histories were developed and used at the end of selected chapters to offer a sense of the practical application of the information in each chapter. The reader may notice some disagreement among contributors in this text. These differences were left intentionally as a reflection of the state of the field itself as well as a reflection of the variety of ways a problem can be explained and solved. Therefore, we hope that these differences will prove of immense value as you study this subject.

This text evolved after a detailed survey was conducted with professors across the country who teach in the areas of substance abuse counseling, addictions, and chemical dependency. The text was based on responses from this group, and is organized in a manner suggested by them. Special thanks and appreciation go to the professors and their institutions who helped shape this text. And we appreciate the insights and comments from the reviewers of our manuscript: David Couch, Southwest Texas State University; J. Scott Hinkle, University of North Carolina-Greensboro; Gerald A. Juhnke, University of North Carolina-Greensboro; Richard C. Page, University of Georgia; Michael J. Taleff, Pennsylvania State University; R. Craig Williams, Northern Illinois University.

We wish to thank our contributors for their effort and willingness to make numerous and often rapid revisions of this textbook. Also, we express appreciation to each of the students who read and critiqued this text before publication for their time, energy, and honesty. We would also like to thank Kevin Davis for his patience and perseverance with us. And last, but certainly not least, we must thank all our family and friends who have been supportive throughout this endeavor.

About the Authors

Dr. Patricia Stevens-Smith is the director of the Marriage and Family Training Program at the University of Colorado at Denver. She is currently the chair of the Ethics Committee for the International Association of Marriage and Family Counselors, and the past co-chair of the Women's Mentoring and Interest Network of the Association for Counselor Education and Supervision. Dr. Stevens-Smith is a clinical member and approved supervisor with the American Association for Marriage and Family Therapy and a Certified Family Therapist. She is also the recent recipient of a Fulbright Scholarship and will be traveling to Malaysia to assist the University there in establishing their training program.

Dr. Stevens-Smith has written and presented extensively at the local, regional, national, and international levels in the areas of marriage and family training, substance abuse, gender issues, and ethical and legal issues in marriage and family therapy. She is an approved presenter with the State of Colorado for their Jurisprudence Workshops, which are required for licensure.

Robert L. Smith is chair of the Counseling Psychology and Counselor Education Division at the University of Colorado at Denver. He completed his Ph.D. at the University of Michigan. As a licensed psychologist, he has worked as a private practitioner and has taught and administered graduate-level courses. He is the author of three books and more than fifty professional articles in counseling and family therapy and in the field of mental health. He is the Executive Director of the International Association of Family Counseling, and founder of the National Academy for Certified Family Therapists. Dr. Smith's professional research interests include the efficacy of treatment modalities in individual psychotherapy, family therapy, and substance abuse counseling.

Dr. Linda Chamberlain is a psychologist in private practice in Denver, Colorado. She teaches graduate courses in substance abuse treatment at the University of Denver and the University of Colorado at Denver. Dr. Chamberlain has co-authored a book titled "Strange Attractors: Chaos, Complexity, and the Art of Family Therapy" (1997, Wiley) and edited a book titled *Clinical Chaos* (1997, Taylor & Francis). In addition to working in the area of drug and alcohol addictions, Dr. Chamberlain is a nationally certified counselor and supervisor for the treatment of compulsive gambling and serves on the board of the Colorado Council on Compulsive Gambling. She is currently writing a text with Dr. William McCown on the assessment and treatment of compulsive gambling, titled *All Bets Are Off.*

Sharon H. Erickson is assistant professor in health and human development and director of the Human Development Clinic at Montana State University. She has 20 years of clinical experience in counseling and has conducted research on alcoholics and adult children of alcoholics, and also taught classes for offenders of driving under the influence with Mississippi State University. She has held adjunct teaching appointments at Mississippi University for Women and St. Mary's University.

A Registered Nurse, Erickson worked as a pediatric and school nurse prior to receiving her degrees in mental health management. She is also a National Certified Counselor, Certified Clinical Mental Health Counselor, Certified Group Psychotherapist, and is a clinical member and approved supervisor in the American Association for Marriage and Family Therapy. She is a Licensed Professional Counselor in Montana and Mississippi and a Licensed Marriage and Family Therapist in Texas. She is a former board member of the Mississippi Association for Marriage and Family Therapy. She received her degrees from Montana State University, Chapman University, and Mississippi State University.

Dr. Cynthia L. Jew is a Licensed Psychologist and Senior Instructor at the University of Colorado at Denver. She is currently teaching courses in the Counseling and School Psychology programs at the University of Colorado at Denver. Her areas of research and interest include assessment and diagnosis of psychiatric disorders and the treatment of children within the family context. Her current line of research is in the development/validation of a measure of resiliency and intervention-based treatment aimed at increasing resiliency.

Christine Manfrin, MA, CACIII, is a clinician with extensive experience in the field. She is a certified addictions counselor as well as a lecturer and trainer in the substance abuse field.

Dr. John Joseph Peregoy is a member of the Salish and Kootenai Tribes of Montana (Flathead). He has more than 20 years of experience in diversity issues. Dr. Peregoy sits on the Executive Board of Directors for the Indian Alcoholism Counseling and Recovery House Program of Salt Lake City Treatment Facility and Health Care Clinic. He currently teaches in the Counselor Education Program at the University of Utah. His specialty area is in multicultural counseling. Research interests include minority identity development, issues in American Indian/Alaskan Native mental health, ethnic/minority experiences in the education system (K-12) and how people seek assistance when in crises (help-seeking pathways). He received his doctorate in Counselor Education from Syracuse University.

Jim Porter, MA, MAC, NCACII, CACIII, is a nationally known speaker and counselor with more than 20 years of experience in the field of addictive disorders. He is co-owner and program director of a licensed outpatient treatment center in Lakewood, Colorado, and is founder of The Institute for Self-Discovery, which offers consultant/educational services for various community sectors that include judicial, employee assistance programs and school systems. Jim conducts over 150 lectures and training seminars to public as well as professional groups on an annual basis.

Dr. Connie Schliebner is an assistant professor in the Department of Counseling at Idaho State University. She holds a doctorate from Syracuse University in Counselor Education, with a concentration in Multicultural Counseling. She also holds a master's degree in secondary school counseling and a bachelor's degree in elementary education. She has taught multicultural counseling for the past six years and has presented at international, national, regional, and state conferences. The main focus of her research and publications has been on providing culturally appropriate and sensitive counseling to ethnic and nonethnic minorities.

Brief Contents

Contents

CHAPTER 2

ETIOLOGICAL THEORIES OF SUBSTANCE ABUSE 25

CHAPTER 3

THE MAJOR DRUGS OF ABUSE AND THEIR ADDICTIVE PROPERTIES 65

CHAPTER 4

ASSESSMENT AND DIAGNOSIS 97

CHAPTER 5

TREATMENT SETTINGS   135

CHAPTER 6

TREATMENT MODALITIES IN SUBSTANCE ABUSE 169

CHAPTER 7

WORKING WITH SELECTED POPULATIONS: TREATMENT ISSUES AND CHARACTERISTICS 193

CHAPTER 8

WORKING WITH DIVERSE CULTURES: TREATMENT ISSUES AND CHARACTERISTICS

CHAPTER 9

CHAPTER 10

Introduction to Substance Abuse Counseling

Patricia Stevens-Smith, PhD

The use of mind- or mood-altering drugs has been described since the beginning of written history. A historical review shows that the use of substances goes back as far as one wants to explore. Every culture used a drug or drugs of choice for a variety of reasons. In tribal societies, mind-altering drugs were commonly used in religious ceremonies and for healing many illnesses. Alcohol consumption was indicated as early as the paleolithic times of the Stone Age culture with the discovery that drinking the juice of fermented berries created a pleasant feeling.

A historical perspective of humankind's use of substances for both analgesic and mind-altering purposes and the multidimensional functions that drugs have played throughout history provide a backdrop for understanding today's substance abuse issues and ensuing ramifications. History may also provide some rationale for the methods of treatment used in the past 50 years.

Substance misuse, abuse, and addiction are multifaceted problems that vary across cultures and families, as well as from individual to individual. No single treatment has evolved for health-distressed individuals experiencing the consequences of substance abuse. Treatment approaches for substance abusers and their families have not been clearly articulated. Research does not support the efficacy of most approaches.

All counselors, whether they work in the field of substance abuse counseling or in the general field of psychotherapy, will encounter many issues of substance abuse with their clients. Considering the economic costs and the price in human suffering, it is imperative that counselors be trained in all aspects of substance abuse intervention and prevention. It is essential that all mental health professionals understand the process of abuse and addiction, the etiology of addiction, and the treatment modalities that are considered the most effective. It is also important that the professional be aware of the psychological and physiological effects of drugs on the human brain and thereby on human behavior. *Substance Abuse Counseling* has been written to guide mental health professionals in their recognition, assessment, and treatment of substance abuse and dependency in their clients.

For consistency throughout this book, we have used the terms *substance abuse* and *substance dependency* whenever possible. These terms coincide with the Diagnostic and Statistical Manual of Mental Disorders-IV (DSM-IV) definitions and are therefore more measurable and consentually defined. We are aware that there are a variety of terms used in the profession including *chemical addiction, chemical dependency, drug abuse, addiction,* and *AOD* (alcohol and other drugs). Our use of the terms *substance abuse* and *dependency* in no way implies that other terms do not have validity; it is merely a way to develop consistency of terminology and meaning throughout the text.

The authors also have used the term *substance* to include alcohol, nicotine, caffeine, prescription drugs, and illegal drugs. We may, however, at times refer to alcohol and other drugs when the distinction is necessary to maintain clarity. It is, of course, relevant to acknowledge that alcohol, nicotine, and caffeine are legal and societally accepted drugs. This lends a different dynamic to the use, abuse, and even dependency issues related to these substances that does not exist for other illegal drugs. It is imperative, however, to acknowledge also that these drugs, particularly nicotine, represent a major threat to physical as well as psychological health.

A BRIEF HISTORY OF DRUG USE

Alcohol

It has been documented that early cave dwellers drank the juice of mashed berries that had been exposed to airborne yeast. When they found that the juice produced pleasant feelings and reduced discomfort, they began to produce this crude wine intentionally (Ray & Ksir, 1990). By the neolithic age, about 8000 B.C. (or almost 10,000 years ago), liquor in the form of beer, wine, or mead was abundant. Egyptian records dating back to 300 B.C. give testimony to beer production. Homer's *Iliad* and *Odyssey* both discussed drinking wine, while Egypt as well as Rome had gods or goddesses of wine. The Bible has many references to the use of wine in sacrificial ritual. Noah was perhaps the first recorded inebriate. In the tenth century the process of distillation was discovered by an Arabian physician, Phazes, who was looking to release the "spirit of the wine" (Kinney & Leaton, 1991).

A 4,000-year-old Persian legend tells about the discovery of wine. A king had vats of grapes stored, some of which developed a sour liquid at bottom. The king labeled these vats *poison* but kept them for future use. One lady of the court was prone to severe headaches which no one could remedy. Her pain was so severe that she decided to kill herself. She knew of the "deadly" grape juice, went to the storage area, and drank the poison. Needless to say, the lady didn't die, but in fact found relief. She continued to drink the "poison" and then confessed to the king.

By the Middle Ages, alcohol was used in all ceremonies from births and marriages to the crowning of kings. Monasteries offered wine to weary travelers who stopped for rest and safety. It was also the basic medicine for all human ailments. In Europe, it was known as the "water of life."

In addition to being used in rituals and for its convivial effect, alcohol has also been used to induce sleep and reduce pain. By 1000 A.D. Italian winegrowers were distilling wine for medicinal purposes. Alcohol has been used as an antiseptic, an anesthetic, and in combinations of salves and tonics. It was one of the few chemicals that was consistently available for physicians to use.

European settlers brought alcoholic beverages in the form of wine, rum, and beer to the New World. The *Mayflower's* log reports, "We could not take time for further search or consideration, our victuals having been much spent, especially our bere" (as cited in Kinney & Leaton, 1991). Spanish missionaries brought grapevines to California before the United States was a nation, and the Dutch opened the first distillery on Staten Island in 1640. In 1790 a federal law was passed allowing each soldier to receive a daily ration of one-fourth pint of brandy, rum, or whiskey.

This brief history of alcohol use indicates the strong presence of alcohol in human history from before written records were kept. It has been used in every aspect of our lives—social, medicinal, religious. The effect of this history cannot be ignored.

Cocaine

Like alcohol, coca has been around for thousands of years. But the active agent, cocaine, was not isolated until 1857. Cocaine was added to wine and tonics in the mid-nineteenth century as well as to snuff, advertised as a cure for asthma and hay fever. Freud experimented with cocaine as a cure for depression, digestive disorders, hysteria, and syphilis. He also recommended cocaine to alleviate withdrawal from alcohol and morphine addiction. Freud himself used cocaine daily for a period of time. However, when he became aware of the addictive effects, he stopped using it for himself and his patients. An American John Pemberton created a medicine that contained cocaine and caffeine. He advertised this product as an "intellectual beverage" or "brain tonic." This product, later known as Coca-Cola, contained about 60 mg of cocaine in an 8 ounce serving until 1903, when it was voluntarily removed (Louis & Yagyian, 1980).

In the twentieth century, cocaine has grown in popularity as it decreased in cost; in recent years it has become available in the intensified form of "crack." The 1995 National Household Survey on Drug Abuse indicates an estimated 1.5 million current cocaine users (defined as having used once in the past month), with 0.3% (or more than half a million) of the U.S. population estimated to be frequent users (defined as having used more than 51 days in the past year). Sixty percent of cocaine users are between the ages of 18 and 34 (Substance Abuse and Mental Health Services Administration, 1995).

Marijuana

Marijuana has been used recreationally and medicinally for centuries. The earliest account of its use is in China in 2737 B.C. (Scaros, Westra, & Barone, 1990). It has been the subject of controversy since its beginnings.

In Europe, in the mid-nineteenth century, cannabis was used extensively by the French romantic literary movement, and through writings, American writers became aware of the euphoric attributes of the drug. Although knowledge of its existence was almost ignored, the primary interest in this drug has been for its euphoric effects. With the beginning of Prohibition, individual use increased as a substitute for alcohol. After Prohibition, its use declined until the 1960s, when it gains significantly in popularity along with LSD and "speed."

It was used as an analgesic, a hypnotic, and an anticonvulsant as well as an anti-nausea drug for individuals undergoing chemotherapy for cancer treatment (Jaffe, 1990).

Marijuana is now the fourth most commonly used drug, after nicotine, caffeine, and alcohol. In 1988 *Playboy* magazine reported that the Asthma and Allergy Foundation had examined air samples in Los Angeles. Nearly 40% of the pollen came from marijuana plants being grown in the area.

Opioids

As early as 1500 B.C. opium was used to quiet crying children. In 129-199 A.D. there are reports of opium cakes being sold in the streets of Rome. In 1729 China, faced with a growing number of opium addicts, found it necessary to outlaw opium smoking. Morphine, a derivative of opium, was freely used in the Civil War and in other wars to relieve pain as well as dysentery. The resulting addiction became known as "soldier's disease." In the last half of the 19th century a wave of opiate abuse hit the United States. The drug was brought in by Chinese laborers who came to work on the railroads. At this time morphine could still be obtained without a prescription and was thought to be nonaddictive.

U.S. statistics on opium imports weren't kept until the mid-1840s. Domestic use increased until the 1890s, when the annual importation of crude opium was half a million pounds (Terry & Pellens, 1928).

Amphetamines

Amphetamines were discovered in 1887 and used in World War II by U.S., British, German, and Japanese soldiers for energy, alertness, and stamina. After the war, amphetamines were prescribed for depression, weight loss, and to heighten one's capacity for work. Soon it was realized that these capsules could be broken open and their contents injected into the body with a needle. Amphetamines also replaced high-priced cocaine. By 1970, 8% of all prescriptions were for some form of amphetamines.

Hallucinogens

Hallucinogens have been around for 3,500 years. Central American Indian cultures used hallucinogenic mushrooms in religious ceremonies. When the New World was discovered, Spanish priests, in an effort to "civilize" the Indians, tried to eliminate the use of the "sacred mushrooms." In 1938 the active ingredient that caused hallucinations was isolated by a Swiss chemist. He was studying a particular fungus in bread that appeared to create hallucinations. The substance he synthesized during this research was LSD (d-lysergic acid diethylamide). Between 1950 and the mid-1970s LSD was well-researched by the government, in the hopes that LSD could be used to view the psychotic mind and the subconscious mind. LSD was used in the treatment of alcoholism, cancer, and schizophrenia. It was also one of the drugs of choice during the 1960s cultural revolution of youth in the United States.

Tobacco

Tobacco was being used by the Indians in the New World more than 2,000 years ago. The use of tobacco was carried across the Atlantic by sailors who had taken up the habit. Smoking became quite popular in Europe and Asia, but faced harsh opposition from the church and the government. Public smoking was punishable by death in Germany and by castration in Russia. In China and Turkey, smokers were put to death (Berger & Dunn, 1982). Despite this early response, people continued to smoke and eventually were at least moderately accepted into society.

With the Industrial Age came the invention of machinery to make the cigarette, a smaller, less expensive, neater way to smoke (Doweiko, 1993, p. 154) making the price affordable to almost everyone. Laws were passed that allowed the decrease in price and after 1910 public health officials began to campaign against chewing tobacco and for smoking tobacco. Smokers also realized that, unlike cigars, cigarette smoke could be inhaled, entering the lungs and the bloodstream (Jaffe, 1990). A few hours of smoking are all that is needed for tolerance to develop. The body immediately begins to adapt to protect itself from the toxins found in tobacco. This results in a rapid development of the need to smoke to stay "normal" (Inaba & Cohen, 1991).

Over time the view of smoking has taken various forms. Early in its use, tobacco was seen as medicinal. In recent history, smoking has been seen as sophisticated. Currently, the view of tobacco use has shifted again. The highly addictive quality of nicotine was acknowledged as a health hazard by the Surgeon General of the United States in his 1964 report on tobacco. In his report, the Surgeon General outlined the various problems that could be related to, or caused by, smoking. Since that report, the relationship between smoking and cancer has continued to be researched and on the whole, is substantiated.

This information has required individuals to rethink their position on cigarette smoking. Many cities now ban smoking in public buildings. The number of smokers has declined since that report, but an estimated 61 million people in the United States, or 29% of the population age 12 and above, continue to smoke regularly, and

6.9 million people use smokeless tobacco. An alarming 4.5 million of our children, ages 12–17, smoke regularly (SAMHSA, 1995).

Caffeine

The legend of the initial caffeine use lies with a goatherder in Arabia about 1,000 years ago, who observed energetic behavior in his goats. He noticed that this happened after they ate the berries of a particular bush. So he tried the berries himself and liked the effect. Usage spread from Arabia to China and Europe. As more easily ingested versions became available, such as coffee, usage increased.

Tea was first mentioned in writing in 350 A.D., but is believed to have been available in China as early as 2737 B.C. Tea came to Europe in 1600 A.D.

Both tea and coffee have had their advocates and detractors throughout history, with debates about usage. Whether it should be categorized as a "drug" comparable to alcohol or opioids continues to be debated (Greden & Walters, 1992).

In low doses, caffeine is a mild stimulant that dissipates drowsiness or fatigue, speeds up the heart rate, raises blood pressure, and irritates the stomach. Tolerance and withdrawal are associated with long term use. Of the 100 million coffee drinkers in the United States, 20% to 30% drink five to seven cups a day. Some researchers report overdose and lethality at 1 g (Inaba & Cohen, 1991). An average cup of coffee contains 85–100 mg of caffeine and cola beverages contain 50–100 mg per 12 ounces. Chocolate has about 25 mg per ounce.

This brief overview of the use of drugs indicates that the desire or need to alter one's consciousness has always been an element of the human experience. However, with the beginning of the 1960s the use of substances, particularly in the United States, became much more widespread. Use and abuse of drugs developed into addiction on a national scale. In the 1980s process addictions such as eating disorders, gambling, shopping, and relationship addictions became prominent. These process addictions are often seen in combination with substance abuse or addiction.

SOCIETAL COSTS AND PATTERNS OF USE

In a 1990 National Institute on Drug Abuse survey, 85% of the households surveyed said they had used alcohol in their lifetime, while 53% said they had used alcohol within the past month. In 1992, nearly 13.8 million (more than 7% of the population) had problems with drinking, including 8.1 million who are alcoholic (National Institute of Alcohol Abuse and Alcoholism, 1994). It is estimated that about 5.5 million people, more than 2% of the population, need treatment for drug abuse (Gerstein & Harwood, 1990).

From 1985 to 1990 the cost of alcoholism and alcohol-related problems rose 40% to $98.6 billion (National Institute of Alcohol Abuse and Alcoholism, 1993) and the cost of other drug use to $66.9 billion with tobacco costing society $72 billion (See Figure 1.1). These costs were broken down into three categories: (1) expenditures of medical treatment (a large portion is for the many medical consequences of alcohol and other drug consumption; the reminder is for treatment of the actual alcohol and drug abuse and dependence), (2) the lost productivity that results from workers' abuse of drugs and alcohol, and (3) the losses to society from premature deaths. (Rice & Kelman, 1989).

Two areas not included in this cost are (1) costs involving the criminal justice system, social welfare administration and (2) property losses from alcohol-related motor vehicle crashes, and lost productivity of the victims of alcohol- and drug-related crime and individuals imprisoned as a consequence of alcohol- and drug-related crime. The inclusion of these categories creates a total cost to society of $237.5 billion for abuse. (Statistical Abstracts of the U.S. Department of Commerce, 1992) (See Figure 1.2). The relationship between drug use and criminal activity is high. Thirty-five percent of state prison inmates report being under the influence when they committed their crimes. "Of those sentenced to prison for robbery, burglary, larceny, or a drug offense, half were daily users and about 40% were under the influence of an illegal drug at the time they committed the crime" (Bureau of Justice, 1986, p. 2).

One in four or approximately 56 million Americans are addicted to nicotine (Centers for Disease Control, 1991; Inaba & Cohen, 1991). An estimated 434,000 people die each year from cigarette smoking (CDC, 1991). According to the American Cancer Society (1990), 83% of all lung cancer and one-third of all cancer is connected to cigarette use. Smoking significantly increases the risk of stroke in men

FIGURE 1.1   The Economic Effect of Substance Abuse

The total costs of substance abuse[1] to society are $237.5 billion— more than the amount spent for all K-12 school education in the United States in 1990.[2]

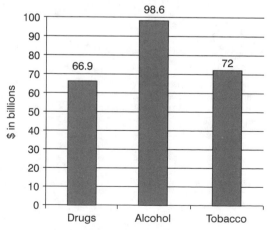

Costs of substance abuse to society

[1] The monetary burden of medical resources, loss of productivity, motor vehicle crashes, and criminal activity; 1990 estimates from *Substance Abuse*, Robert Wood Johnson Foundation, 1993.

[2] *Statistical Abstract of the United States*, U.S. Department of Commerce, 1992.

(Klag & Whelton, 1987). Women who smoke are at risk for "invasive cervical cancer, miscarriages, early menopause, osteoporosis, among other disorders" (University of California, Berkeley, 1990, p. 7), and lung cancer has surpassed breast cancer as the leading cancer-related death in women (Doweiko, 1993).

According to preliminary estimates from the 1993 NIDA National Household Survey on Drug Abuse, 11.7 million people have used illicit drugs, with 5.6% having used in the past month. The most commonly used illicit drug is marijuana, used by about 77% of users. About 103 million people older than 12 had used alcohol in the past month, 50 million smoke cigarettes, and 6.1 million are current users of smokeless tobacco (Substance Abuse and Mental Health Services Administration, 1994). One in 35 Americans older than 12 abuses illicit drugs (Institute of Medicine, 1990). By age 16, 1 in 3 teen-agers has been approached to buy or use drugs; as many as 4 in 10 school children have said that drugs were being sold in their schools; by age 18, more than 1 in 5 teens has used drugs; and 1 in 10 high school seniors has used cocaine at least once (Gallup Poll, 1989; National Institute on Drug Abuse, 1990). Each year more than 6,000 Americans die prematurely due to drug abuse. Economically, each death results in depriving the United States of more than $400,000—the average individual lifetime contribution to national productivity (National Institute on Drug Abuse, 1991).

Research shows that 50% of the patients seen in emergency rooms are there either directly or indirectly because of substance abuse (Evans & Sullivan, 1990). In 1992 an estimated 433,000 people received emergency room treatment for drug-related episodes (Substance Abuse and Mental Health Services Administration, 1993). Substance abuse plays a part in one-third to one-half of the patients seen in psychiatric emergencies (Evans & Sullivan, 1990; Galanter, Castaneda, & Ferman, 1988). The economic cost of substance abuse is more than 2.5 times the cost of all

FIGURE 1.2   The Costs of Substance Abuse

Note: From Statistical Abstract of the United States, Tables No. 211 and 1204, U.S. Department of Commerce, 1992.

• Private construction of residential buildings cost $183 billion.

• All elementary and secondary school education cost $220 billion.

• Substance abuse cost $237.5 billion.

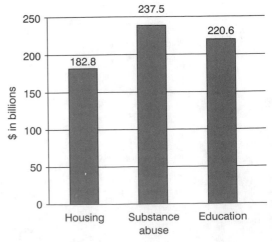

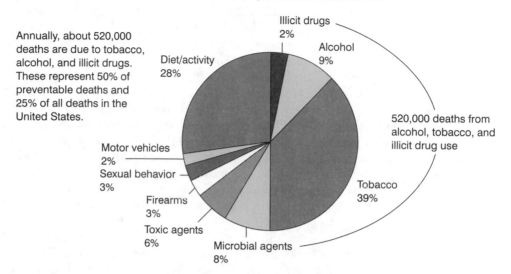

FIGURE 1.3   Is Substance Abuse a Serious Health Problem?

Note: From "Actual Causes of Death in the United States" by J. M. McGinnis, November 10, 1993, *Journal of the American Medical Association.*

other forms of mental illness combined (Group for the Advancement of Psychiatry, 1991) (See Figure 1.3).

The relationship between substance abuse and suicide is well known. About 25% of the successful suicides in any given year are alcoholics (Hyman, 1988). Further, more than 60% of the attempted suicides can be traced, either directly or indirectly, to alcoholism (Beasley, 1987). Additionally, the research shows that some classes of drugs, particularly amphetamines and cocaine, cause suicidal depression after prolonged use.

Minorities are disproportionately represented in these numbers. African Americans represented 29.6% of all deaths related to drugs in 1988. The annual homicide rate for young African American males was five to eight times higher than for young white males, with many of these homicides being drug-related. Also, although the Hispanic population in general has no significantly higher usage than any other population, young Hispanic males tend to have a higher lifetime alcohol and drug use pattern. Within this subgroup, Puerto Ricans tend to have the highest reported cocaine usage of any group.

THE ETIOLOGY OF DRUG USE

As documented by the involvement of human beings with drugs throughout history, drug use is a part of human behavior. As such, it functions by the rule of human behavior. Human behavior, in general, persists when it increases an individual's pleasure or decreases an individual's discomfort. Drugs, then, are used to achieve one of these purposes.

A number of theories are related to the etiology of substance abuse, factors that perpetuate this abuse, and influence methods of treatment. These are discussed at length in Chapter Two. Until recently, substance abuse etiology was viewed from opposite polarities, somewhat akin to the nature/nurture argument. The first model is the disease concept, which sees addiction as a progressive, terminal disease over which the individual has no control as long as the use continues. Treatment aligned with this model emphasizes the biological implications of addiction and requires complete abstinence. The second model is a social learning systems model that regards substance abuse as a learned coping behavior that is regulated and maintained by interacting systems including the family and society. These systems influence the individual in covert and overt ways. Abstinence is preferential in this model, also, but not a necessity.

A third model, the biopsychosocial model has emerged as a holistic way to examine the unproductive behavior of abuse and addiction. This model incorporates all aspects of the individual's life and examines the interactive influences of the physical, emotional, familial, and societal on a person's growth and development. This model allows for the effects of each of these areas individually and collectively in maintaining (as well as treating) abuse and addiction.

Evidence of genetic inclination to addiction certainly exists, as well as evidence supporting addiction as a learned behavior. Some authors believe the only way to prevent drug abuse is for the individual never to come into contact with the drug. Seever (1968) believes the powerful immediate reinforcement achieved by the use of drugs, if offered freely to the populations, would be disastrous. Today this argument continues as society debates the consequences/benefits of legalization of drugs—one contention is that legalization would dramatically decrease drug use, while the other side argues Seever's point of 30 years ago. Many believe that abuse and addiction are a combination of nature and nurture and that the "frightening part of heredity and environment is that . . . parents provide both" (Milkman & Sunderwirth, 1987, p. 14).

Becoming acquainted with these different theories and determining your professional position on these theories is necessary to clinically developing a treatment plan for working with this population.

PHYSIOLOGY, DRUGS, AND THE BRAIN

The discovery of enkephalins in 1974 by John Hughes and Hans Kosterlitz introduced a new dimension to the understanding of human behavior and the physiological aspect of drug use. These enkephalins and related components, endorphines, are naturally produced pain-killing molecules in the brain. Alcohol and opiates bear strong molecular resemblance to these neurotransmitters in the brain and may fool the brain. Drugs such as cocaine, caffeine, and other stimulants also mimic the structure of other neurotransmitters, creating an increased metabolism or a false "high" in the brain.

Chapter Three describes the different drugs of use and abuse and details the effect these drugs have on the central nervous system and the brain. This chapter also gives an overview of how the brain functions and the effect that different drugs have on that functioning. No matter which theory of etiology one believes, with today's medical technology, it is impossible to ignore the chemical effects that any drug has on the brain's functioning. These chemical effects must be considered in developing treatment alternatives.

It is also important to understand the various routes by which a drug can be delivered into the human body. Different routes create different problems and different "highs." A drug can be delivered into the body (1) by mouth, (2) through inhalation, (3), through injection, (4) through contact absorption, and (5) through "snorting."

Oral ingestion of drugs is probably the most familiar method of delivery. When someone drinks a beer or swallows a pill, the substance passes through the esophagus and into the stomach. It is then passed into the small intestine where it is absorbed into the blood vessels lining the walls of the intestines. Any substance taken orally passes through enzymes and acids in the mouth and stomach so its effect is weakened. The reaction time for chemicals taken in this manner is 20 to 30 minutes.

Smoking marijuana, freebasing cocaine, or "huffing" paint are examples of delivering a drug through inhalation. The vapors enter the lungs and are rapidly absorbed by the tiny blood vessels lining the air sacs of the bronchi. This blood is pumped to the heart and directly to the body and the brain. This is the fastest method of chemical delivery, creating a reaction in 7 to 10 seconds.

Cocaine, heroin, speed, and some barbiturates can be delivered with a needle (injection). Drugs can be injected into the bloodstream, the muscle tissue, or under the skin. Reaction time varies from 15 to 30 seconds if injected into the blood stream to 3 to 5 minutes under the skin or in the muscle. This method of delivery also poses the highest health risk. Individuals who inject drugs are exposed to many potential problems such as hepatitis, abscesses, septicemia, and HIV/AIDS.

Some drugs can be absorbed into the body through contact. A small amount of LSD can be dropped into the eye or on a moist part of the body to be absorbed. Morphine is given in a suppository form to terminally ill patients who are too weak for other methods of medication. Reaction time for this method of delivery is 5 to 10 minutes.

Cocaine and heroin are often snorted into the nose and absorbed through the mucus membranes lining the nasal passage. Cocaine may also be rubbed on the gums and absorbed. Reaction time is 3 to 5 minutes and the effect is more intense than ingesting the chemical (Inaba & Cohen, 1991).

ASSESSMENT AND DIAGNOSIS

Chapter Four discusses the assessment instruments and techniques used to diagnosis substance misuse, abuse, or dependence. Assessment is an integral part of the treatment plan, and includes information gathering, clinical evaluation, and diagnosis. Understanding the terminology, as well as the criteria for assessment and diagnosis, is necessary to develop an effective treatment plan for the client.

The terminology used in the field of substance abuse counseling may be confusing to beginning therapists—and at times to the seasoned counselor and the client! This confusion speaks to the changing conceptualization of addiction. Where once we saw individual abuse as either/or—that is, not a problem or addiction/alcoholism—we now understand that substance use exists on a continuum and that individuals are different in their history, pattern of use, and treatment needs. This continuum requires terminology to define the different positions along this spectrum of use. These definitions are provided here for your understanding of future references in this text and in the field.

Definitions: Drugs, Use, Abuse, Dependence

The definition of a *drug* changes with fluctuations in social mores as well as with shifts in the law (Smith, 1970). Cultures also differ considerably on classification of substances such as foods, poisons, beverages, medicines, and herbs (Schilit & Gomberg, 1991). In this text, a *drug* will be defined as any nonfood substance whose chemical or physical nature significantly alters structure, function, or perception (vision, taste, hearing, touch, and smell) in the living organism (Ray & Ksir, 1990). Legality of a substance has no bearing on whether it is defined as a drug. Alcohol, nicotine, and caffeine are legal, but considered a drug in the same way as marijuana, hallucinogens, and narcotics. A *drug user* is a person who intentionally takes legal or illegal drugs to alter his or her functioning or state of consciousness. A drug might be *instrumental* but still abused. Instrumental drugs are used to reduce anxiety, induce sleep, stay awake, and so on. They are usually over-the-counter drugs or may be prescribed by a physician. However, instrumental drugs are often abused and may serve as an entry or gateway to other drug use.

A term closely associated with drug use is *drug of choice*. "A person's drug of choice is just that: Of all the possible drugs available—of all the drugs a person may have used over the years—what specific drug(s) would this person use if given the choice?" (Doweiko, 1993, p. 6). This concept is of particular importance as the number of polydrug users increases. In assessment, diagnosis, and treatment, drug of choice may play an important role.

Drug use, misuse, and abuse are difficult to define. In this text, drug *use* is defined as "the intake of a chemical substance, whether or not the substance is used therapeutically, legally, or as prescribed by a physician" (Schilit & Gomberg, 1991). *Abuse* is defined by Merriam–Webster (1994) as improper use or excessive use, with substance abuse defined as excessive use of a drug or use without medical justification. Further defined, *abuse* is seen as "to will to injure or damage"—all phrases and language that are easily understood. Therefore, *misuse* would be using a substance in a manner that causes detrimental effects in some area of the person's life. *Abuse* would be the **continued** use of a psychoactive drug despite the occurrence of **major** detrimental effects associated with its use, such as social, vocational, health, scholastic, or economic difficulties (Resnick, 1979).

The World Health Organization (1974) defined *addiction* or *dependence* as the following:

> A state, psychic and sometimes also physical, resulting from the interaction between a living organism and a drug, characterized by behavioral and other responses that always include a compulsion to take the drug on a continuous or periodic basis in order to experience its psychic effects, and sometimes to avoid the discomfort of its absence. Tolerance may or may not be present. A person may be dependent on more than one drug. (p. 14)

The DSM-IV (1994), the primary diagnostic tool for the profession, defines substance *abuse* and *dependency* with varying criteria for each category. It is of interest to note that the DSM-IV further divides *dependence* as "with physiological dependence" or "without physiological dependence". This distinction is an addition to the criteria for dependence. Many designer drugs show psychological dependence, but may in fact cause little or no physical dependence.

Two components separate the diagnostic categories of "abuse" from "dependence". These are *tolerance* and *withdrawal*. *Tolerance* means a higher dosage of the drug is needed to produce the same level of effect over a period of time. The length of time may be influenced by the amount and frequency at which the drug is administered.

Schuckit (1989) defines two types of tolerance: (1) *metabolic tolerance* and (2) *pharmacodynamic tolerance*. *Metabolic tolerance* refers to liver function. Drugs are a foreign substance in the body and the liver will assign chemicals to break down or metabolize these chemicals. If the liver is continuously exposed to the chemical, then more cells are assigned the task of metabolizing this chemical. The result is that the chemical is metabolized faster and therefore eliminated from the body more rapidly.

Pharmacodynamic tolerance is the central nervous system's increasing insensitivity to a chemical. As a nerve is continuously bombarded with a chemical, the nerve makes minute changes in its structure to continue normal functioning. The nerve becomes less sensitive to the chemical's effect, creating the need for an increased dosage to achieve the same effect (Doweiko, 1993).

Withdrawal refers to a specific set of symptoms that occur when use of a drug is discontinued—that is, withdrawn from the central nervous system. The particular nature of the withdrawal is contingent on the class or type of drug being taken, the amount and length of time taken, and the health of the individual.

Each class or type of drugs produces certain physical withdrawal symptoms. As the nerves endeavor to *readapt* to their original state of functioning and the body learns to function again without the chemical, the person experiences the physical symptoms of withdrawal. This withdrawal syndrome, also with criteria in the DSM-IV, is strong evidence of dependence or addiction.

It is important to see drug use, misuse, abuse, and addiction as a continuum of behavior. Although this will make assessment and diagnosis more difficult, it will also result in more effective treatment for the individual. An either/or diagnosis may lead to a generalized treatment plan that might be ineffective and usually meets the needs of only the most chronic substance abusers (Lewis, Dana, & Blevins, 1994).

A continuum model does not imply progression of drug use. It does imply that some users may progress, but others may fixate at a particular position on the continuum. This position may, in fact, be problematic for the client but not at a level that could be clinically diagnosed as abuse or dependence.

Looking at substance use on a continuum allows the counselor to design individualized treatment plans. An adolescent who begins to use drugs may need only facilitation in good decision making skills. An adult who is abusing a substance to cope with a recent loss may need facilitation in improvement of coping skills as well as support in a new life stage. These individuals need significantly different clinical intervention than do longtime, daily abusers who have developed a tolerance to a particular drug.

TREATMENT SETTINGS AND MODALITIES

Treatment settings ranging from outpatient care to long-term residential care are discussed in detail in Chapter Five. Settings include halfway houses where clients remain for three to six months and therapeutic communities where individuals may live for two years or longer. As in all areas of health care, the type and length of treatment available is affected by managed health care for individuals with insurance and the continual decrease in federal money available for subsidized programs for individuals who are not insured.

Multiple factors are necessary to assess the type of treatment setting that will best serve each individual. Familiarity with the assessment instruments discussed in Chapter Four will enable the clinician to make a practiced and professional evaluation of the client's needs. The client's familial and social environment also needs to be assessed. Many practitioners in the field believe the best method of explaining the etiology as well as devising a treatment strategy is the biopsychosocial (familial) model. Therefore, in deciding the client's needs, not only does an individual assessment need to be completed but also an assessment of the individual's support systems. These support systems include, but are not limited to, the family, the school, the church, the workplace, and social relationships.

In discussing treatment modalities in Chapter Six, the authors develop the treatment alternatives based on the belief that abuse/addiction is a result of many complicated factors in an individual's life. Therefore, to facilitate lasting changes, it is necessary to therapeutically engage not only the individual but also the existing systems in which the individual exists. It is also necessary to help the individual develop new, supportive systems outside of the context of the client's drug-related social system.

Chapters Seven and Eight discuss assessment of individuals from diverse cultures and selected populations of individuals within cultures. Social and familial as well as personal characteristics that affect treatment are outlined. The multivariate dimensions that these facets add to the equation of assessment, diagnosis and treatment planning create a kaleidoscope of information and consequences.

Chapter Nine discusses an important component of recovery—relapse prevention. Models of relapse planning and control are discussed along with behavioral, psychological, and emotional indicators of relapse. This is an often-neglected aspect in treatment planning, but one that must be addressed to maintain clean and sober living.

Research in the area of substance abuse, the topic of Chapter Ten, is convoluted and skewed. Much of the research on which treatment planning is based was completed on an adult white male population from the mid-1970s to 1980s. Additionally, the population researched has been made up of individuals in treatment for substance abuse problems—and even this research tends to exclude private-care patients (Gazzaniga, 1988).

Yet another flaw in the research is the false assumption that substance abusers in treatment are representative of the general population and therefore that results can be applied to the general population. It is of interest to note, also, that the research often failed to differentiate between *abuse* and *dependence* (Peele, 1991). Another important factor omitted from the research is examination of individuals who have abused or been dependent on chemicals and have stopped using drugs without treatment intervention. It would seem that these individuals might provide valuable insight into the process of recovery. Based on these observation, it would appear that many of the prevailing assumptions concerning etiology, assessment, diagnosis, and treatment of substance abuse/dependency are flawed.

The need to consider cultural and gender norms within the assessment process is imperative. These factors affect the client's development of the problem as well as recovery issues, such as access to services, likelihood of completing treatment, and ability to maintain long-term recovery (Lewis, Dana & Blevins, 1994). The context of society, the media, and the family must also be considered in assessment of a client (Stevens-Smith, 1994). It is obvious from these facts that research on diverse populations is desperately needed. There is a dearth of research on women, adolescents, and the elderly, as well as research that addresses differentiation of type of drug used and frequency of use.

Research also indicates that treatment methods in the area of substance abuse have been slow to change. One study (Miller & Hester, 1985) identified the standard treatment methods in the United States as Alcoholics Anonymous; alcoholism education; confrontation; group therapy; individual counseling; and medications such as Antabuse, which creates a physical reaction (fever, vomiting, and so on) if one drinks. Further research, however, indicates support for aversion therapy, behavioral therapy, community-reinforcement, marital and family therapy, social skills training, and stress management. As you will note, these methods are not currently being used in the majority of programs in the United States.

The recent research in the genetics of addiction are fascinating and certainly an adjunct to working with this populations of clients. Although this research also has its limitations, it has given us extensive physiological knowledge of the effect of drugs on the central nervous system.

HIV/AIDS AND DRUG USE

We would be remiss not to discuss the related higher incidence of HIV infection among drug users. Of the more than 339,500 reported AIDS cases in the United States through September 1993, slightly more than one-third occurred among injecting drug users, their spouses, sexual partners, or their children (Centers for Disease Control and Prevention, 1993). The examination of crack use appears to be associated with increased sexual activity, not only by women but by men as well, and crack use is common among all types of drug users, including needle users. Obviously, this increase in sexual activity creates a greater risk for HIV infection. Studies also indicate that female drug users are involved not only in property crime and drug dealing, but also in prostitution to support their habit (Inciardi, Lockwood, & Pottieger, 1991; Siegal et al., 1992). In the context of HIV infection, prostitution and drug use take on a particularly lethal significance. Because of the effects of drug use on the brain, drug use inhibits the ability of the individual to make rational decisions. Some drugs lower our inhibitions and give the illusion of increasing sexual desire. Because this combination of drugs and sexuality can be lethal, some information concerning sexuality and drug use seems appropriate.

Drug Use and Sexual Activity

Numerous factors may affect the sexual arousal process of individuals using drugs. Some of these are the same factors used to discuss drug effects on an individual: (a) the specific drug being used, (b) the specific amount of drug in the body and bloodstream, (c) body size, (d) food intake, (e) frequency and duration of use, (f) expectation of effect, and (g) potential interactions of drugs in the body. Given these factors, it is apparent that deciding the effect of the drug on sexual desire, performance, or satisfaction is difficult. Although research consistently shows that chemical use is likely to interfere with performance and satisfaction, if not desire, the myth continues that one or the other drug is an aphrodisiac, a substance that enhances sexual pleasure or performance.

Alcohol

As early as Shakespeare's time, the observation was made that alcohol "provokes the desire but . . . takes away the performance (*Macbeth,* Act 2, Scene 3). Alcohol is a disinhibitor and low doses can reduce anxiety and fear. In this case, sexual excitement may increase (Flatto, 1990). With lower anxiety and heightened sexual excitement, individuals tend to engage in sexual activities at a higher rate when intoxicated. Because of this disinhibiting effect, individuals also tend to engage in unsafe sex more times when intoxicated than when not intoxicated. This is particularly problematic in the adolescent population who may be experimenting with both drugs and sex. Research also indicates that this experimentation is happening more frequently at the pre-adolescent age.

But in moderate to high doses, alcohol interferes with desire, performance, and satisfaction (Gold, 1988). Tests show that serum testosterone levels in males decrease as alcohol levels increase (Gold, 1987). Chronic use of alcohol results in a consistently low testosterone level (Flatto, 1990; Gold, 1988), nerve damage to the extremities (this would include the penis), and possible atrophy of the testicles (Geller, 1991). In male alcoholics there appears to be a disruption of spinal cord nerves involved in penile erection.

In women who drink there are lowered levels of vaginal vasocongestion, which will inhibit sexual desire and performance (Flatto, 1990). Chronic female alcoholics also experience menstrual disturbances, infertility, and a loss of secondary sexual characteristics such as body and facial hair, bone-muscle density, body form, and voice pitch (Geller, 1991).

Amphetamines and Cocaine

Both of these drugs have the reputation as aphrodisiacs. Kolodny (1985) suggests that these drugs may be mistaken for aphrodisiacs because they produce a physiological response similar to sexual excitement (increased blood pressure, increased heart rate, and an increase in blood flow to the genitals). Additionally, they bring about a feeling of well-being. It is also possible that central nervous system stimulators might increase compulsive sexual behaviors such as masturbation, sadism, exhibitionism, and possible mutilation of the penis (Lieberman, 1988). Because of the manner in which cocaine affects the brain's pleasure center, cocaine can intensify sexual thoughts, feelings, and fantasies and "(m)any users experience increased sexual desire, prolonged sexual endurance, and markedly reduced inhibitions when high on cocaine (Washton, 1989, p. 34).

Female cocaine users may develop a condition known as anorgasmia, the inhibition of orgasm. It is also known that some women or their partners rub cocaine on the clitoris before intercourse. The belief is that this will enhance the woman's pleasure. Conversely, cocaine is rubbed on the penis for the opposite effect, to reduce responsiveness. Since cocaine is a local anesthetic, it would seem apparent that it would function to reduce responsiveness, not to increase pleasure. Therefore, the expectation of the user plays a significant role in the outcome of effect.

Marijuana

Marijuana alters the individual's perceptions and it is believed that the individual's expectations or subjective perception of the drug's effects is of greater consequence than the actual physiological effects. Another explanation is that marijuana, like alcohol, is a disinhibitor. Sexual feelings normally inhibited may be experienced with the use of the drug. However, there are also physiological problems with use of marijuana. Males who use on a daily basis report erectile problems, lowered testosterone levels, and a disruption of normal sperm production. Prolonged use may result in a reduction of sexual desire for both males and females (Galbraith, 1991). Female marijuana users report vaginal dryness, which may cause pain during intercourse as well as disruption of the menstrual cycle and egg production (Kolodny, 1985).

Amyl Nitrate

Amyl nitrate is a prescription drug used to reduce the pain of angina pectoris. It is a quick-acting (30 seconds in some cases) drug used to cause the blood vessels to the heart to dilate for about five minutes. It has also been used at orgasm to prolong the moment. This feeling may occur by altering the individual's perception of time. It is used frequently in the homosexual population (Masters, Johnson, & Kolodny, 1986). The side effects are nausea, vomiting, headache, and a loss of consciousness. Overuse may result in nitrate poisoning (Lieberman, 1988).

THE PROCESS OF ADDICTION OR PROCESS ADDICTIONS

Another area related to substance abuse that should be addressed is the issue of "process addictions" (Donovan, 1988; McGurrin, 1994; Miller & Rollnick, 1991; Zweben, 1987). *Process addiction* refers to eating disorders, gambling, sexual compulsions, compulsive shopping, workaholism, and any other process (or behavior) where one's behavior fits the criteria for "dependence." Although there may be some differences in each of these behavioral manifestations, the similarity of behaviors leads many in the field to address these issues as abuse and dependency issues. A great deal of evidence also suggests that individuals who have these process addictions come from families with a background of substance abuse and/or have a dual diagnosis of substance abuse/dependency with their process addiction (Carlton & Manowitz, 1988; McGurrin, 1994; Ramirez, McCormick, Russo, & Taber, 1984).

The prevalence of eating disorders has increased by epidemic proportions. Recent studies show that 1% of all adolescent girls develop anorexia nervosa and 2% to 3% develop bulimia nervosa (National Institute of Mental Health, 1996). Both are life-threatening conditions. The obvious commonalities of eating disorders with other dependent behaviors are the compulsive behavior, the sense of powerlessness, the obsessive thought patterns, and the learned ability to avoid feeling through the abuse of food (National Institute of Mental Health, 1996). Bulimics also describe having blackouts during their purging episodes. One major dissimilarity between an eating disorder and a substance abuse problem, of course, is that food is necessary to survive. Treatment, therefore, must be directed toward management of the problem, not abstinence.

Pathological gambling is another process disorder that has much in common with substance dependency. Individuals cannot resist the urge to wager money. The process is chronic and progressive, resulting in unmanageable debt and loss of friends, family, and possibly work. Both eating disorder individuals and pathological gamblers have a high degree of denial as a symptom of the problem.

Although this book focuses on substance abuse and dependence, psychotherapists need to broaden the lens of abuse and dependence to include processes or behaviors other than those involving substances. In assessment, it is clear that examining the possibility of "cross-dependency" is appropriate. In treatment, the substance abuse/dependency issue or the process issues may only be one component of the problem that must be addressed.

CONCLUSION

We have endeavored to organize this material in a logical progression of knowledge about substance abuse and counseling. As a supplement to the knowledge base, we have incorporated the following three brief cases throughout the book to illustrate concepts discussed. The cases assist in understanding the process of assessment and diagnosis, treatment, and relapse-prevention planning. Because we are unable to present you with a "live" case, these cases will allow you to integrate the many concepts presented in the text.

CASE 1 ||||||||||||||||||||||||||||||||||||||||||||||||||||||||||||||||

SANDY AND PAM

Sandy, age 44, and her daughter Pam, age 23, came in to counseling to work on their relationship as well as their relationships with men. They have noticed patterns in their relationships that are similar to each other.

History

Sandy was the middle child of two alcoholic parents. She took on the role of the rebellious child at an early age, drinking, sneaking out of the house, and, finally, getting pregnant at 18. She married Joe, the baby's father who was also an alcoholic and a violent man. She had two children: Pam and, two years later, Henry. When

Pam was five years old, her parents separated. Pam has had a distant and often disappointing relationship with her father since. Sandy admits to continuing to abuse alcohol in her adulthood. She remembers leaving Pam and her brother at home when she thought they were asleep so that she could go to bars. She brought home numerous men and would be sexual with the men. Pam remembers hearing her mother in the bedroom with strangers and feeling frightened and alone. Sandy stopped drinking two months ago and has been trying to make amends to Pam. Pam voices forgiveness, but finds herself following similar patterns.

Pam drinks "too much" but "not as much as a couple of years ago." She is living with a cocaine abuser, Sam, who also drinks and who is emotionally abusive to her. She has used cocaine on "several occasions" with him but says she prefers to drink alcohol. Pam says she is tempted to "sleep around to get even" with Sam.

Pam is a bright young woman. She has a high school degree and two years of community college. Her career counseling indicated that her best fit was in a people-oriented position, but she has been uninspired by any job she has held. Her job history is sporadic, holding jobs for an average of three months as a waitress, receptionist, and bank teller. She quits her job because she "hates it" and usually drinks heavily for several weeks before "getting it together" and finding another job.

Pam recently moved out of her boyfriend's house and back in with her mother. She is attempting to stay away from him but he is pursuing her. She says she "feels drawn to him and wants to make it work."

Pam believes her problem is her inability to commit to anything. Sandy says that is her problem, also, so that "must be where Pam learned it." Pam has recently begun to experience anxiety attacks, which she attributes to her fear of being alone. She says drinking relieves the fear.

CASE 2 ||||||||||||||||||||||||||||||||||||||||||||||||||||||||||||||||||||||

THE SMITH FAMILY

Joe and Jane Smith are in their mid-40s. They have a stepdaughter, Sarah, who is 13, and birth daughter, Karen, who is 6.

Joe and Jane both admit to alcohol and cocaine abuse. Jane works as a bartender and receives free cocaine from her patrons. Joe worked as a bartender at the same place for almost two years but has changed professions. He is currently working as a contractor and is fairly successful.

Both have abused alcohol for 23 years. Jane stopped drinking five years ago for health reasons and remained sober for one year before beginning to drink beer and then wine again. Jane says she drinks only after the children are in bed and does not think Sarah or Karen have ever seen her drunk. Joe drinks mostly beer every evening after work and smokes some marijuana on the weekends. He admits to drinking in front of the girls but not smoking pot until they were in bed or not around.

History

Jane reported a traumatic childhood with an alcoholic and abusive mother. Her father died before she was born. She recalls that when she was 11 or 12, she was sexually abused by an older brother. She left home at age 13 and was placed in a foster home. The home was loving and supportive. Jane says she is grateful for the five years she had in the foster home and that she has made peace with her mother.

Joe is the oldest of five children and had to be the parent to the younger children from about age 10. Both parents drank "a lot" but Joe does not see them as alcoholics. He also left home at an early age and has no relationship with his parents or siblings.

The family came into therapy due to the conflict between Joe and Sarah. Sarah is beginning to act out both at home and in the classroom. Her grades are dropping and she is sneaking out of the house at night. She admits to yelling and screaming at him and turning up the stereo too loud "just to bug him." She also says he drinks too much and when he is drunk he tells her how much he loves her and how he hates it that they fight all the time. Sarah says he yells at her, tells her to get out of his face and that her friends are "dummies." Joe's response to Sarah's behavior (when sober) is to tighten the rules.

Karen is visibly sad. She is quiet and withdrawn from the family fights. Karen spends lots of time in her room playing with her stuffed animals.

Both Joe and Jane admit that being off drugs and alcohol would be difficult but express a desire to stop. The longest they have been able to stop (except for Jane's one year) was nine days. When they started again, both drank to intoxication. Jane is reluctant to give up drugs altogether. She says she feels more socially upbeat when she "does a line or two," and, because she gets it free and has "no ill effects" sees no reason to abstain.

CASE 3 ▌||||||||||||||||||||||||||||||||||||||||||||||||||||||||||||||||||||||

LEIGH

Leigh, who is 15 years old, has been referred due to problems at school and a shoplifting charge. She admits to "smoking some dope" now and then and having a drink or two with friends. She is dressed in black with pierced ears, nose, and lip. Her appearance is disheveled and her hygiene is poor. She appears to be overly thin.

History

Leigh's parents were divorced when she was five. She is the younger of two children. Her brother is five years older. Leigh and her brother lived with her mother in the same town as her father. She saw her father frequently, although she says he was "always busy with work" and she could never talk to him about much of anything. Leigh says her mother was also busy but would "usually" stop and listen. She reports that her mother has a temper and is stressed all the time about money and work. She also reports that her mom and dad still fight about money and "us kids." She feels as if she is in the middle and is always being asked to choose.

Leigh and her mother and brother recently moved to this area and Leigh is at a new school this year. She is in eighth grade and has average grades. Her new friends are "different" from her old friends but they "accept her for what she is."

|||||||||||||||||||||||||||||||||||||||||||||||||||||||||||||||||||||||||||||||||||||||||||||||||||||||

REFERENCES

American Cancer Society. (1990). Data bank. *Breakthroughs, 1*(2), 12.

American Psychiatric Association. (1994). *Diagnostic and Statistical Manual of Mental Disorders* (4th ed.). Washington, DC: Author.

Beasley, J. D. (1987). *Wrong diagnosis, wrong treatment: The plight of the alcoholic in America*. New York: Creative Infomatics, Inc.

Berger, P. A., & Dunn, M. J. (1982). Substance induced and substance use disorders. In J. H. Griest, J. W. Jefferson, & R. L. Spitzer (Eds.), *Treatment of Mental Disorders*. New York: Oxford University Press.

Bland, R., & Orn, H. (1986). Family violence and psychiatric disorder. *Canadian Journal of Psychiatry, 31,* 129–137.

Bureau of Justice. (1986). *State Prison Inmate Survey*. Washington, DC: Author.

Carlton, P. L., & Manowitz, P. (1988). Physiological factors as determinants of pathological gambling. *Journal of Gambling Behavior, 3,* 274–285.

Centers for Disease Control. (1991). Cigarette smoking among adults: United States, 1988. *Morbidity and Mortality Weekly Report, 40,* 757–765.

Centers for Disease Control and Prevention (1993, October). *HIV/AIDS Surveillance Report.*

Donovan, D. M. (1988). Assessment of addictive behaviors: Implications of an emerging biopsychosocial model. In D. M. Donovan & G. A. Marlatt (Eds.), *Assessment of addictive behaviors* (pp. 3–48). New York: Guilford.

Doweiko, H. (1993). *Concepts of chemical dependency*. Pacific Grove, CA: Brooks/Cole.

Evans, K., & Sullivan, J. M. (1990). *Dual diagnosis: Counseling the mentally ill substance abuser*. New York: Guilford.

Flatto, E. (1990). Alcohol and impotence from the doctor's casebook. *Nutrition Health Review, 53,* 19.

Galanter, M., Castaneda, R., & Ferman, J. (1988). Substance abuse among general psychiatric patients: Place of presentation, diagnosis, and treatment. *American Journal of Drug and Alcohol Abuse, 14*(2), 211–235.

Galbraith, R. A. (1991). Sexual side effects of drugs. *Drug Therapy, 23*(3), 38–40, 46.

Gallup Poll, (1989, August 4). (pp. 10, 16)

Gazzaniga, M. S. (1988). *Mind matters*. Boston: Houghton Mifflin.

Geller, A. (1991). Sexual problems of the recovering alcoholic. *Medical Aspects of Human Sexuality, 25*(3), 60–63.

Gerstein, D. R., & Harwood, H. J. (1990). *Treating drug problems*. Volume I. Washington, DC: National Academy Press.

Gold, M. S. (1987). Sexual dysfunction challenges today's addictions clinicians. *Alcoholism & Addictions 7*(6), 11.

Gold, M. S. (1988). Alcohol, drugs, and sexual dysfunction. *Alcoholism & Addictions, 9*(2), 13.

Greden, J. F., & Walters, A. (1992). Caffeine. In J. H. Lowenson, P. Ruiz, R. Milkman, & J. G. Langnod (Eds.), *Substance abuse: A comprehensive text* (pp. 357–370). Baltimore: Williams & Wilkins.

Group for the Advancement of Psychiatry. (1991). Substance abuse disorders: A psychiatric priority. *American Journal of Psychiatry, 148,* 1291–1300.

Hyman, S. E. (1988). *Manual of Psychiatric Emergencies* (2nd ed.). Boston: Little, Brown.

Inaba, D. S., & Cohen, W. (1991). *Uppers, downers, and all arounders: Physical and mental effects of drugs of abuse.* Ashland: CNS Productions.

Inciardi, J. A., Lockwood, D., & Pottieger, A. E. (1991). Crack-dependent women and sexuality: Implications for STD acquisition and transmission. *Addiction & Recovery, 11*(4), 25–28.

Institute of Medicine. (1987). *Causes and consequences of alcohol problems.* Washington, DC: National Academy Press.

Institute of Medicine. (1990). *Broadening the base of treatment for alcohol problems.* Washington, DC: National Academy Press.

Jaffe, J. H. (1990). Drug addiction and drug abuse. In A. G. Gilman, I. S. Goodman, T. W. Rall, & F. Murad (Eds.), *The Pharmacological Basis of Therapeutics* (8th ed.). Upper Saddle River, NJ: Merrill/Prentice Hall.

Kantor, F. J., & Straus, M. A. (1987). The "drunken bum" theory of wife beating, *Social Problems, 34*(3), 214–230.

Kinney, J., & Leaton, G. (1991). *Loosening the grip.* St. Louis, MO: Mosby Year Book.

Klag, M. J., & Whelton, P. K. (1987). Risk of stroke in male cigarette smokers. *New England Journal of Medicine, 316,* 628.

Kolodny, R. C. (1985). The clinical management of sexual problems in substance abusers. In T. E. Bratter, & G. G. Forrest (Eds.), *Alcoholism and substance abuse: Strategies for clinical intervention* (pp. 189–243). New York: The Free Press.

Lewis, J. A., Dana, R. Q., & Blevins, G. A. (1994). *Substance abuse counseling: An individualized approach.* Pacific Grove, CA: Brooks/Cole.

Lieberman, M. L. (1988). *The Sexual Pharmacy.* New York: New American Library.

Louis, G. C., & Yagyian, H. Z. (1980). *The cola wars.* New York: Everest House Publishers.

Masters, W. H., Johnson, V. E., & Kolodny, R. C. (1986). *Human sexual response.* Boston: Little, Brown.

McGurrin, M. C. (1994). Diagnosis and treatment of pathological gambling. In J. A. Lewis (Ed.), *Addictions: Concepts and strategies for treatment* (pp. 123–142). Gaithersburg, MD: Aspen Publishers, Inc.

Merriam–Webster. (1994). *Merriam–Webster dictionary.* Springfield, MA: Merriam–Webster.

Milkman, H., & Sunderwirth, S. (1987). *Cravings for ecstasy.* New York: Lexington Books.

Miller, W. R., & Hester, R. K. (1985). The effectiveness of treatment techniques: What works and what doesn't. In W. R. Miller (Ed.), *Alcoholism: Theory, research, and treatment* (pp. 526–574). Lexington, MA: Ginn Press.

Miller, W. R., & Rollinick, S. (1991). *Motivational interviewing: Preparing people to change addictive behavior.* New York: Guilford.

National Highway Traffic Safety Administration (1988a). *Alcohol involvement in fatal crashes 1986.* (Report No. DOT HS 807 268). Washington, DC: Author.

National Highway Traffic Safety Administration (1988b). *Drunk driving facts.* Washington, DC: Author.

National Institute on Alcohol Abuse and Alcoholism. (1994). *Alcohol Health and Research World, 18*(3), 243, 245.

National Institute on Alcohol Abuse and Alcoholism. (1993). *Alcohol Health and Research World, 17*(2), 133.

National Institute on Alcohol Abuse and Alcoholism. (1991). *Alcohol Alert.* Rockville, MD: Author.

National Institute on Alcohol Abuse and Alcoholism. (1990). *7th special report to U.S. Congress on alco-*

hol and health. Washington, DC: U.S. Government Printing Office.

National Institute on Drug Abuse. (1990). *National household survey on drug abuse: Population estimates 1990*. Rockville, MD: Author.

National Institute on Drug Abuse. (1991). *An economical approach to addressing the drug problem in America*. Rockville, MD: Author.

National Institute on Drug Abuse. (1993). *National household survey on drug abuse: Population estimates 1990*. Rockville, MD: Author.

National Institute of Mental Health. (1996). *Eating disorders*. Washington, DC: Author.

Peele, S. (1991). What we know about treating alcoholism and other addictions, *Harvard Mental Health Letter, 8*(6), 5–7.

Playboy. (1988). *Forum Newsfront, 35*(4), 51.

Ramirez, L. F., McCormick, R. A., Russo, A. M., & Taber, J. I. (1984). Patterns of substance abuse in pathological gamblers undergoing treatment. *Addictive Behaviors, 8,* 425–428.

Ray, O. S., & Ksir, C. (1990). *Drugs, society, and human behavior*. St. Louis, MO: C.V. Mosby.

Resnick, H. S. (1979). *It starts with people: Experiences in drug abuse prevention* (NIDA Publication No. ADM 79-590). Rockville, MD: National Institute on Drug Abuse.

Rice, D. P., & Kelman, S. (1989). Measuring comorbidity and overlap in the hospitalization cost for alcohol and drug abuse and mental illness. *Inquiry, 26,* 249–260.

Scaros, L. P., Westra, S., & Barone, J. A. (1990). Illegal use of drugs: A current review. *U.S. Pharmacist, 15*(5), 17–39.

Schilit, R., & Gomberg, E. S. L. (1991). *Drugs and behavior: A sourcebook for the helping professions*. Newbury Park: Sage.

Schuckit, M. A. (1989). *Drug and alcohol abuse: A clinical guide to diagnosis and treatment*. New York: Plenum.

Seever, M. H. (1968). Psychopharmacological elements of drug dependence. *Journal of the American Medical Association, 206,* 1263–1266.

Siegal, H. A., Carlson R. G., Falck, R., Forney, M. A., Wang, J., & Li, L. (1992). High-risk behaviors for transmission of syphilis and human immunodeficiency virus among crack cocaine-using women: A case study from the Midwest. *Sexually Transmitted Disease, 19,* 266–271.

Smith, J. P. (1970). Society and drugs: A short sketch. In P. H. Blachly (Ed.), *Drug abuse data and debate* (pp. 169-175). Springfield, IL: Charles C. Thomas.

Stevens-Smith, P. (1994). Contextual issues in addiction. In J. A. Lewis (Ed.), *Addictions: Concepts and strategies for treatment* (pp. 11-21). Gaithersburg, MD: Aspen Publishers, Inc.

Substance Abuse and Mental Health Services Administration (1993, September). *Estimates from the drug abuse warning network*. Advance Report No. 4. Rockville, MD: Department of Health and Human Services.

Substance Abuse and Mental Health Services Administration. (1994). *Advance Report No. 7*. Washington, DC: U.S. Department of Health and Human Services.

Substance Abuse and Mental Health Services Administration. (1995). National Household Survey on Substance Abuse. Rockville, MD: Department of Health and Human Services.

Terry, C. E., & Pellens, M. (1928). *The opium problem*. New York: Bureau of Social Hygiene.

University of California, Berkeley. (1990). Women's magazines: Whose side are they on? *The Wellness Letter, 6*(9), 1-2.

Washton, A. M. (1989). Cocaine abuse and compulsive sexuality. *Medical Aspects of Human Sexuality, 23*(12), 32-39.

World Health Organization Expert Committee on Drug Dependence. (1974). *Twentieth report* (Tech. Rep. Series No. 5(51). Geneva: Switzerland: Author.

Zweben, J. E. (1987). Eating disorders and substance abuse. *Journal of Psychoactive Drugs, 19,* 181-192

Etiological Theories of Substance Abuse

Sharon Erickson, PhD

his chapter explores the theories that attempt to explain the phenomenon of substance abuse and discusses the implications for their use in counseling. It must be emphasized, however, that no single model fully explains why substance abuse occurs.

The *etiology* of a disease is the cause of that disease, or the sum of knowledge regarding its causes. Knowing the cause of any disease or condition is essential in five areas: (1) for a general understanding of the condition, (2) selection and implementation of appropriate treatment, (3) prediction of possible outcomes of treatment, (4) construction of appropriate research, and (5) prevention of the condition. In the study of addiction, it can more accurately be said that the etiology is the sum of knowledge regarding its causes, because the cause of addictions and substance abuse has historically been a complex and developing issue. Many theories have been offered, but substantive research is scarce. Multiple factors are often cited, but to date, there is no clear consensus by researchers and clinicians as to why people engage in substance use, and why some people become addicted.

Moreover, alcoholism and other drug addictions appear to be similar in many respects, yet different in others. In spite of the lack of consensus, it is important to have a conceptual framework of the etiology upon which therapeutic assumptions can be based, even if that framework is still evolving.

Viewed from the *moral theory,* substance abuse is the result of willful overindulgence and moral degradation and can be cured with willpower and a desire to abstain. The *disease theory* treats addictions, particularly alcoholism, from a medical viewpoint and looks for biomedical reasons for vulnerability to, and the development of, substance abuse. *Genetic theories* look for biologically inherited reasons for the development of substance abuse. *Systems theories* consider interactions with others, notably the family of origin, as a basis for intergenerational transmission of substance abuse. *Behavioral theories* look to faulty learning patterns and attempts at stress reduction as major components in the establishment and continuation of substance abuse. *Sociocultural theories* examine cultural factors, social pressures, and environmental conditions that foster the development of substance abuse and addictions. And, increasingly, the *biopsychosocial theory* views substance abuse as a complex, interactional condition, to which all of the above theories may contribute.

MORAL THEORY OF SUBSTANCE ABUSE

Until the middle of the 19th century, alcohol consumption was actively promoted. It was assumed that most people would drink, and no one was supposed to suffer from negative results (Metzger, 1988). Alcohol was commonly used as a table beverage in many cultures, and it was a featured part of parties and revelry. As the United States began to move from a largely rural society to the more formal structure of towns in the early 1800s, social-control mechanisms began to emerge (Siegal & Inciardi, 1995). Although alcohol consumption was common and condoned, people were expected to "hold" their liquor, and drunkenness and dependence upon alcohol was considered sinful and a shameful example of lack of willpower. Drunkenness was seen as an individual weakness and a threat to society.

The resulting *moral theory* gained impetus during the Civil War when concern over heavy drinking supported the temperance movement (Nace, 1987). Church and conservative elements of the community made it clear that such moral degradation was inexcusable and not to be tolerated. Imbibing of alcohol was considered sinful and the imbiber morally corrupt. It was assumed that alcoholism was under one's control, and that willpower and desire alone could prevent overindulgence.

The temperance movement reached its pinnacle in 1919 with the passage of the 18th Amendment to the Constitution of the United States, which prohibited the manufacture, sale, and transportation of intoxicating liquors. Prohibition was deemed successful, at first, as alcohol consumption decreased. However, some continued to drink heavily, and a new industry of bootlegging developed. This illegal activity developed into organized crime in the United States (Siegal & Inciardi, 1995). By the 1930s, abstinence was no longer the social norm, and the 18th Amendment was repealed in 1933 (Cox, 1987).

A shift in thinking away from the moral model was accompanied by the development in 1935 of a unique self-help organization for the treatment of alcoholism—Alcoholics Anonymous (AA). AA retained some elements of the moral model in the belief that the help of a Higher Power is needed to achieve and maintain sobriety (Blum, 1991), and that individuals are responsible for seeking their own recovery. However, AA differed from the moral model in that the individual was no longer held responsible for *having* the "disease" of alcoholism, only for seeking help to overcome it. This shift toward the disease model gained validity when the American Medical Association recognized alcoholism as a disease in 1956, followed by the American College of Physicians in 1969 (Nace, 1987). It is this shift in paradigms that has allowed alcoholism and other substance abuse to be scientifically studied, precipitating the development of new theoretical models to explain their causes.

THE DISEASE THEORY OF SUBSTANCE ABUSE

In 1935, two alcoholics, Bill W. and Dr. Bob, came together to seek a solution to their addiction to alcohol (Alcoholics Anonymous, 1976). They noted similarities in their experiences and formulated at least six fundamental points:

- Alcoholics understand other alcoholics.
- Alcoholics can talk to other alcoholics.
- Alcoholics tend to believe other alcoholics.
- It is healing for alcoholics to help other alcoholics.
- Alcoholics need the help of a Higher Power to achieve and maintain sobriety.
- Abstinence is essential to recovery (Blum, 1991).

Jellinek, in his work in the 1950s, more carefully defined alcoholism as a disease, developing the theory that alcoholism is caused by a physiological deficit in an individual that makes the person unable to tolerate alcohol. According to this premise, the only treatment for the disease is abstinence. This is also the foundation of Alcoholics Anonymous, as well as most treatment programs even today (George, 1990). The disease theory also implies that regardless of their history in becoming alcoholic, all alcoholics have the same disease—in other words, the lawyer who is alcoholic has the same disease as the homeless alcoholic, and treatment for all is essentially the same.

Jellinek, in 1950, published a description of the disease of alcoholism, based on a survey of 98 male members of Alcoholics Anonymous (Pratsinek & Alexander, 1992). Jellinek described five types of drinking behaviors (George, 1990; Light, 1985). These are numbered by the first five letters of the Greek alphabet: alpha, beta, gamma, delta, and epsilon.

Jellinek also suggested that there are distinct signs and symptoms of alcoholism, a criterion important if it is to be termed a disease (Light, 1985). These symptoms are clustered into stages of alcoholism: early, middle, and late. According to Jellinek's stages, an individual uses alcohol early in the disease to relieve pain—whether physical or emotional, tension from job or family, or other stress. Driving while intoxicated and memory blackouts can occur during this stage. As the disease progresses to the middle stages, more visible changes occur, such as job or family problems, absenteeism, financial problems, or changes in moral behavior. Physical changes also take place during the middle phase, and treatment is important. If allowed to progress into the late stages, deterioration of the body or brain may make effective treatment impossible. For in-depth reference to Jellinek's theories, see George (1990) or Light (1985).

Generalities from Jellinek's theories should be used with caution because of limitations in the sample population used for his study. The sample was small (98) and homogeneous, being male, late-stage, gamma alcoholics (George, 1990). Females were included only in the control group. Broad conclusions based on such an unbalanced sample cannot be made scientifically. Further, Jellinek's theory did not address the underlying biogenetic causes of alcoholism (Blum, 1991). Nevertheless, Jellinek's contribution in conceptualizing alcoholism as other than a moral problem is an important foundation for other theories.

CASE DISCUSSIONS

Case 1 (Sandy and Pam).   Both Sandy and her daughter, Pam, would be considered to have the disease of alcoholism. Although Sandy is not currently drinking, she is "recovering" and will never be considered "cured." When drinking, Sandy exhibits symptoms of mid-stage alcoholism: problems with relationships and family, and moral changes. Pam is still in the early stages, using alcohol to deal with stress, anxiety, and social problems. Unless she seeks treatment, Pam's dependence on alcohol will increase and the disease will progress to more serious physical and emotional symptoms. Treatment must include abstinence.

Case 2 (Joe and Jane).   Both Joe and Jane are addicted to alcohol and cocaine. Neither is able abstain for long, and once cocaine or alcohol is ingested, it is used compulsively. If intervention does not take place, the addiction and its effects will worsen and the physical, emotional, and social changes will continue. Treatment must include abstinence. Jane continues to deny that her cocaine use is having any untoward effects on anyone, enabling her to continue with its use.

Strengths and Limitations of the Disease Concept

Strengths

1. Acceptance of an addictive disorder as a disease means the substance abuser does not live as a social outcast. Employers and family members are empowered to support treatment and rehabilitation efforts.

2. Relieving the guilt and shame felt by addicts for having the disease may make them more amenable to treatment.

3. Viewing addiction as a disease opens it to research on its etiology, symptomology, progression, and treatment.

Limitations

1. In claiming to have a disease, some addicts may deny responsibility for change, especially since denial is a main symptom of substance abuse. Some may attempt to deny responsibility for entering treatment programs with the attitude of, "What do you expect from a person with a disease?"

2. Alcoholism and other substance abuses are treated in the same way, without recognition of the complex factors which accompany polydrug use.

3. Some authors suggest that a key factor in the maintenance of the myth of the disease concept is that "recovering" alcoholics and addicts commonly work as paraprofessional staff members in treatment and educational programs on substance abuse. The concern is that people in this group, most without scientific or professional training, use their personal experiences and anecdotal stories as evidence that substance abuse is a disease, rather than referring to scientific evidence (George, 1990).

Summary of the Disease Theory of Alcoholism

The concept that alcoholism is a disease gained in popularity in the mid-20th century, lifting substance abuse from the realm of corrupt morals and lack of willpower to a more acceptable and treatable form. The founders of Alcoholics Anonymous followed this theme in 1935 when they began a self-help movement which does not blame alcoholics for having the condition, but holds them responsible for seeking help. Jellinek, in 1960, defined signs and symptoms, as well as progression of the disease. These form the basis of 12-step or Anon-type treatment programs for substance abuse today. Although not universally accepted, the disease concept has allowed research to be conducted on substance abuse, treatment programs to be developed and evaluated, and public and private monies to be applied to the research and treatment of the problem.

GENETIC THEORY OF SUBSTANCE ABUSE

Is substance abuse the result of heredity or environment? Intergenerational studies, twin studies, adoption studies, and a search for trait markers of alcoholism have all been used to attempt to answer this question.

Several caveats must be observed when reviewing current genetic research. Most of the studies have focused on alcoholism and used males as subjects. Generalizations of their findings to chemical dependency and to women may not be accurate. Further, genetic studies for alcoholism and other substance abuse differ in several important ways. Thus, studies on alcoholism and other substance abuse will be discussed separately.

Genetic Studies on Alcoholism

Numerous studies have shown that relatives of alcoholics have a substantially greater risk for alcoholism compared with nonalcoholics, and evidence of genetic predisposition to alcoholism is growing (Anthenelli & Schuckit, 1992; Goodwin, 1985; Vaillant, 1983). Some researchers, such as Schuckit (1983) and Goodwin (1989) believe that at least some of the association between alcohol abuse in parents and in their children is genetically, rather than environmentally, transmitted. However, there is no current evidence of a single gene for alcoholism (Berkowitz, 1996). Berkowitz proposes that several genes, each having a small effect on its own, may interact with each other and with environmental factors, allowing alcoholism to develop.

Intergenerational Studies

Intergenerational studies are useful in detecting patterns of heritability in substance abuse. The basic design compares the risk of developing the disorder among three groups: relatives of individuals with the disorder, relatives of individuals without the disorder, and the general population (Anthenelli & Schuckit, 1992; Vaillant, 1983). Observing a family with a history of alcoholism or substance abuse for several generations can provide clues to the intergenerational transmission of the condition. Several longitudinal studies point to at least a genetic component to the intergenerational transmission of alcoholism (Brown & Creamer, 1987; Cotton, 1978; Vaillant, 1983).

Schuckit (1983) and Goodwin (1989) support the belief that the association between alcohol abuse in parents and their children is genetically, rather than environmentally transmitted. In his study of alcoholic men, Schuckit (1983) found that more than one-third reported alcoholism in a close family member, compared with 5% to 10% of the general population. This finding was unaffected by the loss of an alcoholic parent early in life.

As further support for the theory of genetic transmission of alcoholism, Schuckit (1983) found that almost 60% of the men with primary alcoholism (alcoholism with onset early in life and uncomplicated by other psychological disorders) had histories of alcoholism in close family members. An additional 10% had problems with alcoholism in the extended family, which, Schuckit believes, indicates that alcoholism may skip a generation. In the latter case, Schuckit theorizes, the alcoholic may have been reared in a teetotaling environment or one in which alcohol usage was restricted. Thus, the parents may not have had the opportunity to demonstrate their alcoholic predisposition. He also found that coming from a family with a history of alcoholism appears to increase the risk of having other problems in life.

Twin Studies

Twin studies compare the similarities or concordance rates for alcoholism or substance abuse in monozygotic twins (those developing from one ovum and sperm) with those of dizygotic twins (those developing from two sets of ovum and sperm). If a disorder is genetically influenced or predetermined, monozygotic twins, who share all the same genes, should have a higher concordance rate than dizygotic twins, who develop from two separate fertilized ova (Goodwin, 1985). Environmentally determined disorders, on the other hand, would show no significant difference between the two types of sets of twins, provided the environments were very similar (Anthenelli & Schuckit, 1992). Current twin studies support the theory that genetics influence the transmission of alcoholism, and suggest that inherited factors might affect the quantity and frequency of alcohol consumption (Anthenelli & Schuckit, 1992; Pickens & Svikis, 1991). Unfortunately, the issues of drug abuse other than alcohol are more complicated and the results of twin studies on them are less clear (Anthenelli & Schuckit, 1992).

Adoption Studies

Adoption studies are particularly effective in separating effects of inherited traits and the effects of the environment. If alcoholism were influenced by genetic factors, a high rate of incidence of alcoholism would be found in children of alcoholics, regardless of whether they were raised by their alcoholic parents or by nonalcoholic foster or adoptive parents. Conversely, if the condition were more influenced by the environment, one would expect to find a higher rate of occurrence of alcoholism in children of alcoholics raised by their alcoholic parents when compared with children of alcoholics raised by nonalcoholic foster or adoptive parents.

Recent adoptive studies support the theory that heredity affects development of alcoholism (Anthenelli & Schuckit, 1992; Goodwin, 1985, 1989). Those who had a biological parent with severe alcohol problems were significantly more likely to have severe alcohol problems themselves than those raised by alcoholic surrogate parents. In Denmark, researchers found similar results in a series of adoption studies, beginning in 1970 (Goodwin, 1985).

The generalities on conclusions drawn from the adoptive and twin studies should be reviewed with caution. The population studied has been northern European, and studies have not been replicated on other populations. Further, heritability of alcoholism has been found in males, but has not been seen to the same degree in women. Genetic effects of alcoholism, then, may hold true for northern Europeans and men, but not for other populations (Kumpfer & Hopkins, 1993).

Studies on daughters of alcoholics and children of alcoholic mothers are less conclusive than those on sons of alcoholics or children of alcoholic fathers, as most of the research has been done on father-son samples. Both the number of studies and sample sizes of daughters of alcoholics have been much smaller than those on father-son samples (Searles, 1991).

Research for Genetic Markers for Alcoholism

Results of intergenerational, twin, and adoptive studies have led researchers to look for specific genetic markers for the condition. If found, such markers could indicate physical differences between alcoholics and nonalcoholics, such as physiological predispositions for alcohol abuse, differing rates of alcohol metabolism, or differing chemical breakdowns in the metabolism of alcohol, creating differing reactions to the chemical. A search for biochemical markers holds promise for explaining why, in similar circumstances, some people will develop alcoholism and some will not.

It is, as yet, unclear how genetic components of alcoholism work. Research, however, suggests several possibilities:

1. **Altered metabolism of ethanol or acetaldehyde.**   Several studies have found that alcoholics break down acetaldehyde into acedate at about half the speed of the metabolism in nonalcoholic individuals (George, 1990). Indications are that the metabolic abnormality exists even before heavy drinking. Like their alcoholic parents, children of alcoholics who had never drunk alcohol were unable to convert acetaldehyde to acedate at normal speeds. This may be partially due to liver-enzyme malfunction, causing a buildup of acetaldehyde throughout the body. These large amounts of acetaldehyde interact with the brain amines to form active compounds with morphine-like properties. These, in turn, trigger the alcoholic's need to drink more and more alcohol to counter the painful effects of the high levels of acetaldehyde (George, 1990).

2. **Atypical reaction to ethanol ingestion.**   Another finding related to the metabolism of ethanol is the lack of aldehyde dehydrogenase in some who do *not* drink much alcohol. Aldehyde dehydrogenase (ALDH) is the major enzyme that degrades the first metabolite of ethanol, acetaldehyde, in the liver (Anthenelli & Schuckit, 1992). A lack of isoenzyme forms of ALDH causes affected individuals, after consuming alcohol, to develop higher acetaldehyde levels, resulting in the unpleasant symptoms of facial flushing, tachycardia, and a burning sensation in the stomach. It is estimated that 30% to 50% of Asians lack this enzyme, which may at least partially explain their lower rate of alcoholism and lower consumption of alcohol. Thus, this genetically predicted enzyme system may affect their societal attitudes and habits with regard to alcohol consumption.

Monoamine oxidase (MAO), a major degradative enzyme system for many neurotransmitters, has also come under recent study as a possible deciding variable in the development of alcoholism. Some studies have found a decreased level of MAO in alcohol abusers (Anthenelli & Schuckit, 1992).

Other factors being considered by researchers in the genetic transmission of alcoholism include a search for an increased risk of ethanol-related organ damage in certain people, personality variables, or an increased risk as a result of other psychiatric disorders (Nace, 1987).

From a genetic perspective, alcoholism is a condition that arises from an imbalance in the brain's production of neurotransmitters responsible for our sense of well-being (Blum, 1991) or in the metabolism of ethanol. Physiological studies hold promise for unraveling the mystery of why some people develop alcoholism and others do not. Genetic predispositions could make some people susceptible to development of alcohol abuse and addiction.

Some recent theorists (Devor, 1994; Tartar & Vanyukov, 1994) believe that a search for a genetic basis for alcoholism is simplistic and not reflective of the complex nature of the disease. They believe alcoholism to be a complex developmental disorder that is based on genetic tendencies that are activated by environmental conditions or interactions. Genetic differences in temperament and developing personality traits allow individuals to react differently to environmental factors, leading some to develop alcoholism and others to not have problems with alcohol. This viewpoint greatly complicates research into the causes of alcoholism, as individual factors are extremely difficult to isolate, but it may be more realistic. This view also leans more toward the biopsychosocial theories, discussed later in this chapter, which include all factors that might affect an individual and the development of substance abuse.

CASE DISCUSSION

Case 1 (Sandy and Pam).   Pam comes from a family with a pattern of alcohol abuse. Geneticists would note the alcoholism of her mother, Sandy, and would be interested in looking at aunts, uncles, and previous generations for similar patterns of alcohol abuse. A family genogram (Figure 2.1) might be used to examine substance abuse history across several generations, pointing to a genetic (as well as learned) basis for the abuse.

This might indicate a hereditary component to Pam and Sandy's alcohol abuse. Geneticists would also examine how alcohol consumption makes Pam and Sandy feel, looking for clues to any differences in metabolism from the general population. For example, if they "feel good" only after drinking, disturbances in liver-enzyme function would be suspected, since the morphine-like qualities of the high blood levels of acetaldehyde could cause elevated mood and an increased desire to drink more.

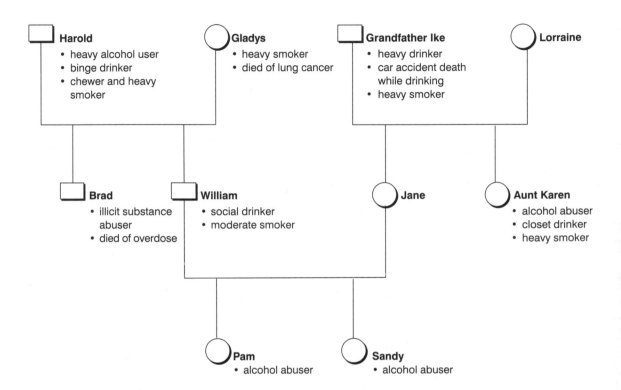

Genogram
Pam and Sandy

Harold
• heavy alcohol user
• binge drinker
• chewer and heavy smoker

Gladys
• heavy smoker
• died of lung cancer

Grandfather Ike
• heavy drinker
• car accident death while drinking
• heavy smoker

Lorraine

Brad
• illicit substance abuser
• died of overdose

William
• social drinker
• moderate smoker

Jane

Aunt Karen
• alcohol abuser
• closet drinker
• heavy smoker

Pam
• alcohol abuser

Sandy
• alcohol abuser

As indicated above, the genogram of Pam and Sandy reveals that alcohol and other substances have been abused for three generations, causing family problems and death throughout the family's history.

FIGURE 2.1   Genogram

Genetic Studies on Other Substance Abuse

It has been more difficult, for many reasons, to conduct research on genetic factors in substance abuse other than alcoholism:

1. While alcoholics comprise a substantial proportion of the population, the number of other-substance abusers fluctuates over the generations, following fads and trends.
2. Alcoholism has been the subject of study for many years, allowing for intergenerational studies. Other substance abuse has been studied only more recently.

3. While the study of alcoholism consists of examination of the effects of only one substance, ethanol, other substance abuse includes a wide range of chemicals, each affecting the body differently.

4. Drug abuse comes in fads, one chemical becoming popular among a certain population for a time, only to be replaced by another.

5. Polydrug use is common, with one chemical compounding the actions of others.

6. People afflicted with some mental disorders, such as antisocial personality disorder, frequently use drugs, making it difficult to distinguish markers for predisposition for drug abuse from the preexisting mental disorder.

Research on substance abuse other than alcoholism is limited and preliminary, at best. There does appear to be a general belief that there is some hereditary risk factor, but identification of a marker and the complicated mechanisms that may convert this predisposition into actual substance abuse lie in the future.

Strengths and Limitations of Genetic Theories

Strengths

1. Research findings on biological differences between those who abuse substances and those who do not lay the foundation for further research and a foundation for theories of treatment.

2. Intergenerational studies are useful in detecting patterns of occurrence in substance abuse. Viewing several generations of a family of an individual who is abusing alcohol or drugs can provide clues to the long-term and intergenerational transmission of the condition.

3. Intergenerational studies give a broad overview of the condition, indicating trends and frequency of substance abuse. Such an overview can suggest areas for further research.

Limitations

1. Intergenerational studies are ineffective in discerning the effects of genetics versus environment, and can only imply genetic transmission.

2. Some authors, such as Fingarette (1988) and Searles (1991), have disputed conclusions on genetic studies. Flaws in the design and results of the studies are cited (Searles, 1991). Further, it is argued that the statistics that indicate a genetic tendency in the intergenerational transmission of alcoholism can be turned around, offering the opposite conclusion. For example, if the findings indicate that one-third of the biological children became alcoholics themselves, it can also be said that two-thirds of the children of alcoholics did *not* become alcoholic (Fingarette, 1988; Searles, 1991).

Summary of Genetic Studies of Substance Abuse

Alcoholism runs in families. A review of the literature reveals a consensus that children of alcoholics run a higher risk of developing alcoholism than children in the general population. Whether this is solely a function of genetics or the product of the environment is open to debate. The results of several studies suggest a genetic predisposition to alcoholism. Others point to dysfunctional dynamics of the alcoholic family in predicting the intergenerational transmission of alcoholism. Perhaps a more reasonable explanation for this phenomenon is a genetic predisposition for alcoholism, which may be triggered or affected by the accompanying and self-perpetuating dysfunction of the alcoholic family (Kaufman, 1980; Woititz, 1983). Regardless, the child of the alcoholic and adult child of the alcoholic appear to be at risk for emotional maladjustment, alcoholism, and multiple life problems. This does not discount the fact that most children of alcoholics do not become alcoholic, or reveal why some children seem to be more resilient to the intergenerational effects of alcohol than others. Genetic components of other substance abuse and addiction are less clear, and research in this area is in its infancy.

SYSTEMS THEORY

The intergenerational transmission of alcoholism has been observed for centuries, although debate continues as to whether it is genetically or environmentally transmitted, or both. Systems theorists would note the replication of family structure and dynamics from generation to generation and seek causative factors in substance abuse from these patterns (Stanton et al., 1982). Stanton and Todd (Daw, 1995) suggest that intergenerational patterns of alcohol abuse are like scripts passed from one generation to another. It may be more accurate to view the family systems etiology more as a description of the dynamics within the substance abusing family and the intergenerational replication of the family dynamics, rather than as an original cause of alcoholism or substance abuse.

Family system theory views parts of a family as a whole, with each member contributing to the tapestry that becomes even more than a sum of its parts (Goldenberg & Goldenberg, 1985). Families, both the family-of-origin and the current family, form a framework for perception of one's place in the world, the roles one must play, and the proper way to interact in it. Systems theorists believe that to view substance-abusing individuals in isolation from their family and environment ignores the influence of the home in which they learn to perceive how they fit in the world, as well as the influences others have on their behavior. It ignores the part that others, who make up the individual's environment, play in maintaining the abuse.

A primary goal of any system is to maintain *homeostasis*, to balance the system and make adjustments to restore that equilibrium whenever it is threatened (Stanton et al., 1982). In a well-functioning family, homeostasis protects the individuals so that the needs of each member can be tended to and the group flourishes as a whole. Any change in one family member will automatically be met with a compensatory change by other family members. Even in dysfunctional families, in which the needs of members are not being met, homeostasis is maintained, keeping the system intact (Berenson, 1978). For example, in a home with an alcoholic wife, the husband will typically take over parenting and household chores formerly done by the wife, thereby assuring that the children are cared for, shopping is done, and so on. Once the system has found stability, great pressure is applied within the system for individuals not to change too much or too fast, for to do so would threaten the integrity of the system and require uncomfortable reciprocal change in other family members (Goldenberg & Goldenberg, 1985).

An alcoholic or substance-abusing system can be described as one in which family life is organized around alcohol or other substance abuse as a homeostatic measure (Berenson, 1978). In effect, the substance becomes the third party in triangulation of relationships, creating stability (Steinglass, 1987). The presence of alcohol or other substance begins to affect roles, interactions, and expectations of the family. For example, a wife may become angry and expect to have to take on the husband's chores when she suspects that her husband has been drinking. Whether he actually has is irrelevant; she *acts* as if he has. It should be noted that this reorganization does not occur in all families in which substance abuse is present, and some families seem to withstand some of the long-term effects of living with a substance abuser. This fact has implications for treatment, particularly in the use of detachment.

In homes where substance abuse is present, individual needs, particularly in times of transition during the family life cycle, may not be met (Berenson, 1978, 1986). Chronic alcoholism can also distort the normative life cycle, interfering with the normal emotional growth and development of individuals within the family (Stanton et al., 1982; Steinglass, 1987). For example, a teen-ager who has assumed parenting chores because his mother is frequently drunk may meet with resistance from parents when attempting to leave home, as his absence will require a shift in the responsibilities and roles of the parents and children remaining in the home.

Malfunctions in the Family System

The family reacts to stresses to the system in ways that will preserve itself (Goldenberg & Goldenberg, 1985). In prolonged chronic illness—such as substance abuse—repetitive, stereotyped patterns of behavior can become integrated into the family's homeostatic mechanisms (Stanton et al., 1982). These patterns thereby paradoxically become associated with long-term family stability. Thus, substance abuse can be seen as being both system-maintaining and system regulating (Steinglass, 1987; Lewis, 1992; Lewis, Dana, & Blevins, 1994). Reactive changes in family dynamics usually occur when substance abuse is introduced into the family. And once the family assimilates these changes and reorganizes around the substance abuse, these changes actually support the addiction or substance abuse. For example, if a 10-year old child begins to watch over a three-year-old sibling because the mother is high on crack, family function is preserved, if imperfectly. However, this assumption of parental roles by the child also makes it easier for the mother to continue with her crack use.

Changes in roles, rules, and boundaries of the family occur in an effort to stabilize the system when a family reorganizes itself in the face of a prolonged crisis such as alcoholism. Behavior of family members within the dysfunctional system, observed from the outside, can appear strange or abnormal while, when viewed within the context of the dysfunctional family, they can be seen as being adaptive or an integral part of maintenance of family homeostasis. In other words, dysfunctional behavior can actually be an attempt to preserve the family system (Stanton et al., 1982; Lewis et al, 1994).

Another characteristic of families with an alcoholic or other substance-abusing member is the high anxiety level of family members. Kaufman (1986) states that "anyone living close to an alcoholic will be psychologically stressed." Other family members of an alcoholic system must assume more of the household tasks and responsibilities as the substance abuser assumes an underfunctioning position in the family. Spouses are affected by the characteristics of their substance abusing partners, as well as the negative consequences of substance abusing behavior, e.g. financial problems, increased social isolation, and family conflicts. Increased depression, anxiety, and physical symptoms have been found in spouses of alcoholics (Kaufman, 1986).

It is important to keep in mind that there is no one prototype for the substance abusing family. The function that alcohol or drug abuse serves for the family may vary and the response of the family may serve to either isolate or magnify its effect. Even so, there are common stresses on the system of the family with a member who is a substance abuser that can, and frequently do, cause certain alterations of functioning and symptoms in the members.

There appear to be substantial differences between families in which a member abuses alcohol and those in which a member abuses another chemical. Therefore, these two types of families will be discussed separately.

Alcoholic Families

Children of alcoholics constitute one of the most prevalent high-risk groups in this country (Werner, 1986). Berkowitz and Perkins (1988) report a parental alcoholism rate of 14% of the adult population, accounting for 21% of all family problems. The New York State Division of Alcoholism and Alcohol Abuse in conjunction with Children of Alcoholics Foundation (Russell, Henderson, & Blume, 1984) estimated that there are about six million youth younger than 18 and 22 million people older than 18 who are children of problem drinkers. This rose to about 6.6 million children younger than 18 living with at least one alcoholic parent (Health ResponseAbility Systems, 1994). This brings the total of children of alcohol-abusing parents in the United States to 28 million, or one out of every eight Americans. Metzger (1988) believes 15% to 20% of the total population would be a more accurate estimation.

Children from alcoholic homes are seen as reflecting some of the dysfunction of the home in which they are raised. Researchers have found a significant proportion of these children exhibit low self-esteem, external locus of control, conduct disorders, learning disabilities, repeated delinquencies, alcohol and drug use, and suicidal tendencies (Russell, Henderson, & Blume, 1984). Additionally, some researchers have found that children of alcoholics were more likely to report drug use than children of depressives or children of "normal" parents (Johnson, Leonard, & Jacob, 1989), have a higher risk of alcohol abuse (Kubicka, Kozeny, & Roth, 1990), and tend to drink at a younger age. Other studies have found more social and personal drinking-related problems at an earlier age than do alcoholics having no history of alcoholism in the family (Penick, Read, Crowley, & Powell, 1978). In general, there is a consistent view that parental alcoholism produces a high risk in children for a variety of emotional and behavioral disorders (Velleman, 1992).

Structural Characteristics of Alcoholic Families

Boundaries. One of the features that allows one family to identify itself, and to be identified by others, is external boundaries. Boundaries can be flexible, allowing for appropriate exit of family members, as in young adulthood; or rigid, restricting movement in and out of the family. Alcoholic families tend to have rigid boundaries, restricting contact with others outside the system. The family uses secrecy to protect the family from shame, and concealment of the problem and silence protect the alcoholic from outsiders (Blum, 1991; Lewis, 1992). However, secrecy also makes the family structure rigid and unable to cope with change.

Coalitions. The family also has internal boundaries. One function of the healthy family is delegation of power, usually along generational lines, forming a hierarchy in which the parents hold the most power. Boundaries normally exist between generations, with the parents clearly separate from the children in terms of rules, roles, and power, and in charge of the caretaking of young children (Goldenberg & Goldenberg, 1985). In couples who abuse substances, this coalition between parents may become strained or damaged (Lewis, 1992; Preli & Protinsky, 1988). Hierarchial reversals in the family, in which mothers and children were placed in lateral positions of power may be found. These intergenerational coalitions, either higher or lower than the alcoholic father in terms of power, suggest that children are enlisted into hierarchically inappropriate caretaking positions in alcoholic families, most often with the nonalcoholic spouse. This blurring of generational boundaries frequently results in the child "parenting" the parent, or meeting intimacy needs that are inappropriate in the parent-child relationship (Lewis, 1992).

Roles. Roles within the family are delegated by the family, and interactions among family members and between the family and the larger social structure are monitored and regulated by the family (Goldenberg & Goldenberg, 1985). Thus, problems of any family member change the dynamics and interactions both within the family and with the larger community social structure.

Several authors (Black, 1979; Wegscheider, 1981; Woititz, 1983) have described roles commonly assumed by children living in alcoholic homes. Although this anecdotal-based theory has not yet been substantiated in research, many treatment programs use the general concepts to treat family members of recovering alcoholics.

Black (1979) describes several roles that children of alcoholics frequently assume: The *responsible child*, who provides structure and stability to an otherwise chaotic family, the *adjuster*, who adapts by withdrawing and detaching from the family; and the *placater*, who smooths over family conflicts to reduce the family pain. These roles reflect Adler's birth order theory in which sibling position affects roles adopted within the family. The oldest child is most likely to adopt a responsible child role, the middle child the role of adjuster, and the youngest child that of placater.

Woititz (1983) adds the roles of the *scapegoat*, who absorbs the blame for the family's dysfunction, and the *clown*, who detracts the family from its pain. The scapegoat, frequently the second child or one who is "different" for some reason, feeling hurt, may engage in delinquency or acting-out behavior. This gives the scapegoat attention, albeit negative attention, and preserves the family system by shifting focus away from the alcoholic.

Wegscheider (1981) describes similar roles. The *hero*, often the oldest child, overachieves out of feelings of inadequacy and guilt, providing self with attention, and the family with a sense of self-worth. Enduring feelings of loneliness, a middle child may assume a *lost child* role, appearing shy and choosing solitariness. In this way family pain may be escaped and the family given some relief. The *mascot*, often the fourth or youngest child, may deal with fear through clowning or hyperactive behavior. This gives the alcoholic family some comic relief and the mascot attention.

Although these roles provide for survival in an unbalanced family, the cost to the child may be great. When carried into adulthood, these roles become dysfunctional. Using Black's (1979) role classifications, responsible or parental children, as adults, take control and continue the pattern of being very serious and unable to enjoy themselves. Moreover, they may be unable to receive help from others. Adjusters may stay in unhealthy situations in adulthood, not having mastered the skill of disengagement and decision-making. This may be partly accountable for the large number of adult children of alcoholics who marry alcoholics. Placaters are not likely to ask others for help in meeting their personal needs and spend time caring for others (Black, 1979). Ackerman (1989) and Pilat and Jones (1984–1985) report that a high percentage of people in the helping professions are adult children of alcoholics. The interest of many therapists in the field of alcoholism may be related to early exposure to parental alcoholism. It is theorized that they may have been responsible, hardworking, sensitive members of the alcoholic family system and carry this role into adulthood.

Scapegoats (Woititz's classification) may continue to see themselves as the cause of problems as adults, with resulting low self-esteem and a self-fulfilling prophesy to continue to place themselves in situations where they will be seen as the cause for the troubles of others. They may perpetuate self-destructive tendencies and may be prone to addiction. Clowns may continue to be the life of the party as adults, but not take themselves seriously (Woititz, 1983). Overuse of humor helps them avoid underlying emotional conflict.

Similarly, using Wegscheider's classifications (1981), the hero, in adulthood, may continue to control and to have a compulsive drive. The lost child may experience social isolation in adulthood, and the mascot may be at risk for immaturity and emotional illness.

A home with inconsistent and confusing parental messages and expectations can be fertile ground for the development of dysfunctional personal attributes among children. These conflicting expectations create double-bind situations and paradoxes in which the child cannot succeed. Attributes frequently reported in studies of adult children of alcoholics are low self-esteem, lack of trust, shame, and no real sense of self, which puts the adult child of an alcoholic parent at risk for alcoholism and other emotional dysfunctions (Ackerman & Gondolf, 1989; Subby, 1987).

There is some disagreement as to whether growing up in a home where there is alcoholism or other substance abuse causes the children to abuse alcohol or other substances. Some researchers and theorists allege that unstable childhoods do *not* predict later alcoholism, although they do predict later regular usage of prescribed medication and mind-altering drugs (Vaillant, 1983). Velleman (1992), in his review of the literature, concludes that although there is ample evidence that children of problem drinkers are at a higher risk for developing a number of childhood problems and disorders, evidence of these differences between children of alcoholics and children of nonalcoholic parents may not carry through into adulthood. Some recent research has supported this conclusion, *not* finding a significant difference in emotional adjustment of adult children of alcoholics and other individuals (Harman, Armsworth, Hwang, Vincent, & Preston, 1995). Others suggest that the emotional differences found are not caused by the presence of alcohol in the family, but by the presence of *any* family dysfunction.

||||||||||||||||||||||||||||||||||||||||||||||||||||||||||||||||||||||||||||||||||||

CASE DISCUSSION

Case 2 (Joe and Jane Smith).   Both Joe and Jane came from alcohol-centered homes, in which emotional and physical abuse were also present. In their current home, alcohol and cocaine use regulate the interactions. Sarah may be seen to be acting as the family scapegoat, detracting from her mother and Joe's drug and alcohol abuse by acting out. Sarah is also reflecting the replication of the abusive and conflictual homes of her mother and stepfather, and is making movements to leave home at an early age. Karen acts as the "lost child," doing her part to stabilize the home by staying out of the way and being quiet.

||||||||||||||||||||||||||||||||||||||||||||||||||||||||||||||||||||||||||||||||||||

Dynamics of Substance Abusing Families

Substance abuse typically begins in adolescence, when tendencies toward risk-taking behaviors emerge and movement toward independence increases reliance upon the peer group. Such a quest for independence and separation from the family is appropriate for the adolescent stage of psychosocial development (Goldenberg & Goldenberg, 1985). As in other stages of transition in family life, the changes of one family member precipitate an imbalance in the family system, initiating reciprocal allowance of some independence by the parents. Ideally, the parents will find a balance between maintaining complete authority over the adolescent and abdicating authority altogether (Goldenberg & Goldenberg, 1985).

Because most substance-abuse families tend to be enmeshed (Kaminer, 1991; Ranew & Serrit, 1992), this differentiation of the adolescent causes a crisis in the family, and an interactive pattern involving drugs may ensue. Rebelling against inappropriately rigid family boundaries, the adolescent may experiment with drugs, which in turn unites the family in an attempt to "help" the drug user. It has been noted by clinicians, however, that when the substance abuser stops using, a familial crisis often erupts, such as marital problems, or the acting out of a sibling (Stanton et al., 1982). This often brings the former substance abuser, finally capable of leaving home, back into the nest where the drug abuse is resumed. Thus, the substance abuse provides a dependency in the user that maintains the rigid family boundaries, preserves the enmeshment of the family, and the substance abuser becomes the symptom-bearer for the family. The addict, in effect, provides the family with a paradoxical resolution to their dilemma of maintaining or dissolving the family.

Children who grow up in homes in which there is substance abuse are at risk for becoming substance abusers themselves (Ranew & Serrit, 1992). The quality of parenting suffers, and the child may experience parental neglect and emotional and physical abuse. Contact with neighbors and others may deteriorate, and the family becomes more socially isolated. And the child is more reluctant to bring others into the home, where they might see the abusive behavior of the parent (Ranew & Serrit, 1992). Thus, in the presence of deteriorating parenting, the family system becomes more closed, exacerbating the effects of the neglect and abuse for the child.

|||||||||||||||||||||||||||||||||||||||||||||||||||||||||||||||||||||||||||||||

CASE DISCUSSION

Case 3 (Leigh).   Leigh can be viewed as the scapegoat of the family. Her rebellion distracts her mother and father from their fighting and unites them as they attempt to control her behavior. It also helps solve the dilemma of whether Leigh should leave home, leaving her mother alone. She distances herself by using drugs and alcohol, but cannot really leave home and her mother because of her irresponsible behavior. Her brother has the role of the hero of the family, doing well and being responsible while the parents are in conflict. Through the use of their roles, the estranged family continues to function, albeit less than satisfactorily.

|||||||||||||||||||||||||||||||||||||||||||||||||||||||||||||||||||||||||||||||||

Strengths and Limitations of Systems Theories

Strengths

1. Identifies relationships that act as underlying factors in maintaining maladaptive behavior, making it more amenable to change.
2. Sociological forces and relationships that influence the development and maintenance of addiction are considered.
3. The dysfunctional parenting that may precipitate the intergenerational transmission of alcoholism and other substance abuse can be assessed and addressed in treatment.

Limitations

1. Although descriptive of the interactions of individuals in the home, systems theory does not provide an empirically based cause for substance abuse.
2. Research is conflicting concerning the intergenerational transmission of substance abuse.
3. In studies that find intergenerational transmission of substance abuse, it is difficult to separate the effects of dysfunctional parenting with that of substance abuse alone.

Summary of the Systems Theory

The intergenerational transmission of alcoholism and substance abuse has long been observed. There is some dispute whether this is due to the presence of substance abuse in the family, or if it might result from living in a dysfunctional family and having inadequate parenting. Systems theory describes the structure and interactions of the substance abusing family, observing the effect of the presence of alcohol or substances on each member. Finding family environment patterns that predispose children for alcoholism and other substance abuse may enable counselors to prevent these conditions in children at risk. Dysfunctional family patterns can be changed through family therapy and parent training. With more nurturing and functional parenting, children in such families have a better chance of becoming well-rounded, resilient adults.

Recent research has pointed out that systems theory is more effective in describing the substance abusing family than in determining a single cause for the condition. However, implications for treatment for all members of the family and prevention of transmission to another generation make it an important theory to consider and increasingly important in treatment programs. For example, family environmental factors not only react to the presence of substance abuse, they also influence the course of the disease (Edwards & Steinglass, 1995). Involvement of the family in treatment would then be extremely helpful, if not critical. Liddle & Dakof (1995), in reviewing studies of family-based adolescent drug-abuse treatment programs, support the efficacy of family therapy in adolescent drug treatment. However, the small number of these studies and their methodological limitations make blanket statements premature.

BEHAVIORAL THEORIES

The behavioral theories, including social learning theory, have their theoretical roots in experimental psychology and learning theory (Bennett & Woolf, 1990). Addictions are viewed as learned, socially acquired behaviors with multiple causes (MacKay, Donovan, & Marlatt, 1991). Substance abuse, like other behaviors, is seen as influenced by biological makeup, cognitive processes, past learning, situational antecedents, and reinforcement contingencies. An assumption is made that all substance abuse, from incidental social use to abuse to addiction, is governed by similar principles of learning and cognition. Early behavioral treatment for substance abuse used chemical-aversion therapy such as daily dosages of disulfiram (Antabuse) for alcoholics to produce a conditioned aversion to alcohol (George, 1990; Ray & Ksir, 1993). While initially effective, it did not prove to be a long-term determent after the drug was discontinued. This approach has largely been abandoned as new behavioral models for substance dependency have been developed. Current behavioral theories have added cognitive factors as mediating variables to the learning patterns believed to be responsible for development of addictions. Other etiological factors, such as genetic elements, sociocultural influences, and physiological factors, are not rejected. Thus, while most behavioralists believe that learning plays an important part in addiction in some individuals, other etiological factors may also play an important role (George, 1990).

Some behavioralists have controlled drinking as a goal, teaching methods that will limit alcohol intake (Ray & Ksir, 1993). They point out that drinking in moderation may be a realistic goal for some early stage problem drinkers (Lewis, Dana, & Blevins, 1994). However, there is much controversy about the effectiveness of controlled drinking strategies in curtailing impulsive behavior or resisting social pressure. Early behavioral research on alcoholism reported operant conditioning to be effective in modifying the alcoholic's pattern of drinking to allow a return to normal drinking in some individuals. A follow-up study, however, showed that those who abstained from alcohol achieved a recovery, while those who attempted controlled drinking had either died or relapsed into alcoholic dependence (George, 1990). Thus, operant conditioning does not appear to allow alcoholics to turn to controlled drinking.

Social learning theory, developed by Albert Bandura (1969), formed the basis of much of the current behavioral theory about substance abuse (Abrams & Niaura, 1987; George, 1990). Cognitive, genetic, and sociocultural factors are thought to predispose or influence the experimentation with alcohol or drugs as well as subsequent usage. It is suggested that abuse of a substance occurs when an individual's coping abilities, through the interaction of personality sets, learned responses, and current circumstances, are overwhelmed; thus, substance abuse can be seen as a coping response to severe stressors. The consequences of substance abuse then become, in themselves, stressors, leading to further substance abuse. A circular behavioral pattern of stress and attempts at stress relief develops. Abrams and Niaura (1987) point out that the immediate tension-reducing properties of alcohol must be measured against the longer term negative consequences of drinking in deciding to control or stop drinking.

Situational antecedents, such as time of day of drinking, place of drinking, and association with certain people or emotional states are all important when analyzing the cause of the behavior (Snow & Wells-Parker, 1986). For example, drinking with friends at the local bar three to four times a week to blow off steam, snorting cocaine at parties with friends once a week, and shooting heroin alone would each be evaluated for behavioral and situational antecedents, associations, and situational settings. Each factor is analyzed so that the maladaptive behavioral sequences can be restructured and changed.

Cognitive processes involved in the behavior are also considered. Anticipation of the desired effects of the drug, remembering past pleasant associations with the behavior and the modeling of the behavior by others are all important (Abrams & Niaura, 1987; MacKay, Donovan, & Marlatt, 1991).

Addictive behavior is maintained by reinforcement, that is, the rewarding aspects of drug consumption and the social setting. Several principles of reinforcement are active in behavior formation and maintenance, including addictive behavior:

1. The more rewarding or positive an experience is, the greater the likelihood that the behavior leading to that experience will be repeated (MacKay, Donovan, & Marlatt, 1991). Thus, a normally shy individual who becomes "the life of the party" after drinking will want to recreate that experience by drinking again.

2. The greater the frequency of obtaining positive experiences through drug consumption, the more likely that drugs will be consumed again (MacKay, Donovan, & Marlatt, 1991).

3. The more closely in time that the behavior (drug consumption) and consequences of the behavior are experienced, the more likely the behavior will be repeated (Childress, Ehrman, Rohsenow, Robbins, & O'Brien, 1992; MacKay, Donovan, & Marlatt, 1991). Conversely, the further in time a consequence of the behavior is experienced, the less likely the consequence will affect future behavior. For example, a lonely man who finds companionship in the bar drinking with others is likely to remember the camaraderie associated with the drinking, and the hangover the next day is more easily attributed to "overdrinking," rather than to drinking with certain friends. It is this reinforcing association of the two events that increase the likelihood of his drinking when feeling lonely or isolated.

The rapid onset of the effects of substances that are inhaled (e.g. cocaine and tobacco) or injected directly into the bloodstream (e.g. heroin) becomes extremely psychologically reinforcing (Ray & Ksir, 1993). Further, a major problem in the rehabilitation of opioid addicts is the long-lasting effect of the chemical—long *after* detoxification (Thomason & Dilts, 1991). Results of heroin-induced brain changes, such as disturbances and problems with bladder control require months to reverse themselves, whereas it only takes a few minutes to get a "high." Unable to feel good without drugs for months during withdrawal, an individual gets immediate reinforcement for drug-taking behavior when feeling good only after drug ingestion.

Alcohol and other substance use can also be viewed as an attempt to relieve stress. *Stress response dampening* is one theory that attempts to explain substance use as stress relief (George, 1990). Alcohol is frequently used as a self-prescribed agent to reduce stress. Stress response dampening, although useful, is generally viewed as only a partial explanation for the abuse of alcohol and other drugs under stress. For example, the stress response dampening theory does not predict that alcohol consumption will reduce stress or which stressful events will initiate usage, nor does it consider individual differences. In situations in which drug use is punished or prohibited, the stress dampening theory may not be predictive of drug use.

Concurrent use of alcohol and other substances is commonly found. There also is a strong correlation between alcohol and tobacco use in the general population, with some estimates of alcoholics who smoke as high as 90% (Sher, 1987). There is also a strong correlation between use of alcohol and tranquilizers or heroin. The high incidence of concurrent multiple drug usage may be due to a common motivation, e.g. reaching for a cigarette and/or a alcohol when under stress, or it may be the result of the effects of one drug upon another (Sher, 1987).

A current trend in behavioral approaches to substance abuse is to address both behavioral excesses (excessive consumption of psychoactive drugs) and a lack of social or behavioral skills (Lewis, 1992; MacKay, Donovan, & Marlett, 1991). Logs of times and circumstances are kept for insight into the antecedent events of the abuse. Contingency contracting, systematic desensitization, covert aversion therapy, relaxation training, and social skills training, including assertion training, may all be included in a behavioral treatment plan to correct social and behavioral deficits.

CASE DISCUSSION

Case 1 (Sandy and Pam).   Sandy appears to be right—Pam has learned how to cope with life and how to relate to others from her mother and is clearly following her example. Both have learned that closeness in a relationship hurts and use alcohol to approach men. Behavior patterns are learned, established, and continuous.

Pam has begun to experience anxiety attacks over being alone. Feeling abandoned as a child, she is afraid of being deserted. At the same time, she distrusts men. Alcohol acts as a stress dampener, relieving, at least temporarily, the anxiety she feels when facing this paradox. The pattern of behavior is replicated.

Cases 2 and 3 (Jane Smith and Leigh).   Both Jane and Leigh use with friends. They have learned that using helps them to fit in—to be "one of the gang." Jane is even supplied by customers at the bar. It would be difficult to stop using without changing friends, and in Jane's case, her job, as well. Being a bartender is also a risky job if sincere about abstaining from alcohol use. Both Jane and Leigh would have to change their behavior and the settings in which those behaviors take place to stay clean. The use of substances has socio-behavioral roots. From a behavioral perspective, both Jane's and Leigh's use is reinforced by the social environment.

Strengths and Limitations of Behavioral Theories

Strengths

1. Behaviors are easily observed.

2. Behaviors are easily measured, as are the results of interventions.

3. Treatment goals for changing the behavior or antecedent reinforcements are easily formulated.

Limitations

1. The individual is treated in isolation from family and family-of-origin. Reinforcing or maladaptive behaviors within the social system of the identified patient will remain, putting pressure on the recovering addict not to change, to "fit" into the maladaptive family or social group.

2. Biological aspects of addiction are not addressed.

3. Genetic predispositions to addiction are largely ignored.

Summary of Behavioral Theories

The behaviorist approaches substance abuse, like all behavior, as the product of learning. Recent theories add cognitive factors as mediating variables to the learning patterns believed responsible for addictions. Addiction and substance abuse are seen as the result of faulty learning patterns, and antecedent actions and situational factors are analyzed to determine the sequence of these patterns. Stress response dampening, or learning to use substances to relieve stress, is one of the more recent behavioral theories.

A major disadvantage of the behavioral approach is that the intergenerational, family, and biological factors are not directly addressed. Critics would claim that, although current behavior of the individual might be changed, long-lasting change requires a change in family patterns and attention to the biological changes involved in addiction, as well as to genetic differences in addicts. Behavioral approaches may not have the total answer to causal factors in abuse of alcohol and other substance, but they do have certain advantages. Relationships between antecedent actions and addictive behavior can be clearly viewed and measured, as can social conditions associated with that behavior. Treatment plans, designed to change these patterns of behavior, can then be planned.

SOCIOCULTURAL THEORIES OF SUBSTANCE ABUSE

Social and cultural influences on substance abuse cannot be ignored. However, most theorists, while recognizing the importance of sociological factors in the initiation and continuation of substance abuse, view them as part of a complex mechanism which supports the whole.

Alcohol Abuse

Environmental support for heavy drinking is an important sociological variable contributing to alcoholism (Smith-Peterson, 1983; Snow & Wells-Parker, 1986). Attitudes toward alcohol consumption and abuse vary from culture to culture and greatly affect the amount and context of alcohol consumption. In general, solitary, addictive, pathologic drinking is more associated with urbanized, industrial societies than with societies that remain largely rural and traditional. Additionally, socially disruptive use of alcohol tends to occur almost exclusively in social settings;

drunken behavior is seldom seen when alcohol is used in a religions context. Non-moralistic attitudes toward alcohol generally accompany nonpathological use in a culture (Smith-Peterson, 1983). For example, in many European countries, such as France and Italy, wine is the beverage of choice with meals and watered wine is served to children as a table beverage. Conversely, cultures with a recent history with alcoholic beverages, which have yet to completely develop a set of values regarding its use, generally experience more alcohol abuse. American Indian tribes are an example (Smith-Peterson, 1983).

Environmental support for heavy drinking is an important factor to development of alcohol abuse. Peers and parents, by example, show how and where to drink, shaping behaviors of others. In conditions of poverty, boredom, and hopelessness, often found in inner cities and American Indian reservations, excessive alcohol consumption, as well as other substance abuse, is common and even expected (Smith-Peterson, 1983). Pressure can be great to conform and to "fit in". To refuse to comply with societal expectations to drink heavily or to seek treatment for alcoholism may mean turning away from previous friends and changing relationships with one's family. Issues raised by cultural and societal norms and expectations must be addressed by the counselor if effective intervention is to take place.

Substance Abuse

Several components of the environment affect the likelihood that an individual will become involved with substance abuse. On a national scale, multiple social crises in recent decades have encouraged expansion of drug use, abuse, and sale of illicit drugs (Johnson & Muffler, 1989). The expansion of the urban ghetto has encouraged the growth of substance abuse as an industry. A decline in labor-intensive jobs has caused unskilled laborers to sink further into poverty. At the same time, the increased cost of adequate housing has created a sizable population with inadequate, or no, housing. The proportion of families headed by single mothers, particularly among minorities, has increased dramatically. Fifty-nine percent of all children younger than 6 who live in mother-headed, single-parent families live in poverty, compared with 13% living in married-couple families. Moreover, the proportion of single mothers who have never married, compared with those who are divorced, widowed, or separated, continues to climb. In African-American households, the proportion of single-parent households in which the mother never married increased from 18% in 1970 to 52% in 1991 (Lamanna & Riedmann, 1997).

Such families are also likely to have inadequate housing or live with relatives in crowded conditions. Inner city youths are less likely to finish high school or to have marketable skills. Child abuse and neglect have increased, and homicide has become a leading killer of young black men. As households experience several of the crises concurrently, which inner-city families do, many are socialized into deviant behavior, such as antisocial acts and child abuse or neglect, or criminal activity (Johnson & Muffler, 1989). In such settings, inner-city families may also experience learned helplessness, and feel disenfranchised from society as a whole (Johnson & Muffler,

1989). Within this realm of hopelessness, opportunity for abuse and sale of drugs becomes attractive.

Use and abuse of drugs follow patterns of popularity and change over time. The popularity of marijuana, psychedelic drugs, opiates, and "designer drugs" as drug of choice have waxed and waned over time (Inciardi & McElrath, 1995; Ray & Ksir, 1993). In the 1960s and 1970s, use of marijuana became popular, peaking in 1979, when just more than 60% of high school seniors stated they had used marijuana at least once. This declined to less than 41% in 1991 (Ray & Ksir, 1993), and continued to drop in the early 1990s. The National Clearinghouse for Alcohol and Drug Information (1996) reports that this trend is reversing, with 37.9% of 1995 high school seniors smoking marijuana. In addition, when they used marijuana, they became more intoxicated than in previous years.

A substantial proportion of the current population has at least experimented with marijuana and may continue to use it as a recreational drug. Marijuana is not only the most commonly used illegal drug in this country, it is currently a common secondary drug used by most drug abusers (Johnson & Muffler, 1989; Inciardi & McElrath, 1995). While about one-half of marijuana users do not use other drugs, virtually all users of other drugs use marijuana. For this reason, it is sometimes known as a "gateway drug" (Johnson & Muffler, 1989; Oetting & Beauvais, 1986; Ray & Ksir, 1993). Moreover, the heavier the usage of marijuana, the greater the likelihood of using cocaine, heroin, or other drugs, or of becoming involved with the sale of illegal drugs (Ray & Ksir, 1993).

Johnson & Muffler (1989) report that the popularity of heroin increased from 1965 to 1973, primarily among inner city youth in large cities. Usage of heroin typically involved injection on a near-daily, or even multiple-daily basis. The national statistics on lifelong heroin use have remained steady since 1979 at about 2 million users, with a reported 196,000 in 1995. However, this estimate is considered conservative, given the possible underreporting by this population. There has been no significant increase except in the area of lifetime heroin smokers, which doubled from 1994 to 1995 to an estimated 1.4 million (SAMHSA, 1996).

Cocaine usage, primarily snorting (nasal inhalation) and freebasing (inhaling fumes from freebase cocaine), gained in popularity from 1979 to 1984 (Johnson & Muffler, 1989). Freebasing caused a rapid increase in frequency of usage, as the rapid euphoria felt after inhaling lasts only about 20 minutes, and is followed by rapid dysphoria, where the user feels worse than usual. Relief of the dysphoria is experienced with repeated freebasing, and the cycle of psychological reinforcement continues.

The time from 1985 to the present can be called the "crack era," for the rock or crystalline form of freebase cocaine sold in vials or bags. In this time, a major expansion of existing drug abuse and sales of drugs in inner cities was seen accompanying the use of crack cocaine (Johnson & Muffler, 1989). Youthful crack users are also commonly involved in sale of drugs and other crimes (Inciardi & Pottieger, 1991).

Developmental and Family Factors of Socialization

A variety of family and social factors affect an individual's decision to start and continue the use of substances, including alcohol. Family factors, such as attitudes and customs of the family involving alcohol and other substances, tolerance toward public intoxication and drug use, and childhood exposure to alcohol and drug use models form a background for adolescent attitudes towards substance usage. Additionally, several types of parenting have been associated with an increase in substance abuse in offspring: the alcoholic parent, the teetotaling parent, the overdemanding parent, and the overprotective parent (Lawson, 1992). Social rewards or punishment for substance usage, coupled with this background, can then influence an individual's decision to begin using or continue to use substances.

Parental substance use and abuse, particularly when viewed by the young child, provides models for later behavior by offspring. This modeling is also one component of the social learning theory (see section on behavioral theories of substance abuse). Parental attitudes toward substance usage, and parent-child interactions are also strongly predictive of future substance use by offspring (Kaminer, 1991; Oetting & Beauvais, 1986). Young people who perceive their family as caring and against drug usage are more likely to choose peer groups with similar standards. They are also more likely to get better grades, which is also a predictor in abstaining from drug use (Oetting & Beauvais, 1986). In addition to providing role models for future behavior and influencing formation of attitudes toward substance use and abuse, family factors such as high stress, poor and inconsistent family management skills, neglect, and lack of interaction among family members are predictive of later substance use and abuse.

The socialization of the adolescent creates factors that influence drug and alcohol experimentation and abuse that may differ from those of adults. Not only does the family exert influence, but the peer group grows increasingly important in the actions and beliefs of the adolescent. Groups of peers, or *peer clusters* (Oetting & Beauvais, 1986; Ray & Ksir, 1993) have great influence on whether an adolescent within that group will use drugs. It may be "cool" to experiment with, or abuse drugs, or it may considered "in" to abstain. Adolescents are at a stage of development in which they not only feel omnipotent and invulnerable to life's tragedies but also are attracted to risk-taking behavior and may feel a rise in self-esteem when accepted by a group who approves of drug usage.

CASE DISCUSSIONS

Case 1 (Sandy and Pam). Sociocultural influences are apparent in their family. Sandy was raised in a home where alcohol was abused and family relationships were distant and abusive. This has continued into Pam's generation. Not only were the nurturing and positive teaching of life skills absent in their homes, but missing also was the modeling of meaningful relationships with others. There was also a great deal of stress and inconsistency in their families, predictors of future substance abuse.

It's difficult to teach someone how to have nurturing relationships when they have neither experienced one nor seen one. This is reflected in their attraction to relationships with abusive men.

Case 2 (Leigh).   Leigh has found acceptance in a counter-culture when she felt rejection at home. With divorced parents, a distant father, overly stressed mother, and parents arguing over the kids, Leigh has poor self-esteem and believes she is the cause of some of the problems. She finds that using drugs with other kids relieves boredom, fear, and loneliness. She feels accepted and acceptable when she is using with them.

Strengths and Limitations of Sociocultural Theories

Strengths

1. Substance abusers are viewed within the larger context of their environment.

2. The importance of social pressure in the development of substance abuse, particularly among adolescents, is recognized.

3. The use of alcohol and drugs is viewed within the cultural context of the individual using them.

Limitations

1. Genetic factors are ignored.

2. Family dynamics are not directly addressed.

3. Individual development and personality factors are not addressed.

Summary of the Sociocultural Theory

Sociological and cultural factors in substance use and abuse cannot be ignored. The early socialization of the child forms the basis for attitudes toward substance use that are acted upon in adulthood. Adolescence—with its striving toward individuation, reliance on the peer group, and penchant for risk-taking behavior—creates an environment conducive to the development of abuse of alcohol and other drugs. In addition, the culture of the inner city can encourage its continuance. However, sociocultural influences alone cannot fully explain the development of substance abuse behavior. Genetic, family, and behavioral/learning factors work together in forming attitudes and probabilities toward substance abuse behavior.

BIOPSYCHOSOCIAL THEORY

The biopsychosocial theory of substance abuse is an integrated theory, conceptualizing behavior as a function of mutual determination and reciprocal effects of a individual, the environment, and behavior. It assumes that many influences combine to create the conditions under which an individual will abuse, or not abuse, alcohol or other substances.

Substance abuse is increasingly seen as a complex, progressive behavior pattern with biological, psychological, and social components (Lewis, Dana, & Blevins, 1994; Pratsinek & Alexander, 1992; Ranew & Serrit, 1992). Support is growing for the belief that alcoholism, for example, may result from the interaction of predisposing factors, biological and constitutional factors, sociocultural factors, and psychological factors (Blane & Leonard, 1987; Nace, 1987). Kumpfer & Hopkins (1993) suggest that addictions are multicausal, involving a complex interaction of genetic, physiologic, and environmental precursors. They include such factors as individual differences in pleasurable reactions to alcohol, psychophysiologic differences, neurochemical differences, cognitive functioning differences, temperament or personality differences, and environmental differences within the family, school, community, and peer groups.

Research in the area of predisposing factors, such as biological and genetic factors, appears particularly promising. Genetic makeup may *predispose* an individual to alcoholism, allowing the disorder to be triggered by other factors. Research on genetic antecedents for other substance abuse is in its infancy and is much more difficult to quantify because of the variety of drugs, often used together, and the faddish nature of their use (Anthenelli & Schuckit, 1992).

Sociocultural influences, too, appear to offer mitigating factors in the development of alcohol abuse. For example, the Irish and American Indians have more social and individual problems with alcohol than do the Chinese (Smith-Peterson, 1983). It is uncertain if these sociocultural differences are due to genetic predispositions or cultural attitudes toward drinking, but the overall effect remains clear: some ethnic groups have more problems concerning alcohol consumption than others.

Psychological factors that may interact with a genetic or biologic predisposition and sociocultural factors include the effects of growing up in an alcoholic home, learned or conditioned drinking and behavior, and cognitive deficiencies. All of the preceding factors—genetic predisposition, sociocultural factors, and psychological factors—may be present, yet an individual may not abuse alcohol or other substances. Researchers are still looking for reasons that a portion of the population seems to be invulnerable or resilient in response to these effects (Harman,

Armsworth, Hwang, Vincent, & Preston, 1995). Some theorize that a trigger, or precipitating factor, must also be present to set off the cycle of substance abuse (George, 1990). Several theories have been presented: that cumulative trauma, a severe loss, or sudden success can initiate a downward progression into substance abuse. For example, an individual made vulnerable by other factors may turn to drink or chemicals as a way of coping when threatened by severe loss of health, or problems with work, school, or family. Other individuals, such as those with masochistic tendencies and disordered character structures, when faced with sudden success, may turn to alcohol or other chemicals. Unconsciously feeling unworthy of success, they may become depressed and turn to substances as a palliative measure. This behavior can be observed in some entertainers, following sudden and overwhelming fame. Interest in research in these areas is growing, and may shed light on the interaction of factors in substance abuse in the future.

CASE DISCUSSIONS

Case 1 (Sandy and Pam).   From a biopsychosocial perspective, Sandy and Pam would be seen as coming from a family in which many members abused alcohol. Genetic components to a predisposition to alcoholism would be suspected. The intergenerational transmission of alcoholism would also be looked at from a systems and learning theory perspective, in which roles and interaction techniques are learned within the home.

Case 2 (The Smiths).   It would be noted that the family has at least several generations of substance abuse in its history. A predisposition to alcohol and possibly drug abuse would be suspected. The intergenerational effects living in the highly dysfunctional homes would also be considered, as would the modeling of the family in how to relate to others. The family is substance-centered, and drastic reorganization would need to take effect for the intergenerational transmission of substance abuse to be stopped.

Strengths and Limitations of Biopsychosocial Theory

Strengths

1. All contributing factors for the development of substance abuse are considered.
2. Treatment can be multifaceted, dealing with many interacting underlying issues.

Limitations

1. It may be too encompassing and too broad to precisely describe the origins of substance abuse.

2. As a combination of other theories, it is difficult to concisely state its basic assumptions and beliefs.

Summary of the Biopsychosocial Theory

Biopsychosocial theories of substance abuse are experiencing growing support for their integrated approach. By accepting the influence of many different factors upon the individual, namely genetic, biological, sociocultural, and familial, a multifaceted approach can be used for treatment, and comprehensive solutions can be sought. It is increasingly accepted that an individual does not live in a vacuum, and behavior has many influences, both from within and from without. An integrated theory (Table 2.1) allows for the exploration of all influencing factors in attempting to explain and to change undesirable behavior, such as substance abuse.

CONCLUSION

The concept of etiology of substance abuse has changed dramatically in this century. Initially, substance abuse was thought to be caused by corrupt morals and a weak will. Society began to soften this critical attitude in the 1930s, allowing Alcoholics Anonymous to form a self-help group to deal with and maintain sobriety. Jellinek refined the disease concept in the 1950s, defining signs and symptoms of alcoholism, stages of the illness, the course of the disease, and delineated types of alcoholics. Later models of substance abuse have included the genetic concept, behavioral models, sociocultural models, systems theory and biopsychosocial models. Each model has strengths in explaining certain aspects of substance abuse.

The behavioral and sociocultural models appear particularly useful in the explanation of drug use, while the genetic model shows promise for identifying predisposing factors in alcoholism. Systems theories are useful in examining the intergenerational aspects of substance abuse and the forces in the family that seem to help perpetuate its transmission. The biopsychosocial theory is rapidly growing in popularity for explaining substance abuse, as the issues involved are exceedingly complex and not easily explained.

Each of the theories has strengths in explaining the origins of substance abuse, yet none is complete in its explanation. Research is particularly difficult, because the factors involved in the abusive behavior are so numerous and complex. Recent trends in treatment of substance abuse reflect this complexity and lean toward the use of combined theories, addressing the interactive aspects of the causative factors.

TABLE 2.1   Comparisons of Etiological Theories of Substance Abuse

	Moral Model	Disease Model	Genetic Model
Characteristics	1. Alcoholism and drug abuse caused by lack of willpower or moral degradation. 2. Willpower and determination are sufficient to overcome addictions. 3. The predominant theory of alcoholism and substance abuse through history until the 1930s.	1. Substance abuse is a disease, with signs, symptoms, and disease progression. 2. As a disease, substance abuse can be treated. 3. Afflicted individual has sole responsibility for the solution.	1. Looks for biological reasons for occurrence of substance abuse through intergenerational studies, twin studies, adoption studies, and a search for genetic markers. 2. Suggests a predisposition for substance abuse can be inherited.
Strengths		1. Removes societal stigma from substance abuser. 2. Relieves feelings of guilt and shame from abuser, facilitating treatment. 3. Allows for research on the disease. 4. Gives hope for a favorable prognosis. 5. Lays the foundation for treatment programs and self-help groups.	1. Research on biological explanations for substance abuse forms a foundation for further research and treatment theories. 2. Intergenerational studies can reveal patterns of occurrence of substance abuse. 3. Intergenerational studies give an overview of trends in type and frequency of substance abuse.

Limitations	1. Does not take into account recent research on families, culture, and genetic transmission of substance abuse. 2. Creates a tendency to blame and belittle the substance abuser.	1. Can be misused by substance abuser to avoid responsibility for seeking treatment. 2. No differentiation between alcoholism and substance abuse is made in treatment. 3. Critics argue that it is an unscientific concept propagated by recovering substance abusers.	1. Intergenerational studies can only imply genetic transmission. 2. There is some dispute over research methods and conclusions of some intergenerational research.
Advocates	Aristotle Temperance Movement Advocates (Predominant theory until 1930s)	Jellinek Alcoholics Anonymous and other Anon groups Light	Goodwin Schuckit Cloninger Pickens

TABLE 2.1, *continued*

	Systems Theory	Behavioral Theory	Sociocultural Theory	Biopsychosocial Theory
Characteristics	1. Considers the family and larger social system for clues to the development of substance abuse.	1. Addictions are learned, socially acquired behaviors with multiple causes.	1. Environmental and social pressures contribute to the development of substance abuse.	1. Substance abuse results from the interaction of predisposing factors, sociological factors, and psychological factors.
	2. Treats the family system as the patient, changing its structure or interactions as part of the recovery process.	2. Substance abuse is influenced by biological makeup, cognitive processes, past learning, situational antecedents, and reinforcement contingencies.	2. Multiple social pressures, such as unemployment, single-parent families, and poverty foster the development of substance abuse.	2. Substance abusers are seen within the larger context encompassing all known influences for development of substance abuse.
	3. Assumes that families change in the presence of a substance abuser. These changes can actually support the substance abuse.	3. Behavioral and learning factors are applied in both determining the cause of substance abuse and in its treatment.	3. Societal attitudes toward alcohol and drugs contribute to their use or non-use.	
	4. Substance abuse can be a symptom of a larger family malfunction within the family.	4. Social learning theory and stress response dampening are behavioral explanation for development of substance abuse.	4. Family and peer attitudes toward substances influence their usage.	
	5. Considers family characteristics such as family member roles, boundaries, and developmental stages when evaluating malfunctions of the family system.	5. Behavioral factors, such as behavioral sequences, situational contingencies, and stressors are analyzed to ascertain the cause of substance abuse.	5. Peer clusters have great influence over adolescent attitudes toward substance usage.	

Strengths	1. More elements of the substance abuser's life are used in treating the condition. 2. Family members are treated, as well as the substance abuser. 3. Family members can support change in the substance abuser.	1. Behaviors are easily observed. 2. Behaviors are easily measured. 3. Treatment goals are easily formulated for changing the behavioral or antecedent reinforcements.	1. Views substance abusers within the larger context of their environment. 2. Acknowledges the importance of social pressure in the development of substance abuse, particularly among adolescents. 3. Views use of alcohol and drugs within the cultural context of the individual using them.	1. All contributing factors for the development of substance abuse are considered. 2. Treatment is multifaceted, dealing with many interacting underlying issues.
Limitations	1. Some critics challenge research that claims an association between children of substance abusers and later development of substance abuse in those children.	1. The individual is treated in isolation from the family and larger social system. 2. Pressures not to change by the family or to conform to peer norms are not addressed directly. 3. Biological aspects of substance abuse are not addressed. 4. Genetic predispositions to alcohol are ignored.	1. Generic factors are largely ignored. 2. Family dynamics are not directly addressed.	1. Is really a combination of theories, which may weaken its applicability. 2. May be so broad and encompassing that too much can be included.

TABLE 2.1, *continued*

	Systems Theory	Behavioral Theory	Sociocultural Theory	Biopsychosocial Theory
Advocates	Haley Stanton Todd Bowen Goldenberg Berenson Steinglass Black Woititz	Bandura Woolf Sher	Lawson Kaminer Johnson Muffler Smith-Peterson	George Nace Blane Leonard

REFERENCES

Abrams, D. B., & Niaura, R. S. (1987). Social learning theory. In H. T. Blane & K. E. Leonard (Eds.), *Psychological theories of drinking and alcoholism* (pp. 131–178). New York: The Guilford Press.

Ackerman, R. J. (1989). *Perfect daughters: Adult daughters of alcoholics*. Deerfield Beach, FL: Health Communications.

Ackerman, R. J., & Gondolf, E. W. (1989, August). *Differentiating adult children of alcoholics: The effects of background and treatment of ACOA symptoms*. Paper presented at the meeting of the Sociological Practice Session of the American Sociological Association, San Francisco.

Alcoholics Anonymous. (1976). *Alcoholics anonymous* (3rd ed.). New York: Alcoholics Anonymous World Services, Inc.

Anthenelli, R. M., & Schuckit, M. A. (1992). Genetics. In J. H. Lowinson, P. Ruiz, R. B. Millman, (Eds.), & J. G. Langrod, (Assoc. Ed.), *Substance abuse: A comprehensive text (2nd ed.)* (pp. 39–50). Baltimore: Williams & Wilkins.

Bandura, A. (1969). *Principles of Behavior Modification*. NY: Holt, Rinehart, & Winston.

Bennett, G., & Woolf, D. S. (1990). Current approaches to substance abuse therapy. In G. Bennett, C. Vourakis, & D. S. Woolf (Eds.), *Substance abuse* (pp. 341–369). New York: John Wiley & Sons.

Berenson, D. (1986). The family treatment of alcoholism. *Family Therapy Today, 1*(6), 1–2, 6–7.

Berenson, D. (1978). Alcohol and the family system. In P. J. Guerin Jr. (Ed.), *Family therapy: Theory and practice* (pp. 284–297). New York: Gardner Press.

Berkowitz, A. (1996). Our genes, ourselves? *Bioscience, 46*(1), 42–51.

Berkowitz, A., & Perkins, H. W. (1988). Personality characteristics of children of alcoholics. *Journal of Consulting and Clinical Psychology, 2*, 206–209.

Black, C. (1979). Children of alcoholics. *Alcohol Health and Research World, 4,* 23-27.

Blane, H. T., & Leonard, K. E. (Eds.) (1987), *Psychological theories of drinking and alcoholism* (pp. 1–11). New York: The Guilford Press.

Blum, K. (1991). *Alcohol and the Addictive Brain*. New York: The Free Press.

Brown, S. A., & Creamer, V. A. (1987-1988, Winter). Implications for intervention of family history of alcohol abuse. *Alcohol Health and Research World, 12*(2), 120–123.

Childress, A. R., Ehrman, R., Rohsenow, D. J., Robbins, S. J., & O'Brien, C. P. (1992). Classically conditioned factors in drug dependence. In J. H. Lowinson, P. Ruiz, & R. B. Millman (Eds.), & J. G. Langrod (Assoc. Ed.), *Substance abuse: A comprehensive text* (2nd ed.) (pp. 56–69).

Cotton, N. S. (1978). The familial incidence of alcoholism: A review. *Journal of Studies on Alcohol, 40,* 89–116.

Cox, W. M. (1987). Personality theory and research. In H. T. Blane, & K. E. Leonard (Eds.), *Psychological theories of drinking and alcoholism,* (pp. 55–89). New York: The Guilford Press.

Daw, J. L. (1995, December). Alcohol problems across the generations. *Family Therapy News,* 19.

Devor, E. J. (1994). A developmental-genetic model of alcoholism: Implications for genetic research. *Journal of Consulting and Clinical Psychology, 62*(6), 1108–1115.

Edwards, M. E., & Steinglass, P. (1995). Family therapy treatment outcomes for alcoholism. *Journal of Marital and Family Therapy, 21*(4), 475–509.

Fingarette, H. (1988). *Heavy drinking: The myth of alcoholism as a disease*. Los Angeles: University of California Press.

George, R. L. (1990). Etiology of chemical dependency. In *Counseling the chemically dependent: Theory and practice* (pp. 22-46). Englewood Cliffs: Prentice Hall.

Goldenberg, I., & Goldenberg, H. (1985). *Family therapy: An overview* (2nd ed.). Monterey, CA: Brooks/Cole.

Goodwin, D. W. (1985). Genetic determinants of alcoholism. In J. H. Mendelson, & N. K. Mello

(Eds.), *The diagnosis and treatment of alcoholism* (2nd ed.) (pp. 65–87). New York: McGraw Hill.

Goodwin, D. W. (1989). The gene for alcoholism. *Journal of Studies on Alcohol, 50,* 397–398

Harman, M. J., Armsworth, M. W., Hwang, C., Vincent, K., & Preston, M. (1995) Personality adjustment in college students with a parent perceived as alcoholic or nonalcoholic. *Journal of Counseling & Development, 73,* 459–462.

Health ResponseAbility Systems. (1994). *Research on children of alcoholics.* Internet newsgroup (alt.recovery).

Inciardi, J. A., & McElrath, K. (1995). Marijuana. In J. A. Inciardi & K. McElrath (Eds.), *The American drug scene: An anthology* (pp. 85–87). Los Angeles: Roxbury.

Inciardi, J. A., & Pottieger, A. E. (1991). Kids, crack, and crime. *Journal of Drug Issues, 21,* 257–270.

Johnson, S., Leonard, K. E., & Jacob, T. (1989). Drinking, drinking styles and drug use in children of alcoholics, depressives, and controls. *Journal of Studies on Alcohol, 50,* 427–431.

Johnson, B. D., & Muffler, J. (1989). In J. H. Lowinson, P. Ruiz, R. B. Millman (Eds.), & J. G. Langrod (Assoc. Ed.), *Substance abuse: A comprehensive text* (2nd. ed.) (pp. 118–137).

Kaminer, Y. (1991). Adolescent substance abuse. In R. J. Frances, & S. I. Miller, (Eds.), *Clinical textbook of addictive disorders,* (pp. 310–346). New York: The Guilford Press.

Kaufman, E. (1986). The family of the alcoholic patient. *Psychosomatics, 27*(5), 347–358.

Kaufman, E. (1980). Myth and reality in the family patterns and treatment of substance abusers. *American Journal of Drug and Alcohol Abuse, 7,* 257–279.

Kubicka, L., Kozeny, J., & Roth, Z. (1990). Alcohol abuse and its psychosocial correlates in sons of alcoholics as young men and in the general population of young men in Prague. *Journal of Studies on Alcohol, 51,* 49–58.

Kumpfer, K. L., & Hopkins, R. (1993, March). Prevention: Current Research and Trends. *Psychiatric Clinics of North America, 16*(1), 11-20.

Lamanna, M. A., & Riedmann, A. (1997). *Marriages and families: Making choices in a diverse society* (6th ed.). Belmont, CA: Wadsworth.

Lawson, G. W. (1992). A biopsychosocial model of adolescent substance abuse. In G. W. Lawson, & A. W. Lawson, (Eds.), *Adolescent substance abuse: Etiology, treatment, & prevention* (pp. 3-10). Gaithersburg: Aspen Publishers.

Lewis, J. A. (1992). Treating the alcohol-affected family. In L. L'Abate, J. E. Farrer, & D. A. Seritella (Eds.), *Handbook of differential treatments for addictions.* Needham Heights, MA: Allyn & Bacon.

Lewis, J. A., Dana, R. Q., & Blevins, G. A. (1994). *Substance abuse counseling: An individualized approach* (2nd ed.). Pacific Grove, CA: Brooks/Cole.

Liddle, H. A., & Dakof, G. A. (1995). Efficacy of family therapy for drug abuse: Promising but not definitive. *Journal of Marital and Family Therapy, 21*(4), 511–543.

Light, W. J. (1985). *Alcoholism: Its natural history, chemistry, and general metabolism.* Springfield, IL: Charles C. Thomas.

MacKay, P. W., Donovan, D. M., & Marlatt, G. A. (1991). Cognitive and behavioral approaches to alcohol abuse. In R. J. Frances & S. I. Miller (Eds.), *Clinical textbook of addictive disorders* (pp. 452–481). New York: The Guilford Press.

Metzger, L. (1988). *From denial to recovery.* San Francisco: Jossey-Bass.

Nace, E. P. (1987). *The treatment of alcoholism.* New York: Brunner/Mazel.

National Clearinghouse of Alcohol and Drug Information. (1996). *Student use of most drugs reaches highest level in nine years—More report getting "very high, bombed, or stoned."* Internet site (www.health.org/pubs/96pride/pr96.htm)

Oetting, E. R., & Beauvais, F. (1986). Peer cluster theory: Drugs and the adolescent. *Journal of Counseling and Development, 65,* 17–21.

Penick, E. C., Read, M. R., Crowley, P. A., & Powell, B. J. (1978). Differentiation of alcoholics by family history. *Journal of Studies on Alcohol, 39,* 1944–1948.

Pickens, R. W., & Svikis, D. S. (1991). Genetic contributions to alcoholism diagnosis. *Alcohol Health & Research World, 15*(4), 272–277.

Pilat, J. M., & Jones, J. W. (1984–1985). Identification of children of alcoholics: Two empirical studies. *Alcohol, Health & Research World, 9*(2), 27-33.

Pratsinek, G., & Alexander, R. (1992). Theoretical perspectives in drug abuse treatment: Models of addiction. In *Understanding substance abuse and treatment* (pp. 9–24). Springfield, VA: Goodway Graphics.

Preli, R., & Protinsky, H. (1988). Aspects of family structures in alcoholic, recovered, and nonalcoholic families. *Journal of Marital and Family Therapy, 14*(3), 311–314.

Ranew, L. F., & Serrit, D. A. (1992). Substance abuse and addiction. In L. L'Abate, J. E. Farmer, & D. A. Serritella (Eds.). *Handbook of Differential Treatments for Addictions,* pp. 84–96. Needham Heights, MA: Allyn & Bacon.

Ray, O., & Ksir, C. (1993). *Drugs, society, & human behavior* (6th ed.). St Louis: Mosby.

Russell, M., Henderson, C., & Blume, S. B. (1984). *Children of alcoholics: A review of the literature.* New York: Children of Alcoholics Foundation.

Schuckit, M. (1983). Alcoholic men with no alcoholic first-degree relative. *American Journal of Psychiatry, 140,* 439–443.

Searles, J. S. (1991). The genetics of alcoholism: Impact on family and sociological models of addiction. *Family Dynamics of Addictions Quarterly, 1*(1), 3-21.

Sher, K. J. (1987). Stress response dampening. In H. T. Blane, & K. E. Leonard (Eds.), *Psychological theories of drinking and alcoholism* (pp. 227-271). New York: The Guilford Press.

Siegal, H. A., & Inciardi, J. A. (1995). A brief history of alcohol. In J. A. Inciardi & K. McElrath (Eds.), *The American drug scene: An anthology* (pp. 45–49). Los Angeles: Roxbury.

Smith-Peterson, C. (1983). Substance abuse treatment and cultural diversity. In G. Bennett, C. Vourakis, & D. Woolf (Eds), *Substance abuse: Pharmacologic, developmental, & clinical perspectives* (pp. 370-383). New York: John Wiley & Sons.

Snow, R. W., & Wells-Parker, E. (1986). Drinking reasons, alcohol consumption levels, and drinking locations among drunken drivers. *The International Journal of the Addictions, 21,* 671–689.

Stanton, M. D., Todd, T. C., Heard, D. B., Kirschner, S., Kleiman, J. I;, Mowatt, D. T., Riley, P., Scott, S. M., & Van Deusen, M. M. (1982). A conceptional model. In M. D. Stanton, T. C. Todd, & Associates. *The family therapy of drug abuse and addiction* (pp. 7–30). New York: The Guilford Press.

Steinglass, P. (1987). *The alcoholic family.* New York: Basic Books.

Subby, R. (1987). *Lost in the shuffle: The co-dependent reality.* Deerfield Beach, FL: Health Communications.

Substance Abuse and Mental Health Service Administration (1996). *The 1995 National Household Survey on Drug Abuse, Advance Report No. 18.* Washington, DC: Author.

Tarter, R. E., & Vanyukov, M. (1994). Alcoholism: A developmental disorder. *Journal of Consulting and Clinical Psychology, 62*(6), 1096–1107).

Thomason, J. H. H., & Dilts, S. L. (1991). Opioids. In R. J. Frances, & S. I. Miller, (Eds.), *Clinical textbook of addictive disorders* (pp. 103–120). New York: The Guilford Press.

Vaillant, G. E. (1983). *The natural history of alcoholism.* Cambridge, MA: Harvard University Press.

Velleman, R. (1992). Intergenerational effects: A review of environmentally oriented studies concerning the relationship between parental alcohol problems and family disharmony in the genesis of alcohol and other problems. I: The intergenerational effects of alcohol problems. *The International Journal of the Addictions, 27*(3), 36–39.

Wegscheider, S. (1981). From the family trap to family freedom. *Alcoholism, 1*(3), 36–39.

Werner, E. E. (1986). Resilient offspring of alcoholics: A longitudinal study from birth to age 18. *Journal of Studies on Alcohol, 47,* 4–40.

Woititz, J. G. (1983). *Adult children of alcoholics.* Deerfield Beach, FL: Health Communications.

The Major Drugs of Abuse and Their Addictive Properties

Jim Porter, MA

A s previously discussed, the causes of substance use, abuse, and addiction in U.S. society are complex and involve many factors. Twenty-five million people have tried cocaine but currently fewer than a million people use this addictive substance daily (Winick, 1992). More than 100 million adults drink alcohol, with 12% to 13% of them meeting the criteria for alcohol abuse, dependence, or both (Substance Abuse and Mental Health Services Administration, 1995). On the other hand, there are more than 51 million smokers in the United States with more than 90% of this population considered dependent or "hooked" on the drug nicotine (National Institute on Drug Abuse, 1989; U.S. Department of Health and Human Services, 1990).

What causes different responses to various substances used by human beings? Why do some people become addicted while others do not? During the last decades research has determined that the primary target of all psychoactive substance use is the brain. To understand drugs and why people use them we need to know how the brain functions and how it interacts with various substances.

THE BRAIN

The human brain has been likened to a 3-pound mainframe computer. The brain is the center of human function and process (Hooper & Teresi, 1986). The brain houses the mechanisms that allow the mind to influence and take charge of the human organism. The mind exists everywhere and somewhere in the brain. Urges,

65

moods, desires, and subconscious forms of learning are all mental phenomena connected within the concept of mind (Fischbach, 1992). Although a modern computer can outcalculate the smartest human brain, it lacks the ability to memorize a new route, plan a party, fall in love, or hate someone. The computer cannot feel, create, or fantasize—in other words, it has no mind.

The brain is divided into two sections called hemispheres, which are separated by the corpus callousum. The left hemisphere is basically concerned with thinking and intellectual functions. It is the site of logic and verbal ability. The right hemisphere is the creative side and houses the intuitive and creative processes. The right hemisphere uses pictures, while the left hemisphere uses words (Andreasen, 1984). The sex of an individual, which is determined hormonally in the brain before birth, will influence the development, organization, and basic shape of the brain (Moir & Jessel, 1991).

It has taken hundreds of millions of years to structurally forge the human brain. The brain's convolutions and inner structures reveal traces of its evolutionary past. As a many-layered spherical organ, the layers have been likened to the layers of an onion.

The brain consists of three basic parts: the *hindbrain* contains the cerebellum and lower brain stem; the *midbrain* houses sensory relay areas from the upper brain stem, and the *forebrain* (See Figures 3.1 and 3.2) (Hooper & Teresi, 1986). Although substance use effects the brain overall, the forebrain houses the mechanisms that most often interact with substances that can cross the blood-brain barrier. The forebrain includes the cerebral hemisphere and the rind or outer covering (about 2 millimeters thick) called the *cortex.* It also includes the *limbic system* and the structures of the *diencephalon,* which contains the *thalamus* and the *hypothalamus* (Fischbach, 1992; Hooper & Teresi, 1986). Most higher states of consciousness take place in the cortex, including thought, perception, motor function, sensory data processing, and vision.

FIGURE 3.1   The human brain

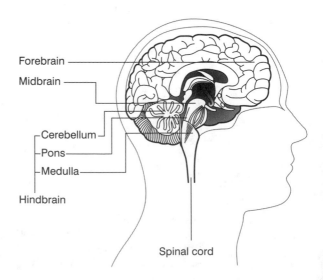

FIGURE 3.2 A cross-sectional image of the brain shows the ventricles, four connected chambers that are filled with cerebrospinal fluid.

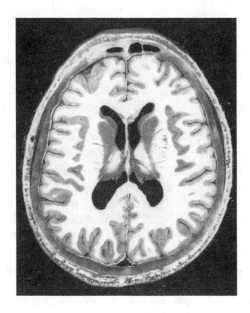

The limbic system lies just below and interconnects with the cortical area. It is involved in emotional behavior and long-term memory, while the hypothalamus regulates more basic, autonomic (primitive) functions such as hormonal activity, thirst, hunger, temperature, sex drive, and sleep.

The brain interfaces with all of these systems in a space about the size of a grapefruit. It accomplishes this through *neuronai* (nerve cell) networking (Cohen, 1988). The brain is composed of about 100 billion neurons (see Figure 3.3), and an astounding amount of structural variation and functional diversity can be found in brain cells (Fischbach, 1992; Shatz, 1992). About one-tenth of these neurons are active nerve cells that have actual or potential links with tens of thousands of others. They compose cellular clusters that form highly specialized centers. These centers are interconnected by bundles of nerve fibers called *tracts,* which link up the different switchboards of the brain.

FIGURE 3.3 The neuron or nerve cell

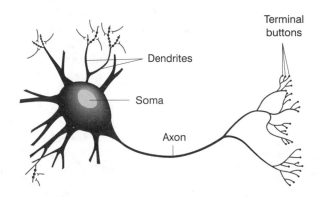

The tracts all conduct information in much the same way. Chemical messengers (molecules) called *neurotransmitters* are released by constant electrical impulses (action potentials) that flash through the brain. These pathways can send thousands of electrochemical messages per second and yet work in harmony, because each cell in a tract responds like a complex, megamicroscopic information processor. It is this process of "blipping" and "dripping" that allows the brain to communicate. Newly sensed experiences (*imprints*) are sifted, rejected, or passed on to appropriate pathways. These imprints are matched to ones already encoded in the data banks directing conscious and unconscious feelings, thoughts, and actions.

A bulk of this encoding is stored at an unconscious level and forms the basic core of a belief system. This belief system will influence how individuals will perceive their own sense of "self" and how they will relate to the world around them (Hooper & Teresi, 1986).

Each neuron has a central body, from which wispy tendrils called *dendrites* appear to sprout at one end and a long slender thread called an *axon* at the other. When stimulated, the axon and dendritic branches generate electrical impulses by the exchange of electrically charged sodium and potassium atoms through ionic channels in the cellular membrane (Cohen, 1988; Hooper & Teresi, 1986). This creates a reversed polarity that allows the impulse to zoom down the axon at speeds up to 300 miles per hour.

A neuron's cell membrane can reverse its polarity from negative to positive and back again in one-thousandth of a second. A strongly stimulated neuron can easily fire 1,000 times per second. When the impulse reaches the button (*terminal*) at the end of the axon, it causes tiny sacs (*vesicles*) to fuse with the membrane (via calcium release) and discharge chemical molecules called (neuro) *transmitters, peptides,* or *hormones* (Cohen, 1988; Hooper & Teresi, 1986).

It is believed that most neurons contain multiple transmitters. The chief chemical messenger may be a neurotransmitter (amine/amino acid) but acts in conjunction with a neuropeptide to modulate the transmission and/or a neurohormone to prolong the transmission (Cohen, 1988). These neurotransmitters discharge from the terminal of one neuron (presynaptic), cross a small gap called the *synapse* and find their way into "receptor" sites on the adjoining neuron (postsynaptic). Each neurotransmitter, peptide, or hormone has a particular shape that allows it to fit into the appropriate receptor site, much like a key fitting into a lock. If the key fits the lock it will turn on a message in the adjoining neuron.

These receptors exhibit a self-regulatory capacity, changing their sensitivity during excessive or infrequent use (Cohen, 1988). It has been well established that the classic neurotransmitters tend to have more than one receptor (Gilbert & Martin, 1978). The classic neurotransmitters include *acetylcholine* (Ach), *dopamine* (DA), *norepinephrine* (NE), *epinephrine* (E), *serotonin* (5-HT), *histamine* (H), *gamma-aminobutyric acid* (GABA) as well as *glycine, glutamate, adenosine* and *adenosine triphosphate* (Cohen, 1988) (See Table 3.1 on p. 76).

The mind that exists within each individual insures the basic survival of that organism. Survival is accomplished by the recall of memory imprints that have been stored in the neo-cortex of the brain. These survival skills become more sophisticated as the organism develops and uses them repeatedly in day-to-day functions. The human brain has many abilities. One of these is the ability to conceptualize and formulate future possibilities, including dangers. In early childhood, the brain forms pathways based on the raw data it receives from the environment. The mind wires up these pathways quickly so that it can avoid or survive potential dangers. For instance, if a child is repeatedly exposed to "fight or flight" situations, whether real or perceived, the association to this stimuli will cause the mind to strengthen developing excitatory pathways. This will allow the organism to be more vigilant and ensure its survival.

Researchers have discovered that the feeling of pleasure is one of the most important emotions connected to survival. The feeling of pleasure is produced and regulated by a circuit of specialized nerve cells in a limbic structure called the *nucleus accumbens*. Dopamine-containing neurons relay pleasure messages through this part of the brain via a circuit that spans the brain stem, the limbic system and the cerebral cortex (National Institutes on Health, 1993). Research scientists know this feeling of pleasure or reward is a strong biological force. If something elicits strong pleasure within the brain, it is wired so that its owner will develop behaviors that will reinforce this good feeling. Basic drives such as eating, sexual activity, and the need for power are activities that evoke rewards in brain. Such rewards become one of the brain's most powerful learning mechanisms (Siegel, 1989; Wise, 1991).

Psychoactive Substances and The Brain

The brain has been the recipient of psychoactive substances allowing human beings to cope with both internal and external stressors for centuries. These substances have offered the user a variety of effects, including pain relief, pleasure, mystical insight, escape, relaxation, stimulation, and ecstasy, as well as a sense of social and spiritual connectedness (Milkman & Sunderwirth, 1986; Siegel, 1989). It has been proposed that the pursuit of intoxication is as powerful a drive in human beings (and many animal species) as the innate survival drives of hunger, thirst, and sex (Wise, 1991; Siegel, 1989)

Substances are considered psychoactive when they can cross the blood-brain barrier and create changes in the brain, and therefore, in the mind and behavior. The primary use of psychoactive substances is to change the neurochemistry of the brain and alter one's consciousness. Substances accomplish this by exciting, quieting, or distorting the chemical and electrical activity of the brain to create a shift in the user's conscious state (Milkman & Sunderwirth, 1986; Siegel, 1989). Substance addiction can include intoxicating substances like ethanol, marijuana, crack cocaine, or heroin that produce rapid neurochemical shifts (8 seconds to 20 minutes) or nonintoxicating substances like nicotine, caffeine, and refined carbohydrates.

Current research has focused on specific sites in the brain that demonstrate a possible neurochemical basis for the ongoing use of substances (Esposito, Porrino, &

Seeger, 1987; Wise, 1991). These sites include the *medial forebrain bundle* (MFB), the *ventral segmental area* (VTA), the *nucleus accumbens,* the hypothalamus and the *locus coeruleus* (LC). The hypothalamus houses multiple nerve centers that are necessary for the maintenance of life. Among them is the "pleasure center" that converges with the MFB as well as the nucleus accumbens and the VTA. There is a profuse convergence of cell bodies, axons, and synaptic terminals among these systems (Khachaturian, Lewis, & Schafer, 1985; Mansour, Khachaturian, Lewis, Akil, & Watson, 1988; Bozarth, 1987; Broekkamp, 1987). The MFB region has been identified as producing the positive reinforcement associated with drugs of addiction by the release of dopamine (DA). This region is activated by the aforementioned systems not containing DA neurons via a myelinated (insulated) fiber system that converges with the MFB. Survival drives such as eating, drinking, copulation, and shelter produce a state of positive reinforcement in the brain. Likewise, it has been found that abusable substances of different pharmacologic categories have a synergistic effect on brain stimulation reward thresholds involving DA systems (Gold, Miller, & Jonas, 1992). This includes all major drugs of abuse except some of the hallucinogenics (Gardner, Paredes, & Smith, 1988; Gardner, Paredes, Seeger, Smith, & Van Praag, 1988).

DEPRESSANTS

This section discusses central nervous system (CNS) depressants including *ethanol, barbiturates, methaqualone, meprobamate* and all *benzodiazepines.* These substances are examined in relation to their effect on the brain and other body organs. At usual doses they dampen central nervous system (CNS) activity while displaying a weak analgesic effect. All drugs in this class can become physically addictive, can be lethal in overdose, demonstrate a cross-tolerance and potentiation of one another and have the ability to induce severe depressions as well as promote extreme anxiety during withdrawal (Radcliffe, Rush, Sites, & Cruse, 1985).

Alcohol

Ethyl alcohol (ethanol) is a clear liquid with a bitter taste. It can be an anesthetic, a poison, a foodstuff, an antiseptic, or a surface blood vessel dilator. It is an unstable central nervous system depressant that for many becomes an addictive substance (Blum & Payne, 1991; Milkman & Sunderwirth, 1986; Wallace, 1985). It is second only to nicotine in the number of deaths that occur yearly because of its use (about 100,000) in U.S. society.

Ethanol is a small organic molecule consisting of only two carbon atoms surrounded by hydrogen atoms, with a hydroxyl group attached to one of the carbons (CH_3-CH_2-OH). This molecular arrangement provides ethanol with water soluble properties as well as lipid- or fat-soluble properties (Radcliffe, Rush, Sites, & Cruse, 1985; Tabakoff & Hoffman, 1992). Alcohol exhibits its most impressive effects on the central nervous system by selectively changing structure and function at the level of the neuronal membrane (Hunt, 1985; National Institute on Alcohol Abuse and Alcoholism, 1987). Ethanol's ability to penetrate the bilipid membrane and disorganize the neuron has resulted in the current hypothesis for intoxication (Lipnick, 1989).

As it passes the blood-brain barrier after ingestion, most people feel their inhibitions quickly disappear and sense a more relaxed social attitude concerning their interactions with others. Although an individual may believe it to be so, experiments have proved that alcohol does not improve mental or physical capabilities (Liska, 1994). Individuals who continue to drink for an extended period of time (two to three drinks per hour for several hours) will disregard their own pain, exhibit poor judgment, and endanger their own or other's safety (Blum & Payne, 1991).

One ounce of absolute alcohol contains about 210 calories which can convert to energy at the cellular level but contains no nutrients to nourish the cell. It can pass through every tissue cluster in the brain and body if enough is consumed. Immediately after drinking, the mouth and esophagus begins to absorb small amounts via the mucous membranes. The stomach will rapidly assimilate about one quarter of a dose, followed by complete absorption through the walls of the small intestine within 20 to 30 minutes (Liska, 1994; Radcliffe, Rush, Sites, & Cruse, 1985; Wallace, 1985).

The cardiovascular system is affected by low doses of alcohol through the dilation of peripheral blood vessels, while severe alcohol intoxication will create a depression of this entire system. Alcohol irritates the gastrointestinal tract through direct contact, as well as by stimulating the secretion of stomach acid and pepsin which can cause gastritis and injury to the mucous membranes of the stomach lining. The presence of food can modify these effects to some extent by slowing down the absorption rate of alcohol. Because alcohol is a diuretic, it overstimulates the production of urine in the kidneys (Liska, 1994; Radcliffe, Rush, Sites, & Cruse, 1985).

Many people erroneously assume that alcohol is a powerful aphrodisiac and a sexual stimulant. This assumption is based on observing people who appear to have a heightened sexual response when drinking (Liska, 1994). This is due to the disinhibiting factor of ethyl alcohol and its immediate influence on the frontal lobes of the brain where the neurochemical mechanisms for exercising judgment are located. A recent study using computer technology to count remaining brain cells in an autopsy demonstrated that alcoholics had fewer brain cells in the frontal cortex than did nonalcoholics (Harper, Kril, & Daly, 1987), confirming alcohol's extensive influence in the frontal lobe area.

Besides the brain, the organ that bears the burden of alcohol ingestion is the liver. This 3-pound organ is the central filter for detoxifying the blood and is the site of 90% of alcohol metabolism. The major pathway for such conversion involves the enzyme *alcohol dehydrogenese* and occurs in two phases in the liver. The first phase produces the metabolite, *acetaldehyde,* and the second converts acetaldehyde to *acetic acid.* With continued heavy intake of alcohol, the liver cells begin to accumulate fatty deposits that destroy the cell and produce scarring called *cirrhosis*. This disease occurs in, and is fatal to, about 10% of chronic alcoholic patients (Liska, 1994; National Institute on Alcohol Abuse and Alcoholism, 1990; Radcliffe, Rush, Sites, & Cruse, 1985).

Nearly every organ in the body is affected by the heavy use of alcohol. Gastricitis, diarrhea, and gastric ulcers are commonly associated with heavy drinking. A single heavy drinking episode can cause the pancreas to hemorrhage. The consumption of large amounts of alcohol also can depress the respiratory center in the medulla, causing death (Goodwin, 1992). Alcohol can be deadly for individuals with epilepsy because it can promote convulsive seizures due to a hyperexcitable rebound condition in the brain after drinking has ceased (Liska, 1994).

The U.S. Department of Health and Human Services (1988) estimates that the use of tobacco with alcohol can increase the risk of cancer fifteen-fold. There is strong evidence for links between alcohol and cancers that occur in the mouth, pharynx, larynx, and esophagus, as well as the liver, pancreas, stomach, large intestine, rectum, and breast. Recent studies suggest that alcohol is typically ingested with co-carcinogens such as tobacco, accounting for 3% of the cancer deaths that occur in the United States annually (Liska, 1994).

Besides liver damage (cirrhosis), alcoholics may develop a pathology of the nervous system due to vitamin deficiencies, as well as experience neurologic complications such as the Wernicke-Korsakoff syndrome. This is a chronic brain syndrome in which the alcoholic has dementia characterized by permanent short term memory loss coupled with the telling of "fanciful" tales (Victor & Adams, 1971). Early studies using computerized tomography (CT) scans produced contradictory results about whether alcoholics produce cortical atrophy (shrinkage) because of alcohol's insult to the brain (Carlen, Wortzman, Holgate, Wilkinson, & Rankin, 1978; Epstein, Pisani, & Fawcett, 1977; Hill, Reyes, Mikhael, & Ayre, 1977). Other medical complications include cardiomyopathy, anemia, myopathy, and breast cancer in women (Gill, Zezulka, Shipley, Gill, & Bevers, 1986; Gorelick, Rodin, & Langengerg, 1987; Regan, 1990; Willett et al., 1987).

The acute withdrawal syndrome generally appears within 12 to 72 hours after drinking has subsided and lasts from five to seven days. During this time the alcoholic will experience profuse sweating, shakes, anxiety, nausea, diarrhea, hallucinations, and general disorientation. In severe cases, the alcoholic may suffer seizures and cardiovascular collapse. This condition is known as delirium tremens (Tabakoff, Sutker, & Randall, 1983).

Alcohol ingested during pregnancy easily passes through the placental barrier and can result in fetal alcohol syndrome (FAS). FAS was first recognized and reported by doctors in 1973 as a pattern of birth defects in children born to alcoholic mothers (Jones, Smith, & Ulleland, 1973). Since that time, numerous studies have established ethanol as a teratogenic agent that produces defects in utero. FAS is characterized by distinct symptoms that can generally be observed in the newborn (Radcliffe, Rush, Sites, & Cruse, 1985). The child is at high risk to be retarded, suffer craniofacial deformities, incur central nervous system damage, and have major organ malformations (Clarren & Smith, 1978; Rosett; 1980). The symptoms can range from gross morphological defects to more subtle cognitive-behavioral problems. FAS is one of the leading causes of mental retardation in newborns.

The nature of the birth defects does not appear to be as related to the teratogen (alcohol) itself as to the toxic effect on the fetus during development (Randall, 1987). Further, animal studies have demonstrated that peak blood-alcohol levels, rather than the amount consumed, represent the critical dosage factor (Pierce & West, 1986b). Thus, alcohol ingestion during pregnancy can result in a wide range of effects from mild mental retardation to the severe expression of Down syndrome in the newborn child (Abel & Soko, 1986a).

Barbiturates

These short-acting sedative-hypnotics are considered primary drugs of abuse by "street addicts." They are taken orally or by injection to produce an intoxication similar to that of alcohol. This intoxicated state produces "disinhibition," elevated mood, a reduction of negative feelings and negative self-concept, and an increase in energy and confidence. This euphoric mood can shift quite suddenly to sadness. Someone who is intoxicated on barbiturates may possess an unsteady gait, slurred speech, and eye twitching, and exercise poor judgment (Wesson, Smith, & Seymour, 1992). Intoxication may vary due to diet, level of emotional excitement, and other drug interactions. Currently, the benzodiazepines have replaced the short-acting barbiturates in medical treatment and many physicians do not prescribe barbiturates for patients as they did in previous years (Wesson, Smith, & Seymour, 1992).

The most commonly used barbiturates include thiopental (sodium pentothal), amobarbital (Amytal), pentobarbital (Nembutal), secobarbital (Seconal), amobarbital in combination with secobarb (Tuinal), butabarbital (Butisol) and phenobarbital (Luminal). On the street, the drug may be assigned a name that correlates with the color of the capsule such as yellow jackets (Nembutal), red birds (Seconal), or rainbows (Tuinal). These particular barbiturates are the ones most often abused on the street. (Radcliffe, Rush, Sites, & Cruse, 1985; Wesson, Smith, & Seymour, 1992). Other sedative-hypnotics include Quaalude, Chloral Hydrate and meprobamate. Methaqualone (Quaalude) is chemically distinct from the barbiturates but is a prime example of a once-approved drug that became a severe social hazard. Through its depression of the CNS, there is a dramatic reduction in heart rate, respiration, and muscular coordination (Liska, 1994).

Barbiturates are lipid-soluble compounds, which allows them to pass the blood-brain barrier. They are also capable of passing the placental barrier and affecting the fetus. Barbiturates depress the central nervous system and inhibit neuronal activity, ranging from anxiety reduction to coma. This depressant action is achieved by potentiation of GABA-ergic transmission, which creates a diminished calcium ionic channel action resulting in a decreased state of neurotransmitters. Barbiturates also reverse the action of glutamate, which induces depolarization and adds to the CNS depression. Barbiturates increase the effects of benzodiazepines or alcohol (Cohen, 1988).

Like all sedative-hypnotic drugs, barbiturates can create tolerance in the user with a single dose. Acute tolerance rarely lasts longer than 24 hours. Chronic tolerance occurs with repeated use. Withdrawal symptoms generally begin 12 to 24 hours after the last dose and peak in intensity between 24 and 72 hours. These symptoms include anxiety, tremors, nightmares, insomnia, anorexia, nausea, vomiting, delirium, and seizures. Death from overdose can occur due to respiratory arrest when centers in the brain that control oxygen intake are severely depressed (Radcliffe, Rush, Sites, & Cruse, 1985; Wesson, Smith, & Seymour, 1992).

Benzodiazepines

The use and abuse of benzodiazepines continues to generate controversy. As a result, the American Psychiatric Association (1990) has reviewed the issue of benzodiazepine dependency and published its findings in a book. Benzodiazepine dependency can occur in many ways including the following: (1) self-administration to produce intoxication; (2) therapeutic doses prescribed by a doctor over a long period of time that eventually develops into physical dependency; (3) patients' escalating their prescribed dosage; (4) self-administration by heroin or cocaine addicts to treat symptoms of withdrawal or toxicity; and (5) intentional overdose in a suicide attempt (Wesson, Smith, & Seymour, 1992)

Benzodiazepines are the most widely prescribed group of drugs in the treatment of anxiety and insomnia. They are considered less lethal than the barbiturates unless used in combination with other drugs like alcohol. Many are capable of achieving a daytime anxiolytic response without excessive drowsiness.

There are more than a dozen varieties of benzodiazepines. The most notorious and controversial are diazepam (Valium), chlordiazepoxide (Librium) and triazolam (Halcion). Alprazolam (Xanax) has been found to be very effective in the treatment of panic attacks (Nightingale, 1990). Busipirone (Buspar) is a new class of anxiolytic that does not act on the GABA receptor, although its mechanism of action is unknown at this time. It is reported that it produces less sedation than the benzodiazepines (Cohen, 1988; Wesson, Smith, & Seymour, 1992).

The benzodiazepines are lipid soluble and absorb into the gastrointestinal tract after oral ingestion. They can also pass the blood-brain barrier and the placental barrier. Peak effects from use occur within two to four hours. By virtue of their specific recognition sites, the benzodiazepines act by potentiating the action of gamma-amino-butyric acid (GABA), which increases neural inhibition. Two types of binding sites are known, which lie next to GABA receptors and are consistent with activity from all members of the benzodiazepine group. Benzodiazepines can produce anxiolytic, anticonvulsant, and muscle-relaxant responses in human beings by enhancing GABA-ergic transmission, which dampens monoamine activity (Cohen, 1988). Withdrawal symptoms from benzodiazepines include seizures, rebound anxiety, panic attacks, delirium, psychosis, mania, and paranoia. Because of the long half-life of these drugs, these symptoms can exist and persist for weeks beyond the last dose (Brown & Hauge, 1986; Levy, 1984; Bleich, Grinspoon, & Garb, 1987).

Beyond prescribed medical uses, benzodiazepines are most often used as street drugs to treat the adverse effects of cocaine, methamphetamine, heroin, or alcohol. Currently, diazepam (Valium) and clonazepam (Klonopin) are the most popular and are sold as black market drugs for $1 to $2 per tablet (Wesson, Smith, & Seymour, 1992).

Opiates

Opium is derived from the poppy flower (*Papaver sominiferum*). The main active ingredient is *morphine alkaloid,* which is widely used because of its ability to relieve pain. It possesses a variety of pharmacologic activities that have been studied by scientists for years (Simon, 1992). Other derivatives include heroin, codeine, hydromorphone (Dilaudid), hydrocodone (Hycodan), oxyymorphone (Numorphan), and oxycodone (Percodan) as well as a number of synthetic medical compounds, including meseridine (Demerol), methadone (Dolophine), fentanyl (Sublimaze), and Propoxyphene (Darvon). There are at least 20 drugs available in the United States that have opioid actions (Cohen, 1988; Jaffe, 1992). It is reported that they may differ in the way they are absorbed, metabolized, and eliminated from the body. According to some sources, the most abused opioid substance is heroin (Liska, 1994).

Currently, about 2 million Americans have tried heroin. It appears to be gaining in popularity again, especially among the young. This may be in response to a new and much purer form of heroin known as black tar (Crider, Gfroerer, & Blanken, 1987). Heroin addicts are most likely to be intravenous (IV) users and there is significant concern about the transmission of HIV in this group.

Recent advances have been made in understanding how opioid drug effects, withdrawal, and relapse phenomena are linked to environmental cues and internal mood states (Childress, McLellan, & O'Brien, 1986; Wikler, 1980). As mentioned in the description of the brain, recent findings indicate that when the opioids occupy binding sites in the ventral segmental area they create an increased activity in the nucleus accumbens and frontal cortex, resulting in a release of dopamine. These findings suggest that there is a common pathway that produces a reinforcing action existing between the opioids and other commonly abused drugs such as cocaine and amphetamines (Jaffe & Martin, 1990; Koob & Bloom, 1988; Wise, 1988).

Tolerance to opioids can develop quite rapidly in frequent users, and experiments have verified that a clinical dose of morphine (60 mg/day) in an individual can be increased to 500 mg/day in as little as 10 days (Jaffe, 1990). The symptoms of withdrawal include feelings of dysphoria, nausea, repeated yawning, sweating, tearing, and a runny nose (Heishman, Sitzer, Bigelow, & Liebson, 1989). It is during this period that subjects experience craving or "drug hunger" for repeated exposure to the drug. Abundant literature suggests that the symptoms of opiate withdrawal are the result of interactions with other neurotransmitter systems including the locus coeruleus, which spikes norepinephrine during this period (Aghajanian & Wang, 1987).

The phenomena of tolerance to and physical dependence (neuroadaption) on opioids appear to be receptor-site specific. In 1975 several endogenous molecules were identified with opioid activity (Hughes et al., 1975). Since then at least 12 peptides have been discovered, including the beta endorphins (Cox, Goldstein, & Li, 1978; Bradbury, Smyth, Snell, Birdsall, & Hulme, 1976) and the dynorphins (Goldstein, Tachiban, Lowney, Hunkapiller, & Hood, 1979). These particular long-chain peptides bind to their own specific opioid receptors (Simon, 1992) and it has been postulated that there are many subtypes of such receptors (Schulz, Wuster, & Herz, 1980; Oka, 1980). Dynorphins appear to be produced throughout the human brain and spinal cord while beta endorphins are found in only two specific areas of the hypothalamus and the brain stem (Watson, Akil, Khachaturian, Young, & Lewis, 1984). Although the evidence is still sparse for a genetic predisposition towards "opioidism", an inherited insensitivity to pain is a possible candidate (Simon, 1992).

TABLE 3.1   Drugs related to neurotransmitters

Drug Relationship to Neurotransmitters	
Drug	**Neurotransmitter**
Alcohol	gamma amine butyric acid (GABA), serotonin, met-enkephalin
Marijuana	acetylcholine
Cocaine/ amphetamines	epinephrine (adrenaline), norepinephrine (noradrenaline), serotonin, dopamine, acetylcholine
Heroin	endorphin, enkephalin, dopamine
Benzodiazepines	GABA, glycine
LSD	acetylcholine
PCP	dopamine, acetylcholine, alpha-endopsychosin
MDA, MDMA (Ecstasy)	serotonin, dopamine, adrenaline
Nicotine	adrenaline, endorphin, acetylcholine

STIMULANTS

This section focuses on drugs of arousal, which include all forms of cocaine, amphetamine, prescription weight-reducing products, amphetamine-like drugs such as methylphenidate (Ritalin), and some over-the-counter weight-reducing drugs. The potential difficulties with frequent use of these drugs include possible overdoses, physical addiction, psychoses, severe depressions, and all anxiety syndromes, including panic attacks and obsessions. Minor psychoactive stimulants include caffeine and nicotine. These substances are considered minor because they can induce and exacerbate anxiety but usually are not capable of producing the more intense psychiatric syndromes such as psychosis and major depression (Liska, 1994; Radcliffe, Rush, Sites, & Cruse, 1985; Siegel, 1989).

Cocaine

Cocaine is an alkaloid drug compound that creates intense central nervous system arousal depending on its level of potentiation. It is processed from an organic source, the coca leaf (Liska, 1994; Siegel, 1989). The natural source for the leaf (*Erythroxylon coca*) comes from two varieties of flowering coca shrubs, the *huanuco* and *truxillo,* which can exist only in the fertile soil of South America. They are grown and cultivated in the mountainous regions of Peru, Bolivia, Ecuador, and Colombia. During the last decade new plantations have been developed in Venezuela and Brazil due to the huge demand for cocaine in the United States and Europe. Local farmers own or lease these plots of land, called *cocals,* which are planted with coca. This business employs hundreds of thousands of impoverished farmers and their families, who harvest the leaves from these shrubs about three to four times a year (Phillips & Wynne, 1980). Each shrub produces no more than 4 ounces of leaves with each picking and it takes an entire family all day to pick 50 pounds of leaves. As it takes more than 200 pounds of leaves to produce a kilo (2.2 pounds) of cocaine paste, the initial processing plants are usually located near the fields (Phillips & Wynne, 1980).

The paste conversion is accomplished through various chemical processes involving mixtures of alcohol, benzol, sulfuric acid, sodium carbonate, and kerosene or gasoline baths combined with several shaking and cooling segments. The final product is a precipitate of crude cocaine called *bazooko.* With the addition of acetone, potassium permanganate, and hydrochloric acid, this pasty sulfate becomes powdery flakes or rocks of nearly pure *cocaine hydrochloride.* At this point it is a white, odorless, crystalline powder that is a member of the tropane family. Most bazooko is converted into cocaine hydrochloride in the jungle laboratories around Colombia. It is then smuggled out through the networks of organized crime to various destinations in other countries including the United States, Europe, and Asia. While en route, it is diluted several times ("stepped on") with various additives such as lactose or dextrose (sugar), inositol (Vitamin B), mannitol (baby laxative), and even cornstarch, talcum powder, and oven flour to stretch the quantity. This "stretching" process increases profits as the now-diluted cocaine finds its way onto the streets of major cities throughout the world (Grinspoon & Bakalar, 1980; Phillips & Wynne, 1980).

During the past few years drug dealers have developed new marketing strategies by processing bazooko or cocaine hydrochloride (powder) into a potentiated form of prefabricated, freebase cocaine called *crack*. This inexpensive method of psychoactive stimulant conversion can be accomplished in one's own kitchen by applying heat to cocaine cooked in a mixture of water, ammonia, baking soda, or liquid drain opener. Crack intensifies the biochemical experience in the brain, but also increases the toxic effect on neurological tissue that is involved with cocaine stimulation (Gold, 1987).

The cocaine experience varies with the user. The factors that will influence this experience include the strength of the drug, the setting, the circumstances under which it is taken, the user's attitude, emotional state, drug taking history, and expectation of what the drug should produce. Most will experience a mild euphoria, an increased heartbeat and a subtle sense of excitement. Some may get little or no reaction from using the drug.

Cocaine is a tremendous mood elevator, filling the user with a sense of exhilaration and well being. It melts away feelings of inferiority while loosening inhibitions and evaporating tensions. It relieves fatigue and imparts the illusion of limitless power and energy. Many compulsive users "treat" themselves for obesity, lack of energy, depression, shyness, and low self-esteem. For those who become addicted, cocaine offers a way of coping with life's difficulties and challenges (Gold, 1992).

The routes of cocaine ingestion include inhalation through the nose, commonly called *snorting* or *tooting;* injection under the skin, into a muscle, or into a vein; and smoking freebase or crack. Death has been reported from all forms of cocaine ingestion (Schweitzer, 1986; Kreek, 1987; Cregler & Mark, 1986; Kosten & Kleber, 1987; Liska, 1994).

When cocaine is snorted, the moist nasal membranes quickly dissolve the powder into microscopic molecules that flood the circulatory system in about 15 minutes (Schweitzer, 1986). These molecules encounter and pass through the protective blood-brain barrier, penetrating the cortical tissue that surrounds the deeper layers of brain. These molecules find their way into stimulatory pathways found in the limbic system, which regulate emotion and connect to primitive pain/pleasure centers deep within the brain (Verebey & Gold, 1988).

One of cocaine's primary effects in the brain is to prevent the reuptake of the neurotransmitters dopamine and norepinephrine. It is believed that the cocaine molecule binds to a receptor which blocks the dopaminergic "reuptake pump" and causes an excess of stimulatory molecules at the postsynaptic site. This blocking action will not allow the excess dopamine to transport back into the presynaptic neuron for future use (Radcliffe, Rush, Sites, & Cruse, 1985; Kuhar, Ritz, & Sharkey, 1988). This process keeps mass amounts of dopamine in the synapse for longer periods. It is this overabundance of the brain's own chemicals that is so rewarding to the individual (Cohen, 1988; Ritchie & Greene, 1985).

This excess of dopamine, called *flooding* or *cascading,* causes a decrease in available receptor sites and may create the phenomena of craving (National Institute on

Health, 1993). The elevated rush of dopamine will trigger the release of another neurotransmitter, norepinephrine, which interferes with the brains ability to synthesize serotonin (Gold, 1992; Schnoll, Karrigan, Kitchen, Daghestani, & Hansen, 1985). This neurochemical response will create a rapid tolerance and dependence (drug hunger) for almost anyone who uses this drug (Kuhar, Ritz, & Sharkey, 1988).

Cocaine acts directly on the heart muscle, causing the heart to beat inefficiently and its vessels to narrow, restricting the oxygen needed for peak performance. The heart has to work harder to keep up with the restricted blood flow in the rest of the body. Heavy use can cause angina, irregular heartbeat, and even a heart attack. As cocaine constricts blood flow, it can injure cerebral arteries. The acute hypertension brought on by cocaine use has been known to burst weakened blood vessels or produce strokes in young people (Liska, 1994). A vicious cycle begins. Soon the blood entering the oxygen-starved heart is not pumped out fast enough and backs up into the lungs. Breathing grows labored and painful as the addict starts to drown in his or her own fluids (Karch & Billingham, 1988).

Each time the effects of cocaine wear off, dopamine levels drop, sending the user into a serious state of withdrawal. Normally, the brain replenishes dopamine from proteins in food. But in cocaine addicts dopamine is quickly depleted, partly because of poor diet and partly because cocaine blocks the mechanism that recycles the neurotransmitter for future use (Adler, 1988; Gawin & Ellinwood, 1988; Merigian & Roberts, 1987). Many individuals depress the action of the central nervous system with alcohol or benzodiazepines to temporarily counter the loss of the brain's dopamine supply. In the long run, this only heightens the need for more cocaine.

It is not uncommon for chronic users to experience seizures that result in a constant tingling sensation of the jaw and neck region. The seizures are a result of neurons firing in synchronous bursts, creating uncontrollable electrical storms in the brain. These seizures can cause a general diminuation of alertness and mental functioning and can induce epilepsy, even in those with no previous signs of it.

Recent studies suggest that 12% to 20% of children born at inner-city hospitals have been exposed to cocaine en utero (Forman, Klein, & Barks, 1994). Many of the abnormalities that have been identified in the offspring of pregnant cocaine users, including low birth weight, are more related to the lifestyle of the drug user than to the pharmacological effect of cocaine (Karch, 1996). There is no doubt, however, that the drug constricts the blood vessels of the placenta, reducing the supply of blood and oxygen that reaches the fetus (Ganapathy & Leibach, 1994). Cocaine is also thought to contribute to premature and stillborn births (Saraf, Drombrowski, & Leach, 1995). Babies born to cocaine-using women may have persistently elevated cocaine levels for days, and the possibility exists that the enzymatic pathway for conversion of cocaine into metabolites may not be fully developed in the newborn (Karch, 1996).

There are many potential difficulties with the chronic use of cocaine. These dangers include possible overdose, physical addiction, psychosis, severe depression, and anxiety syndromes including panic attacks and obsessions. The most common causes of death from cocaine are heart attacks, strokes, respiratory failure, paralysis, heart rhythm disturbances, and repeated convulsions, usually from massive overdoses or at the end of a binge (Dressler, 1990; Loghmanee & Tobak, 1986).

Amphetamines

Amphetamines are psychomotor stimulants that were first investigated in 1927 as a treatment for asthma. Their actions on the central nervous system were not reported until 1933, followed by the first reports of amphetamine abuse (Radcliffe, Rush, Sites, & Cruse, 1985). Methylphenidate (Ritalin) is chemically related to the amphetamines and was first synthesized in 1944. Although its major medical use is for the treatment of hyperactive (attention deficit disordered) children, it is frequently abused. Amphetamines can be orally ingested, intravenously injected, snorted, or smoked. They create intense central nervous system arousal, depending on the level of potentiation. Amphetamine and methamphetamine have a similar but slightly different molecule (Liska, 1994; Radcliffe, Rush, Sites, & Cruse, 1985; Siegel, 1989). Methamphetamine, also called *ice,* is making inroads into the United States from the Pacific Basin and is considered the most hyper-charged analog of this family of drugs (King & Ellinwood, 1992).

During the last three decades, "speed" epidemics have been reported in Japan, Sweden, and the United States (King & Ellinwood, 1992). In the United States, this led to a change in laws when amphetamines were restricted to medical use by the Controlled Substances Act of 1970. This act has been strictly enforced by the Drug Enforcement Administration.

The underground production of amphetamines in North America is largely accomplished through small, clandestine laboratories. They produce more than $3 billion worth of illegal amphetamines per year with a huge profit margin. Law enforcement officials believe these "speed labs" are financed by motorcycle gangs who distribute the final product (King & Ellinwood, 1992). Illicit forms of methamphetamine sold on the street may be called *speed, crystal (meth), crank, batu, slate, glass* or *ice.* (Liska, 1994; Siegel, 1989).

Amphetamines cross the blood-brain barrier easily after oral ingestion. Once the amphetamine molecules pass through the stomach, they absorb into the blood via the intestines where they are able to reach peak levels within one hour. They are lipid soluble, and after absorption, they distribute into the brain, lung, and kidney. Brain levels reach about 10 times the blood levels, which accounts for the intense central nervous system (CNS) effect. Some of the metabolites are active and—if present in sufficient quantity—can cause high blood pressure and hallucinations. Metabolism and excretion are both affected by the acidity of the urine (Radcliffe, Rush, Sites, & Cruse, 1985).

In the CNS, amphetamines mimic cocaine, acting on the neurotransmitters dopamine and norepinephrine. They cause a tremendous release of newly synthesized dopamine from the pre-synaptic neuron to bind and stimulate the post-synaptic neurons (King & Ellinwood, 1992). It also inhibits the action of monoamine oxidase (MAO), the enzyme that ends the action of these neurotransmitters and allows them to remain active in the synapse for a longer period of time. Amphetamines also act on the sympathetic nervous system (SNS) through the stimulation and release of norepinephrine while blocking the reuptake of norepinephrine back into the presynaptic terminal. This action elicits a "fight or flight" response. Thus, the psychostimulants are called sympathomimetic drugs in that they mimic the action of the SNS (Hanson, Sonsalla, & Letter, 1989). High doses of amphetamines have also been found to have a direct effect on serotonergic receptors. Electroencephalogram (EEG) recordings have shown that amphetamine accelerates and desynchronizes neuronal firing rates in the brain even during sleep (Weiner, 1985).

With large doses of amphetamine, extreme symptoms may occur, including rapid heartbeat, hypertension, headache, profuse sweating, and severe chest pain, This generally occurs when dosages exceed 50 to 100 mg per day on a continuous basis, and the user may appear psychotic or schizophrenic. Severe intoxication also can produce delirium, panic, paranoia, and hallucinations. There have been reports of murders and other violent offenses that are attributed to amphetamine intoxication, and it has been found that amphetamine can induce aggression in animal models (King & Ellinwood, 1992). Tolerance develops to specific actions of amphetamine including euphoria, appetite suppression, wakefulness, hyperactivity, and heart and blood pressure effects. During withdrawal, it has been clearly demonstrated that a period of depression, fatigue, increased appetite, and prolonged sleep accompanied by REM (dream sleep) rebound follows the cessation of use. Death occurs due to extreme heat elevation, convulsions, and circulatory collapse (Radcliffe, Rush, Sites, & Cruse, 1985).

CANNABINOLS

Cannibis is known by many names—Indian hemp, marijuana, hashish, pot, grass, or dope—and is a controversial drug in U.S. society (Grinspoon & Bakalar, 1992). Cannabis can be smoked, eaten, or drunk. The strengths of the end products that come from the hemp plant vary due to the climate and soil in which it is grown and the method of cultivation and preparation. Its potency and quality depend mainly on the type of plant that is grown.

Experienced growers identify potency by grading the plant with Indian names. *Bhang* is identified as the least potent and cheapest and is made from the cut tops of uncultivated plants that contain a low resin content. *Ganja* is derived from the flowering tops and leaves of selected, carefully cultivated plants that has a higher content of resin and therefore is more potentiated to the user. *Charas* is the highest grade and is produced from the resin itself, obtained from fully mature plants. This highly potentiated source is generally referred to as *hashish* (Grinspoon & Bakalar, 1992; Liska, 1994).

The potency of marijuana has drastically increased in the United States as California growers have successfully cultivated an unpollinated plant known as *sinsemilla*.

Imported products from Thailand, Hawaii, and The Netherlands have also been tested with incredibly high amounts of tetrahydrocannabinol (THC), the active ingredient in marijuana. Additionally, clandestine laboratories have developed a method of producing a liquid called "hash oil," which has been found to have more than 60% THC content (Grinspoon & Bakalar, 1992; Liska, 1994) compared with an average 30% in regular hashish and 7% to 15% in sinsemilla.

In the United States, cannabis is generally smoked in a cigarette called a *joint* or a *doobie*. A marijuana cigarette contains 421 chemicals before ignition. There are 61 cannabanoids, including delta-1 tetrahydrocannabinol, which is believed to be the active psychoactive agent. There are also 50 different waxy hydrocarbons, 103 terpines, 12 fatty acids, 11 steroids, 20 nitrogen compounds as well as carbon monoxide, ammonia, acetone, benzene, benzathracene, and benzoprene. When ignited, these chemicals convert into more than 2,000 other chemicals. As these are metabolized by the body, they convert to about 600 chemical metabolites. Cannabinoids have a half-life of 72 hours in the human body. When ingested, it appears to be dose dependent. Cannabinoids are lipid soluble and store at megamicroscopic levels for indefinite periods of time in the body (Grinspoon & Bakalar, 1992; Liska, 1994).

The research findings on cannabis are mixed. Some research shows that the chemicals found in marijuana and hashish interfere with the cell's ability to manufacture pivotal molecules, which grossly affects the substances necessary for cell division including DNA, RNA, and proteins. This causes an "aging process" in particular clusters of cells found in the brain, liver, lungs, spleen, lymphoid tissues, and sex organs. These suggestions of long-term damage come almost exclusively from laboratory work with animal models.

Observations of human marijuana users from several studies conducted in this country and abroad do not confirm these findings. Several human studies in the past 20 years reveal little disease or organic pathology found in cannabis-using populations (Gold, 1986; Grinspoon & Bakalar, 1992; Liska, 1994). Unfortunately, many of these studies were conducted at a time when the THC content of cannabis was extremely low (.05% to 4%). With some strains of the drug reportedly reaching THC content that extend into the teens (sinsemilla-14%) and even the twenties (neiterweit-27%) there is concern that cannabis may be doing more damage than previously realized.

One well-confirmed danger of heavy, long-term use is its ability to damage the lungs due to the fact that it burns 16 times "hotter" than tobacco and produces twice as many mutagens (agents that cause permanent changes in genetic material). Biopsies have confirmed that cannabis smokers are at an extremely high risk for the development of lung diseases including bronchitis, emphysema, and cancer (Gold, 1986; Liska, 1994). There is certainly a need for multiple, long-term studies to be conducted on different populations that regularly use cannabis to determine their physiological and medical outcomes.

Cannabis holds some promising uses for the medical community, as it has been used to obtain relief from glaucoma and asthma as well as from the side effects of chemotherapy used in the treatment of specific forms of cancer. This potential has yet to be fully realized, however, because of legal complications involved in doing such research and a resistance to its use by the medical establishment due to its reputation as an intoxicant (Grinspoon & Bakalar, 1992).

Hallucinogens

Hallucinogenic substances that have abuse potential fit into one of two classifications, according to their chemical structure:

1. **Indoles,** which include (a) lysergic acid derivatives and (b) substituted tryptamines such as dimethyltryptamine (DMT) and psilocybin and psilocin.

2. **Substituted phenethylamines,** which include (a) mescaline and (b) phenylisopropylamines such as 2, 5-dimethoxy- 4 methylamphetamine (DOM, STP) or 3, 4-methylenedioxyamphetamine (MDA) or 3, 4-methlenedioxymethamphetamine (MDMA, "ecstasy").

All the indole-type hallucinogens have a structure similar to the neurotransmitter serotonin, while the substituted phenylethylamine-type hallucinogens are structurally related to the neurotransmitter norepinephrine. It is believed that the mechanism of action occurring in the indole-type hallucinogens involves the alteration of serotonergic neurotransmission. Lysergic acid diethylamide (LSD) is probably the best known of the indole-type hallucinogens and is most abused by white males between the ages of 10 and 29 years (Liska, 1994; Ungerleider & Pechnick, 1992). The phenylisopropylamines DOM, STP, MDA, and MDMA (ecstasy) are structurally similar to the psychostimulant amphetamine (Pierce & Peroutka, 1989; Sadzot, Baraban, & Glennon, 1989; Titeler, Lyon, & Glennon 1989; Ungerleider & Pechnick, 1992). A few of the indole-type such as psilocybin and psilocin are found in nature while mescaline is a naturally occurring hallucinogen derived from the peyote cactus (Ungerleider & Pechnick, 1992). The rest are synthetic compounds which are now considered "designer drugs," manufactured in clandestine laboratories and sold on the street as illicit drugs (Kirsch, 1986; National Institute on Drug Abuse, 1987; Ruttenberg, 1986).

The overall effects of many of the hallucinogens are similar, although there is a multitude of variables involving the rate of onset, duration of action, and the intensity of the drug experience. This is due to the wide range of potency available and the amount of the drug that is ingested relative to its specific dose-response characteristics.

Confiscated street samples of LSD can range from 10 to 300 micrograms in a single dose. LSD triggers behavioral responses in some individuals after doses as low as 20 micrograms. Psychological and behavioral effects begin occur about an hour after oral ingestion and generally peak between two and four hours. There is a gradual return to the predrug state within six to eight hours. The subjective effects can be somatic with symptoms of dizziness, weakness, and tremor, followed by perceptual changes of altered vision and intensified hearing, which gradually changes into visual distortions, dreamlike imagery, and synthesia that includes "seeing" smells and "hearing" colors (Liska, 1994; Ungerleider & Pechnick, 1992). LSD is metabolized mainly at the site of the liver to various transformation products, and very little is eliminated as an unchanged product (Liska, 1994).

Phencyclidine (PCP, "angel dust") is considered a hallucinogenic. It was originally developed as a general anesthetic for human application but was found to be unstable. It was then offered as an anesthetic for veterinary applications until 1986 (Liska, 1994; Zukin & Zukin, 1992). At that time, PCP and its chemical analogs were classified as Schedule I drugs under the Anti-Drug Abuse Act. There are extreme penalties for trafficking PCP or attempting to purchase piperidine, a major chemical used in the manufacture of PCP (Liska, 1994).

In its pure form, PCP is a water-soluble white powder. It is often adulterated or misrepresented as a variety of other drugs including tetrahydrocannabinol (THC), cannabinol, mescaline, psilocybin, LSD, amphetamine, or cocaine. On the street, it can be found in powder, tablet, and liquid form. A typical street dose (one pill, joint, or line) is about 5 mg, but confiscated street samples have revealed that purity can run from 5% to 100% depending on the form. This wide variance can create a tremendous risk to the user (Liska, 1994; Zukin & Zukin, 1992).

PCP can be ingested orally, smoked, snorted, intravenously injected, and even inserted vaginally. The mode of administration can drastically alter the onset of effects. Smoking and injection create a rapid onset of effects which usually peak within 30 minutes. The high lasts from four to six hours. Chronic users report doing PCP in "runs" of two to three days, during which time they remain sleepless. When used in this fashion, many of these chronic users may need emergency room treatment to overcome the residual effects of the drug (Zukin & Zukin, 1992).

PCP is a potent compound and extremely lipid soluble. Its psychological/behavioral effects are dose dependent. The dose range for PCP effect on brain stimulation reward enhancement is relatively narrow. At low doses it produces reward enhancement or a "good trip," and at high doses it inhibits brain reward (much like a neuroleptic) and may produce a "bad trip." It is believed that PCP binds to specific sites in the human brain and blocks the reuptake of several major neurotransmitters systems. It also disrupts electrophysiological activity by blocking the ionic exchange of sodium and potassium (Kushner, Lerma, Bennet & Zukin, 1989; Mayer, MacDermott, Westbrook, Smith & Barker, 1987). These serious actions on major brain systems probably accounts for PCP's symptoms of dissociative anesthesia and its ability to create coma and lethal complications in the user. Currently there is no PCP antagonist available to block its effects, and the medical community is forced to use sedatives (benzodiazepines or neuroleptics) to treat toxicity (Zukin & Zukin, 1992).

Volatile Substances or Inhalants

This group contains several chemicals that can be "sniffed," "snorted," "huffed," "bagged" or inhaled. This kind of substance abuse is a much larger problem than most people realize. It has been found to exist in almost every country of the world (Adelekan, 1989; Alvarez, Queipo, Del Rio, & Garcia, 1989; Beauvis & Oetting, 1988; Carlini-Cotrim & Carlini, 1988; Cooke, Evans, & Farrow, 1988; Levy & Pierce, 1989; Medina-Mora & Ortiz, 1988; Pedersen, Clausen, & Lavik, 1989). Although drug use in general has declined in the United States, the use of inhalants in adolescent and preadolescent populations has increased or held constant. It seems to occur at about the same frequency for females as for males. The level of use for inhalants in this population is exceeded only by marijuana, alcohol, and cigarettes (Sharp & Rosenberg, 1992).

Inhalants are widely available, readily accessible, inexpensive, and legally obtained. These reasons account for their extensive use by youths. The toxic vapors make users forget their problems as they obtain a quick high with a minimal hang-over. Chronic solvent abusers tend to be poorer, come from broken homes, and do poorly in school (Oetting, Edwards, & Beauvais, 1988). Disruptive and antisocial behavior as well as self-directed aggression is associated with individuals who abuse inhalants (Sharp & Korman, 1981). It has not been determined whether these groups chose inhalants as their drug of choice because of their predilections or whether the deficiencies came about as the result of their inhalant abuse (Korman, Matthews, & Lovitt, 1981). The majority of inhalant abusers never reach a hospital or a treatment facility (Sharp & Rosenberg, 1992).

Inhalants include glue, gasoline, thinners, solvents, aerosols (found in paint, cooking lubricant spray, deodorant, hairspray), correction fluids, cleaning fluids, refrigerant gases (fluorocarbons), anesthetics, "whippets" (whipped cream propellants), organic nitrites, and cooking or lighter gas.

Acute symptoms associated with the use of inhalants include excitation turning to drowsiness, disinhibition, lightheadedness, and agitation. With increasing intoxication, the user may develop ataxia, dizziness, and disorientation. Extreme intoxication may create signs of sleeplessness, general muscle weakness, dysarthria, nystagmus, hallucinations, and disruptive behavior. After the high wears off, the user may sleep, appear lethargic, and experience headaches. Chronic abusers may experience continued weight loss, muscle weakness, general disorientation, inattentiveness, and lack of coordination. These physical conditions can be complicated by the use of other drugs (mainly alcohol, cigarettes, and marijuana), malnutrition, and respiratory illness.

By contrast, there is an "affluent" group of inhalant abusers that includes dentists, anesthesiologists, and other health professionals. They generally limit their intake of inhalants to organic nitrites (poppers), nitrous oxide (laughing gas), and halothane (Sharp & Rosenberg, 1992).

Neurotoxicity is predominantly related to the type of substance inhaled and the dose and duration of exposure. Acute, high-level exposure to solvents will induce short term effects on brain function but appear to be reversible (Rosenberg, 1992). Chronic, high-level exposure over a longer time slowly produces irreversible neurologic syndromes (Hormes, Filley, & Rosenberg, 1986). There are numerous reports regarding the adverse effects of toxic vapors on the user's kidneys, liver, lungs, heart and blood (Austin, Deizell, & Cole, 1988; Boon, 1987; Davidman & Schmitz,

1988; Horowitz, 1986; McLeod, Marjot, Monaghan, Hugh-Jones, & Jackson, 1987; Rosoff & Cohen, 1986).

It is not clear whether the inhalation of substances during pregnancy creates a "fetal solvent syndrome," because a number of subjects who were studied were also ingesting various amounts of alcohol (Goodwin, 1988; Hersh, 1989). It is highly recommended that pregnant women avoid exposure to solvents to protect their unborn babies.

Nicotine

Cigarette smoking and smokeless tobacco use claim more than 400,000 lives every year in the United States. Tobacco-related health problems include cardiovascular disease, cancer, chronic obstructive lung disease, and complications during pregnancy (U.S. Department of Health and Human Services, 1988; 1990).

Dependence on nicotine resembles that of cocaine, heroin, or alcohol in that it produces compulsive patterns of use and is positively and negatively reinforcing, and the user continues its use in spite of knowing its harmful effects. Nicotine produces tolerance and physical dependence that evolve around an ongoing pattern of craving and relapse after a brief period of abstinence (Hughes & Hatsukami, 1986; Jaffe, 1990; U.S. Department of Health and Human Services, 1988). Most tobacco smokers develop their habit during adolescence, and their risk is increased when friends and family members smoke (U.S. Department of Health and Human Services, 1989). Nicotine smoking has been linked to individuals who suffer from neuroticism, anxiety, alcoholism, depression, and other substance abuse (Anda, Williamson, Escobedo, Mast, Giovino, & Remington, 1990; Glassman, Heizer, Covey, 1990; Kozowski, Ferrence, & Corbit, 1990; Waal-Manning & de Hamel, 1988).

Tobacco smoke contains many toxic compounds. Nicotine is the major reinforcing agent, while tar and carbon monoxide have been identified as physiologically active chemicals. Alone or in combination, they are responsible for most most smoking-related diseases (Honningfield & Nemeth-Coslett, 1988; U.S. Department of Health and Human Services, 1989) with coronary heart disease and lung cancer leading the list (U.S. Department of Health and Human Services, 1989).

Nicotine is readily absorbed in the body from every site it comes in contact with, including the skin. It binds to nicotinic cholinergic receptor sites located in the brain, striated muscle tissue, and autonomic ganglia (Keller, Schwartz, & Martino, 1987). Current research indicates that in the brain, nicotine's reinforcement properties may come from its action on the substantia nigra, ventral segmental area, and projections onto the nucleus accumbens via the release of dopamine as the medium of reward (Clarke, Schwartz, Paul, Pert, & Pert, 1985; London, 1990). Once in the bloodstream, a portion is carried to the liver where it is metabolized into cotinine (90%) and nicotine-N-oxide (10%).

The involuntary inhalation of passive cigarette smoke has been established as dangerous to the health. It has been observed that cotinine levels can be found in children as a result of exposure to cigarette smokers in their family unit (U.S. Department of Health and Human Services, 1990).

Nicotine directly stimulates and inactivates cholinergic receptors in the brain and causes the release of several neurotransmitters and hormones, including dopamine, norepinephrine, and adrenaline (Pomerleau & Pomerleau, 1989). The release of epinephrine at the adrenal medulla causes an increase in free fatty acids, glycerol, and lactate concentrations in the blood. Nicotine is also converted into nitrosonornicotine which has been identified as a carcinogenic (cancer-causing) compound (Hoffman, Brunneman, Adams, & Hecht, 1984). Evidence suggests nicotine is a primary positive reinforcer in the brain and that stimulant and depressant actions are dose dependent and controlled by the smoker (Henningfield & Woodson, 1989). Nicotine produces a euphoria similar to amphetamine and morphine (Jasinski, Johnson, & Henningfield, 1984). It is these pleasurable brain effects that increase cardiac acceleration and can cause sudden death after tens of thousands of self-administered reinforcements (Jarvik & Schneider, 1992).

A major feature of cigarette smoking is its ability to help the smoker lose weight by the aforementioned interaction and drastic release of specific neurotransmitters found in the central nervous system, particularly norepinephrine. This chronic stimulation increases metabolism (Winders & Grunberg, 1990). Smokers who quit have a high rate of relapse during the first two years, citing weight gain, negative emotions, interpersonal conflict, and social pressure as reasons to use again (Benowitz, 1988; Leavitt, 1995).

Caffeine

Caffeine is the most widely consumed psychoactive agent in the world. About 80% of the adults in the United States use caffeine regularly. The chronic overuse of this substance is called "caffeinism." Clinical and epidemiologic data show that its overuse induces an intoxication of the CNS that includes habituation, tolerance, and a withdrawal syndrome (Greden & Walters, 1992).

Caffeine belongs to a chemical class of alkaloids known as *xanthine derivatives* and it was chemically isolated more than 170 years ago (Arnaud, 1984). It is found in coffee, tea, cocoa, chocolate, and a number of soft drinks as well as hundreds of prescription and over-the-counter (OTC) drugs. It is found in more than 60 plant species around the world (Rail, 1980).

A large number of variables make it difficult to research the dose response for developing caffeine dependence. These include a subject's age, body mass, other psychoactive substances in use, amount of stress, level of fatigue, sleep disorders, and varying degrees of sensitivity to the drug. Furthermore, the acute use of caffeine produces very different biologic consequences when compared with chronic use (Greden & Walters, 1992).

Caffeine is rapidly absorbed into the gastrointestinal tract and peak plasma levels occur within 30 to 45 minutes after ingestion. It crosses the blood-brain barrier very quickly and concentrates in brain plasma relative to the amount that is ingested (Kaplan, Greenblatt, LeDuc, Thompson & Shader, 1989).

Data strongly suggest that antagonism of the adenosine receptor accounts for many of caffeine's behavioral effects (Halloway, Modrow, & Michaelis, 1985).

Adenosine has sedative, anxiolytic, and anticonvulsant actions as well as the ability to dilate blood vessels in specific areas in the brain and heart (Snyder, 1984). When caffeine occupies adenosine binding sites, these actions cannot occur and there is a stimulating or anxiogenic effect. Many researchers believe the key reinforcing factor may be caffeine's effects on the pleasure and reward centers found in the hypothalamus and the median forebrain bundle. Caffeine's actions on these centers stimulate the output of dopamine and norepinephrine and appear comparable (although not as intense) to amphetamine and cocaine (Joyce & Koob, 1981). Caffeine increases heart rate and contraction, physiologically creating arrhythmias and mild tachycardia. It increases gastric acidity and is contraindicated for patients with ulcers. Caffeine demonstrates rapid diuretic effects on the urinary tract and is measurable in urine as well as in plasma, saliva, breast milk, cerebrospinal fluid, semen, and amniotic fluid (Christensen & Neims, 1984; Halloway, Modrow, & Michaelis, 1985).

Children do not seem to possess an innate craving for caffeine and most people in our society seem to be exposed to it gradually as their intake eventually progresses to a pattern of frequent or daily use. The daily average dosage of a caffeine user in the United States exceeds 200 mg per day (Barone & Roberts, 1984; Levey & Zylber-Katz, 1983). About one-fourth of this consuming population exceeds 500 mg per day and more than 10% have developed the syndrome of caffeinism. This is manifested by anxiety, sleep disturbances, mood changes, and psychophysiologic complaints. The aforementioned ability of caffeine to stimulate the brain's reward centers may be the most important encouragement for people to move from a controlled phase of caffeine ingestion to the stage of caffeinism (Greden & Walters, 1992).

About 15% of caffeine is metabolized in an hour via the liver (Arnaud, 1984). Its half-life is 3½ to 5 hours in human subjects. Caffeine has a low level of toxicity. It would take 50 to 100 cups of coffee to produce a fatal overdose in an average adult male (Hughes, Higgins, & Bickel, 1991).

CONCLUSION

This chapter has examined how the human brain is the major site for all psychoactive drug interaction. All psychoactive substances manipulate the biochemistry of the brain to some degree and change the neuron's process of communication within its existing structural framework. These changes can alter the user's perceptions, emotions, thoughts, and behaviors over time. Additionally, the effect of drugs on other body organs was discussed.

The current findings were presented on specific drug groups that create dependence and the biological actions that appear to make people reliant on the drugs. Future research involving the neurosciences, psychopharmacology, and new therapeutic strategies with chemically dependent populations will, it is hoped, produce new insights and actions to successfully tackle this problem in society.

REFERENCES

Abel, E. L., & Soko, R. J. (1986a). Fetal alcohol syndrome is now leading cause of mental retardation. *Lancet,* ii, 12–22.

Adelekan, M. L. (1989). Self-reported drug use among secondary school students in the Nigerian state of Ogun. *Bulletin on Narcotics, 41*(1–2), 109–116.

Adler, J. (1988, November 28). Hour by hour crack. *Newsweek,* 64–79.

Aghajanlan, G. K., & Wang, Y. Y. (1987). Common alpha-2 and oplate effector mechanisms in the locus coeruleus: Intracellular studies in brain slices. *Neuropharmacology, 26,* 789-800.

Alvarez, F. J., Queipo, D., Del Rio, M. C., & Garcia, M. C. (1989). Patterns of drug use by young people in the rural community of Spain. *British Journal of Addictions, 84*(6), 647–652.

American Psychiatric Association. (1994). *Diagnostic and Statistical Manual of Mental Disorders* (4th ed.). Washington, DC: Author.

American Psychiatric Association. (1990). *Benzodiazepine dependence, toxicity, and abuse.* Washington, DC: American Psychiatric Association.

Anda, R. F., Williamson, D. F., Escobedo, L. G., Mast, E. E., Giovino, G. A., & Remington, P. L. (1990). Depression and the dynamics of smoking. *Journal of American Medical Association, 264*(12), 1541–1546.

Andreasen, N. (1984). *The broken brain: The biological revolution in psychiatry.* New York: Harper and Row Publishers.

Arnaud, M. J. (1984). Products of metabolism of caffeine. In P. B. Dews (Ed.), *Caffeine* (pp. 3–38). New York: Springer-Verlag.

Austin, H., Deizell, E., & Cole, P. (1988). Benzene and leukemia: A review of the literature and a risk assessment. *American Journal of Epidemiology, 127*(3), 419–439.

Barone, J. J., & Roberts, H. (1984). Human consumption of caffeine. In P. B. Dews (Ed.), *Caffeine.* NY: Springer-Verlag.

Beauvis, F., & Oetting, E. R. (1988). Inhalant abuse by young children. In R. A. Crider & B. A. Rouse (Eds.), *Epidemiology of inhalant abuse: An update* (NIDA Research Monograph No. 85, DHHS Publication No. ADM 88-1577, pp. 30-34). Rockville, MD: NIDA.

Benowitz, N. L. (1988). Clinical pharmacology of nicotine. *Annals of Research Medicine, 37,* 21–32.

Bleich, A., Grinspoon, A., & Garb, R. (1987). Paranoid reaction following alprazolam withdrawal. *Psychosomatics, 28,* 599-600.

Blum, K., & Payne, J. E. (1991). *Alcohol and the addictive brain.* New York: The Free Press.

Boon, N. A. (1987). Solvent abuse and the heart [Editorial]. *British Medical Journal, 294*(6574), 722.

Bozarth, M. A. (1987). Opiate reward mechanisms mapped by intracranial self-administration. In J. E. Smith & J. D. Lane (Eds.), *Neurobiology of opiate reward processes* (pp. 331–359). Amsterdam: Elsevier North Holland Biomedical Press.

Bradbury, A. F., Smyth, D. G., Snell, C. R., Birdsall, N. J. M., & Hulme, E. C. (1976). C fragment of lipotropin has a high affinity for brain opiate receptors. *Nature, 260,* 793–795.

Broekkamp, C. L. E. (1987). Combined microinjection and brain stimulation reward methodology for the localization of reinforcing drug effects. In M. A. Bozarth (Ed.), *Methods of assessing the reinforcing properties of abused drugs* (pp. 479–488). New York: Springer-Verlag.

Brown, J. L., & Hauge, K. L. (1986). A review of alprazolam withdrawal. *Drug Intelligencia and Clinical Pharmacology, 20,* 837-841.

Carlen, P. L., Wortzman, G., Holgate, R. C., Wilkinson, D. A., & Rankin, J. G. (1978). Reversible cerebral atrophy in recently abstinent chronic alcoholics measured by computed tomography scans. *Science, 200,* 1076–1078.

Carlini-Cotrim, B., & Cartini, E. A. (1988). The use of solvents and other drugs among children and adolescents from a low socioeconomic background. As studied in Sao Paulo, Brazil. *International Journal of the Addictions, 23*(11), 1145–1156.

Childress, A. R., McLellan, A. T., & O'Brien, C. P. (1986). Conditioned responses in a methadone population. *Journal of Substance Abuse Treatment, 3,* 173–179.

Christensen, H. D., & Neims, A. H. (1984). Measurement of caffeine and its metabolites in biological fluids. In P. B. Dew (Ed.), *Caffeine* (pp. 39–45). New York: Springer-Verlag.

Clarke, P. B. S., Schwartz, R. D., Paul, S. M., Pert, C. B., & Pert, A. (1985). Nicotinic binding in rat brain: Autoradiographic comparison of [3H] acetylcholine, [3H] nicotine and [1251]-alpha-bungarotoxin. *Journal of Neuroscience, 5*(5), 1307–1315.

Clarren, S. K., & Smith, D. W. (1978). The fetal alcohol syndrome. *New England Journal of Medicine, 298,* 1063–1067.

Cohen, S. (1988). *The chemical brain: The neurochemistry of addictive disorders.* Irvine, CA: CareInstitute.

Cooke, B. R., Evans, D. A., & Farrow, S. C. (1988). Solvent misuse in secondary school children: A prevalence study. *Community Medicine, 10*(1), 8–13.

Cox, B. M., Goldstein, A., & Li, C. H. (1978). Opioid activity of a peptide, B-llpotropin-(61–91) derived from b-llpotropin. *Proceedings of the National Academy of Science, USA, 73,* 1821–1823.

Cregler, L. L., & Mark, H. (1986). Cardiovascular dangers of cocaine abuse. *American Journal of Cardiology, 57,* 1185–1186.

Crider, R. A., Gfroerer, J. C., & Blanken, A. J. (1987, December). Black tar heroin field investigation. In *Community Epidemiology Work Group, Proceedings* (pp. III, 11–34). Rockville, MD: National Institute on Drug Abuse.

Davidman, M., & Schmitz, P. (1988). Renal tubular acidosis: A pathophysiologic approach. *Hospital Practitioner [Office], 23*(1A), 77–81, 84–88, 93–96.

Dressler, F. A. (1990). Quantitative analysis of amounts of coronary arterial narrowing in cocaine addicts. *Journal of the American Medical Association, 263,* 31–97.

Epstein, P. S., Pisani, V. C., & Fawcett, J. A. (1977). Alcoholism and cerebral atrophy. *Alcohol Clinical Experimental Research, 1,* 61–65.

Esposito, R. U., Porrino, L. J., & Seeger, T. F. (1987). Brain stimulation reward: Measurement and mapping by psychophysical techniques and quantitative 2-(14c) deoxyglucose autoradiography. In M. A. Bozarth (Ed.), *Methods of assessing the reinforcing properties of abused drugs* (pp. 421–445). New York: Springer-Verlag.

Fischbach, G. D. (1992). Mind and brain. *Scientific American (Special issue), 267*(3), 48–57.

Forman, R., Klein, J., & Barks, J. (1994). Prevalence of fetal exposure to cocaine in Toronto, 1990–1991. *Clinical Investigations in Medicine, 17*(3), 206–211.

Ganapathy, V., & Leibach, F. (1994). Current Topic: Human placenta: A direct target for cocaine action. *Placenta, 15,* 785–795.

Gardner, E. L., Paredes, W., Seeger, T. F., Smith, D., & Van Praag, H. M. (1988). Mesolimbic DA antagonism by SHTs receptor blockade. *Book of abstracts, World Psychiatric Association regional symposium, the research and clinical interface for psychiatric disorders, October 13-16, 1988* (pp. 222). Washington, DC: American Psychiatric Association.

Gardner, E. L., Paredes, W., & Smith, D. (1988). Facilitation of brain stimulation reward by delta 9-tetrahydrocannabinol. *Psychopharmacology, 96,* 142–144.

Gawin, F. H., & Ellinwood, E. H. (1988). Cocaine and other stimulants. *New England Journal of Medicine, 318,* 1173–1183.

Gilbert, P. E., & Martin, W. R. (1978). The effects of morphine and nalorphine-like drugs in the non-dependent morphine dependent and cyclazocine-dependent chronic spinal dog. *Journal of Pharmacology and Experimental therapy, 198,* 66-82.Ganapathy, V., & Leibach, F. (1994). Current topic: Human placenta, a direct target for cocaine action. *Placenta, 15,* 785–795.

Gill, J. S., Zezulka, A. V., Shipley, M. J., Gill, S. K., & Bevers, D. J. (1986). Stroke and alcohol consumption. *New England Journal of Medicine, 315,* 1041–1046.

Glassman, A. H., Heizer, J. E., & Covey, L. S. (1990). Smoking, smoking cessation and major depression. *Journal of the American Medical Association, 264,* 1546–1549.

Gold, M. S. (1992). Cocaine and crack: Clinical aspects. In J. H. Lowinson, P. Ruiz, R. B. Millman, & J. G. Langrod (Eds.), *Substance abuse: A comprehensive textbook,* (2nd ed., pp. 205–221). Baltimore: Williams & Wilkins.

Gold, M. S. (1991). *The good news about drugs and alcohol.* NY: Villard Books.

Gold, M. S. (1987). Crack abuse: Its implications and outcomes. *Resident & Staff Physician, 33*(8), 45–53.

Gold, M. S. (1986). *The facts about drugs and alcohol.* NY: Bantam Books.

Gold, M. S., Miller, N. S., & Jonas, J. M. (1992). Cocaine and crack: Neurobiology. In J. H. Lowinson, P. Ruiz, R. B. Millman, J. G. Langrod (Eds.), *Substance abuse: A comprehensive textbook* (2nd ed., pp. 222–235). Baltimore: Williams & Wilkins.

Goldstein, A., Tachiban, S., Lowney, L. I., Hunkapiller, M., & Hood, I. (1979). Dynorphin (1–13), an extraordinarily potent opioid peptide. *Proc National Academy of Science, USA, 76,* 6666–6670.

Goodwin, D. W. (1992). Alcohol: clinical aspects. In J. H. Lowinson, P. Ruiz, R. B. Millman, J. G. Langrod (Eds.), *Substance abuse: A comprehensive textbook* (2nd ed., pp. 144–151). Baltimore: Williams & Wilkins.

Goodwin, T. M. (1988). Toluene abuse and renal tubular acidosis in pregnancy. *Obstetrics and Gynecology, 71*(5), 715–718.

Gorelick, P. B., Rodin, M. B., & Langengerg, P. (1987). Is acute alcohol ingestion a risk factor for ischemic stroke: Results of a controlled study in middle-aged and elderly stroke patients at three urban medical centers. *Stroke, 18,* 359–364.

Greden, J. F., & Walters, A. (1992). Caffeine. In J. H. Lowinson, P. Ruiz, R. B. Millman, & J. G.

Langrod (Eds.), *Substance abuse: A comprehensive textbook.* Baltimore: Williams & Wilkins.

Grinspoon, L. & Bakalar, J. B. (1980). Drug dependence: nonnarcotic agents. In H. I. Kapalan, A. M. Freedman, & B. J. Sadock (Eds.) *Comprehensive textbook of psychiatry III* (Volume 2, pp. 16–21). Baltimore: Williams & Wilkins.

Grinspoon, L., & Bakalar, J. B. (1992). Marijuana. In J. H. Lowinson, P. Ruiz, R. B. Millman, J. G. Langrod (Eds.), *Substance abuse: A comprehensive textbook* (2nd ed., pp. 236–246). Baltimore: Williams & Wilkins.

Halloway, F. A., Modrow, H. E., & Michaelis, R. C. (1985). Methylxanthine discrimination in the rat: Possible benzodiazepine and adenosine mechanisms. *Pharmacology and Biochemical Behavior, 22,* 815–824.

Hanson, G. R., Sonsalla, P., & Letter, A. (1989). Effects of amphetamine analogs on central nervous system neuropeptide systems. In K. Asghar & E. DeSouza (Eds.), *Pharmacology and toxicology of amphetamine and related designer drugs* (NIDA Research Monograph No. 94, pp. 259–269). Washington, DC: Government Printing Office.

Harper, C., Kril, J., & Daly, J. (1987). Are we drinking our neurons away? *British Medical Journal, 294,* 534–536.

Heishman, S. J., Sitzer, M. L., Bigelow, G. E., & Liebson, I. A. (1989). Acute opioid physical dependence in postaddict humans: Naloxone dose effects after brief morphine exposure. *Journal of Pharmacology and Experimental Therapeutics, 248,* 127–134.

Henningfield, J. E., & Woodson, P. P. (1989). Doses related actions of nicotine on behavior and physiology: Review and implications for replacement therapy for nicotine dependence. *Journal of Substance Abuse, 1,* 301–317.

Hersh, J. H. (1989). Toluene embryopathy: Two new cases. *Journal of Medicine and Genetics, 26*(5), 333–337.

Hill, S. Y., Reyes, R. B., Mikhael, M., & Ayre, F. (1977). A comparison of alcoholics and heroin abusers: Computerized transaxial tomography and neuro psychological functioning. In F. Sexial

(Ed.), *Currents in alcoholism*. New York: Grune & Stratton.

Hoffman, D., Brunneman, K. D., Adams, J. D., & Hecht, S. S. (1984). Formation and analysis on N-nitrosamines in tobacco products and their endogenous formation in consumers. In K. K. O'Neill, R. C. Von Borstel, C. T. Miller, J. Long, & H. Bartsch (Eds.), *N-nitros compounds: Occurrence, biological effects and relationship to human cancer* (IARC scientific publication 57, pp. 743–762.) Geneva: International Agency for Research on Cancer.

Honningfield, J. E., & Nemeth-Coslett, R. (1988). Nicotine dependence: Interface between tobacco and tobacco-related disease. *Chest, 93,* 37S-55S.

Hooper, J., & Teresi, D. (1986). *The three pound universe: The brain*. New York: Dell Publishing Company.

Hormes, J. T., Filley, C. B., & Rosenberg, N. L. (1986). Neurologic sequelae of chronic solvent vapor abuse. *Neurology, 36*(5), 698–702.

Horowitz, B. Z. (1986). Carboxyhemoglobinemia caused by inhalation of methylene chloride. *American Journal of Emergency Medicine, 4*(1), 48–51.

Hughes, J. R. & Hatsukami, D. K. (1986). Signs and symptoms of tobacco withdrawal. *Archives of General Psychiatry, 43,* 289–294.

Hughes, J. R., Higgins, S. T., & Bickel, W. K. (1991). Caffeine self-administration, withdrawal and adverse effects among coffee drinkers. *Archives of General Psychiatry, 48,* 611–617.

Hughes, J., Smith, T. W., Kosterlitz, H. W., Fothergill, L. A., Morgan, B. A., & Morris, H. R. (1975). Identification of two related pentapeptides from the brain with potent opiate agonist activity. *Nature, 285,* 577–579.

Hunt, W. A. (1985). *Alcohol and biological membranes*. New York: Guilford Press.

Jaffe, J. (1990). Tobacco smoking and nicotine dependence. In S. Wonnacott, M. A. H. Russell, & I. P. Stolerman (Eds.), *Nicotine psychopharmacology: Molecular, cellular and behavioral aspects* (pp. 1–37). New York: Oxford Press.

Jaffe. J. H. (1992). Drug addiction and drug abuse. In A. G. Gilman, T. W. Rail, A. S. Niew, & P. Taylor (Eds.), *Goodman and Gilman's the pharmacological basis of therapeutics* (8th ed., pp. 522–573). New York: Pergamon Press.

Jaffe, J. H. & Martin, W. R. (1990). Opioid analgesics and antagonists. In A. G. Gilman, T. W. Rail, A. S. Niew, & P. Taylor (Eds.), *Goodman and Gilman's the pharmacological basis of therapeutics* (8th ed., pp. 485–521). New York: Pergamon Press.

Jarvik, M. E., & Schneider, N. G. (1992). Nicotine. In J. H. Lowinson, P. Ruiz, R. B. Millman, & J. G. Langrod (Eds.), *Substance abuse: A comprehensive textbook* (2nd ed., pp. 334–356). Baltimore: Williams & Wilkins.

Jasinski, D. R., Johnson, R. E., & Henningfield, J. E. (1984). Abuse liability assessment in human subjects. *Trends in Pharmacological Science, 5,* 196–200.

Jones, K. L., Smith, D. W., & Ulleland, C. M. (1973). Pattern of malformation in offspring of chronic alcoholic mothers. *Lancet, 1,* 1267–1271.

Joyce, E. M., & Koob, G. F. (1981). Amphetamine, scopolamine, and caffeine-induced locomotor activity following 6-hydroxydopamine lesions of the mesolimbic scopamine system. *Psychopharmacology (Berlin), 73,* 311–313.

Kaplan, G. B., Greenblatt, D. G., LeDuc, B. W., Thompson, M. L., & Shader, R. I. (1989). Relationship of plasma and brain concentrations of caffeine and metabolites to benzodiazepine receptor binding and locomotor activity. *Journal of Pharmacology and Experimental Therapeutics, 248,* 1078–1083.

Karch, S. B., & Billingham, M. E. (1988). The pathology and etiology of cocaine induced heart disease. *Archives of Pathology and Laboratory Medicine, 112,* 225–230.

Karch, S. B. (1996). *The pathology of drug abuse* (2nd ed.). Boca Raton, FL: CRC Press.

Kellar, K. J., Schwartz, R. D., & Martino, A. M. (1987). Nicotinic cholinergic receptor recognition sites in brain. In W. R. Martin, G. R. Van Loon, E. T. Iwanmoto, & L. T. Davis (Eds.), *Tobacco smoking and nicotine: A neurobiological approach* (pp. 467–480). New York: Plenum Press.

Khachaturian, H., Lewis, C., & Schafer, M. K. H. (1985). Anatomy of the CNS opioid systems. *Trends in Neuroscience, 8,* 111–119.

King, G. R., & Ellinwood, E. H. (1992). Amphetamines and other stimulants. In J. H. Lowinson, P. Ruiz, R. B. Millman, & J. G. Langrod (Eds.), *Substance abuse: A comprehensive textbook* (2nd ed., pp. 247–270). Baltimore: Williams & Wilkins.

Kirsch, M. M. (1986). *Designer drugs.* Minneapolis, MN: Compcare Publications.

Koob, G. F., & Bloom, F. E. (1988). Cellular and molecular mechanisms of drug dependence. *Science, 242,* 715–723.

Kolsten, T. R., & Kleber, H. D. (1987). Sudden death in cocaine abusers: relation to neuroleptic malignant syndrome. *Lancet, 1*(8543), 1198–1199.

Korman, M., Matthews, R. W., & Lovitt, R. (1981). Neuropsychological effects of abuse of inhalants. *Perceptual Motor Skills, 53,* 547–553.

Kozowski, L. T., Ferrence, R. G., & Corbit, T. (1990). Tobacco use: A perspective for alcohol and drug researchers. *British Journal of Addiction, 85,* 245.

Kreek, M. J. (1987). Multiple drug abuse patterns and medial consequences. In H. Y. Meltzer (Ed.), *Psychopharmacology: The third generation of progress* (pp. 1600–1603). New York: Raven Press.

Kuhar, M. J., Ritz, M. C. & Sharkey, J. (1988). Cocaine receptors on dopamine transporters, mediate cocaine-reinforced behavior. In D. Couet, K. Asghar, & R. Brown (Eds.), *National Institute of Drug Abuse, Research Monograph, 88,* 14–22.

Kushner, L., Lerma, J., Bennet, M. V. L., & Zukin, R. S. (1989). Using the xenopus oocyte system for expression and cloning of neuroreceptors and channels. In P. N. Conn (Ed.), *Methods in neuroscience* (pp. 1–29). Orlando, FL: Academic Press.

Leavitt, F. (1995). *Drugs and behavior* (3rd ed.). Thousand Oaks, CA: Sage Publications.

Levey, M., & Zylber-Katz, E. (1983). Caffeine metabolism and coffee-attributed sleep disturbances. *Clinical and Pharmacological Therapeutics, 33,* 770–775.

Levy, A. B. (1984). Delirium and seizure due to abrupt alprazolam withdrawal. *Journal of Clinical Psychiatry, 6,* 124-125.

Levy, S. J., & Pierce, J. P. (1989). Drug use among Sydney teenagers in 1985 and 1986. *Community Health Studies, 13*(2), 161–169.

Lipnick, R. L. (1989). Hans Horst Meyer and the lipid theory of narcosis. *Trends in Pharmacology Science, 10,* 265–269.

Liska, K. (1994). *Drugs and the human body* (4th ed.). Upper Saddle River, NJ: Prentice Hall.

Loghmanee, F., & Tobak, M. (1986). Fatal malignant hyperthermia associated with recreational cocaine and ethanol abuse. *American Journal of Forensic Medicine and Pathology, 7,* 246–248.

London, E. D. (1990). Effects of nicotine on cerebral metabolism. In *The biology of nicotine dependence. CIBA Foundation Symposium Vol. 153* (pp. 131–146).

Mansour, A., Khachaturian, H., Lewis, M., Akil, H., & Watson, S. (1988). Anatomy of CNS opioid receptors. *Trends in Neuroscience, 11,* 308–314.

Mayer, M. L., MacDermott, A. B., Westbrook, G. L., Smith, S. J., & Barker, J. L. (1987). Agonist- and voltage-gated calcium entry in cultured mouse spinal cord neurons under voltage clamp measured using arsenazo III. *Journal of Neuroscience, 7,* 3230–3244.

McLeod, A. A., Marjot, R., Monaghan, M. J., Hugh-Jones, P., & Jackson, G. (1987). Chronic cardiac toxicity after inhalation of 1, 1, 1-trichloromethane. *British Medical Journal [Clinical research], 294*(6574), 727–729.

Medina-Mora, E., & Ortiz, A. (1988). Epidemiology of solvent/inhalant abuse in Mexico. In R. A. Crider & B. A. Rouse (Eds.), *Epidemiology of inhalant abuse: An update* (NIDA Research Monograph No. 85). (DHHS Publication No. ADM 88-1577, pp. 140–171). Rockville, MD: NIDA.

Merigian, K. S., & Roberts, J. R. (1987). Cocaine intoxication: Hyperpyrexia, rhabdomyolysis and acute renal failure. *Journal of Toxicology and Clinical Toxicology, 25,* 135–148.

Milkman, H., & Sunderwirth, S. (1986). *Craving for ecstasy: The consciousness & chemistry of craving.* Lexington, MA: Lexington Books.

Moir, A., & Jessel, D. (1991). *Brain sex: The real difference between men and women.* New York: Carol Publishing Group.

National Institute of Alcohol Abuse and Alcoholism (1990). *Alcohol Alert, 16,* 1–3.

National Institute of Alcohol Abuse and Alcoholism (1987). *Sixth special report to the United States Congress on alcohol and health.* Rockville, MD: Author.

National Institute on Drug Abuse (1989). *National household survey on drug abuse.* Washington, DC: U.S. Government Printing Office.

National Institute on Drug Abuse (1987). *Drug abuse and drug abuse research: The second triennial report to Congress,* Rockville, MD: Author.

National Institute on Health (1993). *Drugs and the brain.* Rockville, MD: Author.

Nightingale, S. L. (1990). New indication for Alprazolam. *Journal of the American Medical Association, 264*(22), 28–63.

Oetting, E. T., Edwards, R. W., & Beauvais, F. (1988). Social and psychological factors underlying inhalant abuse. In R. A. Crider & B. A. Rouse (Eds.), *Epidemiology of inhalant abuse: An update* (NIDA Research Monograph No. 85). (DHHS Publication No. ADM 88-1577, pp, 137–163). Rockville, MD: NIDA.

Oka, T. (1980). Enkephalin receptor in the rabbit ileum. *British Journal of Pharmacology, 68,* 193–195.

Pedersen, W., Clausen, S. E., & Lavik, N. J. (1989). Patterns of drug use and sensation-seeking among adolescents in Norway. *Academy of Psychiatry of Scandia, 79*(4), 386–390.

Phillips, J., & Wynne, R. D. (1980). *Cocaine: The mystique and the reality.* New York: Avon Books.

Pierce, P. A., & Peroutka, S. J. (1989). The 5-hydroxytryptamine receptor families. *Seminar Neuroscience, 1*(145), 145–153.

Pierce, D. R., & West, J. R. (1986b). Blood alcohol concentration: A critical factor for producing fetal alcohol effects. *Alcohol, 3,* 269–272.

Pomerleau, O. F., & Pomerleau, C. S. (1989). A biobehavioral perspective on smoking. In T. Ney & A. Gale (Eds.), *Smoking and human behavior* (pp. 69–90). New York: John Wiley & Sons.

Rail, T. W. (1980). The xanthines. In A. G. Gilman, L. S. Goodman, & A. Gilman (Eds.), *The pharmacological basis of therapeutics* (6th ed., pp. 592–607). Upper Saddle River, NJ: Merrill/Prentice Hall

Randall, C. L. (1987, Supplement). Alcohol as a teratogen: A decade of research in review. *Alcohol 1,* 125–132.

Radcliffe, A., Rush, P., Sites, C. F., & Cruse, J. (1985). *The pharmer's almanac: Pharmacology of drugs.* Denver, CO: M.A.C.

Regan, T. J. (1990). Alcohol and the cardiovascular system. *Journal of American Medical Association, 264,* 377–381.

Ritchie, J. M., & Greene, N. M. (1985). Local anesthetics. In A. G. Gilman, L. S. Goodman, & T. W. Rail (Eds.), *Goodman and Gilman's the pharmacological basis of therapeutics* (7th ed., pp. 309–310). Upper Saddle River, NJ: Merrill/Prentice Hall.

Rosenberg, N. L. (1992). Neurotoxicology. In J. B. Sullivan & G. R. Krieger (Eds.), *Medical toxicology of hazardous materials* (pp. 145–153). Baltimore: Williams and Wilkins.

Rosett, H. L. (1980). A clinical perspective of the fetal alcohol syndrome. *Alcoholism (NY), 4,* 119–122.

Rosoff, M. H., & Cohen, M. V. (1986). Profound bradycardia after amyl nitrite in patients with a tendency to vasovagal episodes. *British Heart Journal, 55*(1), 97–100.

Ruttenberg, J. (1986, June). Designer drugs. In *Community Epidemiology Work Group* (Vol. 4, pp. 12–20). Rockville, MD: National Institute on Drug Abuse.

Sadzot, B., Baraban, J. M., & Glennon, R. A. (1989). Hallucinogenic drug interactions at humans 5-HT2 receptor: Implications for treating LSD-induced hallucinogens. *Psychopharmacology, 98,* 495–499.

Saraf, H., Drombrowski, M., & Leach, K. (1995). Characterization of the effect of cocaine on catcholamine uptake by pregnant myometrium. *Obstetrics and Gynecology, 85*(1), 93–95.

Shatz, J. (1992). Mind and brain. *Scientific American: Special Issue, 267*(3), 39-48.

Schnoll, S. H., Karrigan, J., Kitchen, S. B., Daghestani, A., & Hansen, T. (1985). Characteristics of cocaine abusers presenting for treatment. *National Institute on Drug Abuse Research Monograph, 61,* 171–181.

Schweitzer, V. G. (1986). Osteolytic sinusitis and pneumondelatinum: Deceptive otolaryngologic complications of cocaine abuse. *Laryngoscope, 96,* 206–210.

Schulz, R., Wuster, M., & Herz, A. (1980). Pharmacological characterization of the epsilon-opiate receptor. *Journal of Pharmacology and Experimental Therapeutics, 216,* 604–606.

Sharp, C. W., & Korman, M. (1981). Volatile substances. In J. H. Lowinson, P. Ruiz, R. B. Millman, & J. G. Langrod (Eds.), *Substance abuse: A comprehensive textbook* (2nd ed.) (pp. 233–255). Baltimore: Williams & Wilkins.

Sharp, C. W., & Rosenberg, N. L. (1992). Volatile substances. In J. H. Lowinson, P. Rulz, R. B. Millman, & J. G. Langrod (Eds.), *Substance abuse: A comprehensive textbook* (2nd ed.) (pp. 303-327). Baltimore: Williams & Wilkins.

Siegel, R. K. (1989). *Intoxication.* New York: Plenum Press.

Simon, E. J. (1992). Opiates: Neurobiology. In J. H. Lowinson, P. Ruiz, R. B. Millman & J. G. Langrod (Eds.), *Substance abuse: A comprehensive textbook* (2nd ed., pp. 195–204). Baltimore: Williams & Wilkins.

Smith, R. G. (1988). Inhalant use and abuse in Canada. *National Institute on Drug Abuse Research Monograph, 85,* 121–139.

Snyder, S. H. (1964). Adenosine as a mediator of the behavioral effects of xanthines. In P. B. Dews (Ed.), *Caffeine* (pp. 129–152). New York: Springer-Verlag.

Substance Abuse and Mental Health Services Administration (1995). National household survey on substance abuse. Rockville, MD: Department of Health and Human Services.

Tabakoff, B., & Hoffman, P. L. (1992). Alcohol neurobiology. In J. H. Lowinson, P. Ruiz, R. B. Millman, & J. G. Langrod (Eds.), *Substance abuse: A comprehensive textbook* (2nd ed.) (pp. 152–185). Baltimore: Williams & Wilkins.

Tabakoff, B., Sutker, P. B., & Randall, C. L., (Eds.) (1983). *Medical and social aspects of alcohol abuse.* New York: Plenum Press.

Titeler, M., Lyon, R. A., & Glennon, R. A. (1989). Radioligand binding evidence implicates the brain 5-HT2 receptor as a site of action for LSD and phenylisopropylamine hallucinogens. *Psychopharmacology, 94,* 213–216.

Ungerleider, J. T., & Pechnick, R. N. (1992). Hallucinogens. In J. H. Lowinson, P. Ruiz, R. B. Millman, & J. G. Langrod (Eds.), *Substance abuse: A comprehensive textbook* (2nd ed., pp. 280–289). Baltimore: Williams & Wilkins.

U.S. Department of Health and Human Services (1988). *The health consequences of smoking. A report of the Surgeon General.* Washington, DC: U.S. Government Printing Office.

U.S. Department of Health and Human Services (1989). *Reducing the health consequences of smoking: 25 years of progress. A report of the Surgeon General.* Washington, DC: U.S. Government Printing Office.

U.S. Department of Health and Human Services (1990). *The health benefits of smoking cessation: A report of the Surgeon General.* Washington DC: U.S. Government Printing Office.

Verebey, K., & Gold, M. S. (1988). From coca leaves to crack: The effects of dose and routes of administration in abuse liability. *Psychiatry Annuals, 18,* 513–521.

Victor, M., & Adams, R. D. (1971). *The Wernicke-Korsakoff syndrome.* Philadelphia: F. A. Davis.

Waal-Manning, H. J., & de Hamel, F. A. (1988). Smoking habit and psychometric scores: A community study. *New Zealand Medical Journal, 88,* 188–191.

Wallace, J. (1985). *Alcoholism: New light on the disease.* Newport, RI: Edgehill Publication.

Watson, S. J., Akil, H., Khachaturian, H., Young, E., & Lewis, M. E. (1984). Opioid systems: Anatomical, physiological, and clinical perspectives. In J. Hughes, H. O. J. Collier, M. J. Rance, & M. B. Tyers (Eds.), *Opioids past, present and future* (pp. 145–178). London: Taylor & Francis.

Weiner, N. (1985). Norepinephrine, epinephrine and the sympathomimetic amines. In A. G. Gilman, L. S. Goodman, T. W. Rail, & F. Murad (Eds.), *The pharmacological basis of therapeutics* (pp. 145-180). Upper Saddle River, NJ: Prentice Hall.

Wesson, D. R., Smith, D. E., & Seymour, R. B. (1992). Sedative-hypnotics and tricyclics. In J. H. Lowinson, P. Ruiz, R. B. Millman, & J. G. Langrod (Eds.), *Substance abuse: A comprehensive textbook* (2nd ed., pp. 271–279). Baltimore: Williams & Wilkins.

Wikler, A. (1980). *Opioid dependence: Mechanisms and treatment.* New York: Plenum Press.

Willett, W. C., Stampfer, M. J., Colditz, G. A., Rosner, B. A., Hennekens, C. H., & Speizer, F. E. (1987). Moderate consumption and breast cancer. *Journal of the National Cancer Institute, 78,* 657–661.

Winders, S. E., & Grunberg, N. E. (1990). Effects of nicotine on body weight, food consumption and body composition in male rats. *Life Science, 46*(21), 1523–1530.

Winick, C. (1992). Epidemiology of alcohol and drug abuse. In J. H. Lowinson, P. Ruiz, R. B. Millman, & J. G. Langrod (Eds.), *Substance abuse: A comprehensive textbook* (2nd ed., pp. 15–29). Baltimore: Williams & Wilkins.

Wise, R. A. (1991). Brain reward circuits and addiction. In J. H. Lowinson, P. Ruiz, R. B. Millman, & J. G. Langrod (Eds.), *Substance abuse: A comprehensive textbook* (2nd ed.) (pp. 86-88). Baltimore: Williams & Wilkins.

Wise, R. A. (1988). The neurobiology of craving: Implication for the understanding and treatment of addiction. *Journal of Abnormal Psychology, 2,* 118–132.

Zukin, S. R., & Zukin, R. S. (1992). Phencyclidine. In J. H. Lowinson, P. Ruiz, R. B. Millman, & J. G. Langrod (Eds.), *Substance abuse: A comprehensive textbook* (2nd ed.). Baltimore: Williams & Wilkins.

Assessment and Diagnosis

Linda L. Chamberlain, PsyD, & Cynthia L. Jew, PhD

ASSESSMENT METHODS AND ISSUES

Accurate assessment and diagnosis of substance abuse are crucial for adequate treatment planning and delivery of services. Improper assessment and faulty diagnosis can lead counselors to create ineffective treatment plans, have inappropriate expectations for therapy, and instill an overall sense of frustration in the client and the therapist. One cannot treat what one does not recognize or understand. As with other diseases and disorders, the earlier a therapist diagnoses a substance abuse problem, the better the prognosis for the client.

This chapter presents a theoretical and practical framework for assessment and acquaints clinicians with several methods and tools that can aid in the diagnosis of substance abuse or dependence. Guidelines for conducting an assessment interview and obtaining a reliable history are also provided. Several major assessment instruments generally available to clinicians will be reviewed. The issue of diagnosis and the problems related to differential and dual diagnosis will be explored. It is the intent of this chapter to give counselors a pragmatic orientation to making an accurate diagnosis of a substance abuse problem.

It may be helpful to note at the onset that the assessment and diagnosis of substance abuse is not an exact science. Currently, there is no single medical or psychological test that can determine with certainty that a person is dependent on drugs or alcohol. Also, the inconsistency in social attitudes about alcohol and drug use, and the imprecise standards for defining a drinking or drug problem often complicate a clinician's awareness and attitudes about a client's substance use. The stigma associated with alcoholism or drug addiction often leads to denial by users, their families, and even health professionals.

Gallant (1987) notes that the beginning therapist must be aware of several other problems that may interfere with the diagnostic process. First, the therapist may have biases about substance abuse clients. Beliefs that substance abusers are uncaring, irresponsible, untrustworthy, dangerous, or untreatable are concepts that are certain to interfere with a clinician's ability to conduct an accurate and sensitive diagnostic interview. Second, the client's attitude about alcohol or drugs and his or her sense of shame in seeking help may create a barrier to accurate assessment. It is not unusual for clients to seek help from clinicians for problems such as depression or anxiety that may be secondary to their drug use or drinking. The stigma of being labeled a "drunk" or an "addict" is still a powerful deterrent to disclosing a pattern of substance use, especially among women.

In large part, a clinician's awareness of common factors and problems related to substance abuse is of great importance. An understanding of the dynamics of denial, tolerance, loss of control, and the diverse medical consequences associated with different drugs of abuse is an essential prerequisite for accurate diagnosis. A familiarity with Jellinek's symptom chart (Jellinek, 1960) for alcoholism and other similar charts that delineate the progression of symptoms for other drugs of abuse can help guide the clinician in the assessment process. Later in this chapter, the behavioral and social characteristics associated with substance abuse will be described in greater detail. Previous chapters have acquainted you with some of the symptoms, effects, and dynamics that should serve as "red flags" for pursuing more formal diagnostic procedures. However, assessment still is somewhat a process of "skunk identification," meaning, if it looks, smells and walks like a skunk, it's probably a skunk.

The process of diagnosing substance abuse is perhaps most relentlessly hindered by the phenomenon of denial. Denial and minimization of the severity of a drug abuse problem is often an essential part of how substance abusers learn to function in their world. Without the mechanism of denial, users could not continue their pattern of substance abuse. Although not all substance abusers exhibit patterns of denial, most minimize or avoid facing the consequences of their use on both themselves and others. Denial or minimization keeps reality at arm's length and allows users to believe that no one is aware of their excessive drug use and the negative effect it is having on their lives. The use of denial to delude both themselves and others tremendously complicates the assessment process. Therefore, establishing a standardized format for assessment and diagnosis is essential in helping clinicians consistently provide appropriate detection and treatment for their clients.

The Diagnostic Interview

The most important aspect of any assessment of substance abuse is the diagnostic interview. A carefully planned and conducted interview is the cornerstone of the diagnostic process. The initial contact with someone for the assessment of substance abuse may occur within the context of individual, family, group, or marital counseling. The clinician may be aware of the possible problem by the nature of the referral or it may be clearly defined as a referral for the purpose of assessing a drug or alcohol problem. Most assessments, however, will initially be undertaken as a part of the clinician's normal interviewing procedure. It is striking how many mental health professionals do not include at least some questions about a client's drug and alcohol use history in their standard interview format. Clinical training programs are often lacking in course work or opportunities for practical experience that expose medical and mental health professionals to the dynamics and treatment of addictions. Given the prevalence of denial on the part of substance abusers, if there is any suspicion about a possible abuse problem, it is important in the first interview to request permission to involve family members, friends, co-workers, and others who may be able to provide more objective information about the client's pattern of substance use and related behaviors.

Initially, it is still important to ask the client directly about his or her use of drugs or alcohol. A useful question is: "Do you believe that your use of alcohol or other drugs has caused problems in your life?" Many clinicians find it helpful to assure the client that they are not asking such questions to make judgments. Often, people will respond less defensively if they are reassured that, "I'm not here to tell you that you are or aren't an addict. I simply need to understand as much about the problem as I can and to help you (and your family) determine whether your drug and/or alcohol use may be playing a role in the current situation." Also interview significant others in the client's life to determine whether they view the client's problems as related to substance abuse.

An interview format that gathers information specific to substance abuse should be a standard part of the assessment process. An example of a structured interview format is the Substance Use History Questionnaire (see Questionnaire 1 in the Appendix at the end of the chapter). This questionnaire may be given to the client to complete or the questions can be asked during the interview. The information from this procedure will help in determining what additional assessment instruments to use. Information regarding work habits, social and professional relationships, medical history, and previous psychiatric history are also necessary for the assessment. Questions related to each of these areas should be included in the standard intake interview.

It is important to note that family members and significant others may be unaware of or reluctant to divulge information about the client's substance use patterns. Like the client, they may be experiencing denial or avoiding a confrontation with the user. Common misinformation about substance abuse may divert the focus of the problem to other factors, which are then presented as the primary problem. For example, a spouse may describe his partner as using alcohol to relieve depression rather than identifying the substance use as a causal or maintaining factor in his partner's emotional turmoil. Due to the shame and embarrassment that frequently accompany the admission of substance abuse, the clinician may need to reassure everyone involved in the assessment that appropriate help can only be made available if the problem is accurately and completely understood.

DSM-IV Diagnosis

One of the primary difficulties encountered in diagnosing alcohol and drug problems may lie in the inadequate definitions commonly used for the symptoms. In an attempt to provide more comprehensive, specific, symptom-related criteria for diagnosis, the American Psychiatric Association (1994) developed categories for "Substance-Related Disorders" in the Diagnostic and Statistic Manual of Mental Disorders, fourth edition (DSM-IV). The term *substance* is used to refer to a drug of abuse, a medication, or a toxin. Substances are grouped into 11 classes: alcohol; amphetamines; caffeine; cannabis; cocaine; hallucinogens; inhalants; nicotine; opioids; phencyclidine (PCP); and sedatives, hypnotics, or anxiolytics (anti-anxiety drugs.) The Substance-Related Disorders are divided into basic groups: the Substance Use Disorders (Substance Dependence and Substance Abuse) and the Substance-Induced Disorders (including Substance Intoxication and Substance Withdrawal). The essential features of Substance Use Disorders are as follows:

Criteria for Substance Dependence

A maladaptive pattern of substance use, leading to clinically significant impairment or distress, as manifested by three (or more) of the following, occurring at any time in the same 12-month period:

1. tolerance, as defined by either of the following:
    (a) a need for markedly increased amounts of the substance to achieve intoxication or desired effect
    (b) markedly diminished effect with continued use of the same amount of the substance
2. withdrawal, as manifested by either of the following:
    (a) the characteristic withdrawal syndrome for the substance
    (b) the same (or a closely related) substance is taken to relieve or avoid withdrawal symptoms
3. the substance is often taken in larger amounts or over a longer period than was intended
4. there is a persistent desire or unsuccessful efforts to cut down or control substance use
5. a great deal of time is spent in activities necessary to obtain the substance (e.g., visiting multiple doctors or driving long distances), use the substance (e.g., chain smoking), or recover from its effects
6. important social, occupational, or recreational activities are given up or reduced because of substance use
7. the substance use is continued despite knowledge of having a persistent or recurrent physical or psychological problem that is likely to have been caused or exacerbated by the substance (e.g., current cocaine use despite recognition of cocaine-induced depression, or continued drinking despite recognition that an ulcer was made worse by alcohol consumption). (American Psychiatric Association, 1994, p. 181)

Criteria for Substance Abuse

1. A maladaptive pattern of substance use leading to clinically significant impairment or distress, as manifested by one (or more) of the following, occurring within a 12-month period:
    (a) recurrent substance use resulting in a failure to fulfill major role obligations at work, school, or home (e.g., repeated absences or poor work performance

related to substance use; substance-related absences, suspensions, or expulsions from school; neglect of children or household)

(b) recurrent substance use in situations in which it is physically hazardous (e.g., driving an automobile or operating a machine when impaired by substance use)

(c) recurrent substance-related legal problems (e.g., arrests for substance-related disorderly conduct)

(d) continued substance use despite having persistent or recurrent social or interpersonal problems caused or exacerbated by the effects of the substance (e.g., arguments with spouse about consequences of intoxication, physical fights). (American Psychiatric Association, 1994, pp. 182–183)

2. The symptoms have never met the criteria for Substance Dependence for this class of substance. (American Psychiatric Association, 1994, pp. 182–183)

The category of Substance Dependence is the more severe diagnosis and is the DSM-IV description of what may otherwise be defined as addiction. The DSM-IV also lists several criteria for rating the severity of the dependence. Clinicians should be acquainted with the physiological and psychological manifestations of both acute drug or alcohol intoxication and withdrawal symptoms as outlined in the DSM-IV. Certain drugs, such as barbiturates, can have serious medical complications associated with withdrawal, and clients must be under a physician's care to assure they will safely complete the detoxification period.

BEHAVIORAL CHARACTERISTICS

Substance abuse almost always occurs within the context of other problems. Common presenting problems related to substance abuse are marital and family conflict, child abuse, unemployment, financial problems, multiple medical problems, depression, suicide, and problems with aggression and violence. In assessing the role of substance abuse within the context of other problems, the clinician needs to understand the dynamics of other behavioral problems and how they can be exacerbated by substance abuse. For example, it is estimated that most domestic violence occurs when one or both parties are abusing some substance. Also, as many as two-thirds of homicides and serious assaults involve alcohol. Criminal behavior such as child abuse or sexual molestation may be committed when the perpetrator is under the influence of a drug or alcohol. One study found that 64% of all child abuse cases in New York City involved a perpetrator who was under the influence of drugs and/or alcohol (Chasnoff, 1988). Although there is some disagreement about the exact nature of the relationship between substance abuse and violence, there is clearly a strong correlation between the two.

An important question for the clinician during a first interview is, "Did all or any of these problems (the presenting problems) occur while you were drinking or using any other type of drug?" If the answer is yes, one can then begin to gather information to determine if there is a pattern of use that is causing or contributing to the client's behavioral symptoms. Again, given the nature of denial, this question should also be asked of significant others who are participating in the assessment.

As a rule, a drug or alcohol problem exists and requires treatment if the use of the substance continues despite significant interference in any one of the six major areas of a person's life:

1. Problems on the job or in school
2. Upset relationships with family
3. Problems with social relationships
4. Legal problems
5. Financial problems
6. Medical problems

Behaviorally, addiction can be considered any use of a psychoactive substance that causes damage to the individual or society or both.

Phases of Chemical Addiction

Becoming dependent on any substance occurs over differing periods of time for different individuals and depends on the substance used. A dependence on alcohol may take several decades to develop while an addiction to cocaine, especially crack cocaine, may occur almost immediately. There are, however, certain phases that individuals are likely to pass through as their dependence on a substance increases. An old proverb regarding alcoholism outlines the progression of addiction: "The person takes a drink, the drink takes a drink, and the drink takes the person." The journey from controlled use to being controlled by their use is the nature of addiction to drugs or alcohol. No one begins using substances with the goal of becoming addicted. A more in-depth, definitive review of the behavioral symptoms will provide a basis for recognizing the path that substance abusers travel.

Phase 1: The Prodomal Phase

In the prodomal phase, casual or social use of a substance begins to change and the first signs of dependence can be charted. In this early phase, the following behavioral changes generally occur:

1. Increase in tolerance of the substance
2. First blackout or loss of significant time to drug use
3. Sneaking drinks or drugs
4. Preoccupation with drinking or drug use
5. Gulping drinks or hurried ingestion of chemicals
6. Avoiding reference to drinking or drug use

The first symptom noted in the prodomal phase is an increase in tolerance. *Tolerance* can be defined as "the adaptation of an organism to a drug, so that the same dose repeatedly produces less and less of an effect" (Palfai & Jankiewicz, 1991, p. 500). Physiologically, the brain and central nervous system adapt over time to the effects of any psychoactive substance. Therefore, the user must increase the amount of the substance or the frequency of use to achieve the sought-after effect. To establish the symptom of tolerance, counselors should ask about any changes in the amount or frequency of drug use.

The second symptom in this phase is the onset of blackouts. A blackout isn't unconsciousness; users remain awake and active, but they later don't remember what was said or done while they were using. It is an indication that the user was able to ingest enough of the substance to "anesthetize" the part of the brain that processes short-term memory. Blackouts do not occur with all categories of substances, but they are prominent features of alcohol abuse.

The third behavioral symptom is sneaking drinks or drugs. This often means users will "pre-use" by drinking or using before a social gathering to assure that they have enough. It also means the users are stockpiling drugs or hiding them from others who might share them. Users typically experience discomfort or irritability with others who are not keeping up with their rate of drinking or using drugs.

The fourth symptom involves a cognitive change in which users become more preoccupied with time spent using. Behaviorally, it is manifested by social plans that increasingly focus on the opportunity to drink or use, leaving work early to have extra time to drink, becoming irritable if there is any interruption in the time set aside to get high, and an increased amount of time and effort spent in assuring that they have plenty of alcohol or drugs available.

The fifth symptom, a more hurried ingestion of drugs or alcohol, is an extension of the development of tolerance. Users become concerned that they won't have enough of the substance to relax or "get a buzz" and use more quickly to get a higher level in their system. Nearly all the behaviors in the first stage can be summarized by describing the user who might develop a serious problem as the one who must "have a drink (or drug), and have it fast" (Blue Cross and Blue Shield Associations, 1979).

The final symptom in the prodomal phase sets the stage for denial. Users begin to feel uncomfortable with others' comments or questions about the changes in their patterns of drug or alcohol use and avoid confrontation. They begin to estrange themselves from others who might express concern about their use and avoid questioning themselves about the changes in their relationship with the substance.

Phase 2: The Crucial Phase

In this middle phase, substance abusers experience some of the more obvious and pronounced behavioral changes associated with addiction. This phase is labeled the "crucial" phase because it offers the most hope for intervention in the growing physical and psychological dependence before some of the more severe medical and social consequences enter the picture. It is also during this phase that family and significant others usually become more aware of the user's growing dependence on drugs or alcohol. In this second phase, the following behavioral symptoms usually occur:

1. Loss of control of substance use
2. Denial and minimization of use
3. Confrontation by others
4. Behavioral loss of control
5. Guilt and remorse
6. Periodic abstinence or change in patterns of use
7. Losses
8. Medical and psychological interventions
9. Growing alienation and resentment
10. More frequent substance use

The first symptom, loss of control of the substance, is often misunderstood and poorly defined. In the dynamics of addiction, loss of control means loss of predictability. For example, an individual who is abusing alcohol begins to experience times when he drinks more than he intends. On one night, he may have only the three beers he planned to drink after work. On the following night, his plan falls apart and he drinks until he passes out. The user cannot predict with any certainty when he will be able to stick to his plan and when he will use more than he intended.

The next set of behavioral symptoms (numbers 2 through 6) will be considered together because they usually occur as part of a pattern of confrontation and denial. At this point, changes in the users' behavior related to drugs or alcohol are generally more obvious. While intoxicated or recovering from a binge, users are more likely to become aggressive, impulsive, extravagant, or otherwise unpredictable in their behavior. If confronted, they are likely to insist that they can control it and stop any time. In fact, they may quit briefly to "prove" they have control. Guilt feelings may begin when they are confronted with the result of some harmful behavior that occurred while they were intoxicated (for example, missing a child's birthday because they were drinking with buddies at the bar instead of picking up the birthday cake and going home as promised). Fear sets in, followed by flashes of remorse and sometimes aggressiveness or isolation to keep others at a distance. The consequences of their actions while using are increasingly difficult to minimize, rationalize, or deny.

The final group of symptoms in the crucial phase (numbers 7 through 10) outlines some of the more overt consequences that users experience as the addiction progresses. These include loss of friends, divorce, loss of a job or financial setbacks, loss of other interests such as hobbies or leisure pursuits, and loss of a normal, daily routine that does not revolve around substance use. Other less clearly observable losses include a loss of ordinary willpower and self-respect, and an abandonment of moral or spiritual values. Often during this phase, users experience some acute medical consequences of their use and will seek medical intervention for secondary symptoms (problems that are secondary to their drug or alcohol use). For example, a cocaine user may experience periodic heart arrhythmias (irregular heartbeat) and seek a doctor's advice for the heart problem, but not for the cocaine use that is causing the difficulty (the primary problem).

Denial creates and perpetuates a vicious circle. Because the users deny that they have a problem, they can't go to anyone else to talk about it, and so may use more to overcome the guilt or anxiety that results from the loss of control of their behavior. As users become further trapped in the cycle of remorse, they externalize their fears through resentment and blame, which leads to increased alienation.

Phase 3: The Chronic Phase

This phase of addiction is typified by a complete loss of behavioral control and by the physical manifestations that accompany chronic drug or alcohol abuse. In the last phase, the following symptoms appear and often continue as a vicious circle until the user either dies or finds help. The general symptoms are the following:

1. Continuous use of the substance for longer periods
2. Indefinable fears and vague spiritual desires
3. Impaired judgment and irrational thinking
4. Tremors, malnutrition, overdoses, decreased tolerance, and/or other physiological problems associated with the drug
5. Obsessive use of the substance until recovery or death

Binges, benders, daily use, and the inability to stop without help are characteristic of this phase. Users engage in prolonged, continuous use and are unable to function without using their drug of choice regularly. They neglect their daily needs to the point of not eating or caring for themselves. Attempts to control their usage are abandoned as the periods of intoxication and recovery encompass most of their time.

Symptoms 2 and 3 reflect the loss of ability to function that accompanies brain deterioration associated with prolonged use of psychoactive drugs and alcohol. Users can't think clearly and often make outlandish claims that are obviously irrational. For example, an addict might claim—and believe—that someone broke into her house and took all her cocaine while she slept. As their fears increase, addicts may experience a vague yearning for some miracle or "divine intervention" to stop them from continuing in the downward spiral that is the course of addiction.

The final two symptoms reflect the absolute deterioration of addicts before death. Especially with alcohol dependence, addicts may experience a "reverse tolerance" in which they once again become very intoxicated by a smaller dose of alcohol. This is an indication that their systems are essentially saturated with alcohol and cannot process the alcohol quickly enough to remove it from their bodies. Obsessive use, if unbroken, ultimately leads to death, either by suicide, homicide, accident, or medical complications. Here, the drug truly "takes the person" by becoming the solitary focus of addicts' lives. They become obsessed with using—not to get high, but to feel normal and avoid the consequences of withdrawal.

Assessing the Behavioral Symptoms

The questions in Figure 4.1 are suggested for helping the clinician evaluate the behavioral symptoms of addiction. They are classified under the headings Preoccupation, Increased Tolerance, Rapid Intake, Using Alone, Use As A Panacea (Cure-All), Protecting Supply, Nonpremeditated Use, and Blackout (for alcohol).

1. Preoccupation

Yes   No

____ ____   Do you find yourself looking forward to the end of a day's work so you can have a couple drinks or your drug of choice and relax?

____ ____   Do you look forward to the end of the week so you can have some fun getting high?

____ ____   Does the thought of using sometimes enter your mind when you should be thinking of something else?

____ ____   Do you sometimes feel the need to have a drink or "hit" at a particular time of the day?

2. Increased tolerance

Yes   No

____ ____   Do you find that you can sometimes use more than others and not show it too much?

____ ____   Have friends ever commented on your ability to "hold your alcohol or drugs"?

____ ____   Have you ever experienced an increased capacity to drink or use drugs and felt proud of this ability?

3. Rapid Intake

Yes   No

____ ____   Do you usually order a double or like to drink your first two or three drinks fairly fast, or use your drug of choice in a way it works the fastest to get you high?

____ ____   Do you usually have a couple of drinks before going to a party or out to dinner or use a drug before going out to "get a head start"?

4. Using Alone

Yes   No

____ ____   Do you routinely stop in a bar alone and have a couple of drinks or go home and get high by yourself?

____ ____   Do you sometimes use alone or when no one else with you is using?

____ ____   Do you usually have an extra drink by yourself when mixing drinks for others or have extra drugs of your own when using with others?

FIGURE 4.1   Questions for Assessing Behavioral Symptoms

5. Use as a Panacea (Cure-All)

Yes	No	
____	____	Do you fairly routinely drink or get high to calm your nerves or reduce tension or stress?
____	____	Do you find it difficult to enjoy a party or social gathering if there is nothing to drink or use?
____	____	Do you often think of relief or escape as associated with your use?
____	____	When encountering any physical or emotional problems, is your first thought to use?
____	____	Does life seem easier knowing your drug of choice will help you out?

6. Protecting the Supply

Yes	No	
____	____	Do you sometimes store a bottle or drug away around the house in the event you may "need" to use, or do you fear you may run out?
____	____	Do you ever keep a bottle or substance in the trunk of your car or office desk or stashed in the house in case you might need it?

7. Nonpremeditated Use

Yes	No	
____	____	Do you sometimes start to have a drink or two or use just a little and have several more drinks or hits than you had planned?
____	____	Do you sometimes find yourself starting to use when you had planned to go straight home or do something else?
____	____	Do you sometimes use more than you think you should?
____	____	Is your use sometimes different from what you would like it to be?

8. Blackouts (for alcohol)

Yes	No	
____	____	In the morning after an evening of drinking, have you ever not been able to remember everything that happened the night before?
____	____	The morning after a night of drinking, have you ever had difficulty recalling how you got home or who you were with and what you did?

The more "yes" answers a client gives, the more indications there are of serious abuse or dependence on substances. In assessing the behavioral components of a client's substance use, it is important to remember that each individual will experience some diversity in the pattern of addiction. Some individuals who are addicted to cocaine will experience periods of profound depression after a binge, and some will not. Not all alcoholics will experience a reverse tolerance, even in the chronic stage of the addiction. The symptoms overlap and occur in a variety of orders depending on the individual situation. The description of the behavioral characteristics and questions about behavioral changes are meant to serve as guidelines and directions for further exploration with the client.

SOCIAL CHARACTERISTICS

Evidence of substance abuse is often initially detected through the investigation of a client's social and family life. As users become more heavily involved in abuse or dependence on a drug, their primary relationship in life eventually becomes the relationship with the substance. As their use becomes increasingly important and central to their lives, other social relationships inevitably suffer.

Abusers learn to focus their lives on social activities that afford them opportunities to indulge in substance use. Especially with the use of illegal substances, to protect themselves from detection, users increasingly socialize with others who also use. Drinkers prefer to drink with others who drink like them. Family members or friends who are "straight" become excluded from a significant part of the users' lives. As their "affair" with a substance grows and the barrier of denial is fortified, the chasm deepens in their important relationships with family and friends. Increasing family conflict related to their substance use, a very constricted social life, lack of involvement in activities that do not afford an opportunity to use, and general withdrawal from "straight" friends are signals that the substance abuse is well under way. The more advanced the dependence on the substance, the more alienated users become from others who don't indulge with them.

Patterns of behaviors are well established in families of abusers (Treadway, 1989). The strength of the addiction is easy to see when users fail to try to prevent family breakups or isolation from significant others to maintain their substance use. Intimate relationships become distorted through the denial or "enabling" behaviors exhibited by the user's family.

FAMILY CHARACTERISTICS

Family members, like the user, progress through different phases in their journey with the addict. Addiction is often classified as a "family illness" because the effects of the addiction on those who are in a close relationship with the abuser also experience symptoms that, while different, are frequently as serious as those suffered by the addict. Essentially, everyone in the addict's family and social system suffers.

Four Stages in the Family System of the Addict

The dynamics that are often seen in families with substance dependent members can be delineated by stages or phases (Washousky, Levy-Stern, & Muchowski, 1993). These are not discrete stages; it is likely that there will be some overlap or that several stages will be in evidence simultaneously. Also, not every family will experience the same intensity or exact set of responses in each stage. Some families may stay in a prolonged state of denial, even to the point of the addict's death. However, the description of the stages can provide some guidelines for assessing the dynamics in the user's family and provide a basis for treatment planning with both the addict and other family members.

Denial

In this stage, family members deny that there is a problem. They try to hide the substance abuse from each other and from those outside the family. Members "cover" and make excuses for the addict's behavior, other explanations are offered, and the family begins to isolate from others who might suspect "something is wrong."

Home Treatment

Family members try to get the addict to stop using. Hiding drugs or bottles, nagging, threatening, persuasion, and sympathy are attempted. Home treatment, or the family's effort to stop the addict from using without seeking outside help, may fail because the focus is on controlling the behavior of someone else. The roles in the family often change significantly, usually with deleterious effects. Children may try to care for a parent, coalitions among family members are formed, and family members ignore or minimize their own problems by focusing on the addict.

Chaos

The problem becomes so critical that it can no longer be denied or kept secret from those outside the family. Neighbors and friends become aware of the addiction. Conflicts and confrontations escalate without resolution. The consequences for family members become more pronounced and a child or partner of the addict may experience serious emotional or physical problems. Threats of divorce, separation, or withdrawal of family support are often made but not acted upon.

Control

A spouse or other family member attempts to take complete control of and responsibility for the user. If still living within the family, the addict becomes an emotional invalid who exists as parasite on the family. Control is often exercised through divorce, separation, or emotional alienation from the family. The family, like the addict, exists in a state of suspended animation; trapped in a cycle of helplessness and futile attempts to control the addict's behavior.

ASSESSING THE SOCIAL AND FAMILY RELATED SYMPTOMS

As previously noted, it is important to have access to family members, friends, or significant others to adequately assess an individual's substance abuse problem. If an addict has somehow entered the mental health system, through a doctor's referral or employer's recommendation, it is highly likely that the situation has become unmanageable enough for significant others in the addict's life to break the barrier of denial. As with the addict, it is critically important to undertake the assessment in a supportive, caring, nonjudgmental manner. Many family members experience a high degree of guilt or shame about the addict's behavior and believe the continuation of the addiction is somehow their fault. They may think they have not been a good enough spouse, child, or parent, or that they have created so much stress in the addict's life that they have promoted the addiction.

The questionnaire in Figure 4.2 can be given to family members or friends to gain important information about the user's pattern of substance use. Information gathered from others can be compared with the responses given by the client to assess the degree of minimization or denial that may be present. A "yes" response to any of the questions indicates some possibility of substance abuse; "yes" to four or more indicates a substance abuse problem.

In addition to gathering information from others who are familiar with the addict, counselors must be alert to some of the common social consequences that often appear in an addict's life. Frequent job loss, a driving under the influence (DUI) arrest or other legal problem (particularly domestic violence), the breakup of important relationships, a series of moves (also called "the geographic cure"), a history of unresolved psychological or medical problems, and a lack of interest in activities that were once important to the individual are all indicators of an addiction. Several of the assessment devices discussed in the next segment of the chapter will help the clinician gather information related to the social characteristics of substance abuse.

MAJOR ASSESSMENT DEVICES

To assist in the diagnosis and assessment of substance abuse, psychometric instruments are often very helpful. A variety of specific psychometric instruments are generally available to counselors. Material from the initial interview should help the clinician select measures that will enhance their understanding of the exact nature,

**Questionnaire: Do You Have a Spouse, Friend, or Loved One
Who Has a Drinking or Drug Abuse Problem?**

1. Do you worry about how much they drink or use drugs?
2. Do you complain about how often they drink or use?
3. Do you criticize them for the amount they spend on drugs or alcohol?
4. Have you ever been hurt or embarrassed by their behavior when they are drinking or using?
5. Are holidays in your home unpleasant because of their drinking or drugging?
6. Do they ever lie about their drinking or drug use?
7. Do they deny that drinking or drugs affect their behavior?
8. Do they say or do things and later deny having said or done them?
9. Do you sometimes think that drinking or drug use is more important to them than you are?
10. Do they get angry if you criticize their substance use or their drinking or drug-using companions?
11. Is drinking or drug use involved in almost all of your social activities?
12. Does your family spend almost as much on alcohol or drugs as it does on food or other necessities?
13. Are you having any financial difficulties because of their use?
14. Does their substance use keep them away from home a good deal?
15. Have you ever threatened to end your relationship because of their drinking or drug use?
16. Have you ever lied for them because of their drug use or drinking?
17. Do you find yourself urging them to eat instead of drink or use drugs at parties?
18. Have they ever stopped drinking or using drugs completely for a period of time and then started using again?
19. Have you ever thought about calling the police because of their behavior while drunk or high?
20. Do you think that alcohol or drugs creates problems for them?

FIGURE 4.2 Questions to Determine Patterns of Substance Use

dynamics, severity, and effects of the client's substance use. For example, several tools focus on alcohol abuse only, while others include abuse of additional or other substances. The measures that are reviewed are only a sample of those available to counselors. They were chosen based on their widespread use and availability, ease of administration and scoring, and reliability and validity. The assessment devices included in this segment include the Michigan Alcoholism Screening Test (MAST) and the Short Michigan Alcoholism Screening Test (SMAST), the Drug Abuse

Screening Test (DAST-20), the CAGE Questionnaire, the Alcohol Use Inventory (AUI), and the Substances Abuse Subtle Screening Inventory-2 (SASSI-2).

The Michigan Alcoholism Screening Test (MAST)

The most researched diagnostic instrument is the self-administered Michigan Alcoholism Screening Test (MAST), which was created in 1971 by M. L. Selzer (1971). The 25-item MAST correctly identifies up to 95% of alcoholics, and the SMAST, a shorter form of the MAST has also been shown to identify more than 90% of the alcoholics entering general psychiatric hospitals (Mendelson & Mello, 1985). The MAST was originally validated with treatment-seeking alcoholics. Many studies have used the MAST to assess adolescent and adult populations in a variety of settings. The MAST may realistically and effectively be used with virtually any population.

The MAST is simple to administer; it is given to clients with instructions to answer all questions either "yes" or "no." After they complete the test, the points assigned to each question are totaled. The MAST sample test form (Questionnaire 2 in the Appendix at the end of the chapter) indicates the number of points assigned for each question. It should be noted that questions 2, 5, 7, and 8 are assigned points for a "no" answer; all other questions are scored for a "yes" answer. A total of 4 points is presumptive evidence of alcoholism; a total of 5 or more points makes it extremely unlikely that the individual is not alcoholic. In addition, given the scoring values, a "yes" response to items 10, 23b, or 24b would be enough to diagnose alcohol addiction. Three questions abstracted from the MAST can also quickly diagnose potential alcohol problems:

1. Has your family ever objected to your drinking?
2. Did you ever think you drank too much in general?
3. Have others said you drink too much for your own good?

The three questions can be easily incorporated into the interview process to serve as indicators for a more thorough evaluation. They may also be adapted to use with clients who are abusing other substances by substituting using their drug of choice instead of "drinking."

Short Michigan Alcoholism Screening Test (SMAST)

The SMAST is administered in the same manner as the MAST, or it can be given verbally. It consists of the following 13 of 25 questions taken from the MAST.

Short Michigan Alcoholism Screening Test

1. Do you feel you are a normal drinker?
2. Does your wife/husband, a parent or other near relative ever worry or complain about your drinking?

3. Do you ever feel guilty about your drinking?

4. Do friends or relatives think you are a normal drinker?

5. Are you able to stop drinking when you want?

6. Have you ever attended a meeting of Alcoholics Anonymous?

7. Has drinking ever created problems between you and your wife/husband, a parent, or other near relative?

8. Have you ever gotten into trouble at work because of drinking?

9. Have you ever neglected your obligations, your family, or your work for two or more days in a row because you were drinking?

10. Have you ever gone to anyone for help about your drinking?

11. Have you ever been in a hospital because of drinking?

12. Have you ever been arrested for drunken driving, driving while intoxicated, or driving under the influence of alcoholic beverages?

13. Have you ever been arrested, even for a few hours, because of other drunken behavior?

The SMAST is easy to score. One point is given for each of the following answers: "no" on Questions 1, 4, and 5; "yes" on all other questions. A score of 0–1 indicates a low probability of alcoholism, a score of 2 points indicates the client is possibly alcoholic, and a score of 3 or more points indicates a strong probability of alcoholism (Selzer, Benokur, & Van Roogen, 1989).

The Drug Abuse Screening Test (DAST-20)

The DAST-20 (Skinner, 1982) is a 20-item, self-report inventory designed to measure aspects of drug use behavior, not including alcohol. It was derived from the Michigan Alcoholism Screening Test (MAST) and reflects similar content (see Questionnaire 3 in the Appendix at the end of the chapter). DAST-20 scores are computed by summing all items positively endorsed for drug use. Higher scores indicate a greater likelihood of drug dependency. The DAST-20 is designed for use with adult male and female drug users.

The DAST-20 is a useful tool for helping to differentiate among several categories of drug users. In clinical trials, the DAST-20 scores demonstrated significant differences among the alcohol, drug, and polysubstance abuse groups. DAST-20 scores were also found to correlate highly with other drug use indices.

The CAGE Questionnaire

The CAGE (Ewing, 1984) is a four-item questionnaire that includes questions related to a history of attempting to cut down on alcohol intake (C), annoyance over criticism about alcohol (A), guilt about drinking behavior (G), and drinking in the morning to relieve withdrawal anxiety, sometimes known as an "eye-opener" (E)

(Gallant, 1987, p. 50). Most questionnaires duplicate information by using different phrases or words to detect similar patterns of behavior. The authors of the CAGE found that they could eliminate many questions and still have a powerful tool for assessing alcohol dependency. This is also an extremely useful questionnaire to use with family members or others participating in the assessment.

The CAGE was originally developed for use with adult alcoholics seeking treatment. Like the MAST, the CAGE may be used to screen for alcoholism in a variety of health-care settings. Effective use of the CAGE questions discriminates alcoholics from nonalcoholics at or above the 90% range.

The CAGE is generally administered verbally as part of the diagnostic interview. Instructions for administering the CAGE include observing clients' attitudes as they respond to the questions. The counselor should ask them to explain any "yes" answer and watch for signs of rationalization, denial, projection of blame, and minimization. The first question deals with the common problem of repeatedly trying to get the drinking under control only to lose control again and again as drinking resumes. The next question detects sensitivity to criticism of the user's drinking behavior. The third question taps into the personal sense of guilt, and the fourth looks at the tendency to drink in the morning as a remedy for excessive drinking the night before.

To administer the CAGE, the client is asked to answer "yes" or "no" to the following questions:

CAGE Questionnaire for Alcoholism
1. Have you ever tried to cut down on your drinking?
2. Are you annoyed when people ask you about your drinking?
3. Do you ever feel guilty about your drinking?
4. Do you ever take a morning eye-opener?

Only "yes" responses are scored on the CAGE. One "yes" response indicates a possibility of alcoholism, two or three "yes" responses indicate a high alcoholism suspicion index, and four "yes" responses indicate an alcoholism diagnosis is highly likely. As with the SMAST, the CAGE questions can be adapted as an assessment tool for other substances.

A variation of the CAGE questionnaire that offers alternative questions to assess abuse of substances other than or in addition to alcohol is also available (see Questionnaire 4 in the Appendix at the end of the chapter). Several follow-up inquiries are noted on this form that can help the clinician get more detailed information if the client answers "yes" to any of the four questions. There also is a version of the CAGE (see Questionnaire 5 in the Appendix at the end of the chapter) for assessing substance abuse problems in youth and adolescents.

The Substance Abuse Subtle Screening Inventory-2 (SASSI-2)

The SASSI-2 (Miller, 1985) is a one-page, paper-and-pencil questionnaire. On one side are 52 true-or-false questions that generally appear unrelated to chemical abuse; on the other side are 26 items that allow clients to self-report the negative effects of any alcohol and drug use. Clients can complete the SASSI-2 in 10 to 15 minutes, the test is easily scored, and training is available in interpretation and use of the SASSI-2 as a substance abuse screening tool.

The primary strength of the SASSI-2 is in identifying abuse patterns that are hidden by the more subtle, but still common, forms of denial. Items on the SASSI-2 touch on topics seemingly unrelated to chemical abuse (for example, "I think there is something wrong with my memory" and "I am often resentful"). The questions are designed to be nonthreatening to avoid triggering clients' defenses and denial. The SASSI-2 is resistant to faking and defeats efforts to figure out the "right" answer. As a result, the SASSI-2 is effective in identifying clients who are minimizing or in denial about their substance abuse. It is also effective in identifying substance abuse regardless of the drug of choice. There are adult and adolescent inventories, and both are adapted to either male or female clients.

The data from research with the SASSI-2 indicates about a 90% accuracy in identifying substance abuse patterns in clients. Thousands of test items were designed or considered, then given to samples of alcoholics, other drug abusers and controls (nonabusers). The inventory was tested for 16 years and is still being adapted and updated. In 1994, the Adult SASSI-2 replaced the adult SASSI. Two scales from the original test were dropped and three new scales were added. Counselors have used the SASSI-2 as a screening tool for court-ordered substance abuse programs, employee assistance programs, and in general mental health settings. Information, training, and materials are available through the SASSI Institute, P.O. Box 5069, Bloomington, IN 47407.

The Alcohol Use Inventory (AUI)

The AUI (Wanberg & Horn, 1983; Horn, Wanberg, & Foster, 1986) is a hierarchically organized set of self-report scales that provides a basis for diagnosing different problems associated with the use of alcohol. The AUI is based on the hypothesis that alcoholism should be diagnosed from a multiple-syndrome model and the scales are designed to provide an operational definition of the multiple manifestations of alcohol-related problems. It should be used to provide a more thorough diagnostic picture if there are clear indications from the MAST or CAGE that an alcohol problem is probable.

The AUI consists of 228 multiple-choice items. The specific areas of assessment of the AUI are motivation for treatment, physical health, anger and aggression management, risk-taking behavior, social relationships, employment or educational situation, family situation, leisure-time activities, religious/spiritual activities, and legal status. The AUI is simple to administer and can generally be given to clients with little additional instruction. Clients should be told that it is important they respond as honestly as possible to all questions and not skip questions or give more than one response per question. Both hand-scored and computer-scored versions of the AUI are available (Horn, Wanberg, & Foster, 1983). A Substance Use Inventory (SUI) is a similar test for assessment of dependence on substances other than alcohol.

DIAGNOSIS

Professionals who have to make decisions about the presence or absence of addiction for their clients must make a series of complex judgments. An adequate conceptualization of substance abuse and addiction emphasizes the interaction among the individual user, the physiological effects, and the social context in which the user functions. Establishing a standard set of rigid diagnostic criteria for addiction is not only improbable, but is not likely to be beneficial to clients. The simple diagnostic definition that "addiction exists when drug or alcohol use is associated with impairment of health and social functioning" is a useful general thesis (Mendelson & Mello, 1985, p. 18).

The diagnosis of substance abuse has always been complicated by inconsistent attitudes and imprecise standards for what constitutes an *addiction*. Inadequate definitions of chemical dependence have often been cited as the primary reason for a lack of success in developing adequate epidemiological, diagnostic, and prognostic assessment tools. As Gallant (1987) notes, "With many medical illnesses . . . the etiology or pathologic abnormality, prognosis, and treatment are known, and no preexisting public or medical concepts interfere with the scientific identification of the illness" (p. 1). This is certainly not the case with the diagnosis of substance abuse. Here, much of the information needed to establish a diagnosis is based on self-reports from an often unreliable population given the preponderance of denial. Making an adequate diagnosis is further complicated by long-standing prejudices and moral attitudes.

Differential Diagnosis

One of the most challenging aspects of diagnosing substance abuse is often the interplay of addiction and other mental disorders. Counselors who effectively treat individuals with a primary diagnosis of substance abuse may be faced with treating additional psychological disorders. Other DSM-IV diagnostic categories such as personality disorders, post-traumatic stress disorder, mood disorders, and thought disorders are common differential or co-existing diagnoses. Symptoms related to other disorders may be accentuated or mollified by a client's substance abuse.

It is important that clinicians working with substance abusers be trained in diagnosing other mental disorders as well as substance abuse. Many symptoms of intoxication or withdrawal from certain substances mimic the behaviors seen in psychiatric disorders. Clinicians who are untrained in the recognition of such problems as depression, mania, psychosis, and dementias may risk misdiagnosing a client. For example, if a client arrives in the counselor's office with symptoms of slurred speech, difficulty with coordination, and difficulty focusing his attention, the counselor might assume this is evidence of a substance abuse problem. These symptoms, however, are also associated with certain neurological diseases such as multiple sclerosis. Differentiating between a bi-polar or manic-depressive disorder and the highs and lows experienced by substance abusers is often a complicated diagnostic process.

Generally, a longitudinal approach is useful in differentiating between psychiatric and substance abuse-related symptoms (Schuckit, 1988). Many symptoms of substance intoxication and withdrawal improve or are alleviated within days or weeks. It is not unusual for substance abusers to appear far more disturbed when initially assessed than after a period of abstinence. Family members or others who can be consulted regarding the client's behavioral history before the onset of abusing substances can also be invaluable in accurately diagnosing and planning for treatment.

A standard rule of practice for counselors working with substance abusers is to refer clients for a thorough physical early in the assessment process. Establishing a good working relationship with a physician who is familiar with drug and alcohol abuse is a mandatory step in providing appropriate and adequate services. A psychologist trained in differential diagnostic techniques for assessing addiction and other psychological and neuropsychological problems also should be a part of the counselor's assessment referral network. Licensed psychologists have a broader range of standardized evaluation techniques that they can administer to help differentiate between emotional, characterological, or psychological disorders and alcohol- or drug-related problems.

Dual Diagnosis

Many individuals diagnosed with substance abuse problems also meet the criteria for other psychological disorders. It is important to discover whether symptoms of a psychological problem either preceded the onset of the abuse problems or persist after the substance abuse has been treated and abstinence has been maintained for several months. For example, alcoholics typically exhibit a high rate of depressive symptomology due to the depressant effects of their chronic use of alcohol. Sleep and appetite disturbances, feelings of helplessness and hopelessness, and loss of pleasure and motivation are symptoms of depression and also part of the pattern of addiction to alcohol. The deterioration of an alcoholic's lifestyle and health, the loss of significant relationships, and other problems related to excessive drinking along with the basic chemical effects of alcohol make it nearly inevitable that an alcohol-addicted client will appear depressed while they are actively drinking. However, this depression is usually reactive and should decrease significantly with abstinence and efforts to resolve life problems that accumulated during the period of addiction. In alcoholics with a primary depression, the symptoms either preceded the onset of alcohol abuse or became more pronounced during periods of abstinence (Mayfield, 1985).

Some clients may have begun using drugs to alleviate symptoms of anxiety or depression. Psychoactive drugs may offer initial relief to individuals who suffer from mood disorders. It is helpful for clinicians to question clients carefully about their psychological history before using drugs or alcohol and to seek information regarding a family history of psychological problems. The learning theory of chemical dependency in fact proposes that the concept of anxiety reduction related to drug or alcohol use is the basis for many addictions.

Research addressing the question of whether substance abusers are more likely to exhibit personality and other psychiatric disorders has produced mixed results. In some studies, the link between substance abuse and passive-dependent, antisocial, or narcissistic personality types have not been confirmed (Westermeyer, 1976). One obvious difficulty is that if a person using an illegal substance such as cocaine, some aspects of their life style necessarily engender the symptoms of an antisocial or paranoid personality. It is a matter of self-preservation for them to become suspicious, secretive, alienated from others who do not use, and, by definition of their cocaine use, involved in illegal pursuits. However, these behaviors may be secondary to their dependence on cocaine and should diminish when they maintain abstinence.

In other research, about one-third of the substance abusing population sampled met the criteria for one of the DSM-IV psychiatric diagnoses (Helzer & Pryzbeck, 1988). Among those with the diagnosis of alcoholism, almost half (47%) had a second psychiatric diagnosis. Phobias were particularly common among males, followed by depression, schizophrenia, panic, and mania. For alcoholic women, phobias and depression, followed by antisocial personality, panic, schizophrenia, and mania were the most prevalent.

Other social and familial factors appear more frequently in substance abusing groups. Also, genetic factors have been clearly related as a predisposing factor for the development of alcohol addiction (Goodwin, 1985). A "lack of family cohesiveness," which involved such factors as an early death or divorce, or separation of parents appears to be associated with an increase in alcohol related problems for offspring of these families. Burnside, Baer, McLaughlin, and Pokorny (1986) found that compared with control groups, adolescents who later became substance abusers were more likely to:

1. Identify with groups who shared alcohol and drugs during adolescence.

2. Be more impulsive.

3. Display greater evidence of rebelliousness and/or nonconformity.

Other researchers (Goldstein & Sappington, 1977) obtained a similar profile of behavioral traits including a tendency for substance abusers to be less likely to learn from experience and less conservative or reserved behaviorally than their peers.

There is also a frequent relationship between substance abuse and suicide. Most surveys report that about 25% of substance abusers entering treatment have attempted suicide in the past (Francis & Miller, 1991). The incidence of completed suicide is probably three to four times higher than that found in the general population (Murphy, 1988). As previously noted, these clients may be using alcohol or other drugs to treat the symptoms of depression. In these clients, it is essential to provide an accurate diagnosis and initiate treatment for the depression as soon as possible. Involvement of a qualified psychologist and physician to assist in diagnosing and providing treatment for these clients is critical at an early stage. The therapeutic importance of assessing depression that is dually diagnosed with substance abuse is summarized by Schuckit (1980).

CASE DISCUSSIONS

Case 1 (Sandy and Pam). Effective assessment and diagnosis would begin with the diagnostic interview. Using the Substance Use History Questionnaire (see Appendix 1), information would be gathered regarding their histories of substance use and abuse. Significant factors to consider about Sandy's substance use are the following:

1. She has a history of alcohol use dating back to junior high school.
2. By self-report, Sandy admitted to continuing to abuse alcohol into adulthood.

In assessing Sandy's substance use, it is apparent that her alcohol use has affected her family life and social relationships. She reports that she married Joe, a violent alcoholic, and that during her drinking days, she left the children at home so she could go to bars and pick up numerous men. This would clearly indicate that Sandy's alcohol abuse affected her judgment and ability to care for herself and her children.

With the information from the Substance Use History Questionnaire, it is possible to assess the phase of abuse/dependence that Sandy is experiencing. The *crucial phase* (see pages 103–105) is characterized by obvious and pronounced behavioral changes. Sandy reported behavioral loss of control coupled with guilt and remorse about her actions while using alcohol.

In diagnosing Sandy's substance abuse, additional information is needed. The CAGE Questionnaire (see page 132) and the MAST (see page 128) would be useful in determining whether Sandy meets the criteria for substance abuse or substance dependence in the DSM-IV.

Sandy's childhood history is indicative of the potential for a personality or mood disorder. Her marriage to Joe may indicate that she has suffered some type of physical or emotional abuse. Post-traumatic stress disorder is also a diagnostic possibility. Differential or dual diagnoses must be considered when evaluating Sandy's substance abuse. After a period of sobriety, additional psychological testing would be indicated to assess whether Sandy needed treatment for other disorders.

Pam's history of substance use included cocaine and alcohol. In assessing Pam's substance use, the significant factors are the following:

1. Pam's employment history
2. Pam's unstable relationships
3. Pam's report of anxiety symptoms

In addition to the diagnostic interview using the Substance Use History Questionnaire, use of the Substance Abuse Subtle Screening Inventory-2 would be useful in identifying treatment issues and potential diagnoses. Clearly, Pam's substance abuse has also affected her judgment regarding relationships. The history with her live-in boyfriend seems to indicate intense conflict resulting in potential negative outcomes.

Pam's history of unsuccessful employment indicates that she may be in the *crucial phase* (see page 103) of the progression of substance abuse/dependence. This pattern of substance abuse after a loss is a clear indicator of the overt consequences of the progression. Other factors that need to be explored are the periodic abstinence or changes in Pam's pattern of substance use.

The information from the SASSI-2 may be helpful in distinguishing between the DSM-IV diagnosis of substance abuse or substance dependence with a focus on polydrug use. Pam's childhood and recent conflicts with her boyfriend may indicate a possible personality disorder or mood disorder. Pam's statement regarding her boyfriend, that she "feels drawn to him" and wants to "make it work" may indicate a dependent personality style. Pam's increasing anxiety could indicate either periodic withdrawal from the substances or an underlying anxiety disorder.

In summary, additional information gathered through an assessment would be needed in both cases to make accurate diagnoses and to plan treatment. Contacting other family members or significant others to gather information would be useful. Once each woman had established abstinence of at least two months, further assessment would help in answering questions about dual diagnoses.

Case 2 (Joe and Jane Smith)   Joe and Jane's substance abuse is of primary importance and must be addressed. It is important to note that Jane and Joe admit to abusing alcohol for 23 years and to recent use of cocaine. Both continue to have ample access to both substances through contacts at work.

In assessing substance abuse/dependence, some psychometric instruments may be valuable in gaining more information. Using the Substance Use History Questionnaire (see Questionnaire 1 in the Appendix) and the Drug Abuse Screening Test (see pages 130–131) would help in evaluating the degree of substance abuse. It is extremely useful to distinguish between substance abuse and substance dependence to plan appropriate treatment. In addition, the questionnaire for families should be given to Sarah, and Karen should be interviewed on an age-appropriate level. This would provide further information regarding the parent's substance use and its effect on the family.

In assessing Jane's substance use, some significant factors are the following:

1. Attempts to stop drinking for health reasons
2. Reluctance to give up drugs completely
3. A traumatic childhood history with an alcoholic/abusive mother, sexual abuse by a brother, and foster home placement

Jane's substance use indicates that she is in the *crucial* to *chronic* phase (see pages 103–105) of substance abuse/dependence evidenced by her denial and minimization of her cocaine use and her five-year periodic attempts at abstinence from alcohol.

Jane's traumatic childhood history needs to be evaluated as to the effect these factors have on her substance use. Diagnostically, Jane would meet the criteria for substance dependence in the DSM-IV (see page 100). Her history may indicate other diagnoses such as a personality disorder, depression and post-traumatic stress disorder are likely.

In assessing Joe's substance use, the significant factors are the following:

1. Frequent substance use
2. His family history
3. Joe and Sarah's increasing conflict over Joe's drinking

Joe's history of daily alcohol use, weekend marijuana use, and his behavioral changes when drinking are indicative of the *crucial* phase of substance abuse/dependence. It is clear that when Joe drinks, he loses control and acts inappropriately toward Sarah. In addition, Joe's longest period of abstinence was nine days and after that, he drank to the point of intoxication. This pattern indicates a tolerance for alcohol, as well as minimization and denial.

Diagnostically, Joe would meet the criteria for substance dependence in the DSM-IV. In addition, diagnoses of depression and personality disorder need to be investigated. Additional information about Joe's childhood experiences should be gathered.

In summary, it is clear that Jane and Joe's substance use is a major factor to be considered in treatment of the Smith family. Sarah's increasing and escalating behavioral problems may be indicative of her response to her parent's drinking and drug use. Sarah may also be at risk for abusing substances. The patterns of both children should be evaluated using information about typical coping styles or roles adopted by children in response to substance abuse problems in the parents.

Case 3 (Leigh).   Leigh's substance use needs to be evaluated in the context of her developmental stage. Coupled with her reported substance use, other factors such as problems at school, shoplifting, parental conflict, parental divorce, and relocation to a new area are issues that need to be examined.

During the diagnostic interview the adolescent version of the Substance Abuse Subtle Screening Inventory-2 can be administered along with other instruments to determine a general level of functioning. More information from parent interviews and school assessment needs to be gathered.

In assessing Leigh's substance use, the significant factors include the following:

1. Her development stage (adolescence)
2. Loss of parental support
3. Increased conflict with her mother
4. Ambivalent feelings toward the conflict between her mother and father

Leigh's "acting out" behavior may indicate substance abuse or the substance use may be an outlet for her problems. This needs to be evaluated before treatment interventions can be implemented. It is clear that Leigh's behavior at school and in the community needs to be addressed. Her appearance of being "overly thin" must be investigated so that a possible eating disorder can be assessed. Referral to a physician for a thorough physical would be indicated.

To diagnose substance abuse/dependence with Leigh, more information needs to be gathered. Family members should be interviewed to assist in obtaining this information. Family conflict and Leigh's feelings of isolation must be addressed. Parent-child conflict, adjustment disorder, and eating disorder are potential dual diagnoses.

In summary, Leigh may be experiencing some *prodomal* phase (see page 102) symptoms related to her substance abuse. It will be important, however, to more carefully evaluate her previous functioning to determine whether her substance use is a temporary, reactive response to conflict and changes in the family.

REFERENCES

American Psychiatric Association. (1994). *Diagnostic and Statistical Manual of Mental Disorders (4th ed.)*. Washington, DC: Author.

Blue Cross and Blue Shield Associations. (1979). *Alcoholism*. Chicago: Author.

Burnside, M. A., Baer, P. E., McLaughlin, R. J., & Pokorny, A. D. (1986). Alcohol use by adolescents in disrupted families. *Alcoholism: Clinical and Experimental Research*, 10, 274–278.

Chasnoff, I. J. (1988). Drug use in pregnancy: Parameters of risk. *Pediatric Clinics of North America, 35*(6), 1403–1412.

Ewing, J. A. (1984). Detecting alcoholism: The CAGE questionnaire. *Journal of the American Medical Association 252*, 1905–1907.

Francis, R. J., & Miller, S. I. (Eds.) (1991). *Clinical Textbook of Addictive Disorders*. New York: Guilford Press.

Gallant, D. (1987). *Alcoholism: A Guide to Diagnosis, Intervention, and Treatment*. New York: W. W. Norton & Company.

Goldstein, J. N., & Sappington, J. T., (1977). Personality characteristics of students who become heavy drug users: An MMPI study of an avant-garde. *American Journal of Alcohol and Drug Abuse, 4*, 401–412.

Goodwin, D. G. (1985). Alcoholism and genetics: The sins of the fathers. *Archives of General Psychiatry, 42*, 171–174.

Helzer, J. I., & Pryzbeck, T. R. (1988). The co-occurrence of alcoholism with other psychiatric disorders in the general population and its impact on treatment. *Journal of Studies on Alcohol, 49*(3), 219–224.

Horn, J. L., Wanberg, K. W., & Foster, F. M. (1983). *The alcohol use inventory (AUI): computerized and paper-pencil forms*. Baltimore, MD: PsychSystems.

Horn, J. L., Wanberg, K. W., & Foster, F. M. (1986). *The alcohol use inventory: test booklet*. Minneapolis, MN: National Computer Systems, Inc.

Jellinek, E. M. (1960). *The disease concept of alcoholism*. New Haven, CT: Hillhouse.

Mayfield, D. (1985). Substance abuse in the affective disorders. In A. I. Alterman (Ed.), *Substance abuse and psychopathology*. New York: Plenum Press.

Mendelson, J., & Mello, N. (Eds.). (1985). *The diagnosis and treatment of alcoholism*. New York: McGraw-Hill.

Miller, G., (1985). *The substance abuse subtle screening inventory*. Bloomington, IN: The SASSI Institute.

Murphy, G. E., (1988). Suicide and substance abuse. *Archives of General Psychiatry, 45*, 593–594.

Palfai, T., & Jankiewicz, H. (1991). *Drugs and human behavior*. Dubuque, IA: Wm. C. Brown Publishers.

Schuckit, M. A. (1988). Evaluating the dual diagnosis patient. *Drug Abuse and Alcoholism Newsletter, 17*, 1–4.

Schuckit, M. A. (1980). Alcohol and depression. *Advances in Alcohol, 1*, 1–3.

Selzer, M. L. (1971). The Michigan alcoholism screening test: The quest for a new diagnostic instrument. *American Journal of Psychiatry, 127*, 1653–1658.

Selzer, M. L., Benokur, A., & Van Roogen, L. (1989). A self-administered Short Michigan Alcoholism Screening Test (SMAST). *Journal of studies on alcohol, 36* (1), 117–126.

Skinner, H. A. (1982). Statistical approaches to the classification of alcohol and drug addiction. *Alcoholism: Clinical and Experimental Research, 77*, 259–273.

Treadway, D., (1989). *Before it's too late: Working with substance abuse in the family*. New York: W. W. Norton & Company.

Wanberg, K. W., & Horn, J. L. (1983). Assessment of alcohol use with multidimensional concepts and measures. *American Psychologist, 38*(10), 1055–1069.

Washousky, R., Levy-Stern, D., & Muchowski, P. (1993, January/February). The stages of family alcoholism. *EAP Digest*, 38–42.

Westermeyer, J. (1976). *Primer on chemical dependency*. Baltimore, MD: Williams & Wilkins.

Appendix: Substance Use Questionnaires

Substance Use History Questionnaire

1. What substances do you currently use? (check all that apply)

   ____ alcohol   ____ amphetamines (uppers)
   ____ cocaine   ____ barbiturates (downers)
   ____ marijuana   ____ nicotine (cigarettes)
   ____ other (specify) _____

2. What are your current substance use habits?

   ____ daily use   ____ social use (with friends or at parties)
   ____ weekend use only   ____ occasional heavy use (to point of intoxication)
   ____ occasional light use
       (not to point of intoxication)

3. How many days ago did you last take a drug or drink? ____ days

4. Have you used daily in the past two months? ____ yes ____ no

5. Do you find it almost impossible to live without your drugs or alcohol? ____ yes ____ no

6. Are you always able to stop using when you want to? ____ yes ____ no

7. Where do you do most of your drinking or drug use? (check all that apply)

   ____ home
   ____ with friends
   ____ bars, restaurants, or other public places
   ____ parties or social gatherings
   ____ other

8. Do you drink or use during your work day? ____ yes ____ no

9. Do most of your friends use like you do? ____ yes ____ no

10. With whom do you use or drink? (check all that apply)

   ____ alone   ____ neighbors
   ____ family   ____ co-workers
   ____ friends   ____ strangers

11. Do you consider yourself to be a

   ____ very light user   ____ fairly heavy user
   ____ moderate user   ____ heavy user
   ____ nonuser

12. Do friends or family think you use more than other people? ____ yes ____ no

13. Have any family or friends complained to you about your drug or alcohol use?
   ____ yes ____ no

Questionnaire 1   Substance Use History Questionnaire For General Use (pp. 125–127)

14. Do you think you use more than other people who use? _____ yes _____ no

15. Were your drug use or drinking habits ever different from what they are now?
_____ yes _____ no

If yes, please explain why the habits changed.

_____

_____

_____

16. Has your drinking or drug use ever caused you to (check all that apply):

_____ lose a job or have job or academic problems
_____ have legal problems (DUI, arrest for possession)
_____ have medical problems related to your use
_____ have family problems or relationship problems
_____ be aggressive or violent

17. Have you ever neglected your obligations, family, or work for two or more days in a row because you were drinking or using drugs? _____ yes _____ no

18. Because of your alcohol or drug use, have you felt (check all that apply):

	often	sometimes	seldom	never
tense or nervous	_____	_____	_____	_____
suspicious or jealous	_____	_____	_____	_____
worried	_____	_____	_____	_____
lonely	_____	_____	_____	_____
angry or violent	_____	_____	_____	_____
depressed	_____	_____	_____	_____
suicidal	_____	_____	_____	_____

19. Do you ever feel bad about things you have done while using? _____ yes _____ no

if yes, please specify: _____

_____

20. People use alcohol and/or drugs for different reasons. How important would you say that each of the following is to you?

	very important	somewhat important	not at all
It helps me to relax.	_____	_____	_____
It helps me be more sociable.	_____	_____	_____
I like the effect.	_____	_____	_____
People I know use dugs or drink.	_____	_____	_____
I use when I get upset or angry.	_____	_____	_____
I want to forget or escape.	_____	_____	_____

Questionnaire 1   (continued)

	very important	somewhat important	not at all
It helps cheer me up.	_____	_____	_____
It makes me less tense or nervous.	_____	_____	_____
It makes me less sad or depressed.	_____	_____	_____
It helps me function better.	_____	_____	_____
I use to celebrate special occasions.	_____	_____	_____

Other (please specify): _____

_____

_____

21. Have you tried to stop using drugs or alcohol in the past two months? _____ yes _____ no

If yes, did you experience any medical or physical problems when you stopped? (please explain)

_____

_____

_____

22. Have you ever gone to anyone for help about your drinking or drug use? _____ yes _____ no
If yes, please explain:_____

_____

_____

23. Have you ever attended a meeting of Alcoholics Anonymous (AA), or any other self-help group because of your drug or alcohol use? _____ yes _____ no

24. Do you think you have an addiction to alcohol or drugs? _____ yes _____ no

25. Do you want help with a drug or alcohol problem at this time? _____ yes _____ no

Mast Test

Yes   No

____   ____   1.   Do you enjoy a drink now and then?

____   ____   2.   Do you think you are a normal drinker? (By normal, we mean you drink less than or as much as most other people.)

____   ____   3.   Have you ever awakened the morning after drinking the night before and found that you could not remember part of the evening?

____   ____   4.   Does your wife, husband, a parent, or other near relative ever worry or complain about your drinking?

____   ____   5.   Can you stop drinking without a struggle after one or two drinks?

____   ____   6.   Do you ever feel guilty about your drinking?

____   ____   7.   Do friends or relatives think you are a normal drinker?

____   ____   8.   Are you able to stop drinking when you want to?

____   ____   9.   *Have you ever attended a meeting of alcoholics Anonymous (AA)?

____   ____   10.   Have you gotten into physical fights when drinking?

____   ____   11.   Has your drinking ever created problems between you and your wife, husband, a parent, or other near relative?

____   ____   12.   Has you wife, husband (or other family member), ever gone to anyone for help about your drinking?

____   ____   13.   Have you ever lost friends because of your drinking?

____   ____   14.   Have you ever gotten into trouble at work because of drinking?

____   ____   15.   Have you ever lost a job because of drinking?

____   ____   16.   Have you ever neglected your obligations, your family, or your work for two or more days in a row because you were drinking?

____   ____   17.   Do you drink before noon fairly often?

____   ____   18.   Have you ever been told you have liver trouble? Cirrhosis?

____   ____   19.   After heavy drinking have you ever had delirium tremens (DTs) or severe shaking, or heard voices or seen things that weren't there?

____   ____   20.   Have you ever gone to anyone for help about your drinking?

____   ____   21.   Have you ever been in a hospital because of drinking?

Questionnaire 2   The Michigan Alcohol Screening Test (MAST)

_____ _____ 22. Have you ever been a patient in a psychiatric hospital or on a psychiatric ward of a general hospital where drinking was part of the problem that resulted in hospitalization?

_____ _____ 23. Have you ever been seen at a psychiatric or mental health clinic or gone to any doctor, social worker, or clergyman for help with any emotional problem, where drinking was part of the problem?

_____ _____ 24. Have you ever been arrested for drunken driving, driving while intoxicated, or driving under the influence of alcoholic beverages?
(If yes, how many times? _____)

_____ _____ 25. Have you ever been arrested, taken into custody, even for a few hours, because of other drunken behavior? (If yes, how many times _____)

*If you went to an AA meeting because you were concerned about your drinking, answer the question yes; if not, answer no.

Source: "The Michigan Alcoholism Screening Test: The Quest for a New Diagnostic Instrument" by M. L. Selzer, 1971, _American Journal of Psychiatry, 127,_ pp. 1653–1658. Used by permission.

Name_____ Date _____

Drug Use Questionnaire (DAST-20)

The following questions concern information about your potential involvement with drugs, *not including alcoholic beverages,* during the past 12 months. Carefully read each statement and decide if your answer is "yes" or "no." Then circle the appropriate response beside the question.

In the statements, *drug abuse* refers to (1) the use of prescribed or over-the-counter drugs in excess of the directions, and (2) any nonmedical use of drugs. The various classes of drugs may include cannabis (marijuana, hash), solvents, tranquilizers (such as Valium), barbiturates, cocaine, stimulants (such as speed), hallucinogens (such as LSD), or narcotics (such as heroin). Remember that the questions *do not* include alcoholic beverages.

Please answer every question. If you have difficulty with a statement, choose the response that is mostly right.

Questionnaire 3 The Drug Use Questionnaire (DAST-20) (pp. 130–131)

These questions refer to the past 12 months.   Circle Your
                                                                    Response

1.   Have you used drugs other than those required for medical reasons? ....Yes   No

2.   Have you abused prescription drugs? ....Yes   No

3.   Do you abuse more than one drug at a time?...Yes   No

4.   Can you get through the week without using drugs? ....Yes   No

5.   Are you always able to stop using drugs when you want to?.......................................Yes   No

6.   Have you had "blackouts" or "flashbacks" as a result of drug use? ....Yes   No

7.   Do you ever feel bad or guilty about your drug use? ....Yes   No

8.   Does your spouse (or parents) ever complain about your involvement with drugs?..Yes   No

9.   Has drug abuse created problems between you and your spouse or your parents? Yes   No

10. Have you lost friends because of your use of drugs?..Yes   No

11. Have you neglected your family because of your use of drugs? ....Yes   No

12. Have you been in trouble at work because of drug abuse? ....Yes   No

13. Have you lost a job because of drug abuse? ....Yes   No

14. Have you gotten into fights when under the influence of drugs? ....Yes   No

15. Have you engaged in illegal activities in order to obtain drugs? ....Yes   No

16. Have you been arrested for possession of illegal drugs?...Yes   No

17. Have you ever experienced withdrawal symptoms (felt sick) when you stopped
     taking drugs? ....Yes   No

18. Have you had medical problems as a result of your drug use (e.g. memory
     loss, hepatitis, convulsions, bleeding, etc.)?..Yes   No

19. Have you ever gone to anyone for help for a drug problem?......................................Yes   No

20. Have you been involved in a treatment program specifically related to drug use? ....Yes   No

© 1982 by the Addiction Research Foundation. Author: Harvey A. Skinner, Ph.D. For information on the DAST, contact Dr. Harvey Skinner at the Addiction Research Foundation, 33 Russell St., Toronto, Canada, M5S 2S1.

The CAGE Questionnaire

C Have you ever felt a need to CUT DOWN on your drinking/drug use?

Alternative questions—Have you ever tried to cut down on your usage? Were you successful? What was it like? Why did you decide to cut down or go on the wagon? Are you able to drink as much now as you could a year ago? Five or ten years ago? How do you feel about your drinking or use of drugs now? Has anyone ever commented on how much you are able to consume?

A Have you ever been ANNOYED at criticism of your drinking/drug use?

Alternative questions—Have you ever been concerned about your usage? Has anyone else been concerned about your drinking or use of drugs? What caused the concern or worry? Do you get irritated by their concern? Have you ever limited how much you use in order to please someone?

G Have you ever felt GUILTY about something you've done when you've been drinking/high from drugs?

Alternative questions—Do you feel that you are a different person when you are high? How would you compare yourself when you're using and when you're not? Have you ever been bothered by anything you have said or done while you have been high/drunk? Has anyone else been bothered by your usage?

E Have you ever had a morning EYE OPENER—taken drink/drugs to get going or treat withdrawal symptoms?

Alternative questions—Do you ever get a hangover? How often? Have you ever felt shaky after a night of heavy drinking? Have you ever had a drink to relieve the hangover or the shakiness? Have you ever had trouble sleeping after a heavy night of drinking or getting high? Do you ever have difficulty remembering what happened while you were high? How many times has this occurred?

Questionnaire 4 The CAGE Questionnaire for Adults

Source: "Detecting Alcoholism: The CAGE Questionnaire" by J. A. Ewing, 1984. *Journal of the American Medical Association, 252,* pp. 1905–1907. Used by permission.

Cage for Youth and Adolescents

1. Have you ever used before or during school?

2. Have you ever missed school (or been truant) because of use or just to use?

3. Have you ever lied in order to use?

4. Have you ever avoided nonusers?

5. About how often do you get intoxicated?

6. About how often do you use more than one drug when you get intoxicated?

Questionnaire 5   The CAGE Questionnaire for Youth and Adolescents

Treatment Settings

Christine Manfrin, MA

SETTINGS AND SERVICES

Treatment *services* come in many forms and refer to what is provided for the clients and their significant others. They may be in the form of *prevention* activities within communities; *intervention*, such as the Hazelden model; *education*, such as those provided within Driving Under the Influence (DUI)/Driving While Ability Impaired (DWAI) programs; or *counseling* and *psychotherapy*. Treatment services are designed to meet the varied and special needs of individuals who are abusing or addicted to alcohol, drugs, and assorted combinations of chemicals, or a combination of substances along with mental disorders. There are also programs to treat addictive behavioral disorders, such as gambling, compulsive eating and dieting, sex addiction, obsessive working, co-dependency, and dysfunctional relationships, as well as to treat those affected by an individual suffering from any of those dependencies.

Treatment *settings* are the facilities, sites, and programs in which services are delivered. As opposed to mental health settings, which have a moderate range of facility differences, chemical dependency services can be delivered in hospitals, converted houses, basements of nonhospital detoxification centers, jails and prisons, youth centers, community centers, locked and unlocked psychiatric units, rural dwellings, and almost any setting that will house an alcohol or drug counselor with clients. Most treatment services delivered within settings are based on the current philosophy that addiction to chemicals, particularly alcohol and barbiturates, is a primary illness, and that secondary problems can range from mild to moderate depression to severe anxiety or from living in a continual state of fear to pathological diagnosable mental conditions. Services are also based on the idea that the primary addictive condition affects not only the chemically dependent clients, but also the

135

individuals who are significant in their lives—spouses, co-workers, children, employers, and even the public domain.

The evaluation or initial interview can take place in many places, such as employee assistance programs (EAPs), school counselors' offices, courtrooms, hospital emergency rooms, social services offices, or jails. The primary addicted or dependent individual (client) and significant others arrive at evaluation points with myriad issues. Clients and their families come to any of these sites with distinct histories of substance use, as well as the primary and secondary effects of that use. The severity of those histories varies, and all parties arrive with defenses and denial that compound the issues for even the most sophisticated and probing of inquiries.

The assessment of drug-affected and well-defended individuals must be thorough to determine the most appropriate setting or type of program. When all the components of an individual's situation are scrutinized by a trained counselor, the result is an accurate matching of the client with the appropriate treatment services, modality (counseling approach), and the setting that best fits the evaluator's recommendations (see chapter 4).

Because a client's presenting issues can be extensive and complex, the counselor should have an operational understanding of treatment approaches as well as the settings available within the client's geographic region and local community. Counselors need to know what is meant by a range of services, or what is referred to as a *more-* or *less-intensive setting*. Thus, to individually treat and maintain clients in any type of treatment program, there should optimally be what is termed "continuum of care" or a range of services that allows the client to move from a more-restrictive environment to a less-restrictive one as appropriate, or in reverse when the problems indicate. For instance, in **Case 1,** Pam may benefit from a stay in a halfway house, not because her drinking is continuous and she cannot function adequately in the outside world, but because of her symbiotic relationship with her mother, her episodic job history, and her anxiety-producing fear of being alone. In the halfway house, she will receive reinforcement for (1) not drinking, (2) setting limits with the boyfriend within a safe environment, and (3) encouragement to maintain a job. Her care begins with a setting of moderate intensity, and the movement along the continuum of care helps the recovery process.

To design and implement a continuum of care in a variety of settings, such as detoxification, ¼-day intensive services, and so on, the treatment staff must be sensitive to their program's geographic location, the clients that emerge from that location, and the resources readily accessible to the recovering individuals. Program designers and staff must continually review client demographics, and usually can obtain current information through local and state health departments.

Treatment planning and selection of the setting is thought to be best done on an individualized basis. This can be accomplished even if a treatment program predominantly uses the *group* modality or if the setting is structured. Individualized treatment planning is necessary to meet specific and individual needs presented by clients during evaluation and admission to the treatment program. Every treatment program or setting has similarities. For example, most free-standing, residential programs will be less-structured than hospital-based inpatient programs. Outpatient counseling and methadone maintenance will have less weekly contact with clients than intensive out-patient programs. But most programs, regardless of design, will always attempt to meet the individual needs of clients as well as the collective needs of the population they serve, such as crack/cocaine addicts versus drinking drivers.

Most alcohol and drug treatment settings share the common value that most chemically dependent people respond best to a therapy conducted in the *group* setting. Thus, the program will have most of its psychoeducational activities (skills-building, such as assertiveness training), education, and counseling provided through that modality.

The second commonly shared value is that individual therapy should be more often used as an *adjunct* to group treatment. The individual case manager or coun-selor, or the treatment team will evaluate the situation to determine if individual/family therapy outside the group is (1) necessary and beneficial to the current treat-ment plan within the respective setting, and (2) necessary to the individual's treat-ment process. The recommendation for one-to-one work is most often made by the treatment team in a "patient staffing," or by the primary counselor who is an addic-tions specialist. For hospital settings, it is often mandated by the professional who assumes responsibility for the care of a client, such as the admitting physician.

The third common belief is that the defense mechanism of *denial* is a key issue in the treatment of many disorders, whether chemical, behavioral, or emotional. Thus, for most settings, it is preferred that clients be admitted on voluntarily. Addictions pro-grams and specialists still refer to the client as "ready," or open and amenable to treat-ment approaches, while others argue that a state of "readiness" is not necessary for a successful treatment outcome. Readiness is an attitude, a frame of mind, a susceptibil-ity that implies a degree of openness and willingness on the part of the participant. In **Case 3,** Leigh's evaluation indicates no openness to intervention, nor is she there vol-untarily. However, the fact that she has a new peer group that "accepts her as she is" may give the counselor an opportunity to create that therapy opening. Counselors generally believe that this attitude ensures a more positive outcome in treatment.

Substance use, abuse, and addiction affect *all* individuals associated with the sub-stance abuser. To provide the best ongoing recovery for everyone involved, the coun-selor should be familiar with continuum of treatment services within each geo-graphic community. This continuum should be made readily known and easily accessible to all clients, and the specifics of their transition along that continuum, (for example, all the details and who is responsible), should be incorporated into all discharge planning.

CONTINUUM OF CARE

In chemical dependency treatment, the continuum of care spans a wide range of pro-gram designs and settings. This includes the following:

- Short-term, inpatient care (IP) lasting three to seven days
- Intensive outpatient programs (IOP) in which clients stay eight to twelve weeks

- Halfway houses (HWH), where the client lives in a moderately structured, supportive residence for three to six months
- Therapeutic communities (TC), where residents may remain up to two years
- Outpatient alcoholism programs lasting four to six months
- Opiate and methadone clinics that a client may attend for two to five years

Managed Care Influence

As the managed-care approach to insurance benefits provided for mental health and chemical dependency treatment increases in popularity, a focal point for insurance companies and managed care companies has been what is termed the *least-restrictive environment* or the least patient-restricted level of care. The definitions of the various levels of intensity within the continuum of care are increasingly accepted and used by EAPs, insurer "gatekeepers" such as pre-authorization specialists or primary care physicians (PCPs), preferred provider organizations (PPOs), discharge planners, and others. The "gate" is the point at which individuals begin to access their mental health or alcohol and drug abuse benefits, and the role of "gatekeeper" is a common one in health-care systems today.

The changing system of care has forced individual providers (addictions counselors, therapists) and programs to establish criteria that define precisely what symptoms and behaviors a client must present to be admitted into one of the levels of care. It has forced mental health counselors and health care providers to:

- Be more knowledgeable in the behavioral symptoms of the addictive disorders.
- Be able to assess a client's symptoms within DSM criteria and terminology.
- Have a working understanding of the wide range of program designs.
- Know the limits and strengths of each setting.

Setting Models (GCHA)

To meet the increasing demand for this program "matching," groups, facilities, health departments, and professional organizations have attempted to write standard definitions of settings, models, and designs. One of the most well-defined models resulted from a collaborative research and pilot project in 1987. It was published by the Greater Cleveland Hospital Association for the Northern Ohio Chemical Dependency Treatment Directors Association, and one of its objectives was to identify three levels of criteria associated with treatment settings: admission, discharge, and transfer. Funding for the project to develop standard criteria came from both public and private sources, including the Ohio Department of Health. The resulting document, titled *The Cleveland Admission, Discharge, & Transfer Criteria, A Model for Chemical Dependency Treatment Programs*, (1987) was available for a fee to individuals and programs.

The Cleveland group recognized that there were no professionally or regionally standard definitions and criteria for admission into treatment, and that those being used varied greatly. Terminology was affected by "local usage variance." The group's initial document, which they distributed to a wide range of programs for feedback, addressed the problem of varying definitions and terminology:

> Terminology can encounter local variance that may result in confusion.
>
> One intent is to provide a framework in which to accumulate more objective data.
>
> The use of terms may not be compatible with conventions in . . . U.S.
>
> No single uniform set of criteria has been adopted by the insurance industry.
>
> Treatment providers [programs] are confronted with an array of confusing and conflicting guidelines. (pp. 3–5)

The project's outcome was a model that divided the chemical dependency continuum of care into six distinct levels of program designs. For both adolescents and adults, the levels ranged from low-intensity, nonprofessional support to the highest or most intense level—medically based inpatient care. The primary difference between adults and youth was in Level III as the adolescents were more often being treated on an after-school basis.

Level I: Mutual and self-help

Level II: Low intensity outpatient treatment

Level III: (Adolescents) Intensive after-school treatment

Level III: (Adults) Intensive outpatient

Level IV: Structured all-day treatment

Level V: Medically supervised intensive inpatient treatment

Level VI: Medically managed intensive inpatient evaluation units

Each treatment level was briefly defined. Then the programs and professionals who submitted contributions arrived at a consensus on broader, more inclusive definitions for each level.

Level I

This level, the *mutual, self-help* setting, requires no professional staff and typically is a *12-step, 12-tradition* program (see Appendix at the end of the chapter). Self-help groups often meet weekly, and may be specialty groups, (i.e. gay and lesbian; women only; young adult), or aftercare and "alumni." They are composed mainly of individuals who have experienced a common difficulty and who consider themselves recovering or in the process of healing. They attend voluntarily and regularly, and provide support to other recovering individuals. Most often, the groups are loosely organized and democratically run. Records are not kept.

Level II

An outpatient setting is the least-restrictive professional environment. It generally requires professional staff trained in one or more areas of substance abuse issues and respective treatment. Specialty areas include the addictive process, relapse identification and prevention, codependency and enmeshment, domestic violence as a primary or secondary syndrome, methadone maintenance, and so on. Because the licensing or certification requirements for chemical dependency professionals varies from state to state, the definition of *licensed professional* also varies. As opposed to other mental health professionals, it is not always required that outpatient counseling staff be licensed or certified to function as a primary case manager in many settings. At the outpatient level of treatment and above, records are kept and documented, and formal treatment planning begins (see Outpatient Program section later in this chapter).

Level III

An *intensive outpatient* design is a mid-level intensity between outpatient and inpatient. The number of staff required to deliver the care increases with the treatment intensity, and this level more often has treatment teams rather than individual providers. To participate in intensive outpatient, the client needs to be predominantly physically stable and reasonably free from regular use of substances, yet demonstrate that she or he requires three to five groups per week to maintain the recovery process. Usually a medical specialist determines whether the client is (1) medically clear or sufficiently stable, (2) able to benefit from intensive outpatient care, and (3) able to tolerate the treatment intensity. However, if the client does not have an adequate support system or home environment, or the physical and psychological difficulties are such that she or he is a high risk for relapse to the substance or behavior of choice, then a more restrictive and intensive level of care should be considered.

Level IV

Day treatment, or partial hospitalization, generally requires more intense staffing and offers more on-site clinical supervision than intensive outpatient. Typically, the parameters of one full day of partial hospitalization are five hours of treatment time, or patient involvement, on site. The parameters of half-day are no less than three hours, and there can be any combination of partial days in the client's treatment prescription. Some programs offer ¼ days, which may be mornings or evenings.

The insurance industry in many states recognizes both a full- and half-day partial hospitalization as a billable unit of service and will often convert one inpatient day to two partial hospitalization days. Treatment groups within the day treatment design range from general support and counseling groups to skills-building and recreation. All groups are facilitated by staff trained in their field of specialty, for example, an occupational therapist, recreation specialist, addictions counselor, psychiatric nurse, and so on. For facilities that are licensed or accredited, all staff members will have minimum education and licensing requirements in their fields of specialty.

Levels V & VI

Inpatient treatment is the most restrictive setting and maintains the more intense staffing patterns. Settings vary from medical and psychiatric hospitals to nonmedical, residential settings. The staffing requirements vary with the licensing requirements. Most medical and psychiatric hospital facilities are accredited by the Joint Commission on Hospital Accreditation and staffing for treatment units will need to meet those stringent requirements. Residential, or community-based, free-standing facilities offering intensive care will have requirements that meet other standards or licensing. Most often, those are dependent upon the health department statutes of the state in which they are located.

Setting Model (NAATP)

About the time the document of standard definitions of the levels of intensity was being written in Ohio, the Chemical Dependency Recovery Committee of the Hospital Council of Southern California (HCSC) and a group of licensed clinicians studied the standards developed by the National Association of Alcohol Treatment Programs (NAATP), and they drafted an adaptation of those standards. This massive research effort included all licensed inpatient chemical dependency providers in the South, multicorporate institutions that owned or managed facilities, and independent clinicians. Their document, the *Model Criteria for Adult Inpatient and Intensive Outpatient Dependency Treatment* was formally recognized and adopted in 1988.

The Hospital Council identified observable, mostly measurable symptoms for admission into levels of care, and they especially addressed the inpatient setting. (While the average inpatient length of stay has been dramatically reduced since 1988, diagnostic criteria used to indicate the need for *some* form of nonoutpatient treatment remains constant and reliable. Adults typically participated in 30-day programs; 45-60 days for adolescents.) The criteria for inpatient admission in the *Model Criteria* handbook specifically states the client "must meet *at least* three" of the symptoms. It further states that for the counselor's diagnostic workup to be reliable, those symptoms must have "persisted for at least one continuous month and have occurred repeatedly over a longer period of time." These symptoms are similar to the DSM-IV-R criteria for abuse and dependence.

The handbook lists symptoms that the counselor or assessment professional must look for when evaluating and assessing a client for admission into any level of treatment. These are the same symptoms for diagnosis specified in other textbooks and general assessment instruments, and are considered the primary issues related to chemical abuse and dependency. The general categories of symptoms include the following:

1. Issues of tolerance to the chemical.
2. Loss-of-control over one's use.
3. Intense desire for the drug of choice (cravings).

4. Attempts to control one's use to convince others that his/her use is not out of control.

5. Withdrawal symptoms.

6. Continued use despite increasing and recurring problems and conflicts.

7. Other symptoms of dependence and progression typically recognized by clinicians.

In reviewing these characteristics, or symptomology, of drug use, counselors can see the treatment program implications. Chemical dependency programs will treat—through intervention, confrontation, education, talk therapy, and other modalities—all those issues and many more. Most programs will also introduce clients and their families to the principles and philosophy of a self-help recovery program, such as AA or Rational Recovery, while at the same time recognizing and supporting individual differences. Built into programs is a requirement that clients regularly attend self-help groups.

Many individuals who are chemically dependent, or who are "dual diagnosed," benefit from a short-term (four to seven days) inpatient stay. Dual diagnosis, or comorbid conditions, which often accompany substance abuse, can mean that there is a concomitant psychiatric condition, chronic medical condition, or more than one dependence disorder (Frances & Sheldon, 1991). Each condition must be assessed independently and in relation to the other presenting conditions or symptoms. This is done to withdraw the affected individual safely from chemicals, stabilize the client emotionally and physically, and identify and treat those concomitant disorders. For the more severely disturbed and affected client, a short-term stay is 7 to 10 days.

When a counselor is responsible for the transition of a client along the continuum of care, it is important that the counselor have access to all evaluations for concomitant conditions. The counselor will want to know the following:

- That medical and psychiatric staff have evaluated all presenting conditions.
- The client is thoroughly withdrawn from self-administered substances.
- The client is stabilized on only those medications that are necessary to treat the condition(s).
- Staff have had sufficient time and opportunity to watch for the development of another condition or mental health problem.
- The counselor has had sufficient time with the client to make appropriate treatment setting suggestions.
- The treatment setting has the capacity, through staffing and physical design, to monitor the client for emerging conditions, guarantee the client's safety, and provide for continuing assessment and treatment planning.

Clients with a dual diagnosis should be encouraged to participate in the inpatient setting. Whereas many substance abuse clients can successfully withdraw on an outpatient basis, the client with concomitant conditions should not attempt detoxification outside of a safe, restrictive environment. This client often requires milieu therapy and a program with a multidisciplinary team. The team's inpatient experience can provide differential assessment, a comprehensive and appropriate evaluation, intervention, and treatment services while the client safely withdraws from mood- and mind-altering chemicals. Based on the results of such a thorough evaluation, if it is determined that the client requires longer inpatient care, the counselor will have to make a referral to an appropriate treatment facility. The evaluating staff, then, has the ethical responsibility to know about various treatment program designs (options), and to follow through with the disposition as much as possible.

The Minnesota Model

The Minnesota model of alcohol treatment (Anderson, 1981; Laundergan, 1982) is an integration of the self-help approach with professional or addictions-trained counseling staff. This is now a well-recognized treatment design, and the model is nationally distributed through publications from the Hazelden Foundation. From this model, levels of care are identified as a *three-phase* continuum of care: (1) detoxification, (2) rehabilitation, and (3) aftercare (Straussner, 1993).

The descriptions of the three phases follow (Straussner, 1993; Wallace, 1992):

1. *Detoxification* can take place in a hospital-based setting, acute-care facility, or community-based nonhospital facilities. Its purpose is to safely and thoroughly relieve symptoms of intoxication. Each setting must provide medical management directly or assure it is immediately available, as withdrawal from alcohol and a combination of chemicals can be life-threatening, unpredictable, and unique to the individual's physiology. Alcohol withdrawal usually lasts three to five days in an acute hospital setting; the average stay for nonhospital detox centers is one to three days, with a median withdrawal time of three days. Other substances may require longer withdrawal stays.

2. *Rehabilitation* can occur in either an inpatient (residential) or outpatient setting. The daily routines for the structured inpatient setting are the same for all clients, but the length of stay varies from 21-28 days after detoxification. Before the emergence of extreme cost-containment approaches by the insurance industry, the average stay was 21 days for adults and 35 days for adolescents within this model. Although *rehabilitation* is a treatment *outcome*, it has become a descriptive term identifying a *setting*.

In the outpatient setting, clients with sufficient support systems are seen one to three times per week, in groups or individually. Clients maintain their usual social and family functioning, but commit to abstinence. If, however, that cannot be accomplished on an outpatient basis, the addictions counselor facilitates an intervention of some kind in an effort to have them admitted to inpatient care.

3. *Aftercare* is synonymous with continuing recovery or ongoing treatment. It may take the form of individual and family therapy, or alumni and support groups. It is based on the belief that to maintain successful abstinence, clients completing intensive treatment should have continuing contact with other recovering individuals.

The Minnesota model (Straussner, 1993) can be seen throughout the type of program design where treatment is "integrated." This means that clients being treated in the same setting may have different chemical preferences, such as alcoholism, heroin addiction, and chronic marijuana use. It also means that clients who have a dual diagnosis can be treated in the same group treatment when the matter of substance abuse is addressed.

There are common assumptions in the treatment philosophy of many residential recovery facilities (Straussner, 1993). Some of these assumptions are as follows:

1. Chemical dependency is a disease, and all clients have the same disease.
2. The disease is progressive and should be thought of as the primary problem.
3. The characteristics of that disease are primarily loss of control and denial.
4. Treatment staff should include recovering (two years or more) counselors.
5. Education and therapy are essential to program effectiveness.
6. Families (significant others) must be included in treatment.
7. Self-help groups are essential.

To adequately discriminate among the many symptoms presented by the new client and how those symptoms meet criteria for levels of care, it is necessary to have a set standard for collecting assessment and admission information. The procedure most often used by inpatient facilities is the collection of an *admission database*. This is done as soon as the client is chemical-free or at a low point of the compulsive behavior. It enables the counselor to conduct a *differential assessment,* or to have a basis on which to recommend one type of setting over another. For the counselor to make that recommendation, it is necessary to have as much accurate information as possible. Much of this information has been discussed in chapter 4's Clinical Interview. The counselor needs information regarding:

1. Social and support system, living situation.
2. Client and significant other's chief complaint(s).

   (After 1 and 2, the addictions counselor can make a preliminary assessment as to the most appropriate setting.)
3. History of *current* conditions.
4. Symptoms and events leading to this evaluation—physical, behavioral, and personality changes.
5. Substance abuse related to present symptoms and problems.
6. Substance use patterns over the past six months.
7. Family, social, and job changes related to substance use during past six months.
8. List client and family's strengths and weaknesses. Identify coping skills, support system, risk for relapse, and vocational functioning. (After 3-8, the second level of assessment is completed.)

The counselor will then need to assess critical components regarding the selection of the appropriate setting or level of care:

1. Is this client capable of maintaining behavioral and emotional stability for more than 72 hours?

2. Has the client failed at outpatient treatment recently? If so, she or he may meet criteria for admission into a more intense and restrictive setting.

3. Are there symptoms, either self- or other-reported, of a mental or emotional disturbance that is impairing the general functioning of this client?

4. Does the client have a living situation that will provide adequate support or maintenance while in the nonresidential setting?

5. Is this client able to perform the activities of day-to-day living? If not, the counselor may need to consider placement in day treatment or look for a transitional living situation, such as a halfway house.

6. Is this client's history *adequate* for determining the setting? Is the history *reliable* at this point in time? If the client is an adolescent, the history information will come from school counselors, peers, teachers, friends, and others not immediately related.

DETOXIFICATION AND STABILIZATION

Withdrawal from alcohol, barbiturates, hallucinogens, and other selected chemicals is typically completed in an inpatient setting. Hayashida et al. (1989) identified major objectives of detox treatment:

1. To resolve acute . . . problems and prevent the development of more severe symptoms

2. To arrest . . . abusive use of substances(intervention)

3. To help the patient become engaged in . . . rehabilitation

4. To prevent a need for redetoxification

5. The confrontation of defenses

Medical necessity must be established before admission. Facilities and insurance carriers typically will provide the definition of medical necessity, some criteria implying more acuity than others. Trained staff must make the assessment in accordance with the accepted definition. Although it is standard practice to withdraw clients from certain chemicals on an inpatient basis, it is not uncommon for clients to be withdrawn from their chemicals on an outpatient basis when they can be seen frequently.

The detoxification setting is used with individuals who are incapacitated or intoxicated as a result of their substance abuse. When counselors are making a detox program determination for a client, they should look for the following elements:

1. The program maintains a *structured* and *supportive environment*. That environment provides protection for both the client and the family from the effects of drinking or drugging behavior.

2. The program provides *protection* from the mental or physical consequences of the habitual and excessive use of alcohol or other mood-altering chemicals.

3. The program staff conduct a thorough *screening* for the presence of severe withdrawal symptoms and/or psychiatric conditions.

4. While inpatient, the client receives encouragement, education, and counseling for help in eliminating the use of alcohol or other mood-altering chemicals.

5. The program provides on-site or readily accessible professional medical and psychiatric care (Johnson, Wanberg, Carducci, & Manfrin, 1987).

Safe and complete withdrawal (detoxification) are the immediate goals of both hospital and nonhospital or free-standing units. In most settings, detox is measured by a reduction in the blood-alcohol content to .00; in other settings, stabilization is determined when the client is lucid, the intervention has been completed, and a beginning treatment plan is in place. The placement of a client in the inpatient setting for detox is based on the philosophical concept that many individuals who are chemically dependent or who have a dual diagnosis do better in that setting, but that transition plans (discharge planning) should begin the day after admission (Weiner, 1991).

The benefit and argument for having a substance abuser go through withdrawal (detox) on an inpatient basis (Weiner, 1991) are the following:

1. The inpatient experience provides more comprehensive and immediate assessments; clinical and medical staff are more readily available and can respond to the patient more quickly.

2. It is an optimal modality when offered in conjunction with an intensive outpatient track; thus, while the patient is at the end of the withdrawal stage and *before* discharge, she or he begins attending the outpatient or intensive outpatient service and is assigned a primary counselor.

3. Often the admission has been based on the results of an *outpatient* assessment. This procedure aids in supporting the basis for the inpatient admission.

Medical necessity simply describes the elements that should be measurable and observable to justify admission. It is a commonly used term in managed care, the insurance industry, and standard admission criteria, and must be included in counselor assessments. It includes (1) impaired physical and neurological functioning, (2) functioning having elements of major depression, (3) a disorientation of self, (4) observable and measurable alcohol/drug toxicity, (5) altered level of consciousness, and, (6) risk of seizure.

Criteria for Counselors to Use When Recommending Detox

1. Individual is incapacitated or intoxicated, and is exhibiting withdrawal symptoms.
2. Individual is involved in a chaotic or turbulent family system or other social system, which by its negative influence inhibits the individual's beginning recovery.
3. Individual is in need of intensive assessment/diagnostic services to differentiate between symptoms attributable to chemical dependency and symptoms attributable to psychiatric illness (Weiner, Johnson et al., 1991).

Withdrawing From the Effects of Abuse and Addiction

What are the withdrawal symptoms most likely to be seen in the inpatient setting? Because an aggregate of the symptoms is used in substantiating the admission to a more intense setting, it is important to be familiar with the more common ones (Weiner, 1991; Frances & Sheldon, 1991).

Common Withdrawal Symptoms: Alcohol

- **Physical evidence.** Shakes; increased sweating; increased heart rate; elevations in body temperature or blood pressure; nausea/vomiting; difficulty sleeping (relaxation techniques are useful before medication is given).
- **Psychological disturbances.** Euphoria; anxiety; depression; suicidal activity.

Common Withdrawal Symptoms: Cocaine, Crack, Speed, and Other CNS Stimulants.

- **Physical evidence.** Hyperactivity; tremors; pupil dilation; "the crash" may last from nine hours to four days; experiences of intense cravings; high need for frequent exercising; disturbed sleep and eating patterns.
- **Psychological disturbances.** Euphoria; severe depression; emotionality will seem, at times, unmanageable, but it may pass without needing medication.

The withdrawal syndrome in this category may last one to ten weeks or longer. During this period, the client may report intermittent depressions, low energy, a decline in interest and enjoyment of normal activities, anxiety, and increased cravings. This will pass when brain neurotransmitters return to normal. When the client returns to regular sleep, normal or more manageable moods, and reports a general decrease in craving, it is safe to assume that detox has been completed.

Common Withdrawal Symptoms: Marijuana

- No specific withdrawal *syndrome* when detoxifying from cannabis that would routinely indicate inpatient detox; marijuana is absorbed by the fatty tissues and it may take weeks to months for the body to rid itself of it and any other byproducts.

- **Physical disturbances.** Mild to moderate symptoms of hyperactivity and tremors.
- **Psychological disturbances.** Euphoria; delusions; mild to moderate depression, anxiety, and irritability.

Role of the Counselor in the Hospital Setting for Detoxification

The expectations of the primary counselor or attending staff member is that she or he either *directly* provides for the client assessment, or assures that it is completed by another professional staff member. The elements of the detox phase will include but not be limited to the following:

1. An in-depth evaluation of the patient's physical and mental condition; this is usually completed by medical personnel, although the evaluation of the mental condition can be completed by a trained counselor.
2. A measurement of the degree of intoxication, generally using urine screens and blood samples; counselors are usually required to observe patients for changing symptoms.
3. The chemical history through reports from the client and others: extent, including duration, frequency, and amount of involvement with chemicals.
4. A comprehensive plan for the management of any possible physical complications and psychological disturbance.
5. The interpretation of chemical dependency inventories for the purpose of discharge planning and continuing care.
6. Administering of lifestyle questionnaires that will be used for both client and family intervention and treatment strategies.
7. Assure that medical and psychiatric testing is interpreted for patient and family while she or he is an inpatient.

Accessing Care

Clients access levels of care through a variety of sources. Accessing a detoxification or other residential setting does not occur just through physicians. Clients sometimes admit themselves voluntarily, termed a *self-referral* or *voluntary admit*. Or a recommendation is made by a mental health or other professional, members of community self-help groups who often do an intervention and transport the client to the facility, or law enforcement.

In some cases, a medical or psychiatric commitment is made, termed an *involuntary referral*, or a *hold-and-treat*. Admitting a client on an involuntary basis can be done more easily in detox than in other settings where the risk of harm is greater and more immediate. It is increasingly more difficult to detain a client in residential settings, even though their substance use is imminently a danger to themselves and others.

OUTPATIENT SETTINGS

Outpatient is viewed as the least-restrictive setting for treatment. In states where programs must be *licensed* or *certified,* basic elements of the outpatient system and range of services must be in place for the setting to be defined as *outpatient*.

States vary widely in their licensing requirements, although a program designated as *drug-free* and one designated as a *narcotic treatment service* will differ in their licensing requirements and program design regardless of the state in which they operate. The former is based on a drug-free model, meaning no nonpsychiatric medications and especially no methadone will be dispensed. A narcotic treatment program will be allowed, under federal standards and regulations, authorization for dispensing and monitoring a controlled substance, such as methadone. This authorization requires a special license in all states, a physician, and strict, written drug screening protocols to which all staff and clients must adhere.

Common Elements of Outpatient Licensing

For an individual counselor, professional group, or program to post outpatient services, they may have policies and client notices that specify the following:

1. Clinic hours of operation and provisions for off-hours and emergency services.
2. Staffing patterns and staff-to-client ratios.
3. State mandates for counselor training, credentialling, and continuing education.
4. Criteria for allowing a client to remain in outpatient.
5. Criteria for identifying the treatment modality as "outpatient" and not "aftercare."
6. Record-keeping, confidentiality regulations, and disclosure requirements.
7. Duty-to-warn statements, or exceptions to confidentiality required by law.

Although professional staff ideally would prefer these mandates to be applied uniformly among states and programs, they clearly are not and may vary considerably.

Some statutes can be expected to be applied to an outpatient modality or setting in any state. Federal statutes regarding legal rights, confidentiality, and anti-discrimination will be constant, for example. Individual programs may have rules in place that have come from the experience of professionals working with substance abusers.

One can expect to see certain basic clinical services provided in outpatient setting with a full range of substance abuse services. These optimally include the following elements:

Crisis Intervention

Crisis intervention usually includes on-call staff available to assist in either the direct or indirect disposition of clients needing evaluations and referral. Often, trained staff are available to work with family members, friends, employers, and significant others in setting up and conducting interventions. The purpose of intervention is to enable substance abusers to seek treatment before they experience significant losses or "hit rock bottom." This technique has been proved successful in motivating the substance abuser and family into treatment; it may be in the form of caring confrontation and "tough love," the Johnson Institute model of intervention, family and clergy conferences, or education. No matter what the avenue, having the capability to provide crisis interventions is important to the outpatient design.

Individual Counseling

One-to-one counseling or psychotherapy are available in outpatient clinics, but not always to the same degree or with the same emphasis. Therapies range from basic addiction counseling with another recovering individual to more intense psychotherapy with a trained clinician. Standards have few mandates in the alcohol and drug field.

Family Counseling

Family counseling will deal with changes in significant others, family, and living situations. A vital part of the services involves working with members of a client's family. This allows family members the opportunity to deal with problems they have experienced as a result of the substance abuse and to begin their own program of recovery. Again, due to the heavy emphasis on the group setting, couples' and family services may or may not be readily available within the outpatient setting, but may be referred out to community practitioners.

Specialty Groups

Whenever possible, group therapy will be the design of choice. Groups may include education on special topics, grief and loss counseling, social skills building, and other didactic sessions relative to life issues; they may simply be "recovery talk" groups, support groups, and even monthly pot-luck "speaker's meetings." They may take any form, and will be dependent upon the geographic location, availability of community resources, philosophy of the program, and staff resources.

Ancillary Services

Ancillary services are often provided by social workers or discharge planners. These may include on-site work with family systems, consultations with employers, back-to-work conferences, assistance with transportation to and from support groups, and personal aid in finding contacts in self-help recovery groups, and guidance around changing physical and nutritional needs.

Education

Education includes classes on alcohol, drugs, abuse, addiction, self-medication, and the many ways that chemical dependency or substance abuse affect one's life.

Evaluation and Referral

Evaluation and referral are an important part of the outpatient service. This is the assessment of a client's readiness to enter the outpatient setting from a more intense level of care, or his or her ability to maintain sobriety in an aftercare group. Counselors in this setting must have skills in differential assessment for the levels of care as well as the ability and time to follow through on client referrals.

Outpatient settings in which narcotics are dispensed have special requirements. They include, but are not limited to the following:

1. A physician or designated medical personnel must evaluate all admissions.
2. A *complete* and current medical history and physical must be done.
3. The medical history must include a history of the narcotic dependence, recent lab reports, and documentation of physiological dependence upon drugs.
4. Complete physical examinations must be submitted annually or semi-annually.
5. Clients *voluntarily* participate in methadone maintenance.
6. The program should specify a communicable disease resource person who will ensure that AIDS/HIV and other disease information is routinely offered to all clients.
7. Urine drug screening should have written protocols for counselors and clients.
8. Drug screening should be scheduled as well as random to minimize the opportunities to falsify results.
9. Drug screening may take place over a period as long as two to five years.
10. Clients will be guaranteed confidential records and treatment in accordance with federal statutes, and counselors will adhere to those regulations.

OUTPATIENT DUI/DWAI/DUID PROGRAMS

Driving Under the Influence, Driving While Ability Impaired, and Driving Under the Influence of Drugs are some of the titles of state legislation to address drunken driving. With the onset of mandated drunken driver programs, states have actively sought to define and standardize treatment and penalties of the driver impaired by the use of chemicals. Many states now have well-defined, detailed, and judicious systems. Outpatient drunken-driver designs have been in development since the mid-1970s, when the National Institute on Alcohol Abuse and Alcoholism funded many pilot projects known as alcohol-driving countermeasures (ADC) programs. These were most often administratively placed under motor vehicle divisions or highway safety departments. In the early 1980s and with the onset of action groups such as MADD (Mothers Against Drunk Drivers) and SADD (Students Against Drunk Drivers), treatment programs and citizen advocacy groups collaborated to influence the development of more formalized and strictly mandated programs targeting this population.

Often outpatient treatment programs adopt alcohol education tracks from the requirements of "intervention education" for the drunken driver. These tracks have elements common to all education courses on driving under the influence. The basics are the following:

1. The physiological effects of alcohol and other drugs, their interactions, and the effects on behaviors and driving.
2. The possible psychological consequences of use/abuse/addiction to the client and significant others.
3. Blood alcohol concentration levels, their definition and implications, and the state's legal penalties and impaired-driver laws.
4. The current theories and practices of chemical abuse and addiction, treatment approaches, and self-help groups.
5. Alternatives to drinking/drugging and driving.

Outpatient group therapy tracks have the following common elements:

1. Clients make a minimum 12-week commitment to group, and groups meet for 90 minutes or longer.
2. Counseling follows completion of an education series.
3. Peer pressure and confrontation are used in groups.

INTENSIVE OUTPATIENT SETTING

The intensive outpatient setting (I-OP) allows clients to maintain vocational and family responsibilities while participating in a treatment experience that has both inpatient and outpatient elements. This program design is typically structured to be completed in phases or levels. Each phase has a set of requirements for the client to fulfill before moving to the next. Family services in the I-OP setting are often structured so that significant others attend classes or groups for one full week, or periodically during the entire treatment episode. This encourages family members to deal quickly and intensely with issues they have experienced as a result of the substance abuse and to begin their own program of recovery. The result is often an intervention for the entire family system.

Any individual admitted to the intensive education/treatment model should be assessed as being capable and able to benefit from such a setting and experience. At the time of admission, a *primary counselor* is often assigned to each client. This person will attend to the counseling need of a given number of clients, yet those clients will receive education and therapy services from many members of the multidisciplinary staff.

It is important for the continuity of treatment planning and the safety of the client that each individual have one assigned and primary addictions counselor. It is not uncommon for a client to be evaluated by trained substance abuse counselors, medical personnel, or related mental health staff, to be in need of specialty or more intense services, and to be referred to the appropriate modality. That may include detoxification, psychiatric stabilization, or a residential program. The obligation for the appropriate referral rests with the primary counselor. The counselor knows that the first history obtained from the client will not be the most accurate or complete one and that it is important to closely supervise the client in this setting.

Intensive Outpatient Model

All substance abusers receive an in-depth assessment of their physical and mental condition, the degree of current and recent intoxication, the extent of involvement with chemicals, particularly in the previous three to six months, and the degree of social and personal dysfunction.

They will then be given a treatment plan for the management of any withdrawal syndrome. At the point of entry in a treatment group, the primary counselor will have the responsibility of assuring that the clients receive (1) motivational counseling, (2) education relative to mood-altering chemicals, (3) introduction to self-help, community-based programs, and (4) treatment planning for discharge and post-discharge.

The treatment process in the intensive outpatient setting will be typically conducted in phases or levels. Each phase has particular requirements for clients at the point of entry.

Phase or Level One

Schedule.   Three to five evenings per week, two to four hours each night, for an average of six weeks.

Goal.   Client admits to self and to the peer group the extent of substance abuse; demonstrate compliance with all treatment requirements, and a reduction in denial.
Requirements for entry into Level One:

1. Client makes arrangement for a complete medical evaluation. Recommendations are made based on the results of this physical.
2. Interviews are conducted with all significant others. Treatment recommendations are made to significant others.
3. Treatment contracts are signed by clients and significant others.

4. Assessment instruments are completed by client within the first seven days. Treatment planning is completed after review of instruments.

Outcomes of Level One must be met before client transitions to the next level:

1. Completion of personal history, genogram, family history, or similar task.
2. Written history of all substance use, including details of the kinds of substances used, a history of any other compulsives or addictions, the frequency of use (participation), and the amount of each substance.
3. Assigned readings must be completed and discussed with the primary counselor.
4. Verification of abstinence. Clients agree to random drug screens and monitored disulfiram (Antabuse) if indicated.
5. In self-help settings, clients are required to attend community-based self-help meetings, get a sponsor, and purchase conference-approved literature ("the Big Book," *One Day at a Time,* and so on).

Phase or Level Two

Schedule.   May be two nights per week, 1½ to three hours each night, for six to 12 weeks. Family attends on a separate night, or the program may offer a large multifamily component on a third night.

Goals.   Uninterrupted abstinence for at least three months; replacement of drinking behavior with other routines and activities.
Requirements for entry into Level Two:

1. What was once *compliance* with the program requirements is now seen as *surrender* to the therapeutic process, a *willingness* to change.
2. Completion of the first three steps of a self-help program. Selection of a "home group" in the recovery program of choice. Acknowledging to the peer group that one has begun listing all the harm one has caused, is making restitution, and is doing "depth work" into one's personality,
3. Maintains all treatment contracts made with the primary counselor or peer group.
4. Demonstrates positive and significant changes in self-care, shows care and respect toward others, and identifies effect of actions on self and others.
5. Assumes consequences for own actions. Can identify and complete corrective actions.

Phase or Level Three

Schedule.   Reduction to one night per week, 1½ to three hours in length. May be unstructured in the form of an aftercare group, or facilitated by clinicians in a structured format.

Goals. Evaluated as having both external and internal commitment to a substance-free lifestyle; has identified on-going treatment issues and has a plan for making changes; has made positive life changes socially, psychologically, and spiritually.

Outcomes expected before discharge from treatment:

1. Actively using community-based recovery and support groups; has begun after-care process.
2. Demonstrates an acceptance of self and others, of appropriate and inappropriate behaviors.
3. Has completed a relapse prevention education series or program.
4. Is volunteering to help others in the beginning phases of treatment. Has identified ways to be of service to family, community, and significant others.

PARTIAL HOSPITALIZATION AND DAY TREATMENT

Admission to a partial hospital setting requires the counselor to have the ability to determine the risk or presence of withdrawal symptoms as well as serious, debilitating mental health conditions, and risk of continuing relapse. If clients have sufficient disturbances in their family and work lives, and insufficient social support to maintain recovery or abstinence, it is likely they will meet criteria for *partial hospitalization* or *day treatment*. Scales for determining the appropriateness of day treatment specify criteria for admission and what are considered the necessary elements of partial care. These are similar to the questions asked at admission into intensive outpatient. To conduct a differential assessment, counselors need to determine the following:

1. **What is the current or presenting problem? Duration?** The problem may represent a recent crisis, but the individual gives little or no history of similar difficulties. If this current problem is representative of a chronic or long-term condition, then it is likely the counselor would not use day treatment. If the long-term condition appears to be one of a dual-diagnosis, then partial hospitalization in the psychiatric setting might be appropriate.

In the context of substance use, if the counselor determines that there is no presenting need for medical stabilization that would require inpatient care, or that the client is not significantly toxic enough to need detox, then partial care may be acceptable.

2. **What are the observable, disruptive behaviors?** The current behaviors may be disruptive, but the client is showing almost no psychotic features. The acting-out behavior is manageable within the daycare structure and clinical support provided by trained staff.

3. **What is the suicide or homicide potential?** This is a question always asked at any stage of treatment or admission into any setting. It is particularly impor-

tant in the partial-care setting. The counselor must determine the risk of imminent danger to self or others, and that the risk is either low-level or absent.

Often, substance abusing clients have suicidal ideation present, but they have made no recent attempts and have no specific plan. The assessment of ideation or harm will need to be related to recent episodes of the drug-affected condition so the counselor can make a reliable evaluation. If the client is assessed as capable of maintaining self-preservation during this time of crisis, and support is readily available, then the partial hospital setting is considered.

4. What is the previous six months' pattern of alcohol and other drug involvement? The client may report no recent history of substance use but may present as being a high risk for relapse. Recent onset—sudden or gradual—of deterioration in life/coping skills can often lead to relapse and self-medication.

The client may indicate that there has been episodic use within the past six months, and that it is caused or aggravated by changes in life situation, such as employment, divorce, or illness. There is recent evidence of psychological reliance on one or more chemical substances, and the degree of physical dependence present is mild to moderate, not acute. However, if the client's use is chronic with indications of high tolerance to the drug of choice, and there is clear evidence of loss of control, it is unlikely that partial care will be an appropriate setting.

5. How does the counselor assess the system's and/or member's motivation? Partial-care clients need adequate motivation to remain in treatment. If they are ambivalent, but the family or employer is highly motivated and can exert sufficient pressure, the setting is workable. However, if the current situation is a crisis, and all parties demonstrate minimal motivation, another setting must be considered.

6. What is the support system and living situation? If the clients live in emotionally supportive environments, even though they may live alone, partial care can be a supportive adjunct to their social network.

7. What is the means of transportation? Clients must be able to drive or take public transportation daily. Or they can arrange to get a consistent ride and can rely on that transportation for periods of time, such as four to six weeks.

If day treatment is in a setting that has medical consultation and supervision, for instance a psychiatric hospital, it will have a different appearance than treatment within a community-based, nonhospital residential program. The medical model may have an supervising therapist who is a psychiatrist or psychologist, but client's primary counselor will be a trained counselor. Day treatment often has a multidisciplinary team overseeing the program services and the direct management of the clients. Nursing staff and on-site regular observation may be required, particularly in settings where clients have psychiatric disorders (see Figure 5.1 on p. 162).

In the residential, nonmedical facility, the "attending" may be a trained therapist or addictions counselor, or both. Nursing staff may be available during all hours of operation in case of emergencies, but not be on-site daily. The treatment team may direct program design and services, but not manage the client on a daily or direct basis. It may oversee all client care and assure quality programming, but not be directly responsible for the client's treatment. Medications may be monitored depending on the disciplines of the staff members and the philosophy of the program. It is incumbent upon the referring counselor to thoroughly research the particular model and setting before directing clients to day treatment.

HALFWAY HOUSE

Within the halfway house (HWH) setting, the resident's daily routine is a part of the treatment activity. Successful living within that environment becomes a part of the treatment plan. Managing daily functions becomes, as part of the therapeutic setting, a participatory exercise for all residents, and often counselors as well.

In the early development of HWHs, it was expected that staff and clients were treated equally and democratically, and that both would participate in all social situations and functions. In the 1950s, the purpose of a HWH was to support alcoholics in the early stages of recovery who needed food, shelter, and a sober social support. This indicated more of a "family" or boarding house atmosphere. Residents were made up of recovering "counselors" and recovering residents, all in different stages of recovery. The supportive relationship was not identified as "client-counselor" in the way it is now. The model has evolved to a more "benevolently authoritarian" structure with more clearly delineated staff-patient boundaries.

HWHs have continued to evolve in the area of their client population. Even in the early 1970s, most HWHs would not admit residents who were taking psychiatric medications, or who had a primary diagnosis of a mental disorder with alcoholism secondary. Rarely would they accept a client who had a primary drug dependence problem, even if the alcoholism was concomitant. Halfway houses for recovering drug addicts were clearly separate from those assisting alcoholics. Client populations were never intermingled.

By the 1990s, the admission criteria had altered to meet the ever-changing profile of the substance abuser. A new resident may have completed some intensive treatment program as opposed to just having detoxified before self-referring. A prospective resident would be less often denied admission on the basis of having a drug problem, although the primary presenting problem most typically needed to be an alcohol abuse. Drug issues could be secondary. Some medications were allowed, primarily the milder anti-depressants, Antabuse, and/or Lithium. Most clients on other medications who might need medical supervision were referred to mental health clinics and elsewhere.

The common model for a HWH setting is best described in literature from the Johnson Institute in Minnesota (Stuckey & Harrison, 1982). Many state health departments publish, for the public, manuals for the licensing of facilities. In those manuals are more detailed descriptions of treatment models and required elements.

Elements common to halfway house setting:

1. It is a transitional living facility for people who have completed primary treatment in another modality or setting.

2. It provides a supportive environment with the primary emphasis on social rehabilitation.

3. It services a population not completely prepared to re-enter the community, and it assists in making a successful transition.

4. It accepts clients who require removal from a high-risk environment, but do not need intensive medical or psychiatric services.

5. It has an informal atmosphere, thus easing transition from primary care to community-based support systems.

6. The length of stay is significantly longer than inpatient, short-term intensive, or day treatment, particularly for those with no environmental advantages or social supports.

7. Staff is identified as "paraprofessional," most often recovering alcoholics.

8. The HWH emphasis is on returning to work, re-entering the social system, and becoming contributing members of the community.

9. There is always a strong link with 12-step programs; often a required activity.

10. The HWH maintains a referral system for medical, psychiatric, and psychological services; these are not provided on-site.

Today, there is an emerging need for transitional care between the halfway house setting and reintegration into the community. For the later-stage alcoholic and drug abuser, this is particularly crucial in preventing relapse. This has resulted in the emergence of the three-quarter way house (TQH).

A TQH is funded primarily by the residents themselves, although most must have predictable income in the way of public or private funding to support routine operating costs. The setting is usually a community-based home or a building next to a residential facility. Residents need the limited safe and supportive structure of a transitional living arrangement, but need less social support and less monitoring of recovery. They most often are working and have some history of maintaining employment, or they are in vocational rehabilitation and able to function independently.

RESIDENTIAL AND INPATIENT PROGRAMS

A typical residential facility can be similar to a therapeutic community in setting and rules. Otherwise, they can be quite different and serve the needs of a different clientele. They both offer a structured and supportive environment, the latter being defined differently in settings such as the community-based residential facility and the hospital-based inpatient modality. Similarly, and in contrast to the therapeutic community, residential and inpatient programs provide the following:

1. Protection from the effects of drinking and drugging behavior on self and others.
2. Support in dealing with the physical, mental, emotional, and social consequences of habitual and excessive use.
3. Temporary cessation from a chaotic or turbulent family and social system which, by its negative influence, inhibits the individual's beginning recovery and creates a high risk for relapse.
4. Evaluation for those in need of intensive diagnostic services to differentiate between those symptoms attributable to chemical dependency and those attributable to psychiatric illness.
5. A safe environment in which to assess and monitor serious emotional problems (Johnson, Wanberg, Carducci, & Manfrin, 1987).

All residential programs have rules. The number of rules and the consequences will vary, particularly when seen in relation to those in the therapeutic community setting. All consider deliberate rule violations a serious matter, one which should be handled at the level of the treatment team or peer group. As rules are specifically geared to patient/client safety and well-being, violations of the rules is seen as "jeopardizing the welfare and treatment of all residents" (Johnson, Wanberg, Carducci, & Manfrin, 1987). Upon a serious infraction, the client may be discharged from the program and allowed to return only when she or he offers behavioral evidence of more honesty and an open frame of mind; states to staff that "I am ready," indicating a state of willingness; and signs a contractual agreement with the program to concede to organizational structure or community values.

In all residential settings, counselors and clients know there are immediate consequences to serious infractions of program rules. A common consequence is discharge from the facility. Not all addictions counselors support the conviction, however, that immediate termination from the setting is a therapeutic consequence. Regardless, facilities must provide patient handbooks to all residents that outline the more serious violations such as:

1. Use/possession of drugs or alcohol either on or off the premises.
2. Abusive behavior, threats, or physical violence toward anyone.
3. Sexual activity or any inappropriate physical contact.
4. Absence without permission from the facility or assigned groups.
5. Patient is not in control of own behavior, refuses to accept the agreed-upon consequences, and may be a danger to self or others.
6. A deliberate effort to not cooperate, or to interfere with or inhibit the work of others in recovery.

Residential programs also have requirements that are atypical of partial hospital *psychiatric* programs, but are expected in the substance abuse milieu. These include, but are not limited to, the following:

Abstinence. Few programs endorse or attempt to teach controlled drinking as a treatment outcome, thus abstinence from all chemicals at all times is the standard.

Drug screens. Usually taken at random, and always after passes off a unit. Consequences have been announced to patients as part of the regulations they agree to when entering the setting, and carrying out of those consequences is both a team and unit issue.

Medications. All are turned in for medical or team review, counting, and to prevent other patients from self-medicating. This includes vitamins. Self-medicating is a behavior.

Diversions. Radio, TV, or anything that might deter focusing on treatment issues is discouraged, often strictly prohibited, although this prohibition has not been an entirely proven positive element.

Interaction. Disclosing one's family, drug, and related history to others may be a program requirement. It is often incumbent upon the assigned counselor to monitor the frequency of interaction with other residents, the type of interaction, and the purpose.

Participation. Active engagement with elements of the program is encouraged in some settings, mandatory in others.

THERAPEUTIC COMMUNITIES

The therapeutic community is a structured residential treatment, long-term, and highly intense. It has a broad goal of social and life skills rehabilitation as well as drug addiction recovery. This highly structured design evolved from treating addicts with significant psychosocial deficits and histories of criminal behavior, as well as poor impulse control and low levels of self-concept.

The first therapeutic community in the United States was Synanon, started in California in 1958 (Straussner, 1993). Similar to the inpatient residential model, it is highly structured, intensely supervised, and relies heavily on a strong peer culture. Most of the counselors are recovering addicts, and "graduates" of the community often stay on in the capacity of senior peer, counselor, or adviser. Because one of its common goals is to re-socialize the addict, it is usually a long-term living arrangement with extremely limited connections outside the community for the first six months of residency.

While the free-standing residential facility is suitable for the alcoholic, it is not as successful for high-dose, high-frequency drug users who have had severe psychological, social, and legal deterioration (Wallace, 1992). These users often have long-standing, habitual chemical-use patterns with problematic attitudes, poor impulse control, insufficient internal controls, and a history of negative behaviors ranging from domestic violence, theft, drug sales and distribution, and habitual legal entanglements. They are also victims of multiple stressors, including family members who use and sell drugs, housing problems, unemployment, broken homes, and drug- and crime-saturated neighborhoods. The therapeutic community developed as a safe haven for those with even a minimum of motivation toward rehabilitation.

Therapeutic communities share the following elements:

1. They are drug-free and have a code of strictly supervised abstinence.

2. Heavy confrontation about attitudes and behaviors is commonplace.

3. The emphasis is on peer self-help and daily role modeling by peers.

4. Residents actively participate in *all* responsibilities and functions; no treatment is "optional."

5. Counseling and treatment outcomes include personal accountability and socially responsible behavior.

6. Residents ultimately share a common belief, a pro-social value system emphasizing re-socialization and rehabilitation.

7. The community expectation of the individual and the group is the maintenance of a strong commitment to the treatment environment, its customs, and its culture.

8. There is a continual stream of feedback and self-disclosing.

9. Punishments and assignments are routine, as are immediate consequences for behaviors.

10. The treatment focus is on *current* behaviors, recognition and acknowledgment of personal motivations, and a minimum of blaming on one's past or family of origin.

11. The setting has a strict rule of limited access to family and friends during early treatment (Biase, 1985; Frances & Sheldon, 1991; L'Abate, Farrar, & Serritella, 1992; Sullivan & Biase, 1988; Wallace, 1992).

The staffing design of most residential and hospital-based programs is considered multidisciplinary. Under accreditation standards and recommendations, a multidisciplinary team is one in which several health professionals work with the patient and family during the inpatient stay. This staff is ultimately responsible for monitoring patient care during the entire inpatient stay, help family members make necessary decisions, provide direct services such as face-to-face counseling, and develop discharge and aftercare plans.

Attending Physician or Provider

In a medical/hospital setting, the physician, psychologist, or other approved mental health professional who "attends" the patient's stay, is responsible for approving course and methods of treatment, and will assume dispensing or monitoring of correct medications; credentialed by the hospital medical staff.

Medical Director

Typically, an addictions-trained physician who oversees the delivery of services in the unit; not necessarily a direct provider of patient care; assumes general supervision of the nursing staff; occasionally directly involved with addictions counselors directly assigned to patient care.

Nursing Staff

Generally responsible for day-to-day patient care; often 24-hour per day on site or directly supervising nonmedical unit staff members; will help determine program procedures, patient care, treatment, and discharge planning.

Social Worker

Will provide required transition, discharge, or placement planning; will assure all record documentation meets standards; often has a portion of his or her time allocated from the social services department to the C/D unit; not required to be "addictions certified." Will conduct assessments and make treatment recommendations. Often not the primary counselor or assigned therapist.

Mental Health Workers

Mental health professionals trained in the delivery of general mental health and counseling services; not typically the primary provider or attending practitioner; assist in treatment planning, conducting education portions of the IP milieu, co-facilitating, activity, therapy, or skill-building groups; on Dual Diagnosis units, need not be certified in addictions treatment.

Certified Substance Abuse or Addictions Specialists; or, Primary-Care Counselors

In a medical facility, a member of the treatment team under the direction of the attending practitioner; certified by the state as a trained counselor in the field of addictive disorders. In residential, nonmedical setting, often the primary counselor/therapist directly responsible for clinical care, treatment planning, education sessions, group treatment, and aftercare planning. In residential, free-standing units, may be a recovering individual with no primary or advanced degrees, but with technical, approved training in the field of substance abuse treatment.

Clinical Director

Generally a trained, advanced-degree mental health professional who is a certified or licensed addictions specialist; oversees the delivery of clinical care to patient and significant others; may directly provide group and specialty services, such as CD education, couples' group therapy, multifamily therapy, and so on; supervises primary counseling staff; if advanced in training, may supervise all medical and clinical functions.

FIGURE 5.1   Inpatient and Partial Hospital Modalities: Common Staffing Patterns

EVALUATING THE SETTING: WHAT DETERMINES
THE DESIGN OF A PROGRAM?

A treatment program cannot be designed in a vacuum, nor can one be selected for a client without the counselor knowing precisely what type of client is entering the system. State health departments publish annual demographics for public use. Program managers are strongly encouraged to review those statistics, match the client profile with the services offered within the program, and regularly modify the design. In theory, this assures that demographics are considered when treatment programs are designed. It is irresponsible to select a treatment setting for a client without reasonable knowledge of client characteristics, patterns of use, and type of drug use patterns within each geographic area. To even begin selecting intervention and treatment approaches for a client requires that the counselor have some knowledge of the treatment population. The population changes regularly, and reviewing health department data is necessary to providing appropriate and effective services.

Self-Help Groups

Counselor effectiveness can be increased by knowing and understanding the tenets of 12-step, 12-tradition programs, Rational Recovery, and the many self-help groups available to recovering individuals (see Appendix at the end of the chapter). Self-help resources are also sponsored by churches, community organizations, treatment programs, and mental health centers. The basic principles of these organizations and groups are increasingly more common in every modality and setting. Being able to relate to and identify the tools of recovery within those programs is important in effectively treating the substance abusing client, because it gives the counselor an indication of strengths the client will be able to draw on in the recovery process. It also simplifies the therapeutic process by reducing a great deal of psychological jargon to some simple, easy-to-remember slogans, affirmations, and tenets. Whether a mental health specialist is an advocate of those particular self-help groups or not, being familiar with its principles can significantly enhance the counselor's approach and treatment outcomes. A sample of slogans in Figure 5.2 is taken from the most common self-help printed materials.

1. Stay away from the first drink/drug/person/behavior.
2. Use the 24-hour plan.
3. Incurable, progressive, fatal.
4. Live and let live.
5. Become involved.
6. Problems are common to all.
7. Change routines.
8. Nutrition, exercise, and rest; caring for the body as well as the soul.
9. Use the telephone.
10. Choose positive actions.
11. Correct the events of the past; restitution and amends.
12. Follow the directions.
13. First things first.
14. You are not alone.
15. Remove self-pity.
16. Seek professional help.
17. Adversity is opportunity.
18. Relate to others in an honest and sincere manner.
19. The answers are within.
20. Keep spiritually active.
21. Detachment.
22. Keep an open mind. Think!
23. Suspend judgment of self and others.
24. Be responsible for your actions; thought produces action.
25. Guard individuals' right to think, talk, and act as they see fit in accordance with their own values and principles.
26. Relapse prevention is the cornerstone of continuing sobriety.

FIGURE 5.2　Self-Help Slogans

REFERENCES

Anderson, D. (1981). *Perspectives on treatment: The Minnesota experience*. Center City, MN: Hazelden Foundation Publications.

Biase, D. V. (1985, June). Daytop miniversity: A multi-year therapeutic community treatment project fund report. Baltimore: National Institute of Drug Abuse, No. r-18 DA 03382.

Frances, R. J., & Sheldon, I. M. (1991). *Clinical textbook of addictive disorders*. New York: The Guilford Press.

Hayashida, M., Alterman, A. I., McLellan, A. T., O'Brien, C. P., Purtill, J. J., Volpicalli, J. R., Raphaalson, A. H., & Hall, C. P. (1989). Comparative Affectiveness and cost of inpatients and outpatients with mild-to-moderate alcohol withdrawal syndrome. *New England Journal of Medicine, 320*(6), 358–365.

Hospital Council of Southern California (1988). *Model criteria for adult inpatient and intensive outpatient dependency treatment*. Los Angeles: Author.

Johnson, J., Wanberg, K., Carducci, R., & Manfrin, C. J. (1987). Chemical Dependency Program Manual. Denver, CO: Horizon Hospital.

Koenigsberg, H. W., Kaplan, R. D., Gilmore, M. M., & Cooper, A.M.. (1985). The relationship between syndrome and personality disorder in DSM-III: Experience with 2,462 patients. *American Journal of Psychiatry (142)*2.

L'Abate, L., Farrar, J. E., & Serritella, D. A., (Eds.). (1992). *Handbook of differential treatments for addictions*. Boston: Allyn and Bacon.

Laundergan, J. (1982). *Easy does it: Alcohol treatment outcomes, Hazelden and the Minnesota model*. Minneapolis, MN: Hazelden Foundation.

Ohio Department of Health. (1987). The Cleveland admission, discharge, & transfer criteria: A model for chemical dependency treatment. Cleveland: Author.

Straussner, S. L. A. (Ed.). (1993). *Clinical work with substance-abusing clients*. New York, NY: The Guilford Substance Abuse Series, Guilford Press.

Stuckey, R. F., & Harrison, J. S. (1982). The alcoholism rehabilitation center. In *Encyclopedic Handbook of Alcoholism*. New York: Gardner Press.

Sullivan, A., & Biase, D. V. (1988). *Daytop therapeutic community concept at the quarter century mark*. New York: Daytop, Inc., Department of Research and Development.

Wallace, B. C. (Ed.). (1992). *The chemically dependent: Phases of treatment and recovery*. New York: Brunner/Mazel Publishers, Inc.

Weiner, N. (1991). *Handbook for Detoxification and Stabilization*. Denver, CO: Author.

Weiner, N., Johnson, J., & Manfrin, C. (1991). Alcohol and drug manual for Bethesda PsycHealth. Denver: Bethesda PsycHealth.

Appendix: 12-Step, 12-Tradition Groups

Alcoholics Anonymous (AA)
Central Office: Box 459, Grand Central Station, New York, NY 10163
Directories available for U.S., Canada, and International

Al-Anon and Alateen
Central office: Al-Anon Family Group, P.O. Box 182, Madison Square Station, New York, NY 10010
Directories available for U.S., Canada, and International

Adult Children of Alcoholics (ACoA)
P.O. Box 3216, Torrance, CA 90510. (213) 534-1815

Cocaine Anonymous (CA)
Central office: P.O. Box 1367, Culver City, CA 90239
Also listed: 6125 Washington Blvd, No. 202, Los Angeles, CA 90230. (213) 559-5833

Codependents Anonymous (CoDA)
P.O. Box 33577, Phoenix, AZ 85067-3577. (602) 277-7991

Codependents of Sex Addicts (CoSA)
Central office: P.O. Box 14537, Minneapolis, MN 55414. (612) 537-6904

Co-Dependents of Sex/Love Addicts Anonymous (Co-SLAA)
P.O. Box 614, Brookline, MA 02146-9998

Debtors Anonymous (DA)
P.O. Box 20322, New York, NY 10025-9992. (212) 642-8222

Drugs Anonymous (DA)
P.O. Box 473, Ansonia Station, New York, NY 10023. (212) 874-0700

Emotional Health Anonymous (EHA)
P.O. Box 429, Glendale, CA 91209. (818) 240-3215

Emotions Anonymous
P.O. Box 4245, St. Paul, MN 55104. (612) 647-9712

Gamblers Anonymous (GA)
Central office: P.O. Box 17173, Los Angeles, CA 90017. (213) 386-8789
Directories available for U.S., Europe, and Australia

Gam-Anon Family Groups
P.O. Box 157, Whitestone, NY 11358

Incest Survivor's Anonymous (ISA)
P.O. Box 5613, Long Beach, CA 90805-0613. (213) 428-5599
National organization: (213) 422-1632

Narcotics Anonymous (NA)
P.O. Box 9999, Van Nuys, CA 91409. (818) 780-3951

Nar-Anon Family Group
P.O. Box 2562, Palos Verdes, CA 90274-0119. (213) 547-5800

Nicotine Anonymous (formerly Smokers' Anonymous)
2118 Greenwich Street, San Francisco, CA 94123. (415) 922-8575

O-Anon Family Group (Family Group for OA)
P.O. Box 4305, San Pedro, CA 90731

Overeaters Anonymous (OA)
Central office: 2190 190th Street, Torrance, CA 90504
Also listed: P.O. Box 92870, Los Angeles, CA 90009. (800) 743-8703

Parents Anonymous (use volunteer professionals as resources)
6733 S. Sepulveda Blvd., No. 270, Los Angeles, CA 90045. (800) 421-0353

Pill Addicts Anonymous
P.O. Box 278, Reading, PA 19603. (215) 372-1128

S-Anon (patterned after Al-Anon)
P.O. Box 5117, Sherman Oaks, CA 91913.
(818) 990-6910

Sex Addicts Anonymous (SAA)
Central office: P.O. Box 3038, Minneapolis, MN
55403. (612) 339-0217

Sex and Love Addicts Anonymous (SLAA)
Central office: P.O. Box 529, Newton, MA
02258
Also listed: P.O. Box 119, New Town Branch,
Boston, MA 02258. (617) 332-1845

SexAholics Anonymous (SAA)
Central office: P.O. Box 300, Simi Valley, CA
93062. (818) 704-9854

Sexual Compulsives Anonymous (SCA)
P.O. Box 1585, Old Chelsea Station, New York,
NY 10011. (212) 439-1123

Survivors of Incest Anonymous (SIA)
World service: P.O. Box 21817, Baltimore, MD
21222

Workaholics Anonymous
P.O. Box 661501, Los Angeles, CA 90066.
(310) 859-5804
Note: *Central office* and *World service* are terms
used to identify central locations for national
and international information.

Treatment Modalities in Substance Abuse

PATRICIA STEVENS-SMITH, PH.D.

This chapter will examine the treatment modalities used to work with substance abusers and individuals who are dependent on substances. Of course, some factors vary from setting to setting. If a program or setting is basically an alcohol treatment facility, then the use of methadone maintenance will not be of interest to the administrators or participants. Some programs have detox facilities, some do not. Also, as in every aspect of the mental health field, the theoretical basis on which the program is grounded will in many ways determine the components used in treatment.

The biopsychosociofamilial model of the etiology of substance use is an effective treatment model. Anecdotal as well as empirical research substantiates that the use of substances interferes with every aspect of an individual's life. It seems reasonable, therefore, that a treatment program would endeavor to incorporate every aspect of the individual's life in the solution.

It is beyond the scope of this chapter to provide a thorough review of each theory or model presented; rather, the purpose of this chapter is to introduce you to the modalities of treatment that appear to be most effective with substance abusers. A collaborative framework of therapy appears to result in the highest rate of success. This framework includes individual work, group work, and family work. Therefore, aspects of each of these modalities will be discussed. Before treatment can begin, however, the individual must be engaged in the therapeutic process.

GETTING THE INDIVIDUAL INTO TREATMENT

For any type of treatment to be successful, the individual must stop using any substances. Therefore, the first order of business in treatment is to interrupt the substance using behaviors (Lewis, Dana, & Blevins, 1994). This may be a voluntary process whereby the individual has reached the point he or she decides that change is necessary, or an employer, spouse, or significant other may demand action.

Coercive versus Voluntary Treatment

Much has been said about the influence of motivation in recovery. Is motivation present when users are coerced into treatment rather than voluntarily choosing to stop their substance use? Note that the term *voluntary* may be a misnomer. Individuals who are substance abusers or are substance dependent will often continue to use in spite of the consequences. It is only under intense external pressure to address the issue of use that treatment might be considered. This may come in the form of family intervention, legal intervention, employment intervention, or medical intervention.

Court-ordered treatment usually occurs after the individual is arrested for a drug-related charge such as driving under the influence or possession of an illegal chemical substance. The judge may offer treatment as an alternative to incarceration. Court-ordered intervention can be a powerful motivation for treatment (Moylan, 1990). Studies indicate that individuals who are court-ordered into treatment do as well or better than those who come to treatment "voluntarily" (Collins & Alison, 1983; Matuschka, 1985).

Another form of coercive intervention is through employers. Many times the user's job will be in jeopardy if the substance use is not discontinued. An "either/or" ultimatum is given: Either you go to treatment or lose your job. In a 1989 study of alcoholics, Adelman and Weiss found that employees coerced into treatment actually had *better* outcomes than those who entered voluntarily.

Other forms of coercive intervention come from the spouse or significant other or the medical profession. The loved one may also offer an "either/or" situation, in which either the individual enters treatment or the relationship ends. In some states, substance abusers can be involuntarily committed by medical professionals. In such a case, there must be sufficient evidence of imminent harm to self or others. However, *harm to self* may be defined as neglect or when the chemical use puts the client or others at risk.

Intervention: Voluntary or Coercive?

One method of confronting an individual about substance abuse problems is called intervention. This process was pioneered by V. E. Johnson of the Johnson Institute. He defines *intervention* as a:

. . . process by which the harmful, progressive, and destructive effects of chemical dependency are interrupted and the chemically dependent person is helped to stop using mood-altering chemicals, and to develop new, healthier ways of coping with his or her needs and problems. (Johnson Institute, 1987, p. 61)

This process involves all the significant others in the substance abuser's life. This may include spouse/significant other, children, siblings, parents, friends, supervisors and co-workers, minister, medical professionals and any other support people in the person's life. The planning and completion of an intervention is usually performed under the supervision of a substance abuse counselor who is trained in the process of intervention.

The purpose of an intervention is to get the abuser to look at the rationalizations, denial, and projection (or externalization of blame) they are using to justify the substance use. The result of an intervention is, ideally, the individual's agreement to seek immediate treatment (Doweiko, 1993). Interventions should be structured to let the substance abusers know they are cared for but that there are limits or consequences to their continued substance use.

Individuals involved in an intervention "break the silence" concerning the individual's substance abusing behaviors. It is important to have many significant people involved in the intervention. Anyone who has ever tried to challenge a substance abuser one on one knows the frustration and power of the abuser's excuses, rationalizations, projection, and denial. Each person should bring specific situations or incidents involving the abuser to the intervention. With a group of people present at the intervention, it becomes difficult for the abuser to manipulate the facts of any situation.

Remember that the purpose of the intervention is not to confront the individual with negative behaviors. It is an act of caring for the substance abuser and for the people involved with the abuser (Johnson Institute, 1987). It is a place where significant others can address their feelings about the person's chemical use (Twerski, 1983). The purpose of the intervention is to break through the individual's denial and to have the person accept the need for immediate treatment (Doweiko, 1993; Johnson Institute, 1987; Williams, 1989).

Interventions should be supervised by a substance abuse counselor who is trained in this treatment technique. They should be planned and rehearsed before the actual intervention. Individuals participating in the intervention should be clear as to the purpose of the intervention. Additionally, these individuals should know how they will respond if the substance abuser refuses treatment. They may choose to detach from the person, for example. Detachment may take many forms, such as excluding the person from family functions, refusing to give the individual money, and divorce. For the employer it may mean putting the person on leave or firing him or her. The medical professional may choose to seek involuntary commitment.

Any of these actions should be well thought out before the intervention begins. Any consequence will be difficult and should not be thought of as punishment for the substance abuser or as a way to manipulate the person into seeking treatment. It is, rather, an alternative behavior for significant others when the abuser denies treatment and "an opportunity for healing" (Meyer, 1988, p. 7). The abuser obviously has the choice to seek treatment or not; similarly, the significant others can choose whether to continue to engage with the individual who continues chemical use.

Ethical and Legal Concerns of Intervention

In today's litigious society, it behooves the substance abuse counselor to move carefully. Rothenburg (1988) addresses the need for a diagnosis of substance dependency before an intervention begins. Should this be an independent diagnosis? Are there legal sanctions for a counselor who supervises an intervention without this diagnosis? (Doweiko, 1993). As there are no precedent cases, this question has not been answered in a court of law.

The individual's right to leave at any time may also be a legal as well as ethical question. Should the substance abuser be informed that he or she has the right to leave at any time? What might be the legal difficulties if this information is not provided?

Counselors need to be aware of the ethical and legal implications of these situations and others that may emerge. Because interventions are, by their nature, high-stress activities, clear rules or action should be established and agreed on beforehand. The substance abuser should be made aware of his or her rights and responsibilities in this situation.

Once the individual decides to enter treatment, no matter which path that is taken, treatment should engage all aspects of the individual's life—the individual, the family, and the sociocultural milieu. Types of treatment should be complementary and coordinated to best serve the client.

INDIVIDUAL THERAPY

A variety of treatment approaches can be used in therapy with substance abusers. These include *cognitive-behavioral therapy,* (Lesser, 1976; Ulmer, 1977; Emick & Aarons, 1990), *reality therapy* (Schuster, 1978–1979), *aversion therapy* (Miller, 1990), and *social skills training* (Emick & Aarons, 1990; Lewis, Dana, & Blevins, 1994). There is no empirical research that indicates that one theory or model is more effective than any other theory or model or under what conditions one theory or model may be more effective than another (Schilit & Gomberg, 1991).

It appears, however, that in the early stages of recovery, the tasks that need to be accomplished seem to respond best to the cognitive-behavioral schools of thought. With prolonged recovery, many of the other more insight-oriented models work in conjunction with the cognitive-behavioral models. The therapist's job in early recovery is to act as a coach in these behavioral strategies for abstinence. Another important responsibility is to assist in the establishment of structure. Since recovering individuals are usually not as intact as they appear on the surface, establishment of structure is vital to continued recovery (Yalom, 1995).

Miller and Hester (1986a) reviewed controlled studies and found that the most effective strategies or models fell into two categories: direct-effect strategies and broad spectrum strategies.

Direct-Effect Strategies

The first category has a direct effect on the discontinuation of chemical use. Three therapies that appear to be effective are aversion therapy, behavioral self-control training, and medication.

Aversion therapy is designed to help an individual lose the desire to perform a particular act, in this case, use chemical substances. This therapy has the longest history in the field and has been used most frequently with alcoholics. Several different aversion approaches have been used. Electric shock, nausea-producing drugs, and covert sensitization. Neither electric shock nor nausea-producing drugs have consistent positive outcome results (Cannon, Baker, Gino, & Nathan, 1986). The reported outcome results with alcoholics appear modestly positive, but the results are unclear due to the lack of controlled studies (Baker & Cannon, 1979; Blake, 1965). There are also no substantiated studies with drug abusers showing positive results using electrical or chemical aversion therapy (Lesser, 1976; Lieberman, 1969; Wolpe, 1965). However, covert sensitization using imagery appears to produce positive effects (Miller, 1985; Rimmele, Miller, & Dougher, 1990).

In some studies using covert sensitization techniques it is suggested that conditioned nausea responses can occur and that subjects (about 69% of those treated) who develop these responses maintain significant periods of abstinence (Elkins, 1975, 1980). Again, there are no controlled studies using covert sensitization with drug abusers, but positive outcomes have been shown in single-subject studies with drug-free periods of up to 18 months (Palakow, 1975; Wisocki, 1973).

This technique is used in conjunction with other interventions and is simple to use. It is based on the desensitization techniques developed by Wolpe (1965). Counselors train individuals in relaxation and then have them imagine aversive scenes that include the use of chemicals. Scenes of nausea, vomiting, sweats, cramps, and so on are paired with the smell, sight, and taste of the drug. Repetition of this pairing results in conditioned aversion to the chemical.

Covert sensitization and imagery is easy for clients to learn and use when they think they might begin using again. It can also be tailored to individual drug use, particular patterns of behaviors, and environment (Lewis, Dana, & Blevins, 1994).

Behavioral self-control training teaches clients a variety of self-regulating techniques to modify their chemical use patterns (Miller, 1990). Recognizing, analyzing, and monitoring situations that the individual associates with chemical use is imperative in recovery. As these situations are identified, individuals can develop coping strategies that maintain recovery. Coping strategies need to be both cognitive and behavioral. Cognitive strategies include self-statements and alternative planning. Behavioral techniques include relaxation training, assertive training, covert sensitization, and the use of alternatives behaviors such as exercise.

The third technique in this category is the use of medication. The most commonly used drug in the treatment of alcoholism is disulfiram (Antabuse). If this drug is taken regularly, individuals will become violently ill when they drink alcohol. There are other significant physical effects possible from the combination of disulfiram and alcohol that should be communicated the individual when the drug is prescribed, such as seizures, high fever, nausea, and possible death. Also, initial monitoring by medical personnel is recommended. Studies show compliance when the drug is taken regularly and indicate that the drug is effective in working with couples (involving the significant other or spouse as a monitor) (Azrin, Sisson, Meyers, & Godley, 1982).

The use of methadone with heroin addicts is another example of medication as treatment. Methadone mimics the production of endorphins in the body, producing a feeling of satisfaction without the high of heroin. Once methadone has occupied these receptor sites, subsequent heroin or morphine produces no psychoactive effects. It also occupies these receptor sites much longer than heroin or morphine. Methadone must be administered under the supervision of a medical professional. Therefore, the individual is required to come to a treatment facility to receive a daily dose. Tolerance does develop and therefore withdrawal symptoms will appear if the drug is stopped all at once. For these reasons, methadone use has been criticized as simply trading one addiction for another. It is, however, a medication that can be used as an adjunct to other treatment modalities. Or in the case of repeated relapses, it is possible to place an individual on a long-term methadone maintenance program.

Broad-Spectrum Strategies

The second category of strategies falls under what Miller & Hester (1986a) term *broad spectrum strategies*. These strategies include social skills training, stress management, marital therapy, and the community reinforcement approach (Azrin, Sisson, Meyers, & Godley, 1982). These strategies focus on life problems and circumstances rather than on the discontinuation of the chemical use. The purpose of these strategies to help the individual learn to cope with situations and circumstances that elicit the chemical use. The discontinuation of the substance is a secondary goal.

Social skills training, or assertiveness training, is well established as a successful strategy in the treatment of substance abuse (Chaney, O'Leary, & Marlatt, 1978; Ferrell & Galassi, 1981; Monti, Abrams, Kadden, & Cooney, 1989). Many substance abusing individuals failed to learn social skills and may report that the use of the substance "eases the way" in social situations. Still others may have lost their social skills through many years of substance use. In either case, re-learning assertiveness and social skill behaviors is an important concept in learning coping mechanisms to avoid substance use. Monti, Abrams, Kadden, & Cooney (1989) list a variety of social skills to be taught in treatment, beginning with starting conversations to forming close and intimate relationships.

Social skills can be taught through modeling, role play, and demonstration. Various forms of these techniques are available in treatment. For example, other clients can be used as appropriate role models for specific behaviors. Audiotapes and video-tapes are also available for demonstration purposes and learning. Role play and role taking help the client to increase skills. (George, 1990).

Refusal skills and assertiveness training are closely related. "Assertion is the behavior or trait that allows people to appropriately express their personal rights and feelings" (Lewis, Dana, & Blevins, 1994, p. 115). Assertive training is most often practiced in the group setting. Being assertive means you can express thoughts and feelings in direct, honest, and appropriate ways. Being assertive means that you defend yourself when necessary and express your needs and wants. It also means, particularly for the substance abuser, that you identify situations in which you will need to be assertive in order not to resume substance use. Examining the illogical beliefs related to these situations, developing new strategies to cope with the situation, and practicing these strategies lead to new strength for the abuser (George, 1990).

Assertive behavior can be contrasted with other behavioral responses: aggression, passive-aggressive behavior, and passive behavior. Helping the client recognize assertive behavior as well as practice assertive responses is an important part of treatment. Assertive behavior increases self-esteem and personal power while decreasing feelings of self-pity, thereby decreasing the cues for substance use (Lewis, Dana, & Blevins, 1994).

Another skill necessary for clients to develop is the skill to refuse drugs and alcohol. Goldstein, Ragles, & Amann (1990) have a list of core skills they believe to be essential in the recovery process. These include asking for help, knowing your feelings, dealing with fear, dealing with being left out, responding to persuasion, and making a decision. The teaching model includes role playing, performance feedback, modeling, and transfer of this learning into real life situations.

Anxiety is often a precursor to substance use. Anxiety occurs through a combination of factors including social, environmental, cognitive, and affective components. Substance abusers usually manage anxiety through the use of their drug of choice. Learning to manage this anxiety through other means is an important individual consideration in treatment. Relaxation training is one mechanism for anxiety or stress management. Although relaxation does not facilitate resolution of the underlying problems, it is a way the client can deal with the outward aspects of stress (George, 1990). Relaxation is incompatible with anxiety. In other words, one cannot be anxious and relaxed at the same time. Therefore, it is an easy-to-use, positively reinforcing technique for clients that appears to yield long-term results of decreased substance use (Chaney, O'Leary, & Marlatt, 1978; Ferrell & Galassi, 1981; Lewis, Dana, & Blevins, 1994).

Progressive relaxation training methods teach individuals to tense and relax a particular set of muscles, then another and another, until the entire body is relaxed (Jacobsen, 1968). Audio tapes of relaxation techniques are also available for individual use. Imagery can also be used as part of the relaxation training. Relaxation and imagery are two strategies that the client can use easily after leaving treatment.

Community reinforcement approaches combine an assortment of strategies such as medication, marital therapy, and assistance with job searches. A program that uses a variety of methods appears to have the most effectiveness (Azrin, Sisson, Meyers, & Godley, 1982; Miller & Hester, 1986a) while traditional treatment approaches (educational films and lectures, medication, confrontational therapy, and AA) appear to be the least effective (Annis & Chan, 1983; Miller & Hester, 1986b; Powell, Penick, Read, & Ludwig, 1985). In spite of the availability of this outcome information, most treatment programs continue to use the traditional models. The reasons for this continuation remain a mystery. Perhaps it is associated with the plethora of recovering individuals in counseling positions in the field or rooted in the financial structure of the facilities.

Another individual strategy to be discussed is involvement in a self-help group, such as Alcoholics Anonymous, Narcotics Anonymous, Cocaine Anonymous, or Rational Recovery. Involvement in these groups is controversial and difficult to assess. These groups are easy to find and cost-effective. As a supplement to treatment, they are invaluable if the individual is motivated to participate. When individuals are forced to attend (as in some treatment programs) the result can be resistance and treatment failure (Lewis, Dana, & Belvins, 1994). There have been no empirical studies of outcome that do not have methodological flaws (Brandsma, Maultsby, & Welsh, 1980; Stimmel et al., 1983).

None of these self-help groups profess to be treatment groups. They were established as, and remain, support groups for recovering substance users. The need for support is a central issue in recovery. Self-help groups provide peer support; their members understand the feelings and problems faced by a recovering person. These groups confront when necessary and offer encouragement when it is needed (George, 1990). As such, they are an invaluable tool in treatment and recovery.

The last individual strategy or technique to be discussed is solution-focused, brief therapy. Much of our treatment planning today has become economically driven by managed-care systems. Managed care, insurance companies, employers, and other third-party providers have put limits on the number of sessions or amount of financial compensation available for care. Research indicates that the mean number of sessions attended by clients is between five and six.

Additionally, there is an increased competitive marketplace as more and more facilities offer treatment programs. It is wise to investigate techniques that are cost-efficient and effective. Numerous studies have shown no appreciable difference between short- and long-term treatment outcome. In fact, this research shows that alcohol abusing clients respond positively and rapidly to only minimal or brief intervention when treatment is "targeted, individualized, and focused" (Berg & Miller, 1992; Berg & Gallagher, 1991, Hester & Miller, 1989).

The steps in solution-focused brief therapy for substance abuse are outlined by Berg and Miller (1992):

1. Develop a cooperative client-therapist relationship

2. Develop "well-formed" treatment goals

3. Implementing goals

4. Interviewing for change

5. Delivering Treatment Interventions

6. Developing strategies for maintaining progress (p. v)

These six steps are, of course, built on the framework of solution-focused therapy. The emphasis is on the exception to the problem; in other words, how to strengthen and maintain those times when the individual was not using drugs. Client strengths, resources, and abilities are emphasized. This therapy also maintains that change is inevitable and that the therapist need only "tip the first domino" (Rossi, 1973, p. 14) to begin that change.

Solution-focused therapy is atheoretical and client-determined. This means that sessions are not devoted to figuring out why a problem exists. A client's view is accepted and the task of finding solutions begins immediately (Berg & Miller, 1992). Goals are measurable and attainable—which also suits managed-care requirements.

The central philosophy of solution-focused therapy is stated in three simple rules:

1. If it ain't broke, DON'T FIX IT!

2. When you know what works, DO MORE OF IT!

3. If it doesn't work, then don't do it again, DO SOMETHING DIFFERENT! (Berg & Miller, 1992, p. 17)

Obviously, the criticism of solution-focused brief therapy with substance abusers is the same as with other populations. Many believe it to be only a "band-aid" for the problems that clients bring to therapy. While some professionals believe that it discounts the immense pain that clients may have, others praise the embrace of strength and wellness that underlies this therapy. Solution-focused therapy is an alternative to the traditional means to this end.

In summary, individual therapy may take many forms. As with all therapy, it is based on the unique problems and situations presented by the individual. The underlying goal of therapy with this population, however, is the minimization of, or at best the discontinuation of, the use of chemical substances to cope with life. Whether one believes in the moral model, the disease model, or the biopsychosocial model, increasing the individual's healthy coping skills will help the individual toward this goal.

GROUP THERAPY

Group therapy traditionally has been the most popular form of treatment for substance abusers. Whether this popularity rests on the efficacy of group therapy or on the fact that group treatment is less expensive is an issue yet to be determined, because measurable benefits are inconsistent (Miller & Hester, 1985; Galanter, Castaneda, & Franco, 1991). In fact, it *is* less expensive than individual or family therapy and it also *appears to work*. Anecdotally, the literature is enthusiastic regarding the effectiveness of group therapy. Early on group was touted as "the treatment of choice for the psychological problems of the alcoholic" (Stein & Friedman, 1971, p. 652) and more recently as "the treatment of choice for chemical dependency" (Matano & Yalom, 1991, p. 269) as well as "the definitive treatment for producing character change" (Alonso, 1989, p. 1). Some explanation of why group therapy works may lie in the basic nature of humankind—the on-going and constant participation in groups of all kinds throughout our lives—and on the characteristics of substance abusing clients themselves (George, 1990). Matano and Yalom (1991) attribute this to the power of the group: "the power to counter prevailing cultural pressures to drink, to provide effective support to those suffering from the alienation of addiction, to offer role modeling, and to harness the power of peer pressure, an important force against denial and resistance" (pp. 269–270). Despite these positive descriptions, research on efficacy in group therapy is sparse.

Bowers and al-Redha (1990) found that group therapy with couples was more effective than individual therapy in both lowering alcohol consumption and in reported increased marital adjustment. Another study of schizophrenic substance abusers in group therapy found that during a one-year period they had a marked decrease in hospitalization days (Hellerstein & Meehan, 1987). Some types of substance abusing patients appear to respond more positively to group therapy than do others. In one such study it was determined that group therapy is more useful for alcoholic clients with dependent personality disorder than with clients who have antisocial disorders (Poldrugo & Forti, 1988).

Therapeutic Factors in Group Therapy

There appears to be more consistency in the research that addresses the factors that influence the group experience as well as agreement on the skills that are important in the group process. Yalom (1975) developed a Q-sort technique which he used to study basic curative factors in psychotherapy groups. Using this process, Yalom constructed a ranking of interpersonal input, catharsis, group cohesiveness, and insight. These four curative factors were ranked highest in the assortment. A replication of this Q-sort with inpatient alcoholics resulted in an identical outcome for the first four curative factors (Feeney & Dranger, 1976). Another model of therapeutic factors was developed by George and Dustin (1988). Although titled differently, these factors seem to coincide with Yalom's factors with the addition of vicarious learning. They include the following:

1. Instillation of hope
2. Sense of safety and support
3. Cohesiveness
4. Universality

5. Vicarious learning

6. Interpersonal learning

Yalom's interpersonal input refers to the feedback received from other group members and the therapist as to the client's personal interactions. Cohesiveness is the feeling of being accepted by other group members. As previously stated, interpersonal relationships are an area in which substance abusers have great difficulty, whether it is from a deficit in early learning or in the paucity of intimacy resulting from years of chemical use.

Clients frequently come into therapy feeling isolated and distrustful of others. Because of their consistent substance use, client may have a distorted perception of themselves and the world (Lewis, Dana, & Blevins, 1994). Group therapy reduces the sense of isolation and allows clients to gain knowledge and learn new behaviors from each other. Group therapy is also beneficial in altering the client's distorted world view through the interactions and reinforcement in the group setting (Vanicelli, 1992).

The feeling of being accepted by other group members increases the feeling of safety for the client. While individual therapy may increase anxiety, group therapy may permit the client to be more open and less anxious in treatment. It may also enable the client, in this supportive atmosphere, to admit and explore the abuse problem.

Catharsis, or the release of strong feelings, can be therapeutic by virtue of releasing previously repressed feelings. The knowledge that others in the group now are aware of these intense feelings and the situations that brought them about can be a step toward self-acceptance (George, 1990). However, catharsis alone has limited merit. Insight into the individuals' participation and responsibility in these situations as well as their ability to make personal choices and changes is imperative in the recovery process.

The factors isolated by George and Dustin (1988) incorporate many of the same characteristics as Yalom's factors. Instillation of hope, safety and support, cohesiveness, and universality are related to group acceptance. Hope is instilled by the fact that others share the same concerns as the client, accept the client as an individual, and continue to be supportive. Safety also comes from acceptance. As group members continue to interact in a mutually supportive manner, trust builds. As trust grows, so does the sharing of issues, problems, and concerns. Clients learn that they are not unique in their problems and feel a sense of relief. Interpersonal learning is the process of input or feedback and output, or developing more effective models of interaction with others (Bloch, 1986). As the group continues, members become more aware of the effect of their behavior on others, both positive and negative. This learning can then be used in the world outside the group to facilitate change in interpersonal relationships. The circle is completed as this knowledge brings more hope.

Group therapy provides a fertile ground for vicarious learning. It is an optimum experience for molding appropriate behavior. As group members try new behaviors in the process of recovery, modeling and feedback by the group can reinforce the desirability of these behaviors. Individuals learn through observation of others what works and does not work for them (George, 1990; Gladding, 1991).

The Content of Group Therapy with Substance Abusers

Group therapy with substance abusers has many of the same components as group therapy with any individuals. As the process begins and continues, many of the tasks and accomplishments are consistent. Groups "supply a mixture of therapeutic forces not available in any other single modality of treatment" (Washton, 1992, p. 508). Features that are imperative to group success in any setting include structure or ground rules; goal setting; a sense of trust, safety, and cohesiveness; confrontation and support; immediacy; and role playing.

Setting the Ground Rules

Establishing the structure, purpose, and rules in group therapy is an important task in the first phase of the group setting. This is particularly true when working with substance abusers. Two areas in which substance abuse clients frequently need change is in their sense of personal responsibility and in clear boundary setting. Establishing rules of attendance, conduct, and participation early in the process allows clients to begin the change process immediately.

Allowing group members to participate in this decision-making process is an empowering exercise. Many of these groups are time-limited due to treatment mandates, and are closed, so that the same members will participate during the complete group therapy process. When the group members negotiate, compromise, and set limits about the group, they develop a higher investment in the process. Also, a group-set rule carries more intrinsic weight that does a leader-set rule.

Setting Goals

Goal setting for the group can also be an experiential learning process. Many of these individuals have no experience in setting goals for the day or for their lives. In the beginning sessions, have the group members discuss their expectations for the group as well as their individual recovery goals. During this period of discussion, common themes and goals will emerge (Lewis, Dana, & Blevins, 1994), which will foster feelings of commonality and trust among the group members.

Self-disclosure by the group leader can be used as a therapeutic tool during the goal-setting stage. This is when the group leader "expresses his or her feelings, values, opinions and beliefs to the group." (George, 1990, p. 155). Self-disclosure is used to express feelings about what is happening in the here-and-now experience of the group, including reactions to the interactions within the group. Self-disclosure also serves as a way to "personalize the leader within the group" (George, 1990, p. 155). It allows group members to see the leader as genuine and human, facilitating trust between the leader and the group members.

Trust, Safety, and Cohesiveness

Again, the process of mutual goal setting increases trust and cohesion within the group. Trust is difficult for a substance abusing client, as is cohesiveness. As members develop a sense of each other as well as the commonality of their problems and concerns, a feeling of belonging grows. This sense of belonging may be the first time the client has felt accepted and protected.

Obviously, these behaviors lead to a more beneficial group experience for the members. As members of the group become more cohesive, intimacy develops. Members become aware of how they have created barriers to intimacy and trust. Within the group experience, they learn new behaviors that can be used in the outside world.

Confrontation

As the group process moves into the working stage, the activities within the group also change. Confrontation of conflictual behaviors or talk and behavior is important. Substance abusers are often unaware of the inconsistencies in their lives. Presenting an individual with this awareness can be an effective therapeutic tool. Inconsistency may result from a person saying one thing and doing another, saying one thing and nonverbally contradicting it (smiling when saying, "I am angry"), or from making contradictory statements on different occasions.

The primary purpose of conformation is to provide insight and allow the individual to grow. Confrontation should never be used in a hurtful or negative manner, but in a caring, supportive, and thoughtful way. Leaders should model appropriate confrontation for the group members. Group leaders should always be aware of managing the anxiety that confrontation stimulates within the group (Golden, Khantzian, & McAuliffe, 1994). An essential component of confrontation is assertiveness. In addition to confrontation, the group leader will also be modeling appropriate assertive behaviors, an important aspect of recovery.

Immediacy

Immediacy, or the awareness of one's emotional experiences in the present, is an essential component of recovery. Substance abusers often have difficulty feeling and identifying their emotions. When they do feel, a learned coping mechanism is to cover the feeling by using a substance. In a cohesive group setting, members learn to recognize a feeling, name it, and to appropriately manage the feeling. They are supported and encouraged in the group setting as they struggle.

Role-Playing

Many of the behaviors we have mentioned can be developed and strengthened in the group experience through role-play. Bandura (1989) emphasizes the importance of role-play in his steps for changing high-risk behaviors. He believes that practicing new behaviors is fundamental for change. He further believes that practicing these new behaviors within a safe environment will reinforce the ability to attempt these behaviors in a less-than-safe environment.

Group members can role-play a variety of situations. They can practice new behaviors for high-risk relapse situations. Members can act out the roles they currently play in different situations and the roles they would like to play in these same situations. Learning new assertive skills and intimacy skills as a means of relating to others is useful for group members. The group leader may use role-play to illustrate alternative behavioral responses to the same situation and the consequences of each of these responses.

As group members role-play new behaviors within the group, they experience success. This experience of success further empowers the individual to experiment with the behavior in other settings. Repeated role-play also lends a level of comfort to the new behavior that encourages repetition outside of group.

Other Types of Groups

The previous discussion described a modified psychotherapeutic group used in many treatment settings. Other types of groups are also available within the field of substance abuse treatment. These groups serve a different purpose than the therapeutic group previously described.

Psychoeducational groups are also commonly used in this field. These groups can be used with the public, with individuals who engage in high-risk behaviors such as driving under the influence of alcohol or other drugs, and with individuals who are diagnosed as substance abusers or substance dependent (Schilit & Gomberg, 1991). The purpose of these group is primarily to present information. They are usually time limited and closed ended groups. A lecture/discussion format is common. Members can be either voluntary or court-mandated. Many times, follow-up treatment is recommended. As stated earlier, these groups do not have a high level of effective outcome. There are some instances, however, when they are the only treatment modality available or mandated.

Self-help groups have been previously discussed in some detail. These groups include Alcoholics Anonymous, Al-Anon, Narcotics Anonymous, Nar-Anon, Cocaine Anonymous, Overeaters Anonymous, Gamblers Anonymous, Rational Recovery, and so on. The primary purpose of these groups is support of the individual in recovery. Serving as a social support for the individual, thereby reducing isolation and loneliness is an important function of a self-help-group.

In summary, individual therapy, group therapy, and self-help groups may certainly work together in a treatment plan. Individual therapy allows the person the attention to specific areas of concern and skill building that is necessary. Group therapy provides the affective support and an opportunity to practice the skills developed in individual therapy.

FAMILY THERAPY

Systems theory and the addiction field have often been at odds with one another. Much of this disagreement has focused on whether addiction is an individual or a family problem. In other words, is the addiction secondary to the dysfunction in the family, or the primary cause of the dysfunction? Bateson (1971) believes it is not an "either/or" proposition but a "both/and" problem. Basing this position on the already stated philosophy that the etiology of abuse/dependency is biopsychosociofamilial, it makes sense to incorporate family therapy into the treatment model.

Over the years, research in the use of family therapy in the substance abuse field has been delineated into two separate tracks: Working with the "alcoholic family" and working with the "substance abuse family." Research in the area of alcoholism has tended to focus on families of white middle-class males in their mid-forties. Research on families of substance abusers (individuals whose primary drug is not alcohol) has tended to focus on adolescents or young adults. Unknowingly, researchers might have been studying the same family from two different perspectives (Schilit & Gomberg, 1991). Many young-adult, polydrug users have parents who are alcoholics, further substantiating the need to address family issues along with individual issues in the treatment plan.

During the past two decades it has become increasingly apparent that family structure and dynamics play an important role in the continuation of substance use within a family (Bennett, Wolin, & Reiss, 1987; Jacob & Seilhammer, 1987; Moos, Fenn, & Billings, 1989; Steinglass, 1994; Wolin, Bennett, & Noonan, 1991). Conversely, the substance use increases other dysfunctional patterns of behavior in families, such as domestic violence (Gondolf & Foster, 1991), child abuse, and incest (Sheinberg, 1991). It has also been shown that biomedical models account for "less than half of the expressed variance in incidence and course of the condition" (Plomin, 1990, cited in Steinglass, 1994). Clinicians need to address the fact that not only does the family influence the substance abuser but also that the substance abuser influences the family.

Many of these families share characteristics. Secrecy is extremely important. Denial of the problem is also paramount. Family members will go to extreme measures to keep the secret and avoid dealing with the issue of alcohol/drug use. The family will readjust itself and redistribute responsibilities to accommodate the user. In fact, Ackerman (1983) states that the "key to surviving in an alcoholic home is adaptation" (p. 16). Hypervigilance is also a characteristic of individuals in these families. Never knowing when or where the abuser will act out creates a constant state of fear for other family members. Lack of trust is a byproduct of this unstable and uncertain atmosphere. Another feature of addictive families is the inability to express feelings. Since the user/abuser is the feeling carrier and the only one allowed to express feelings in the family, other family members lose the ability to identify and express appropriate feelings.

With compelling evidence of the effect of the family in the etiology and maintenance of abuse and dependency, it seems appropriate to incorporate family systems therapy in the treatment process. Outcome research supports the efficacy of family therapy in working with substance abusers. Studies (Collins, 1990; Oxford, 1984; Steinglass & Robertson, 1983) show that family therapy consistently has a better outcome than individual therapy. Other studies have shown that family involvement increases client engagement in both detoxification and treatment stages (Jacobson, Holtzworth-Munroe, & Schmaling, 1989; Liepman & Nirenberg, & Begin, 1989; Sisson & Azrin, 1986).

However, many treatment programs do no more than pay lip service to family therapy. Partially, this may be due to the politics and available money through managed care for substance abuse treatment today. Treatment programs tend to compartmentalize individual and family therapy, offering a time-limited family component to augment the on-going individual treatment. This artificial compartmentalization itself denies a systems approach to treatment.

Additionally, many treatment facilities do not have clinicians trained in family systems theory. Therefore, the "family therapy" component is being offered by counselors who are minimally trained in the theory and techniques of family therapy. Regardless of these problems, family therapy can be a powerful adjunct in the treatment of substance abusers from assessment, to detoxification, through treatment to aftercare.

An underlying principle of system theory, no matter which school of family therapy one adheres to, is that systems (families) are self-regulating and self-maintaining. (For an overview of differential theories in family systems theory see Goldenberg & Goldenberg, 1991, and Nichols & Schwartz, 1991). This one sentence speaks volumes for the inclusion of family members in treatment. The identified patient (IP) or substance abuser would be unable to continue the behavior without a system to support the behavior. This in no way implies that the system prefers the individual's continued use of drugs, but that the system accommodates and adjusts itself to the individual's use. The family may be traumatized by the consequences of the abuse but at the same time find it essential that the individual continue using to maintain the family system. Therefore, when the individual decides to stop abusing, the family balance is disrupted. Without intervention, the system will seek to return to its previous homeostasis or balance, which includes a substance abusing family member.

The value of including the family in assessment lies in the multiple perspectives that become available when the family members are included. The clinician does not have to rely on the individual abuser's information about drug use, but has access to a variety of information about the individual's patterns of behavior. Additionally, the clinician has information concerning the effects on the family's problem-solving skills, daily routines, and rituals (Steinglass, 1994), or more specifically, how the family maintains itself in the face of the dysfunctionality.

It may also be important for the counselor to address the difference in the family's behavior patterns when an individual is using and when the individual is not using ("wet" and "dry" conditions). Developing a clear understanding of these behavior patterns can be essential in assisting the family in change.

Many practitioners in the field believe that meaningful psychotherapy can begin only after an individual ceases using mind-altering drugs. Therefore, detoxification is a fundamental beginning for treatment. The family therapy approach to detoxification includes a contract with the entire family for detoxification, which includes not only abstinence by the individual but also a shift in the self-regulating patterns of behavior that have developed around the use of drugs in the family (Steinglass, 1994).

When an individual stops using alcohol or other drugs, the family is destabilized. Many times this creates a crisis within the family. Sometimes other problems increase: An adolescent will begin to act out; a physical illness will become worse; or another family member's drug use will worsen. A systems approach recognizes the family's attempt at striving for balance, and addresses these issues from that perspective. Just as the family learned to organize itself around the substance use, it must now reorganize itself when there is no substance use in the family. This will require the restructuring of family rituals, roles, and rules. For many families, daily routines will be significantly altered without the presence of alcohol or other drug use. In cases of long-term substance use, families may have no concept of how to function other than as a group that revolves around the abuser's behavioral shifts.

As treatment continues, new behaviors are learned and integrated into the family system. These new behaviors can be both empowering and frightening for family members as well as the substance abuser. Change creates a destabilized system and confusion. This destabilized system will seek to find a comfortable balance, which may include relapse. Aftercare support and relapse prevention techniques for the individual and the family are a necessary component for long-term change.

In summary, to be most effective, treatment should be addressed at three levels: individual, group, and family. Individual therapy addresses the intrapsychic conflict and issues of the individual. Group therapy allows a platform for change and support on the interactional level. Family therapy addresses the systemic circumstances in which the individual exists. If we as clinicians belief that the etiology of substance abuse encompasses every aspect of the individual's life, then it is only reasonable that our treatment modalities mirror this belief.

CASE DISCUSSIONS

Case 1 (Sandy and Pam).   Neither Sandy nor Pam would be referred to residential treatment at this time. Although Pam may need detoxification, more information concerning her drug use pattern would be necessary to make this decision.

Sandy is an example of an individual who has made the decision to stop drinking and now needs someone to facilitate structure and develop a plan of action to avoid a relapse. Using the biopsychosocial model of treatment, Sandy would be involved in individual therapy to address relationship issues and the possibility of post-traumatic stress disorder. Using a solution-focused model of therapy, the therapist would build on Sandy's strengths, emphasizing the fact that she has quit drinking on her own. The therapist would ask for other exceptions to times when Sandy was drinking and explore how she managed to stay sober during those times. A plan to continue these behaviors would be developed.

Because Pam and Sandy came in together to work on their relationship, the therapist would want to honor this request and continue to work with them from a systems perspective. Using the genogram previously developed, issues of transgenerational patterns of use would be explored. From a solution-focused model, the question would be how did others in the family handle stress other than drinking.

Pam would be asked to contract to decrease her drinking and not to use cocaine for a negotiated period of time and also agree not to come to session having had alcohol or cocaine. The goal would be complete abstinence as soon as possible. It would also be effective to ask Pam to contract not to see Sam for a given period of time. During this time frame, the therapist would work with Pam on relationship issues, transgenerational patterns of coping, and developing alternatives to using alcohol and cocaine. It would also be appropriate to work with Pam on relaxation techniques for the anxiety attacks. Referral for medication is possible, but not preferable because the goal of therapy is to learn to live productively without drugs.

The therapist would recommend that both Pam and Sandy attend 12-step meetings, using the 90/90 schedule (90 meetings in 90 days). If an outpatient group was available, the therapist might suggest attendance for additional support and therapeutic involvement not available through the 12-step program.

Case 2 (The Smith Family). As noted in Chapter Four, both Jane and Joe meet the criteria for substance dependence. Their chronic use of drugs span 23 years. If possible, the therapist would suggest short-term residential treatment for Jane and Joe. This decision is based on the admitted inability to stop using, the environment in which Jane works, and the admitted lack of desire to completely quit using. Placing the Smiths in a setting to at least detoxify might enable the therapist to begin to develop an abstinence plan. Additionally, it would allow a breathing space to work with Sarah and Karen to explore what is actually happening with them.

Residential treatment may not be practical for both adults in the family and if not, intensive outpatient treatment would be recommended. A regiment of individual, family, and group sessions would be designed. Both adults need to address transgenerational substance abuse and child abuse issues as well as parenting issues in the present. A contract to remain clean and sober should be developed and a structure constructed with the Smiths to implement the plan.

Sarah's acting out behavior is an indication of the imbalance in the system. Also, Joe's inappropriate behavior with Sarah when drinking must be explored thoroughly. Although Karen is the quiet one, her "disappearance" from the family is also a concern for the therapist. Boundary issues and hierarchy should be discussed. Again, transgenerational patterns of abuse can be discussed and the implications for Karen and Sarah brought into the session.

The therapist must also be aware of the possibility that Sarah is already involved in drug use. Individual sessions with the girls would be an important asset in the treatment plan. The therapist would want to gather information about the day-to-day activities in the home, at school, and in other situations. Information about peers and activities would also be helpful. Referring Sarah to Alateen and Karen to a group for children would be beneficial if available.

Couples group therapy for Jane and Joe would prove extremely beneficial. In this setting, couple and family issues as well as parenting can be discussed freely and with others in the same situation as well as benefiting from the facilitation of a professional. Certainly a 12-step program would be an appropriate support for both Joe and Jane.

Case 3 (Leigh).   In working with Leigh, several factors need to be considered. The first factor is Leigh's developmental stage. Normal adolescent growth includes rebellious and sometimes dangerous behavior. It most certainly includes behaviors that are unacceptable to the parents. Additionally, there have been many changes in Leigh's life recently—her brother left for college and she has moved to a new area and a new school. Her mother's stress appears to have increased, creating more conflict between Leigh and her mother.

The therapist might address Leigh's drug use and acting out behavior as a symptom of her discontent with her current situation. An additional important concern, and also a symptom, would be the fact that Leigh is overly thin. The possibility of an eating disorder combined with the other issues must be evaluated. If the therapist determines that an eating disorder exists, a referral to an eating disorder specialist might be appropriate. Safety issues must be addressed in regard to all of Leigh's current behaviors.

Addressing Leigh's drug use as a symptom, rather than the problem, requires a different approach to treatment. Normalizing some of her behavior with Mom might take pressure off the situation. A "no-drug" contract would be negotiated. Sessions with Mom would be scheduled to decrease the conflict and establish boundaries as well as connections. If possible, this therapy would also include the father. How to schedule these sessions would be determined after conversations with Leigh, Mom, and Dad. Mom and Dad appear to need some assistance with their relationship, because Leigh feels in the middle of this situation. So, parenting skill work would be one goal of therapy. Also, developing a plan in which Leigh spends quality time with her parents would be advantageous.

Leigh does not appear to need a 12-step program at this time. If there were a teen group available, however, the support of other clean and sober teenagers might be beneficial.

REFERENCES

Ackerman, R. J. (1983). *Children of alcoholics: A guidebook for educators, therapists, and parents.* Holmes Beach, FL: Learning Publications, Inc.

Adleman, S. A., & Weiss, R. D. (1989). What is therapeutic about inpatient alcoholism treatment? *Hospital and Community Psychiatry, 40* (5), 515–519.

Alonso, A. (1989, September). Character change in group therapy. A paper presented at Psychiatric Grand Rounds, The Cambridge Hospital, Cambridge, MA.

Annis, H. M., & Chan, D. (1983). The differential treatment model: Empirical evidence from a personality topology of adult offenders. *Criminal Justice and Behavior, 10,* 159-173.

Azrin, N. H., Sisson, R. W., Meyers, R., & Godley, M. (1982). Alcoholism treatment by disulfiram and community reinforcement therapy. *Journal of Behavior Therapy and Experimental Psychiatry, 13,* 105-112.

Baker, T., & Cannon, D. S. (1979). Taste aversion therapy with alcoholics: Techniques and evidence of a conditioned response. *Behavior Research and Therapy, 17,* 229-242.

Bandura, A. (1989). Perceived self-efficacy in the exercise of control over AIDS infection. In V. M. Mays (Ed.), *Primary prevention of AIDS: Psychological approaches* (pp. 128-141). Newbury Park: Sage Publications.

Bateson, B. (1971). *Steps toward an ecology of the mind.* New York: Ballentine Books.

Bennett, L. A., Wolin, S. J., & Reiss, D. (1987). Couples at risk for alcoholism recurrence: Protective influences. *Family Process, 26,* 111-129.

Berg, I.K., & Miller, S. D. (1992). *Working with the problem drinker: A solution-focused approach.* New York: W. W. Norton & Company

Berg, I. K., & Gallagher, D. (1991). Solution focused brief treatment with adolescent substance abusers. In T. Todd & M. Selekman (Eds.), *Family therapy approaches with adolescent substance abusers.* Boston: Allyn & Bacon.

Blake, G. B. (1965). The application of behavior therapy to the treatment of alcoholism. *Behavior Research and Therapy, 3,* 75-85.

Bloch, S. (1986). Therapeutic factors in group psychotherapy. In A. J. Frances & R. E. Hales (Eds.), *Annual Review* (Vol. 5, pp. 678-698). Washington, DC: American Psychiatric Press.

Bowers, T. G., & al-Redha, M. R. (1990). A comparison of outcome with group/marital and standard/individual therapies with alcoholics. *Journal of the Study of Alcoholism, 51,* 301-109.

Brandsma, J. M., Maultsby, M. C., Welsh, R. J. (1980). *The outcome treatment of alcoholism: A review and comparative study.* Baltimore: University Park Press.

Cannon, D. S., Baker, T., Gino, A., & Nathan, P. E. (1986). Emetic and electric shock alcohol aversion therapy: Assessment of conditioning. *Journal of Consulting and Clinical Psychology, 49,* 2-33.

Chaney, E. F., O'Leary, M., & Marlatt, G. A. (1978). Skill training with alcoholics. *Journal of Consulting and Clinical Psychiatry, 46,* 1092-1104.

Collins, R. L. (1990). Family treatment of alcohol abuse: Behavioral and systems perspectives. In R. L. Collins, K. E. Leonard, & J. S. Searles (Eds.), *Alcohol and the Family: Research and Clinical Perspectives* (pp. 285-308). New York: Guilford.

Collins, J. J., & Alison, M. (1983). Legal coercion and retention in drug abuse treatment. *Hospital & Community Psychiatry, 34,* 1145-1150.

Doweiko, H. F. (1993). *Concepts of chemical dependency* (2nd ed.). Pacific Grove, CA: Brooks/Cole.

Elkins, R. L. (1975). Aversion therapy for alcoholism: Chemical, electric, or verbal imagery. *International Journal of the Addictions, 10,* 157-209.

Elkins, R. L. (1980). Covert sensitization treatment for alcoholism: Contribution of successful conditioning to subsequent abstinence maintenance. *Addictive Behavior, 5,* 67-89.

Emick, C. D., & Aarons, G. A. (1990). Cognitive-behavioral treatment of problem drinking. In H. B. Milkman & L. I. Sederer (Eds.), *Treatment Choices for Alcoholism and Substance Abuse* (pp. 265-286). New York: Lexington.

Feeney D. J., & Dranger, P. (1976). Alcoholics view group therapy: Process and goals. *Journal of Studies on Alcohol, 38(5),* 611-618.

Ferrell, W. L., & Galassi, J. P. (1981). Assertion training and human relations training in the treatment of chronic alcoholics. *International Journal of the Addictions, 16(3),* 959-968.

Galanter, M., Castaneda, R., & Franco, H. (1991). Group therapy and self-help groups. In R. J. Frances & S. D. Miler (Eds.), *Clinical textbook of addictive disorders* (pp. 431–451). New York: Guilford.

George, R. L. (1990). *Counseling the chemically dependent: Theory and practice*. Upper Saddle River, NJ: Prentice Hall.

George, R. L., & Dustin, D. (1988). *Group counseling: Theory and practice*. Upper Saddle River, NJ: Merrill/Prentice Hall.

Gladding, S. T. (1991). *Group work*. Upper Saddle River, NJ: Merrill/Prentice Hall.

Golden, S. J, Khantzian, E. J., & McAuliffe, W. E., (1994). Group therapy. In M. Galanter & H. D. Kleber (Eds.), *The American Psychiatric Press Textbook of Substance Abuse Treatment*, (pp. 303-314). Washington, DC: American Psychiatric Press.

Goldenberg, I., & Goldenberg, H. (1991). *Family therapy: An overview*. Pacific Grove, CA: Brooks/Cole.

Gondolf, E. W., & Foster, R. A. (1991). Wife assault among VA alcohol rehabilitation patients. *Hospital Community Psychiatry, 42*, 74-79.

Goldstein, A. P., Ragles, K. W., & Amann, L.L. (1990). *Refusal skills: Preventing drug use in adolescents*. Champaign, IL: Research Press.

Hellerstein, D. J., & Neehan, B. (1987). Outpatient group therapy with schizophrenic substance abusers. *American Journal of Psychiatry, 144*, 1337-1339.

Hester, R., & Miller, W. (1989). *Handbook of alcoholism treatment approaches: Effective alternatives*. New York: Pergamon Press.

Jacob, T., & Seilhammer, R. (1987). Alcoholism and family interaction. In T. Jacob (Ed.), *Family interaction and psychopathology: Theories, methods, and findings* (pp. 535-580). New York: Plenum.

Jacobsen, E. (1968). *Progressive relaxation*. Chicago: University of Chicago Press.

Jacobson, N. S., Holtzworth-Munroe, A., & Schmaling, K. B. (1989). Marital therapy and spouse involvement in the treatment of depression, agoraphobia, and alcoholism. *Journal of Consulting and Clinical Psychology, 57*, 5-10.

Johnson Institute (1987). *The family enablers*. Minneapolis, MN: The Institute.

Lesser, E. (1976). Behavior therapy with a narcotics user: A case report. Ten-year follow-up. *Behavior Research and Therapy, 14(5)*, 381.

Lewis, J. A., Dana, R. Q., & Blevins, G. A. (1994). *Substance abuse counseling: An individualized approach*. Pacific Grove, CA: Brooks/Cole.

Lieberman, R. (1969). Aversive conditioning of drug addicts: A pilot study. *Behavior Research and Therapy, 6*, 229-231.

Liepman, M. R., Nirenberg, T. D., & Begin, A. M. (1989). Evaluation of a program designed to help families and significant others to motivate resistant alcoholics into recovery. *American Journal of Drug and Alcohol Abuse, 15*, 209-221.

Matano, R. A., & Yalom, I. D. (1991). Approaches to chemical dependency: Chemical dependency and interactive group therapy—a synthesis. *International Journal of Group Psychotherapy, 41*, 269-293.

Matuschka, P. R. (1985). The psychopharmacology of addiction. In T. E. Bratter & G. G. Forrest (Eds.), *Alcoholism and substance abuse: Strategies for clinical intervention* (pp. 85–106). New York: The Free Press.

Meyer, R. (1988). Intervention: Opportunity for healing. *Alcoholism & Addiction, 9(1)*, 7.

Miller, W. R. (1985). Motivation for treatment: A review of special emphasis on alcoholism. *Psychological Bulletin, 98*, 84-107.

Miller, W. R. (1990). Alcohol treatment alternatives: What works? In H. B. Milkman & L. I.Sederer (Eds.). *Treatment choices for alcoholism and substance abuse* (pp. 253-264) New York: Lexington.

Miller, W. R., & Hester, R. K. (1985). The effectiveness of treatment techniques: What works and what doesn't. In W. R. Miller (Ed.), *Alcoholism: Theory, research and treatment* (pp. 526–574). Lexington, MA: Ginn Press.

Miller, W. R, & Hester, R. K. (1986a). Inpatient alcoholism treatment: Who benefits? *American Psychologist, 41*, 794-805.

Miller, W. R., & Hester, R. K. (1986b). The effectiveness of alcoholism treatment: What research reveals. In W. R. Miller & N. Heather (Eds.),

The addictive behaviors: Processes of change. (Pp. 121-174). New York: Plenum Press.

Monti, P. M., Abrams, D. B., Kadden, R. M., & Cooney, N. L. (1989). *Treating alcohol dependence: A coping skills training guide.* New York: Guilford Press.

Moos, R., Fenn, C., & Billings, A. (1989). Assessing life stressors and social resources: Applications to alcoholic patients. *Journal of Substance Abuse, 1,* 135-159.

Moylan, D. W. (1990). Court intervention. *Adolescent Counselor, 2(5),* 23-27.

Nichols, M. P., & Schwartz, R. C. (1991). *Family therapy: Concepts and methods.* Boston: Allyn and Bacon.

Oxford, J. (1984). The prevention and management of alcohol problems in the family setting: A review of work carried out in English-speaking countries. *Alcohol, 19,* 109-122.

Palakow, R. L. (1975). Covert sensitization treatment of a probationed barbiturate addict. *Journal of Behavior Therapy and Experimental Psychiatry, 6,* 53-54.

Plomin, R. (1990). The role of inheritance in behavior. *Science, 248,* 183-188.

Poldrugo, F., & Forti, B. (1988). Personality disorders and alcoholism treatment outcome. *Drug and Alcohol Dependency, 21,* 171-176.

Powell, B. J., Penick, E. C., Read, M. R., & Ludwig, A. M. (1985). Comparison of three outpatient treatment interventions: A twelve-month follow-up of men alcoholics. *Journal of Studies on Alcohol, 46,* 309-312.

Rimmele, C., Miller, W. R., & Dougher, M. (1990). Aversion therapies. In R. K. Hester & W. R. Miller (Eds.), *Handbook of alcoholism treatment approaches: Effective alternatives* (pp. 215–235). New York: Pergamon Press.

Rossi, E. L. (1973). Psychological shocks and creative moments in psychotherapy. *American Journal of Clinical Hypnosis, 16(1),* 9-22.

Rothenburg, L. (1988). The ethics of intervention. *Alcoholism & Addiction, (9)*1 22-24.

Schilit, R., & Gomberg, E. S. L., (1991). *Drugs and behavior: A sourcebook for the helping professions.* Newbury Park: Sage.

Schuster, R. (1978–1979). Evaluation of a reality therapy stratification system in a residential drug rehabilitation center. *Drug Forum, (7)*1, 59-67.

Sheinberg, M. (1991). Navigating treatment impasses at the disclosure of incest: Combining ideas from feminism and social constructionism. *Family Process, 31,* 210-216.

Sisson, R. W., & Azrin, N. H. (1986). Family member involvement to initiate and promote treatment of problem drinkers. *Journal of Behavior Therapy and Experiential Psychiatry, 17,* 15-21.

Stein, A., & Friedman, E., (1971). Group therapy with alcoholics. In H. I. Kaplan & B. J. Sadock (Eds.), *Comprehensive group psychotherapy.* Baltimore: Williams and Wilkins.

Steinglass, P. (1994). Family therapy: Alcohol. In M. Galanter & H. D. Kleber (Eds.), *Textbook of substance abuse treatment.* (pp. 315-329). Washington, DC: American Psychiatric Press.

Steinglass, P., & Robertson, A. (1983). The alcoholic family in the biology of alcoholism (Vol. 6). In B. Kissin, & H. Begleiter (Eds.), *The pathogenesis of alcoholism: Psychosocial factors.* (pp. 243-307. New York: Plenum.

Stimmel, B., Cohen, M., Sturiano, V., Hanbury, D., Forts, D., & Jackson, G. (1983). Is treatment of alcoholism effective in persons on methadone maintenance? *American Journal of Psychiatry, 140,* 862-866.

Twerski, A. J. (1983). Early interventions in alcoholism: Confrontational techniques. *Hospital & Community Psychiatry, 34,* 1027-1030.

Ulmer, R. A. (1977). Behavior therapy: A promising drug abuse treatment and research approach of choice. *International Journal of the Addictions, 12(6),* 777-784.

Vannicelli, M. (1982). *Removing the roadblocks: Group psychotherapy with substance abusers and family members.* New York: Guilford Press.

Washton, A. M. (1992). Structured outpatient group therapy with alcohol and substance abusers. In J. H. Lowenson, P. Ruiz, R. B. Millman, & J. G. Langrod (Eds.), *Substance abuse: A comprehensive textbook* (pp. 508–519). Baltimore: Williams & Wilkins.

Williams, E. (1989). Strategies for intervention. *Nursing clinics of North America, 24*(1), 95-107.

Wisocki, P. A. (1973). The successful treatment of a heroin addict by covert conditioning techniques. *Journal of Behavior Therapy and Experimental Psychiatry, 4,* 55-61.

Wolin, S. J., Bennett, L. A., & Noonan, D. L. (1991). Disrupted family rituals: A factor in intergenerational transmission of alcoholism. *Journal of Studies on Alcoholism, 41,* 199-214.

Wolpe, J. (1965). Conditioned inhibition of craving in drug addiction: A pilot experiment. *Behavior Research and Therapy, 2,* 285-287.

Yalom, I. D. (1975). *The theory and practice of group psychotherapy* (2nd ed.). New York: Basic Books

Yalom, I. D. (1995). *Treating alcoholism*. San Francisco: Jossey-Bass Publishers.

Working with Selected Populations: Treatment Issues and Characteristics

CONNIE SCHLIEBNER, PH.D.
JOHN JOSEPH PEREGOY, PH.D.

This chapter will address treatment issues and characteristics of five groups of individuals. The underlying criteria for selecting the groups was the power differential among these groups and the influence of societal perceptions and actions that have limited the full participation of these groups in mainstream society. Obviously, as with Chapter 8 on cultural diversity, other groups could be included in this selection, but because of the space constraints of this text, we have chosen to discuss women, people with disabilities, the gay/lesbian community, adolescents, and the elderly.

WOMEN

The problem of substance abuse in women has become a growing concern for society. Although fewer women than men use alcohol and drugs, the number still is significant. Estimates indicate that of the 15.1 million people who abuse alcohol or are alcohol dependent, 4.6 million—or about one-third—are women (Office for Substance Abuse Prevention, 1991). Even with this significant number, women continue to be underrepresented and undertreated in treatment programs (Mondanaro, 1989).

Sumners (1991) stated that women of today face pressures and stressors that differ from those of 25 years ago when women's roles in the family and society were clear and well-defined. Women are supposed to meet past role expectations as well as the current demands of society. Regardless of whether they believe they successfully balance all their roles, their work may be devalued, which often places them in no-win situations or a double bind. "Society conveys to women that they should find their greatest happiness and fulfillment in giving to, and serving others, and at the same time conveys on another level that they are not really valuable for doing this, or that they should be more like men" (Heriot, 1983, pp. 11–12).

Being a female in our society increases the risk of adverse psychological and social factors that can lead to depression, isolation, loneliness, and powerlessness. Faludi (1991) stated that women in the United States represent two-thirds of all poor adults and are far more likely to live in poor housing, receive no health insurance, and draw no pension. "The feminization of poverty" (Pearce, 1979, p. 103) is due to the increase in women living below the poverty level because of their disadvantaged economic status, the rise in female-headed households, and occupational segregation. The workplace is overrepresented by women in traditional female jobs (secretaries, administrative support, and clerks) whose salaries are as far below a man's as they were 20 years ago.

Worell and Remer (1992) noted sex-role stereotyping has changed little over time. Women are still described as being more emotional, submissive, dependent on others, and devoted to nurturing. Ruble (1983) described "competency" characteristics of self-confidence, independence, and decisiveness being attributed to men. These societal conceptions affect how individuals feel and think about themselves and have serious implications for individuals' well-being (Worell & Remer, 1992). For these many reasons, women may seek relief by using drugs and alcohol (Sumners, 1991). See Figure 7.1 for statistics about women and their use of drugs.

- Almost half of all women ages 15 to 44 have used illicit drugs as least once in their lives.
- 10.3 million women age 12 and older have used at least one illegal drug in the past year.
- More than 4.4 million women age 12 and older currently use illegal drugs.
- 4 million women have taken prescription drugs nonmedically during the past year.
- An estimated 221,000 women who gave birth in the United States in 1992 used illicit drugs while they were pregnant.
- AIDS is the fourth leading cause of death among women ages 25 to 44 in the United States.
- More than 34,000—about 67 percent—of the AIDS cases among women are drug related.

FIGURE 7.1   About Women, Drug Abuse, and AIDS

Note: From 1993 National Household Survey on Drug Abuse; NIDA National Pregnancy and Health Survey; and Centers for Disease Control and Prevention *HIV/AIDS Surveillance Report,* June 1994. In NIDA Notes, January–February, 1995.

Risk Factors

There is no single profile that characterizes women who become dependent on alcohol or drugs, although several subgroups have emerged from research conducted by Wilsnack (1989) and Hamlett, Eaker, and Stokes (1989). They found that young women, ages 21-34 report the highest rates of drinking-related problems. Many of these women will resolve these early problems without developing chronic dependence. Women between the ages of 35-49 appear to have the highest rates of alcohol problems. Wilsnack (1989) found additional subgroups of women at risk, including those who are unmarried or cohabiting, unemployed or part-time employed, depressed, suffering sexual or reproductive disorders, and physically or sexually abused, as well as women with nontraditional gender-role orientations and dysfunctional families of origin.

Hafen and Brog (1983) cited several stresses women face that are related to their substance abuse; home stress, work stress, multiple role strain, empty-nest stage of life, menopausal crises, and post-partum depression. The stresses of marriage or non-marriage, work, and childbearing often lead to feelings of loneliness, emptiness, resentment, and failure that may be dealt with through the use of alcohol, tranquilizers, and other drugs (George, 1990).

Laidlaw and Malmo (1990) stated that women often feel divided in their lives and experience conflict in their many roles as a result of the demands and expectations placed on them. "Women feel divided inside as they struggle to meet their own needs while battling old rules or messages that tell them that they should accommodate others, serve, sacrifice, nurture, or be passive and selfless" (p. 288).

Physiological Factors

It has been noted that several physiological factors seem to be important in the number of women who become alcoholic (Fellios, 1989; George, 1990; Lawson & Lawson, 1989; Mondanaro, 1989). This may indicate women are more vulnerable to physical consequences than men. These consequences result in more medical complaints as a result of their use than do dependent men. There appears to be a direct connection between hormonal status and the development of addiction to alcohol. Women tend to develop cirrhosis earlier than men and also the metabolic rate of women leads to a quicker reaction to alcohol than for men. Women appear to get ill more quickly with less alcohol than men. Hill (1984) found that women show a shorter average duration of excessive drinking before first signs of liver disorders, hypertension, obesity, anemia, malnutrition, gastrointestinal hemorrhage, and ulcers requiring surgery.

Mondanaro (1989) stated that when women present to their physicians with physical complaints, often neither the women nor the physicians emphasize the role that alcohol and drugs may be playing in creating these symptoms. When a woman seeks help for these physical complaints it is often related to the stress in her life and a tranquilizer is prescribed to reduce anxiety—which does not heal the underlying cause of her distress. Walker (1990) said there is a greater awareness today of the misuse of prescribing tranquilizers in the treatment of women, but many who work with women do not believe it is being seriously addressed.

> Being sedate and tranquil have traditionally been viewed as desirable feminine attributes . . . this high level of prescribing reflects society's desire to maintain women in this quiet role. It is easier than uncovering the variety of social ills that lie beneath the symptoms. (Walker, 1990, p. 65)

Barriers to Treatment

Women have a greater reluctance than men to admit they have a problem with alcohol or drugs. According to George (1990), Mondanaro (1989), and Sumners (1991), women are faced with a double standard, a social stigma, and sense of failure that contribute to the resistance to seek help. Those closest to a woman are often the most reluctant to admit there is a problem. Women encounter opposition to treatment from family and friends significantly more than men. If family members are supportive the effectiveness of treatment is improved (Beckman & Kocel, 1982; Efinger, 1983; Lisansky, 1989). The reluctance of the family is grounded in shame and fear of societal rejection.

Other barriers to treatment exist apart from social-stigma and gender-related issues. The Colorado Women's Task Force on Substance Abuse Services (1990) compiled the following list to help professionals understand the difficulty of many women to reach treatment services:

- Lack of finances
- Lack of child care
- Lack of transportation
- Lack of family treatment
- Lack of information regarding services
- Lack of treatment sensitive to women's issues
- Lack of outreach to women
- Lack of affordable services
- Attend to needs of others more than their own
- Too many other responsibilities

Prevention and Intervention

Understanding the social, gender, and economic barriers to treatment for women is a important step in creating programs to meet their needs. The approach to treatment also should take into account the different physiological development of addiction for women. Mondanaro (1989) and Reed (1985) stated that treatment programs were initially designed by and for men without regard for the particular needs of women. Ford (1987) found that at the Betty Ford Center women did better in therapy when the group was all female. She found that women in mixed-gender groups tended to take on the nurturing role and hang back while encouraging the men to do all the talking.

Worell and Remer (1992) encouraged helping professionals to realize the need for a specialty in counseling and therapy with women. The issues that need to be addressed are (1) the special problems women bring into therapy, (2) sex-role socialization in the development of women, (3) the inadequacies of theory, research, and practice in addressing the lives of women, and (4) the development of alternative approaches to intervention with women.

Successful treatment programs for women build on nurturance, empowerment, importance of relationships, and a safe environment for women to heal (Prevention Center, 1992). Services that have been found to be valuable for women are (1) child-care availability (Beckman & Kocel, 1982); (2) medical services (Marsh, 1982); (3) assertiveness training, help dealing with unexpressed emotions, social skills training, coping skills training, cognitive restructuring and modeling (Beckman & Kocel, 1982; Ogur, 1986; Wilson, 1987); (4) self-esteem building (Boyd & Mast, 1983); and (5) rehabilitation program including family therapy, support groups, and individual therapy (Lester, 1982).

Because relationships are important to women, their treatment should include significant people in their lives (Sumners, 1991). The support of family and friends emphasizes the importance of the family structure and their efforts should be enlisted in the recovery process. Involving the entire family in treatment can reduce the anxiety about a new self-image (Travis, 1988). The pressures to conform to a variety of roles in and out of the home has led women to overwork and stress (Sandmaier, 1982). Travis (1988) noted that substance abusing women often have no sense of themselves as individuals outside of being a wife or mother. She suggested that treatment include exploring role options and alternatives, with their families, that can encourage women to move in a direction that feels comfortable.

PEOPLE WITH DISABILITIES

Estimates of the number of Americans with disabilities range from 35 million (Pope & Tarlov, 1991) to 43 million (Americans with Disabilities Act, 1990). These estimates vary depending on how *disability* is operationally defined. Data from the National Center for Health Statistics indicates that from 1983 to 1985, 14% of the civilian population had some degree of limitation in their ability to perform activities suitable to their age, this differs from the Bureau of Census data which indicates that 20% of the population fell into this category (Kraus & Stoddard, 1989). People with disabilities have been identified as one of the nation's largest populations at high risk of alcohol and other drug abuse problems (Prendergast, Austin, & Miranda, 1990).

The words *handicapped* and *disabled* have been used synonymously, but many in the disability community distinguish between the two. A *disability* is a medical condition that interferes with a person's development, sight, hearing, dexterity, mobility, learning, or psychological adjustment. A *handicap* is a situational or social barrier or obstacle to the person with a disability in achieving his or her maximum level of functioning. For example, "a person using a wheelchair is handicapped in traveling throughout the city not because of the wheelchair, but because of the inaccessibility of buses or buildings. The disability cannot be changed, but the handicapping condition can be" (Prendergast, Austin, & Miranda, 1990, p. 2). Disabilities include blindness or vision impairment; cleft palate; congenital disabilities; deafness or hearing impairments; spinal cord injuries, paraplegia, or quadriplegia; mental disabilities, which include developmental disabilities; head injuries or head trauma; learning disabilities; and retardation or cognitive impairment (Research and Training Center on Independent Living, 1990).

Risk Factors

One of the major issues in diagnosis of substance abuse in people with disabilities is that the abuse is viewed as a secondary diagnosis with the disability being recognized first, if the abuse is recognized at all (Benshoff & Riggar, 1990; Kircus & Brillhart, 1990). Although studies have suggested that substance abuse is problematic, and estimated to be as high as 80% among some subgroups within this population (Boros, 1989; Heinemann, Donohue, Keen, & Schnoll, 1988; Edgerton, 1986), there is still limited research on prevalence and effective intervention and prevention strategies.

Contributing factors to high rates of abuse include self-perception, environmental and social stress factors, myths, enabling attitudes of family, friends, and professionals in service agencies, social skills, and a general lack of knowledge by members of the abled world (Helwig & Holicky, 1994). Substance abuse behaviors need to be identified as to whether they are a consequence or a response to the disabling event, or whether individuals participated in the same behaviors before the disability. Heinemann, Doll, and Schnoll (1989) found that after certain injuries resulting in a disability, clients who developed substance abuse responded better than those who experienced abuse problems before a disabling event.

All too often substance abuse behaviors are viewed as secondary disabilities (Benshoff, 1990) or not recognized at all in medical settings (Shipley, Taylor, & Falvo, 1990). Helwig and Holicky (1994) pointed out that in many independent living centers the majority do not regularly ask their clients about alcohol or drug use. They further point out that the lack of assessment influences appropriate treatment and hence outcomes. One of the reasons pointed to for inadequate assessment of substance abuse is the lack of cross-training among rehabilitation counselors (Shipley, Taylor, & Falvo, 1990; Rehabilitation Brief, 1990).

Other contributing factors to substance abuse behaviors and lack of assessment and treatment include negative attitudes of society towards those with disabilities. These attitudes include the perception of the abled toward those with disabilities as being less than normal or "hopeless, helpless, fragile, and sick" (Schaschl & Straw,

1989, p. 150). "In a society where fitness and sports are revered, individuals with white canes, hearing aids, crutches, wheelchairs, walkers, speech problems, or developmental disabilities are at best shunned, and at worst, hidden" (Helwig & Holicky, 1994, p. 4).

With these social labels of deviance, which are personally discrediting, people with disabilities become double outcasts when diagnosed with substance abuse. Schaschl and Straw (1989) have suggested that the professional working with this population may view addressing substance abuse issues as an additional burden for the client—cruel, pointless, and a waste of time.

Prevention and Intervention

Early identification of substance abuse in rehabilitation counseling or after entry into a Center for Independent Learning is imperative (Hepner, Kirshbaum, & Landes, 1980-81). "Unless the abuse-addiction is addressed, dealing with the adjustment to a disability will most likely not occur" (Helwig & Holicky, 1994). All too often substance abuse stands in the way of total rehabilitation and is one of the few disabilities that can be totally eliminated (Burbeck, 1981). This requires professionals in the field to become aware of rehabilitation concerns, substance abuse issues, and the development of the ability to address these issues openly, grounded in an informed foundation of cross-training.

People with disabilities experience the same social pressures and psychological stressors that contribute to substance abuse as do people who are not disabled. In addition, they experience the stressors related to social stigma and the additional psychological, emotional, and social problems of their disability, which can increase their risk for abuse. The etiology of substance abuse among people with disabilities is complex (Schaschl & Straw, 1989). Substance abuse histories need to be evaluated in relation to the development of a disability, and the onset of abuse should be scrutinized as to its function in the daily life of individuals with disabilities. This will facilitate assessment and the choice of appropriate interventions.

Interventions need to be designed that are sensitive to the particular disability and life circumstance of the individual. Accommodations, such as American Sign Language interpreters or educational audiotapes for the visually impaired need to be used in psychoeducation components of therapy. When working with any person with a disability, depending on the length of the disability (congenital or traumatic), it is paramount for counselors to remember that they are in a cross-cultural setting.

Areas for intervention that have been identified in the literature include psychoeducation on a variety of issues. Prendergast, Austin, and Miranda (1990) have suggested that clients be provided with information about specific drugs and their contraindications, independent living skills, active alternatives to substance use, parent education and involvement, counter-enabling education, self-esteem, peer pressure, and the development of constructive forms of sensation and fantasy seeking. The client should be assisted in developing new social support networks in conjunction with the above. At the same time, the client's support system should receive psychoeducation on issues they may encounter due the traumatic demands of unsuspected life changes.

ADOLESCENCE

Adolescence is a developmental period characterized by psychological, social, and biological changes. This stage of development is viewed as the transition between childhood and adulthood. It is considered by many as a critical period in development (Dusek, 1987). Hall (1940), the founder of developmental psychology, described adolescence as one of "storm and stress." Erikson (1968) viewed adolescence as a critical period of identity development. Adolescent behavior often reflects the emotional difficulty of this stage of development. This especially important period of transition between childhood and adulthood (Dusek, 1987), presents the adolescent with challenges that can have positive or negative outcomes.

Although most adolescents move through this period without excessively high levels of storm and stress, many individuals do experience difficulty (Eccles et al., 1993). In conjunction with the storminess of this period, adolescents often take part in risk-taking behavior, such as smoking, drinking, and illicit drug use (Quadrel, Fischhoff, & Davis, 1993). These authors concluded that adolescents tend to take more risks as they ignore or underestimate the likelihood of negative outcomes and view themselves as invulnerable to the negative consequences. This misunderstanding or lack of knowledge about the consequences results in the perception that "it couldn't happen to me."

Youths involved with alcohol and drugs pose a major problem not only to themselves, but the community as a whole. It has been estimated that at least 15% of students age 12-17 have serious problems with alcohol or drugs. Another 5% become chemically dependent. Furthermore, about 25% of all school-age youth are children of alcoholics. All in all, between one-fourth and one-third of all school-age children are seriously affected by their own or someone else's substance use (Anderson, 1988). Some may be experimenting with drugs, others attempting to ease the stress of adolescence, and others modeling the behavior of family members and peers. Newcomb and Bentler (1988) stated that the negative outcomes of such behavior put youths at risk for school failure or dropping out, poor occupational adjustment, crime, and mental and physical disorders. See Figure 7.2 for statistics on the use of marijuana among high school students.

Risk Factors

No single profile identifies who will or will not use alcohol and drugs. Adolescent substance abusers have different personality types, family histories, socioeconomic

FIGURE 7.2 Marijuana Use
Among High School Students
Note: From NIDA Notes,
January–February, 1996.

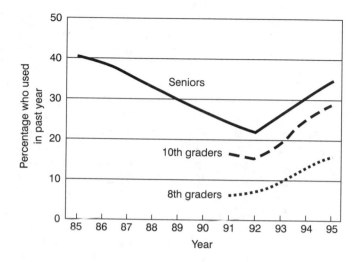

Marijuana use among the nation's 8th-, 10th-, and 12th-grade students
rose in 1995, continuing a trend that began in the early 1990s. The
graph shows past-year use of marijuana since 1985 for 12th graders
and since 1991 for 8th and 10th graders, who were surveyed for the
first time that year.

levels, and life experiences. However, research has indicated that there are variables
associated with substance abuse that can be categorized as environmental or individual (Brounstein, Hatry, Altschuler & Blair, 1990; Hawkins, Catalano, & Associates,
1992; Lawson & Lawson, 1992; Rhodes & Jason, 1990; Towers, 1987). The main
environmental factors include family issues, peer influences, and the school environment. The individual factors associated with substance abuse are personality variables, low self-esteem, low achievement expectation, lack of support networks,
parental substance use, and early initiation of substance use, particularly cigarettes
and/or marijuana. The researchers concluded that the more factors an adolescent is
exposed to, the higher the risk of involvement with alcohol or drugs.

Environmental Factors

Rhodes & Jason (1990) stated that adolescents may initiate substance use to cope
with various stressors and influences that may arise from within the family, school,
peer group, or the community. Individuals are less likely to engage in problematic
early substance use if they are members of prosocial, supportive social networks.

Family members are a significant factor in adolescent development, because they
are role models and major sources of support. Families exhibiting disturbed functioning with high levels of conflict, lack of cohesion, support, and encouragement
are related to levels of substance use (Kumpfer, 1987). In particular, Towers (1987)

noted that characteristics common to families of substance-using adolescents were negative communication (criticism, blaming, lack of praise), inconsistent and unclear limits of behavior, unrealistic parental expectations, denial of drug use, and over- or underdominating parental styles. In addition, families experiencing the stress of poverty, unemployment, despair (Schliebner & Peregoy, 1994), and lack of access to mental and physical health care also put adolescents at risk for substance abuse.

As children enter into adolescence, the influence of peers greatly increases. There is an increasing conformity to peers as the importance of parents as a reference source decreases (Curtis, 1979). Peer groups offer security and a feeling of importance, but also demand conformity to group behavior norms (Dusek, 1987; Horrocks & Benimoff, 1967). Hawkins, Catalano, & Miller (1992) stated that one of the strongest predictors of adolescent substance use is association with drug-using peers. Bandura (1977) stressed that most social learning occurs through observation of behaviors that tend to be modeled. If the observed norm behavior is drinking alcohol or using drugs, this behavior will be modeled (Lawson & Lawson, 1992). Newcomb and Bentler (1986) found that the influence of peers was a stronger influence than that of parents for white, African American, Asian Americans, and Hispanic American youth using drugs. Even when children come from healthy functioning families and do not experience other risk factors, merely associating with friends who use drugs greatly increases their risk. However, if an adolescent has inattentive and unconcerned parents, he or she may turn to peers to receive emotional support (Wodarski, 1990).

The second most important socializing agent for children, after the family, is the school. What is happening or not happening in schools has an effect on youths using illicit drugs. Towers (1987) has noted that even though parents have the primary responsibility for dealing with their children's substance use, many students spend more waking hours with their teachers than their parents. Several factors have been identified as predictors of substance abuse related to the school environment: peer pressure to use substances, rejection by peers, academic failure, low degree of commitment to education, and lack of interest in school subjects and activities (Coie, 1990; Gottfredson, 1981; Hawkins, Catalano, & Miller, 1992). In addition, schools that do not have clear and unambiguous drug policies that are fairly enforced send messages to the students that drugs are not a problem.

Individual Factors

Certain personality characteristics and psychological factors are associated with a greater risk of adolescent alcohol and drug use. Aggressiveness, attention-deficit disorders (when combined with conduct problems), alienation from the dominant values of society, rebelliousness, a strong need for independence, low self-image, negative attitudes, and a high tolerance for deviance are all factors that affect substance use (Bennet & Woolf, 1991; Hawkins, Catalano, & Miller, 1992; Lawson & Lawson, 1992). Robins (1978) found that when these behaviors and factors are serious and occur frequently in childhood, the more likely they will occur in adulthood. In addition, the earlier the onset of drug use, the greater the frequency of use and increased possibility of extensive and persistent involvement.

Problems also may occur in adolescents who lack role models, have low involvement with family, and have inadequate social skills, such as communication, cooperation, decision making, and judgment skills (Lawson & Lawson, 1992). To deal with these stressors and influences, adolescents often will use substances as a means of coping. Hence, Rhodes and Jason (1990) encourage the development of supportive networks within the family, school, peer group, and community that can assist in developing social competencies to offset negative influences.

Parents are important role models for their children and transmit values, attitudes, and beliefs. The result of this imitation is an important factor in adolescents' early and continued use of alcohol and drugs. Research has found a high correlation between parental substance use and use patterns among their children (Jessor & Jessor, 1975; Johnson, Schoutz, & Locke, 1984). Parents who conform to either heavy use or abstinence are more likely to have children who abuse substances than those whose parents are moderate drinkers or model appropriate use (Barnes, Farrell, & Cairns, 1986). In other words, the adolescent learns appropriate or inappropriate behaviors from the family unit by modeling and reinforcement.

Parental relationships, personality characteristics, existence of role models, and social skills are often directly related to the environmental factors that affect the development of alcohol and drug use. It is difficult to determine which risk factors or combination of factors are specific to drug use behavior. Knowledge that certain variables do exist and have some effect on use or abuse points professionals in directions for effective intervention strategies.

Prevention and Intervention

Effective identification and assessment of substance abuse is a crucial early step in both treatment and prevention programs. Hawkins, Catalano, and associates (1992) suggested that prevention strategies require counselors to pay attention to the risk factors associated with substance abuse and then focus on protective mechanisms that will inhibit the use of drugs. Prevention efforts should be interrelated activities that include the home, school, and community. Prevention efforts need to extend beyond providing information and specifically address the individual and environmental risk factors.

Family Support Programs

A key to making adolescents less vulnerable to alcohol and drug use is the involvement of the parents. Regardless of the parents' relationship to their child, they need to be involved in the solution. Snyder and Ooms (1992) stated that the treatment of adolescent problems that do not include the family is unlikely to be successful. An initial first step in the treatment of the adolescent and the family is to assess the system. Snyder and Ooms (1992) have developed a checklist to gain a profile of the adolescent and the family's background. The checklist can help the counselor in assessing strengths, weaknesses, problem areas, and family functioning before developing a plan of treatment to meet the specific needs of each family.

It is important for the therapist to immediately involve the family in the therapeutic process. Encourage the family members to describe their efforts to solve problems, confirm that they are caring and competent, and assure them that failure to solve the problem is not blamed on them, but on the difficulty of the problem. Tell them their efforts have been well intended, and encourage them not to give up (Combrinck-Graham, 1992).

Various treatment modalities and therapeutic orientations can be used depending on the stage and severity of the abuse. However, it has been suggested that the goals of therapy, along with other appropriate treatment, directly involve the parents in the following ways; provide clear lines of support by involving the adolescent in creating rules and consequences, offer positive discipline in a nurturing environment, show interest in their children's activities, promote family values, maintain open channels of communication, recognize the signs of substance abuse and discuss openly with their children, and encourage achievement by raising levels of expectation to achieve reasonable aspirations (Brounstein, Hatry, Altschuler, & Blair, 1990; Lawson & Lawson, 1991).

School-Based Programs

Parents have the primary responsibility for dealing with their child's substance abuse, but active involvement of the school will enhance the chances for success (Towers, 1987). There needs to be a consolidated effort among administrators, teachers, and staff to (1) acknowledge that a problem may exist in their school, (2) understand the debilitating consequences of adolescent substance abuse, (3) be familiar with the signs and symptoms of such abuse, and (4) be willing, within their professional role, to help combat drugs in the schools.

Schools need to set clear, positive, and firm policies on drug use and enforce rules that will provide a safe and secure environment for all students. The National Institute on Drug Use has copies of effective school system policies (LaChance, 1989). Drug education curriculums that provide information should be initiated as early as kindergarten, and special efforts at prevention should be made during vulnerable times, such as transition to middle school and high school. To assure the effectiveness of the curriculum, inservice training for teachers is an essential component. In addition to providing information, successful educational programs incorporate self-esteem building, decision-making, assertiveness training, and refusal skills. Instructional materials and media are available through commercial outlets, government agencies, school districts, and public service groups.

As noted earlier, one of the strongest correlates of adolescent alcohol and drug use is the influence of peers. Towers (1987) noted that the need to be accepted and have friends is paramount during this developmental period. Although this influence can have negative effects, particularly among adolescents who are not emotionally strong, peer influence can also have positive effects. Student or peer-led intervention programs have been successful in reducing drug use among students (Hawkins, Catalano, & Miller, 1992). They can act as peer counselors, lobby against drug and alcohol use, and work to change the norms regarding use in the school community (Towers, 1987).

Schwieshiemer and Walberg (1976) found advantages to peer counseling. Peer counselors may have more empathy for each other and model behaviors more appropriate for personal growth. Schaps (1980) found that a common component of successful alcohol and drug abuse programs included peer counseling. Lawson and Lawson (1992) suggested that peer counselors be assessed for their problem-solving skills, empathy, genuineness, immediacy, and unconditional positive regard. Oster (1982, as cited in Lawson & Lawson, 1992) stressed that training for peer counselors involve identifying the problem, exploring solutions, selecting and implementing a solution, and evaluating the process. The peer counselors should be closely supervised by a professional counselor and learn basic counseling skills (Lawson & Lawson, 1992).

THE GAY AND LESBIAN COMMUNITY

The psychosocial stress of being a homosexual man or woman (hereafter referred to as gay and lesbian) in a society dominated by a heterosexual orientation, places gay and lesbian individuals at high risk for alcohol and drug abuse. Paul, Stall, and Bloomfield (1991) indicated that research has produced inconclusive alcohol abuse rates (10% to 30% for the gay and lesbian community compared with 10% for the general population), but it appears that a substantial number of gays and lesbians drink problematically. Early studies indicated heavier drinking and alcoholism among gay men and lesbians than the general population (Fifield, Latham, & Phillips, 1977; Lohrenz, Connelly, Coyne, & Spare, 1978; Morales & Graves, 1983). However, Paul, Stall, and Bloomfield (1991) cautioned that early studies often had methodological limitations and tended to oversample bar patrons. Whether the studies overestimated the prevalence of substance abuse among the homosexual community is not clear.

It has been estimated that gays and lesbians make up 10% to 15% of the overall population or 22 million individuals (Atkinson & Hackett, 1988; Rudolph, 1989). The figure remains an estimate due to the often hidden or invisible status of gays and lesbians. The impetus not to pass as a sexual orientation minority is driven by fear of rejection from the full participation in mainstream society.

Gibson (1989) suggested that stigmatized sexual identity places gays and lesbians in direct conflict with traditional institutions and support systems in our society. The experience of being bicultural (participating in two cultural realities) and living a marginal existence (being an outsider), may lead to psychological and psychosocial maladjustment (Brown, 1989; Dworkin & Gutierrez, 1992). Gays and lesbians may internalize these societal rejections and learn to hate themselves. This lonely journey of social isolation may lead to depression, drug and alcohol abuse, or suicide.

Much of our current thinking regarding the nonacceptance of homosexuality has been shaped by intolerant Western religious views, particularly Christianity, which has influenced social, legal, and religious discrimination against the gay community (Atkinson & Hackett, 1988; Bullough, 1979; Fassinger, 1991). Whitlock (1989) stated that homophobia—the fear or hatred of gay and lesbian people—has inevitably caused many gays and lesbians to remain "in the closet" and silent for fear of rejection by families, friends, neighbors, employers, service providers, and others.

Gay and Lesbian Identity Development

The development of a positive gay/lesbian identity can be a lengthy and difficult process. Substance use often begins in early adolescence, when youths first experience conflicts around their sexual orientation (Gibson, 1989). O'Bear and Reynolds (1985) pointed out that there seems to be sixteen-year span between awareness of homosexual feelings and the synthesis of ones' sexual identity. They noted an eight- to ten-year gap between first awareness of same-sex feelings and self-labeling as gay or lesbian. This developmental process of "coming out" varies considerably depending on gender, race, ethnicity, social class, age, religion, geographic location, and other factors (Fassinger, 1991). Navarro (1989) stated that the process is effected by a lack of role models, inadequate support systems, and lack of legal protection. For gay and lesbian individuals of some racial/ethnic groups, added isolation and possible loss of ones' primary community may also occur.

Cass (1979) proposed a theoretical Model of Homosexual Identity Formation for understanding six stages of development that an individual moves through in developing an integrated identity as a gay or lesbian person. The model is based on two broad assumptions: (1) Identity is acquired through a developmental process, and (2) change in behavior stems from the interaction between individuals and their environment.

The first stage of identity confusion is characterized by turmoil and doubt as the individual begins to question his or her sexual orientation. Identity comparison, the second stage, occurs when one has accepted the possibility that he or she may be homosexual. In the third stage, identity tolerance, individuals increase their commitment to a homosexual identity, but keep public and private identities separate. The fourth stage, identity acceptance, involves accepting ones' homosexual identity rather than tolerating it. Disclosure of ones' homosexual identity remains selective. Identity pride is the fifth stage, characterized by anger, pride, and activism, which lead to immersion into the homosexual culture and rejects the values of the heterosexual community. Finally, identity synthesis occurs with a fusion of ones' homosexual identity with all other aspects of self and no longer dichotomizes the heterosexual and homosexual world.

This model can assist both clients and professionals in understanding and normalizing the process of developing a gay/lesbian identity (Fassinger, 1991). Counselor awareness of the coming out process and individual differences (race/ethnicity, gender, age, religion, geography, socioeconomic status) are necessary to understand the effect of the developmental tasks. O'Connor (1992) cautioned that although the model represents an orderly developmental sequence, not all gays or lesbians move that predictably from awareness to integration of identity. However, the model is useful in approaching the complexity of sexual orientation that occurs in the context of societal prejudice, discrimination, and lack of support (Coleman, 1982; Fassinger, 1991).

The struggles of developing a gay/lesbian identity and adjusting to a stigmatized and minority sexual status, can lead to low self-esteem and serious depression. Kus (1988) concluded that lack of acceptance of oneself as gay was the prime factor in alcoholism in gay men in the United States. Coleman (1982) noted that alcohol and other drugs may be used by gays and lesbians to manage and escape the conflict, confusion, and turmoil that surrounds the developmental process of forming a homosexual identity—hence forestalling the coming out process. However, Israel-stam and Lambert (1989) noted that the liberating effect of accepting one's gay or lesbian identity and eventual coming out may lead to many practical pursuits away from alcohol and drug use.

Risk Factors

Historically the gay bar has been the protected place where gays and lesbians could meet, socialize, make sexual contacts, and be the dominant culture (Blume, 1985). Zehner and Lewis (1985) stated that the bar is often the only social institution in a community specifically for gay and lesbian people where they don't have to worry about feeling different or whether they will be accepted. While today there are alternatives to the gay bar: bookstores, coffee houses, churches, and social networks (Hastings, 1982), the bar remains an integral part of the gay and lesbian culture (O'Donnell, Leoffler, Pollock, & Saunders, 1980).

The use of alcohol and other drugs can become abuse if individuals rely on these substances to maintain denial of their identity, to cope with the rejection of an oppressive society, and deaden the feelings of alienation, guilt, anxiety, and depression (Blume, 1985). While the gay bar can provide solace from a hostile world, it also can lead to a diminished quality of life. Professionals working with gay and lesbian clients need to be aware not only the inner psychological factors affecting these individuals, but the effect of external societal factors on their clients' lives.

Intervention and Prevention

The gay or lesbian client seeking therapy is still often faced with homophobia, heterosexual bias, and misinformation (American Psychological Association, 1990). Although DeCrescenzo's (1984) research indicated that mental health professionals generally have more positive attitudes about gays and lesbians than do the general population, other research has also indicated that mental health professionals have heterosexist assumptions and societal stereotypes about gays and lesbians that lead to distorted beliefs about their clinical concerns (Cabj, 1988; Casas, Brady, & Ponterotto, 1983). Faltz (1992) stated that therapists may incorrectly conclude that the cause of substance abuse is the client's homosexual orientation rather than exploring issues of depression, relationships, anxiety, and self-esteem that are related to all of areas of the client's life.

Sensitive counseling with gays and lesbians focuses on the external as well as internal sources of problems and develops nontraditional interventions to assist clients (Fassinger, 1991). Clark (1987) and Fassinger (1991) suggested that therapists implement affirmative counseling for gays and lesbians. Counselors should feel comfortable with and appreciate their own sexuality and eliminate homophobic feelings that will interfere with therapy. Clients asking to change their sexual orientation may really be asking for acceptance. The willingness to engage in such a therapeutic contract implies that homosexuality is pathological and undesirable.

Counselors can encourage clients to establish a gay and lesbian support system, be familiar with community resources, and make the information available. They can help their clients become aware of the effects of oppression and discrimination and encourage their clients to free themselves of stereotypes and negative conditioning. In showing acceptance and affirmation of their clients' preferred lifestyle, counselors will assist in desensitizing their feelings of shame and guilt.

Issues of homosexuality and intimacy are often not addressed in chemical dependency treatment programs that are often crucial in dealing with alcohol and drug abuse (Coleman, 1987). There is evidence that gay and lesbian clients are more willing to seek treatment programs that address gay and lesbian issues, have visible gay and lesbian staff members, and provide culturally relevant interventions (Colcher, 1982; Paul, Stall, & Bloomfield, 1991).

Faltz (1992) recommended that therapists be aware of clues of problematic use such as difficulties in intimate relationships, employment, finances, and social life. She suggested assessing for frequency or amount of use, preoccupation with drugs or alcohol, self-medication for anxiety, drinking while alone, and hoarding or hiding of drugs or alcohol.

Fassinger (1991) stated that a variety of theoretical approaches and techniques may be effective with gay and lesbian clients. Cognitive approaches can assist in overcoming negative self-talk, whereas client-centered approaches encourage expression of repressed affect. Gestalt techniques can help clients vicariously confront family, friends, and co-workers about their sexual identity. Feminist therapy can use self-empowerment to deal with societal oppression and discrimination. Family and systems approaches and couples counseling can work on relationship issues and group therapy can help clients develop social networks and overcome feelings of self-contempt, isolation, and depression.

The significant increase of membership in Gay and Lesbian Alcoholics Anonymous indicates the need for nonjudgmental peer groups that provide alternatives to existing groups and values (Blume, 1985). Jones, Latham, and Jenner (1980) surveyed gay alcoholics in recovery and found that 68% of the respondents believed the recovery process would be easier if they could openly discuss their sexuality at general AA meetings. These responses are indicative of Gay and Lesbian AA becoming the largest special-interest group within the AA fellowship, with about 500 gay and lesbian groups in the United States (Bloomfield, 1990).

THE ELDERLY

The extent of alcohol use, drug misuse, and drug abuse among the elderly is an important area of concern for families and society in general. Demographic trends project that the number of older people will increase from about 27 million (12% of the population), to 32 million by the year 2000 (Gurnack & Thomas, 1989) and by the year 2010 one out of five will be 65 or older. In the next few decades this number will exceed 50 million (Gambert, 1992). Crawley (1993) stated that substance abuse among the elderly is unique compared with other age groups, due to the many medications taken for a range of health conditions that surface later in life interrelated with the body's own aging process.

About 1.5 billion prescriptions are written in the United States, with one-third of these for the elderly. During the past 25 years, the average number of prescriptions per person for the general population has increased from 2.4 to 7.5 annually. The elderly average 13 prescriptions per year (Stall, 1996).

A common concern for the elderly using prescription or over-the-counter (OTC) drugs is drug misuse. This can involve underuse, overuse, and erratic use leading to adverse consequences (Gurwitz & Avorn, 1991). Misuse can also take the form of medication swapping between spouses, partners, and/or peers in independent living or care facilities (Chapman, 1996). Another concern is the interaction between prescription and OTC drugs taken concomitantly without medical supervision or knowledge.

While the use/abuse of alcohol generally declines in old age, it still remains a major problem for some elderly and is an often underreported and/or hidden problem (George, 1990). Hazelden (1996) identified that 20 percent of hospitalized older adults are diagnosed with alcoholism, and nearly 70 percent are hospitalized with alcohol-related problems. As with other age groups, there are more male alcoholics than female with about two-thirds being early-onset drinkers (Robertson, 1992). This group is considered high risk for successful treatment, while late-onset drinkers have a good chance of recovery.

George (1990) stated that the greatest proportion of abused drugs in this population, other than alcohol, continues to be OTC drugs, nicotine, and caffeine. The percentage of elderly abusing illegal drugs continues to be rather low unless you categorize use of a prescription drug without proper physician direction as illegal. If so, there is a great concern about the elderly using drugs in this manner (Gambert, 1992).

Risk Factors and Barriers to Treatment

The elderly are at risk for a number of physiological, psychological, social, and economic factors that can lead to substance abuse and/or misuse. These include the physical changes in the body due to normal aging, lack of social support, decreased work-related activities, and failing heath combined with a medical system that does not address the specific needs of the elderly population. Older adults are also the least likely of all age groups to seek treatment, which only compounds the problem.

Physical changes take place in the body as it ages. Some of these changes directly relate to the body's ability to metabolize drugs. With normal aging there is a decrease in total body water content and an increase in the proportion of body fat. Alcohol is rapidly distributed in body water after ingestion. With the decrease in body water as we age, there is a decrease in the volume for distribution and therefore an increase in the amount of alcohol that reaches the central nervous system.

Additionally, the parts of the brain that deal with motor skills and cognition age faster than other areas of the brain. Therefore, when these areas are affected by alcohol the impairment is significant at lower levels of use than at an earlier age. Alcohol affects the cardiac muscle, increasing heart rate and output. Again, when coupled with normal age-related cardiovascular problems, the result can be disastrous. The elderly are also particularly susceptible to alcohol-induced hypoglycemia. Many diseases in the elderly result in reduced dietary intake and, coupled with alcohol intake, can result in severe problems (Levy, Duga, Girgis, & Gordon, 1973).

A second major risk factor is the change in social support and work-related activities for the elderly. Older adults have fewer family responsibilities and work-related duties. Many families live far apart, and when older friends begin to die, the person is left with little or no social-support network. Also, many older adults are retired, leaving the days empty of structured activity and creating the need for a substitute activity. Sometimes the activity is alcohol or other drug consumption.

Loss of family and friends coupled with loss of job (status), economic instability, and failing health creates another problem for the elderly. Reports show that more than 50% experience depression or severe anxiety. Add the possibility of dementia, and mental illness becomes a common occurrence. Dementia is present in 10% of this population older than 65 and 22% to 47% of those older than 85 (Evans, 1989).

The elderly have a prevalence of diseases that predispose them to substance use: Arthritis, osteoporosis, recurrent gout attacks, neuropathies, and cancer, among others. These diseases all involve chronic pain that must be managed every day. Most people have easy access to prescription drugs for these problems. Physicians are quick to prescribe and not so quick to evaluate medications being taken by the person before prescribing others. Managed-care systems create an atmosphere where the individual is often passed from doctor to doctor. None of these professionals has a true sense of the medications or problems in the person's life. Frustration with the system and anger at being dependent on it prompt further depression and anxiety in the elderly. (Gambert, 1992).

In even the best of medical circumstances, many elderly live alone, and as dementia increases, over- or undermedication is common. Diagnosing substance abuse in the elderly is complicated. Common signs and symptoms such as anxiety, constipation, depression, malnutrition, restlessness, fatigue, or falling, are many times attributed to senility and therefore ignored. Milder symptoms, such as memory loss or drowsiness, may be confused with simple aging. Even withdrawal symptoms such as tremors or unsteadiness can be mistaken for Parkinson's disease (Hazelden Corporation, 1996).

Prevention and Intervention

Many elderly people are unaware of the effects of aging in combination with the use of alcohol and other drugs. Therefore, beginning with an educational discussion may be extremely helpful. Counselors should ask specifically about the frequency and quantity of use, as well as over-the-counter medications, prescriptions, and alcohol use. Possible symptoms of use should not be ignored. Hesitancy to confront an older adult and not wanting to take away "their last pleasure" sets the stage for denial and enabling behavior on the part of the clinician or family member.

Medical personnel should be made aware of what is happening with the person. If dietary supplements are necessary, the individual should have access to appropriate vitamins and that an adequate diet plan is followed.

The older adult should be engaged in a social-support system. This may be a 12-step group, although resistance to attendance may be high. Other community activities such as senior citizens groups might provide reinforcement for the individual. Family members should be educated about the dangers of substance abuse and self-medication in the elderly.

Few studies have been undertaken of treatment for substance abuse in the elderly (Gambert, 1992). Our society's negative feelings about the elderly may be in part to blame for this. However, if the problem is acknowledged and treated, older adults have a very high rate of success in treatment. It is getting them into treatment that is difficult.

Also, clinicians have a moral obligation to practically consider the complications of aging diseases. Although substance abuse is not the answer, without other options, controlled addiction may be the only solution without "callous disregard for comfort and well-being" (Gambert, 1992, p. 850).

The goal of treatment should be the highest quality of life possible for the longest time possible. The problem must be recognized to be treated. And before that, counselors and families need to be aware of elderly persons who are at high risk. They need to be identified and counseled with as many risk factors eliminated as possible (Gambert, 1992; Hazelden Corporation, 1996).

CONCLUSION

Among women, the differently abled, gays and lesbians, adolescents, and the aged we are witnessing a growth in increased alcohol and drug abuse (AOD) behaviors. It is clear that a shared theme among these groups is identification and early intervention. All these groups share the experience of being marginalized within our society, which in turn influences self-esteem as well as self-efficacy skills. These issues then are not only individual issues but are issues of social importance. Interventions need to be designed to meet individual and group needs, as well as professionals acting as change agents within their communities and society. As change agents, helping professionals can assist in challenging myths and in educating the community of particular individual and group needs revolving around AOD behaviors and risk factors for the groups presented in this chapter.

REFERENCES

American Psychological Association, Committee on Lesbian and Gay Concerns. (1990). *Final report of the task force on bias in psychotherapy with lesbian women and gay men.* Washington, DC: Author.

Americans with Disabilities Act. (1990, July 26). Public Law 101-336.

Anderson, G. L. (1988). *Enabling in the school setting.* Minneapolis, MN: Johnson Institute.

Atkinson, D. R., & Hackett, C. (1988). *Counseling non-ethnic American minorities.* Springfield, IL: Charles C. Thomas.

Bandura, A. (1977). *Social learning theory.* Englewood Cliffs, NJ: Prentice Hall.

Barnes, G. M., Farrell, M. P., & Cairns, A. (1986). Parental socialization factors and adolescent drinking behaviors. *Journal of Marriage and the Family, 48,* 26-36.

Beckman, L. J., & Kocel, K. M. (1982). The treatment delivery system and alcohol abuse in women: Social policy implications. *Journal of Social Studies, 38,* 139-151.

Bennet, E. G., & Woolf, D. (Eds.). (1991). *Substance abuse: Pharmacologic, developmental, and clinical perspectives.* Albany, NY: Delmar.

Benshoff, J. J. (1990). Substance abuse: Challenges for the rehabilitation counseling profession. Editorial. *Journal of Applied Rehabilitation Counseling, 21*(3), 3.

Benshoff, J. J., & Riggar, T. F. (1990). Cocaine: A primer for rehabilitation counselors. *Journal of Applied Rehabilitation Counseling, 21*(3), 21-24.

Bloomfield, K. A. (1990). *Community in recovery: A study of social support, spirituality, and volunteerism among gay and lesbian members of Alcoholics Anonymous.* Unpublished doctoral dissertation, University of California at Berkeley.

Blume, E. S. (1985). Substance abuse (of being queer, magic pills, and social lubricants). In H. Hidalgo, T. L. Peterson, & N. J. Woodman (Eds.), *Lesbian and gay issues: A resource manual for social workers* (pp. 79-87). Silver Spring, MD: National Association of Social Workers.

Boros, A. (1989). Facing the challenge. *Alcohol Health and Research World, 13*(2), 101-103.

Boyd, D., & Mast, D. (1983). Addicted women and their relationships with men. *Journal of Psychosocial Nursing and Mental Health Services, 21,* 10-13.

Brounstein, P. J., Hatry, H. P., Altschuler, D. M., & Blair, L. H. (1990). *Substance use and delinquency among inner city adolescent males.* Washington, DC: Urban Institute Press.

Brown, L. S. (1989). New voices, new visions: Toward a lesbian/gay paradigm for psychology. *Psychology of Women Quarterly, 13,* 445-458.

Bullough, V. L. (1979). *Homosexuality: A history.* New York: New American Library.

Burbeck, T. (1981). Alcoholism: The extra burden. *American Rehabilitation, 7*(2), 3-6.

Cabj, R. P. (1988). Homosexuality and neurosis: Considerations for psychotherapy. *Journal of Homosexuality, 15,* 13-23.

Casas, J. M., Brady, S., & Ponterotto, J. G. (1983). Sexual preference bias in counseling: An information processing approach. *Journal of Counseling Psychology, 30,* 139-145.

Cass, V. C. (1979). Homosexual identity formation: A theoretical model. *Journal of Homosexuality, 4,* 219-235.

Chapman, R. J. (1996, October 10). Personal communication.

Clark, D. (1987). *The new loving someone gay.* Berkeley, CA: Celestial Arts.

Coie, J. D. (1990). Towards a theory of peer rejection. In S. R. Asher & J. D. Coie (Eds.), *Peer rejection in childhood* (pp. 365-398). New York: Cambridge University Press.

Colcher, R. W. (1982). Counseling the homosexual alcoholic. *Journal of Homosexuality, 7,* 43-52.

Coleman, E. (1982). Developmental stages of the coming out process. *Journal of Homosexuality, 7,* 31-43.

Coleman, E. (1987). Chemical dependency and intimacy dysfunction: Inextricably bound. *Journal of Chemical Dependency Treatment, 1,* 13-26.

Colorado Women's Task Force on Substance Abuse Services (1990, August). Center for Applied Prevention Resource, Boulder, CO.

Combrinck-Graham, L. (1992). Family assessment and treatment planning for adolescents with alcohol, drug abuse, and mental health problems. In W. Snyder & T. Ooms (Eds.), *Empowering families, helping adolescents: Family-centered treatment of adolescents with alcohol, drug abuse, and mental health problems* (pp. 43-51). Rockville, MD: U.S. Department of Health and Human Services.

Crawley, B. (1993). Self-medication and the elderly. In E. M. Freeman (Ed.), *Substance abuse treatment: A family perspective* (pp. 217–238). Newbury Park, CA: Sage.

Curtis, R. C. (1979). Parents and peers: Serendipity in a study of shifting reference sources. *Social Forces, 52,* 368-375.

DeCrescenzo, T. A. (1984). Homophobia: A study of the attitudes of mental health professionals toward homosexuality. *Journal of Social Work and Human Sexuality, 2,* 115-136.

Dusek, J. B. (1987). *Adolescent development and behavior.* Englewood Cliffs, NJ: Prentice Hall.

Dworkin, S. H., & Gutierrez, F. J. (1992). *Counseling gay men and lesbians: Journey to the end of the rainbow.* Alexandria, VA: American Association for Counseling and Development.

Eccles, J. D., Midgley, C., Wigfield, A., Buchanan, C. M., Reuman, D., Flanagan, C., & MacIver, D. (1993). Development during adolescence: The impact of stage-environment fit on young adolescents', experiences in schools and families. *American Psychologist, 48*(2), 90-101.

Edgerton, R. B. (1986). Alcohol and drug use by mentally retarded adults. *American Journal of Mental Deficiency, 90*(6), 602-609.

Efinger, J. M. (1983). Women and alcoholism. *Topics in Clinical Nursing, 4,* 10-19.

Erikson, E. H. (1968). *Identity: Youth and crisis.* New York: W.W. Norton.

Evans, D. A. (1989). Prevalence of Alzheimer's disease in a community population of older persons. *Journal of the American Medical Association, 262,* 2551.

Faltz, B. G. (1992). Counseling chemically dependent lesbians and gay men. In S. H. Dworkin & F. J. Gutierrez (Eds.), *Counseling gay men & lesbians: Journey to the end of the rainbow* (pp. 245-258). Alexandria, VA: American Association for Counseling and Development.

Faludi, S.(1991). *Backlash: The undeclared war against American women.* New York: Doubleday.

Fassinger, R. E. (1991). The hidden minority: Issues and challenges in working with lesbian women and gay men. *The Counseling Psychologist, 19,* 157-176.

Fellios, P. G. (1989). Alcoholism in women: Causes, treatment, and prevention. In G. W. Lawson and A. W. Lawson (Eds.), *Alcoholism and substance abuse in special populations* (pp. 11-36). Rockville, MD: Aspen.

Ford, B. (1987). *Betty: A Glad Awakening.* New York: Doubleday.

Fifield, L. H., Latham, J. D., & Phillips, C. (1977). *Alcoholism in the gay community: The price of alienation, isolation, and oppression.* Los Angeles, CA: Gay Community Services Center.

Gambert. S. R. (1992). Substance abuse in the elderly. In J. H. Lowinson, P. Ruiz, R. B. Millman, & J. G. Langrod (Eds.), *Substance abuse: A comprehensive textbook* (pp. 843-851). Baltimore: Williams & Wilkins.

George, R. L. (1990). *Counseling the chemically dependent: Theory and practice.* Upper Saddle River, NJ: Prentice Hall.

Gibson, P. (1989). Gay men and lesbian youth suicide. In M. Feinleib (Ed.), *Report of the secretary's task force on youth suicide* (pp. 3-11). Washington, DC: U.S. Department of Health and Human Services.

Gottfredson, G. D. (1981). Schooling and delinquency. In S. D. Martin, L. B. Sechrest, & R. Redner (Eds.), *New directions in the rehabilitation of criminal offenders.* Washington, DC: National Academy Press.

Gurnack, A. M., & Thomas, J. L. (1989). Behavioral factors related to elderly alcohol abuse: Research and policy issues. *International Journal of Addictions, 24,* 641-654.

Gurwitz, J. H., & Avorn, J. (1991). The ambiguous relation between aging and adverse drug reactions. *Annals of Internal Medicine, 114,* 952-965.

Hafen, B. Q., & Brog, M. J. (1983). *Alcohol* (2nd ed.). St. Paul, MN: West.

Hall, G. S. (1940). *Adolescence.* New York: Appleton.

Hamlett, K., Eaker, E. D., & Stokes, J. III (1989). Psychosocial correlates of alcohol intake among women aged 45-64 years: The Framingham study. *Journal of Behavioral Medicine, 12,* 525-542.

Hastings, P. (1982). Alcohol and the lesbian community: Changing patterns of awareness. *Surveyor, 18,* 3-7.

Hawkins, J. D., Catalano, R. F., & Miller, J. Y. (1992). Risk and protective factors for alcohol and other drug problems in adolescence and early adulthood: Implications for substance abuse prevention. *Psychological Bulletin, 112*(1), 64-105.

Hawkins, J. D., Catalano, R. F., & Associates. (1992). *Communities that care.* San Francisco: Jossey-Bass.

Hazelden Corporation (1996). Alcoholism and drug abuse: A growing problem among the elderly. *On the World Wide Web,* 1-2.

Heinemann, A. W., Donohue, R., Keen, M., & Schnoll, S. (1988). Alcohol use by persons with recent spinal cord injuries. *Archives of Physical Medicine and Rehabilitation, 69,* 619-624.

Heinemann, A. W., Doll, M., & Schnoll, S. (1989). Treatment of alcohol abuse in person with recent spinal cord injuries. *Alcohol, Health and Research World, 13*(2), 110–117.

Helwig, A., & Holicky, R. (1994). Substance abuse in persons with disabilities: Treatment considerations. *Journal for Counseling and Development, 72,* 227-233.

Hepner, R., Kirshbaum, H., & Landes, D. (1980-81). Counseling substance abusers with additional disabilities: The center for independent living. *Alcohol Health and Research World, 5,* 11-15.

Heriot, J. (1983). The double bind: Healing the split. In J. H. Robbins & R. J. Siegel (Eds.), *Women changing therapy* (pp. 11-28). New York: Harrington Park Press.

Hill, S. Y. (1984). Vulnerability to the biomedical consequences of alcoholism and alcohol-related problems among women. In S. C. Wilsnack & L. J. Beckman (Eds.), *Alcohol problems in women: Antecedents, consequences, and intervention* (pp. 45-54). New York: Guilford Press.

Horrocks, J. E., & Benimoff, M. (1967). Isolation from the peer group during adolescence. *Adolescence, 2,* 41-52.

Israelstam, S., & Lambert, S. (1989). Homosexuals who indulge in excessive use of alcohol and drugs: Psychosocial factors to be taken into account by community and intervention workers. *Journal of Alcohol and Drug Education, 34,* 54-78.

Jessor, R., & Jessor, S. L. (1975). Adolescent development and onset of drinking. *Journal of Alcohol Studies, 36,* 27-51.

Johnson, G. M., Schoutz, F. C., & Locke, T. P. (1984). Relationships between adolescent drug use and parental drug behavior. *Adolescence, (74)19,* 295-298.

Jones, K. A., Latham, J. D., & Jenner, M. (1980, May). *Social environment within conventional alcoholism treatment agencies as perceived by gay and nongay recovering alcoholics: A preliminary report.* Paper presented at the National Council on Alcoholism Forum, Seattle, WA.

Kircus, E., & Brillhart, B. A. (1990). Dealing with substance abuse among people with disabilities. *Rehabilitation Nursing, 15,* 250-253.

Kraus, L. E., & Stoddard, S. (1989). *Chartbook on disability in the United States: An Inhouse Report.* Washington, DC: National Institute on Disability and Rehabilitation Research, U.S. Department of Education.

Kumpfer, K. (1987). Special populations: Etiology and prevention of vulnerability to chemical dependency in children of substance abusers. In B. Brown & A. Mills (Eds.), *Youth at high risk for substance abuse* (pp. 1-72). Rockville, MD: National Institute on Drug Abuse.

Kus, R. (1988). Alcoholism and non-acceptance of gay self: The critical link. *Journal of Homosexuality, 15,* 25-41.

LaChance, L. L. (1989). *Alcohol, drugs, and adolescents.* Ann Arbor MI: ERIC/CAPS.

Laidlaw, T. A., & Malmo, C. (1990). *Healing voices: Feminist approaches to therapy with women.* San Francisco: Jossey-Bass.

Lawson, G. W., & Lawson, A. W. (1991). *Alcoholism and substance abuse in special populations.* Rockville, MD: Aspen.

Lawson, G. W., & Lawson, A. W. (Eds.). (1992). *Adolescent substance abuse.* Maryland: Aspen Publishers.

Lester, L. (1982). The special needs of the female alcoholic. *The Journal of Contemporary Social Work,* 451-456.

Levy, L. J., Duga, J., Girgis, M., & Gordon, E. E. (1973), Keroacidosis associated with alcoholism and nondiabetic subjects. *Annual of Internal Medicine, 78,* 213.

Lisansky, E. S. (1989). Special issues of women. *U.S. Journal of Drug and Alcohol Dependence, 13,* 9-12.

Lohrenz, L., Connelly, J., Coyne, L., & Spare, K. (1978). Alcohol problems in several Midwestern homosexual communities. *Journal of Studies on Alcohol, 39,* 1959-1963.

Marsh, J. C. (1982). Public issues and private problems: Women and drug use. *Journal of Social Issues, 38,* 153-165.

Mondanaro, J. (1989). *Chemically dependent women.* Lexington, MA: Lexington Books.

Morales, E. S., & Graves, M. A. (1983). *Substance abuse: Patterns and barriers to treatment for gay men and lesbians in San Francisco.* Report to Community Substance Abuse Services, San Francisco Department of Public Health.

National Center for Educational Statistics. (1992). Digest of education statistics. Washington DC: U.S. Government Printing Office.

Navarro, M. (1989, June). Special problems for gays of color. In reprint of published series, *San Francisco Examiner.*

Newcomb, M. D., & Bentler, P. M. (1988). *Consequences of adolescent drug use: Impact on the lives of young adults.* Newbury Park, CA: Sage.

Newcomb, M. D., & Bentler, P. M. (1986). Substance use and ethnicity: Differential impact of peer and adult models. *Journal of Psychology, 120,* 83-95.

O'Bear, K., & Reynolds, A. (1985, March). Opening doors to understanding and acceptance: *A facilitator's guide for presenting workshops on lesbian and gay issues.* Workshop and manual presented at the American College Personnel Association convention, Boston.

O'Connor, M. F. (1992). Psychotherapy with gay and lesbian adolescents. In S. H. Dwrokin & F. J. Gutierrez (Eds.), *Counseling gay men and lesbians: Journey to the end of the rainbow* (pp. 3-21). Alexandria, VA: American Association for Counseling and Development.

O'Donnell, M., Leoffler, V., Pollock, K., & Saunders, Z. (1980). *Lesbian health matters*. Santa Cruz, CA: Women's Health Center.

Office for Substance Abuse Prevention (1991, October). *Prevention Resource Guide: Women*. National Clearinghouse for Alcohol and Drug Information. Rockville, MD: Author.

Ogur, B. (1986). Long day's journey into night: Women and prescription drug use. *Women and Health Review, 11*, 99-115. Oster, R. A. (1983). Peer counseling: Drug and alcohol abuse prevention. *Journal of Primary Prevention, 3*.

Paul, J. P, Stall, R., & Bloomfield, K. A. (1991). Gay and alcoholic: Epidemiologic and clinical issues. *Alcohol World, 15*, 151-160.

Pearce, D. (1979). Women, work, and welfare: The feminization of poverty. In K. W. Feinstein (Ed.), *Working women and families* (pp. 103-124). Beverly Hills, CA: Sage.

Pope, A. M., & Tarlov, A. R. (Eds.). (1991). *Disability in America*. Washington, DC: National Academy Press.

Prendergast, M., Austin, G., & Miranda, J. (1990). *Substance abuse among youth with disabilities*. Wisconsin Clearinghouse, University of Wisconsin-Madison.

Prevention Center: Center for Applied Prevention Research (1992). *Profile of the Chemically Dependent Woman*. Boulder, CO: Author.

Quadrel, M. J., Fischhoff, B., & Davis, W. (1993). Adolescent (in)vulnerability. *American Psychologist, 48*(2), 102-116.

Reed, B. G. (1985). Drug misuse and dependency in women: The meaning and implications of being considered a special population or minority group. *International Journal of the Addictions, 20*(1), 13-62

Rehabilitation Brief (1990). Vol XII, No. 12.

Research & Training Center on Independent Living (1990). *Guidelines for reporting and writing about people with disabilities*. Berkeley, CA.

Rhodes, J., & Jason, L. (1990). A social stress model of substance abuse. *Journal of Consulting and Clinical Psychology, 58*(4) 395-401.

Robertson, N. (1992). The intimate enemy: Will that friendly drink betray you? *Modern Maturity, 35*, 27-30.

Robins, L. (1978). Sturdy childhood predictors of adult antisocial behavior: Replications from longitudinal studies. *Psychological Medicine, 8*, 611-622.

Ruble, T. (1983). Sex stereotypes: Issues of change in the 1970's. *Sex Roles, 9*, 397-402.

Rudolph, J. (1989). The impact of contemporary ideology and AIDS on the counseling of gay clients. *Counseling and Values, 33*, 96-108.

Sandmaier, M. (1982). *Helping women with alcohol problems: A guide to community care givers*. Philadelphia: Women's Health Communications.

Schaps, E. (1980). *A review of 127 drug abuse prevention program evaluations*. Lafayette, CA: Pacific Institute for Research Evaluation.

Schaschl, S., & Straw, D. (1989). Results of a model intervention program for physically impaired persons. *Alcohol Health and Research World, 13*, 150-153.

Schliebner, C. T., & Peregoy, J. J. (1994). Unemployment effects on the family and the child: Interventions for counselors. *Journal of Counseling and Development, 72*, 368-372.

Schwieshiemer, W., & Walberg, H. J. (1976). A peer counseling experiment: High school students as small group leaders. *Journal of Counseling Psychology, 23*, 398-401.

Shipley, R. W., Taylor, S. M., & Falvo, D. R. (1990). Concurrent evaluation and rehabilitation of alcohol abuse and trauma. *Journal of Applied Rehabilitation Counseling, 21*(3), 37-39.

Snyder, W., & Ooms, T. (Eds.). (1992). *Empowering families, helping adolescents: Family-centered treatment of adolescents with alcohol, drug abuse, and mental health problems*. Rockville, MD: U.S. Department of Health and Human Services.

Stall, R. S. (1996). Drug abuse in the elderly: Major issues. *On the World Wide Web*, 1-3.

Sumners, A. D. (1991). Women in recovery. In E. G. Bennett & D. Woolf (Eds.), *Substance abuse:*

Pharmacologic, developmental, and clinical perspectives (pp. 280-292). Albany, NY: Delmar.

Towers, R. L. (1987). *How schools can help combat student drug and alcohol abuse.* Washington, DC: National Education Association.

Travis, C. B. (1988). *Women and health psychology.* Hillsdale, NJ: Lawrence Erlbaum Associates.

Walker, M. (1990). *Women in therapy and counselling: Out of the shadows.* Philadelphia: Open University Press.

Whitlock, K. (1989). *Bridges of respect: Creating support for lesbian and gay youth* (2nd ed.). Philadelphia: American Friends Service Committee.

Wilsnack, S. C. (1989). Women at high risk for alcohol abuse. *Counselor, 20,* 16-17.

Wilson, G. T. (1987). Cognitive studies in alcoholism. *Journal of Consulting and Clinical Psychology, 55,* 325-331.

Wodarski, J. S. (1990). Adolescent substance abuse: Practice implications. *Adolescence, 25,* 667-688.

Worell, J., & Remer, P. (1992). *Feminist perspectives in therapy: An empowerment model for women.* New York: John Wiley & Sons.

Zehner, M. A., & Lewis, J. (1985). Homosexuality and alcoholism: Social and developmental perspectives. In R. Schoenberg, R. S. Goldberg, & D. A. Shore (Eds.), *With compassion toward some: Homosexuality and social work in America* (pp. 75-89). Binghamton, NY: Harrington Park Press.

Working with Diverse Cultures: Treatment Issues and Characteristics

CONNIE SCHLIEBNER, PH.D.
JOHN JOSEPH PEREGOY, PH.D.

The intent of this chapter is to present a background for viewing factors that affect diverse cultural groups related to substance use and abuse, prevalence, and effective prevention and intervention strategies. The diverse groups discussed in this chapter are limited to minority cultures that are prevalent in the United States. The assumption at the foundation of this chapter is simple, yet often overlooked in the implementation of individual and community alcohol and other drug interventions. Simply stated, intervention programs designed for particular groups *need* to be developed within the sociocultural worldview in which they are applied. Imposing dominant middle-class, white male interventions in communities not reflecting these values would be tantamount to changing cabins on the Titanic.

The chapter is divided into sections by sociocultural group. Each section has subsections that include a demographic overview, which may present cultural values and sociocultural perspectives; risk factors affecting each group; barriers to treatment; and finally, considerations in prevention and intervention with each group.

AMERICAN INDIANS AND ALASKAN NATIVES

American Indians and Alaskan Natives are a heterogenous group, made up of 547 federally recognized tribes and a number of tribes that are not federally recognized (LaFromboise & Groff Low, 1989). The most recent census data indicate that there are 1,959,234 American Indians and Alaskan Natives (U.S. Department of Commerce, 1992). According to the 1990 census, there are 625,136 American Indians and Alaskan Natives younger than 15 and 41% of this population is 20 years of age or younger.

Each tribe maintains its own unique customs, values, and religious practices. Tribes range from very traditional, in which members speak their tribal language at home, to tribes that use English as their first language (Peregoy, 1993). About 63% of all American Indians and Alaskan Natives live outside of a reservation. With this shift to the cities, an increase in interethnic and intertribal marriages has occurred. This diversity is also compounded by the fact that more than 60% of all Indians are of mixed background, the result of intermarriages among African American, white, Hispanic and Asian populations (Trimble & Fleming, 1989).

The shift to the urban setting has also separated the enrolled tribal member from treaty-obligated services such as health and human services. A person who meets tribal enrollment criteria and is registered on the rolls of the tribe is entitled to services from the tribe, has voting rights within tribal elections, and has eligibility for government services provided by treaty agreements. Enrolled tribal members who have moved to the city are subject to many of the same social pressures and urban survival problems as other ethnic minorities (Vallo, Frogg, Garcia, & Baker, 1980).

Reliable data on extent and pattern of drug use (including alcohol) among American Indians have been scarce (Gurnee, Vigil, Krill-Smith, & Crowely, 1990). Lemert (1982) suggested that Indians/Natives are more likely to be either abstainers or heavy drinkers than members of the general population. Lewis (1982) cited an Indian Health Services Task Force on Alcoholism report, which concluded "(1) by age 15, most Indian youth have tried alcohol, (2) men were heavy drinkers, outnumbering women by a factor of three, (3) the frequency of drinking reaches a peak between the ages of 25 and 44, and (4) there are few if any older Indians drinking excessively" (p. 35). Even though substance abuse behaviors may taper off with age and the data indicate that there is a slight decrease in lifetime prevalence, the rate is much higher than for non-Indian people (Beauvais & LeBoueff, 1985).

Alcohol and other drug use in the Indian/Native communities takes a drastic toll. Many Indian/Native deaths, including accidental deaths, homicides, and suicides are attributed to alcohol and substance abuse (May, 1988). Brod (1975) found alcoholism death rates for Indians/Natives to have ranged from 4.3 to 5.5 times that of national average. May (1982) found that of the 10 leading causes of death in the Indian/Native communities from 1978-1980, alcohol use was directly implicated in four: accidents, cirrhosis of the liver, homicides, and suicides. Nearly one-third of all outpatient visits to Indian Public Health Services are related to substance abuse or dependence (Sue & Sue, 1990). Snake, Hawkins and LeBoueff (1976) concluded that alcohol and drugs cause 80% to 90% of the problems for Indians/Natives. Clearly, substance abuse is a killing behavior in the Indian/Native communities.

Fetal alcohol syndrome (FAS) and fetal alcohol effects (FAE) are consequences of women consuming large amounts of alcohol during pregnancy. The child can then suffer from neurosensory and developmental disabilities (Plaiser, 1989). Although FAS and FAE occur in every cultural community and socioeconomic group, the occurrences vary by subpopulation. FAS is estimated to occur in the general population at about 1 in 750 live births. May (1982) found that the incidence ranged from 1.3 in 1,000 live births for the Navajo tribe to 10.3 in 1,000 live births for the Southwestern Plains tribes.

Risk Factors

The elements underlying Indian/Native substance abuse are complex and fall into three primary categories: biological, psychological, and sociocultural (Mail, 1989). Biological factors include physiology or the body's response to substances that influence substance dependence. Psychological factors include an individual and community's response to the stresses of oppression and other stressors that assist in sobriety or abuse. Sociocultural factors encompass culturally influenced perceptions in response to larger social pressures as they relate to substance use.

Educational levels are low, the average education is completion of the ninth grade (Gurnee, Vigil, Krill-Smith, & Crowely, 1990), unemployment rates exceed 90% on some reservations, and family income is about one-third of the national average (Peregoy, 1993). The comparison of family income is faulty in that it does not take into the consideration cultural obligations to extended family members and is therefore an overestimate of available resources in many instances.

The literature on Indian/Native substance use often cites stress as a precipitating or causal factor in alcohol and drug abuse (Braroe, 1988; Edwards & Edwards, 1990; Mail, 1989). This stress has been referred to as *acculturative stress,* defined as the demands to integrate into and identify with a more dominant culture (Mail, 1989). Simultaneously, deculturative stress takes place and is defined as stress resulting from the loss or devaluation of historical tradition (Brod, 1975).

Phillips and Inui (1986) viewed acculturation as the outcome of processes that occur at multiple levels in a society, and stated that the acquisition of foreign (mainstream) beliefs and values produces stress that may be alleviated by substance use and abuse. These authors have also identified high rates of substance abuse, family disruption, criminal behavior, and mental illness as attributes of deculturative stress. "To be between two worlds forces individuals into conflicts of choice and produces casualties among those who cannot embrace either the old or new ways" (Braroe, 1988, p. 8).

May (1982) has developed a social integration model for understanding how communities influence substance use. He hypothesized that cohesive and well-integrated communities provide mitigating influences on stress, while poorly integrated communities tend to demonstrate high levels of stress and concomitant substance abuse. Mail (1989) has pointed out that alcohol may become a primary coping response for some individuals and communities, and peer groups may be as powerful an influence as a genetic susceptibility.

The costs of substance abuse goes beyond the emotional and physical dangers and include the use of scarce economic resources. When money is spent on drugs and alcohol it is unavailable for individual or family purchases (Loretto, Beauvais, & Oetting, 1988). Also, reservation economies are affected by economic leakage, the drain of reservation resources being spent outside of the reservation economy (Peregoy, 1993). Loretto, Beauvais, & Oetting (1988) projected that the national expenditure for 7th- to 12th-grade Indian/Native youth for alcohol, marijuana, cocaine, and other drugs was about $8,298,395.

Barriers to Treatment

Guilmet and Whited (1987) pointed to barriers in services offered in the non-Indian community, including historical distrust; difficulties in cross-cultural communication stemming from a lack of shared meaning; the use of extended family systems, which can be misunderstood as child neglect or social instability within the family unit; and unfamiliarity of non-Indian counselors with Indian/Native conversational styles among traditional and transitional family groups. These groups do not emphasize personal issues and may refer only peripherally to matters of great importance to the family.

It has also been pointed out that non-Indian agencies have not demonstrated the ability to cross-culturalize their services to benefit Indian/Native families (Guilmet & Whited, 1987). There is some resistance to providing home-based services, which is interpreted by the Indian community as a fear of cultural differences on the part of non-Indian providers. This speaks to the need for cultural sensitivity on the part of the non-Indian service provider. For further information on Indian/Native cultures, including value orientations, refer to Courtney (1986), Peregoy (1993), and Trimble and Flemming (1989).

Prevention and Intervention

All programming, from prevention to rehabilitation, needs to be developed within the context of the community and the individual. Many programs aimed at American Indian clients emphasize traditional healing practices, including the sweat lodge and other traditional ceremonial or religious activities. These programs appear to be successful for clients who have a strong attachment to traditional Indian/Native cultures. These approaches would not be applicable to clients who do not have a strong attachment to Indian/Native culture and religion. Before implementing services for any client it is important to understand their level of acculturation and their commitment to traditional Indian/Native religions.

Prevention programs using "educational methods" on reservations have failed when they were based on scare tactics. Such programs have actually led to the increase of drug use in adolescent populations (Neligh, 1990). Prevention programming could take several other paths to be effective, including offering alternatives to substance use by strengthening community projects such as recreational opportunities, cultural heritage programs, and employment opportunities and training.

ASIAN AMERICANS

The Asian and Pacific Islander population is growing rapidly in the United States and has doubled in size since 1970, now constituting 2% (5 million) of the total U.S. population (Ho, 1992). This is a diverse population, consisting of at least 32 national and ethnic groups (such as Chinese, Filipino, Japanese, Korean, Hawaiians, and refugees from Vietnam, Cambodia, Thailand, Laos, and Indonesia) with language, religious, historical, social, and economic differences (Ho, 1992; Trimble, Padilla, & Bell, 1987).

Data regarding Asian Americans often present them as a single group with similar characteristics. But it is difficult to make generalizations about this population given the between-group differences and within-group differences—such as migration or relocation experiences, degree of assimilation or acculturation, identification with home country, use of native and English languages, family composition and intactness, amount of education, and degree of adherence to religious beliefs. (Sue & Sue, 1990; Wong, 1985).

Research and information on alcohol and other drug use among Asian Americans is scant (Austin, Prendergast, & Lee, 1990; Trimble, Padilla, and Bell, 1987). This can be attributed to the "model minority" stereotype held by drug researchers and mental health professionals that Asians do not have drug problems, and therefore are in little need of study. Ho (1992) noted that some observers have predicted that alcoholism among Asian-Americans may increase in the future due to urbanization, cultural conflicts, and changes in family structure.

Cultural Values

To fully understand the Asian American client, a mental health professional must be responsive to the culture of the client in a racial/ethnic context in combination with the dominant U.S. culture (Ho, 1992; Lee & Richardson, 1991). Although Asian immigrants and refugees form diverse groups, certain commonalities can be generalized to the Asian populations. Ho (1992), Kinzie (1985), and Sue and Sue (1991) have discussed salient cultural values operating among Asian Americans:

Filial Piety

Filial piety is the respectful love, obligation, and duty to one's parents. Asian children are expected to comply with familial and social authority even if they must sacrifice their personal desires and ambitions. As children become acculturated into the dominant U.S. culture, pressure to meet parental obligations and expectations can lead to stress and conflict.

Shame As a Behavioral Control

Traditionally, shaming is used to help reinforce familial expectations and proper behavior within and outside the family. Individuals who behave inappropriately will "lose face" and may cause the family to withdraw support. With the importance of interdependence, the withdrawal of support can cause considerable anxiety in having to face life alone.

Self-Control

The Confucian and Taoist philosophies emphasize the need for moderation—to maintain modesty in behavior, be humble in expectations, and restrain emotional expression. Love, respect, and affection are shown through behaviors that benefit the family and its members. Hence, the Asian American client may lack experience in identifying and communicating emotional states.

Awareness of Social Milieu

Asian American individuals tend to be very sensitive to the opinions of peers and allow the social norms to define their thoughts, feelings, and actions. One subordinates to the group to maintain solidarity. Social esteem and self-respect are maintained by complying with social norms.

Fatalism

Asian Americans accept their fate and maintain a philosophical detachment. This silent acceptance contributes to their unwillingness to seek professional help. A "what will be will be" view of life is often misconstrued by mental health professionals as resistance to treatment.

Roles and Status

The hierarchy of the Asian family and community is based on cultural tradition of male dominance. Men and elders are afforded greater importance than women and youths. The father makes the major decisions and the mother is responsible for the children. The greatest responsibility is placed on the eldest son, who is expected to be a role model for younger siblings and help raise them. Upon the death of the father, the eldest son takes on the family leadership. Fewer demands are placed on daughters, because they leave their family of origin upon marriage. Therapy with Asian Americans must take into account family hierarchy and the demands placed on each member.

Somatization

Generally Asian Americans perceive problems as difficulties with physical health. Physical illness is believed to cause psychological problems. Complaints such as headaches, stomach aches, and muscle aches are often expressed in response to stressors. Mental health professionals must take into account physical complaints as real problems to improve other aspects of the client's life.

Risk Factors

As noted earlier, the lack of national surveys regarding the drinking patterns of Asian Americans makes it difficult to generalize about the population's substance use. Austin, Prendergast, and Lee (1990) noted that most surveys of Asian American adults have been conducted in Hawaii and California. The results of these studies indicated (1) Asian Americans drink less than whites, (2) there is a large percentage of abstainers (particularly among women), (3) most drinking is done by men, but at moderate levels, and (4) drinking patterns vary considerably among different Asian groups. Kitano, Hatanaka, Yeung, and Sue (1985) found that Asian drinking is often situational (banquets and festivals), and generally takes place in the company of others, usually accompanied by food and with moderation strongly encouraged.

Chi, Lubben, and Kitano, (1989) examined drinking among Chinese, Japanese, Koreans, and Filipinos in Los Angeles and found similarities among all four groups who drank heavily: they were most likely to be men younger than 45, of relatively high social status and educational levels, in professional occupations, with permissive attitudes toward substance use, and with friends tolerant of drinking. Even those who drank heavily exhibited little evidence of alcohol problems, such as arrests for drinking, personal impairment, or changes in life styles.

As Asians acculturate into the dominant culture of the United States, the drinking patterns of the group tend to approximate the standard white norm (Kitano, Hatanaka, Yeung, & Sue, 1985). The stress of acculturation brings challenges of adjustment and the demands of two conflicting cultures. Lee and Cynn (1991) observed that children of immigrating parents are quick to adapt to U.S. cultural values, attitudes, and lifestyle. The difference in rate of acculturation between the parent and child can be a source of stress and conflict.

Sue and Sue (1971) proposed three ways used by Asian Americans to adjust to the conflicts of acculturation. The traditionalist maintains loyalty to their ethnic group by retaining traditional values and living up to the expectations of the family. The marginal person views his or her ethnicity as a handicap and attempts to become over-Westernized by rejecting traditional Asian values. This type of adjustment often leads to an identity crisis and a marginal existence, because the individual cannot completely shed certain traditional ways.

Individuals who are attempting to develop a new identity incorporate positive aspects of the Asian culture with the current situation. They have a need to attain self-pride by reversing the negative of racism and discrimination in the Unites States.

They may become politically or militantly involved to expose and change cultural racism in the United States.

Accurate assessment of an individual's acculturation level assist the therapist in data collection, analysis, interpretation, and determination of whether the client will return for future therapy (Ho, 1992). Understanding the culture of Asian Americans and potential adjustment problems is a necessary first step in providing sensitive interventions to facilitate a positive therapeutic experience.

Prevention and Intervention

Asian Americans do not generally seek out mental health services because of the stigma and shame of talking about one's problems (Sue & Sue, 1990). Austin, Prendergast, and Lee (1990) suggested that in addressing substance abuse, the focus needs to be on prevention. Many Asian American substance abusers may not enter treatment until the late stages of the problem, because it is kept hidden by their families. Chang (1981) recommended that prevention programs include information to identify resources and organizations within the Asian community that lead to developing self-help networks. Publication of drug information literature in Asian languages needs to be available.

Prevention programs can provide education to young people on ethnic heritage and customs to promote positive cultural identity, self-esteem, and family communications. Education for parents on U.S. life and substance abuse issues will help them understand their children's acculturation and the stressors related to that process.

It has been suggested (Prendergast, Austin, & Miranda, 1990) that key organizations and leaders in Asian communities be identified and involved in the programs for successful implementation. Ishisaka, Nguyen, and Okimoto (1985), Lorenzo and Adler (1984), Tung (1985), and Sue and Sue (1990) have suggested that culturally sensitive therapeutic strategies be available when working with Asian American clients.

Because of cultural expectations and lack of experience with counseling, the Asian American client may expect the counselor to furnish direction. An active and directive therapeutic role may best meet these expectations with focus on concrete resolution of problems. Time-limited or brief therapy that deals with the current or immediate future is a positive model that can assist clients in immediate change.

In working with families, it is necessary for the therapist to consider intergenerational conflicts due to role changes, levels of acculturation, and culture conflict. Awareness of the vertical and hierarchial family structure (which is determined by age, sex, generation, and birth order), role responsibilities, and expectations is essential to limiting conflicts and problems within the family system.

AFRICAN AMERICANS

African Americans constitute 12.4% of the United States population, which translates into about 30 million people of African descent in the United States today

(U.S. Department of Commerce, 1991). The African American population more than doubled between 1967 and 1987. (Ho, 1987).

Wide gaps exist between African Americans and the general population in the arenas of education, employment, and income. In 1990 the average educational attainment for African Americans was only slightly below that of whites (12.2 years and 12.6 years respectively). But the education gap widens when examining post-secondary education experiences. For example, when examining the 1972 high school graduates in 1986, it was found that only 4% of African Americans had been conferred advanced degrees, compared with 8% of the white population (U.S. Department of Education, 1992).

This gap in higher education attainment sheds light on the median income for African Americans. The median income for African American families was only 60% of the median income of white families, with no appreciable increase in this difference during the past decade (Sleeter & Grant, 1993).

In 1990, about 50.2% of all African American families had both a husband and wife, yet 43.8% were headed by women. Of these families, 31.9% of the husband-and-wife families and 50.6% of the families headed by women only lived in poverty (U.S. Department of Commerce 1992). Unemployment rates remain high in this population, about twice that of the general population (U.S. Bureau of Commerce, 1992). Ogle, Alsalam, and Rogers (1991) have pointed out that the percentage of African American children living below the poverty level was three times that of white children in the United States.

The toll taken by alcohol and other drugs in the African American community is disproportionate to their numbers. Of all deaths caused by drug abuse in 1988, African Americans represented 29.6% of the fatalities across the nation. In examining deaths attributable to cirrhosis of the liver caused by alcohol abuse for the same year, African Americans again represented a disproportionate percentage of the total equaling 14.9% (National Institute on Drug Abuse, 1989).

Annual homicide rates for young African American males from 1978 to 1987 were 4 to 5 times higher than for African American females, 5 to 8 times higher than for young white males, and 16 to 22 times higher than for young white females (Staff, 1991). Many of these homicides are attributed to substance abuse-related behaviors. Young African American males are at higher risk in a variety of categories within the larger population.

Risk Factors

Environmental risk factors related to African Americans include a disproportionate number of families at or below the poverty level, high levels of unemployment and a bleak employment outlook. The vast majority (86%) live in urban areas (Sue & Sue, 1990), subjected to covert and systematic practices of discrimination from racist elements in mainstream society.

Sociocultural risk factors include acceptance of behaviors related to substance use within the community and peer groups. Robins and Pryzbeck (1985) noted that statistics from an epidemiological study suggested that African Americans were not more genetically vulnerable than whites to alcoholism and that socioeconomic level and cultural norms can change alcohol use. This can be viewed through lifetime prevalence rates. Rates were substantially higher in young adult white males (29%) than African American males (13%). Among elderly whites and African Americans, whites showed lower usage rates (13%) compared with elderly African Americans (24%). These researchers have suggested cultural factors in the increased use with age in the African American community.

Cultural Values

To understand cultural factors in the African American community it is important understand the "extended self", which is validated only in its functioning in relationship and harmony with a collective whole (Butler, 1992, p. 30). The concept of self-identity in relation to the other is perhaps captured best by Mbiti (1970): "I am because we are; and because we are therefore I am" (p. 103). This orientation is grounded in the value and importance of concern for one another. Self-identity in relation to the other begins with the family.

The family has been described as a social system interacting with a number of social systems, each affected by historical influences that must be understood before family and cultural values can be understood (Billingsley, 1968; McAdoo, 1988). The African American family has been identified as operating under themes that help overcome oppressive societal conditions and contribute to both family and community cohesiveness. These themes include (1) strong kinship bonds across a variety of households; (2) strong work, education, and achievement orientation; (3) a high level of flexibility in family roles; (4) a strong commitment to religious values and church participation (Solomon, 1976); and (5) an endurance of suffering (Ho, 1987).

Strong kinship bonds stem from African traditions and values (Nobles, 1988) while also a functioning as a response to demands from unwelcome and oppressive environments (Franklin, 1988). The strong family and kinship system helps the family cope with environmental threats to ensure survival, security, and self-esteem of its members (Ho, 1987).

Kinship systems are found in an extended family network composed of older children, relatives, close family friends (Sue & Sue, 1990), and within the church—its members and services (Ho, 1987). Kinship systems have served in functional and nurturing roles providing financial aid, child care, emotional support, and guidance (Ho, 1987). The church provides religious and social services and helps maintain family solidarity, status conference, leadership development, a safe haven for the release of emotional tensions, social/political activity, and amusements (Manns, 1988).

Elements of the African American worldview include ways of knowing, oral patterns, and thought. Ways of knowing for African Americans are influenced by what is known via the senses and in an extrasensory fashion (Butler, 1992). "Spirit gives essence to the life form, which in turn provides concreteness to the spirit; the two are one" (p. 32). This worldview embraces the co-existence and interconnectedness of opposites, which allows for the characterization of material phenomena and spiritual forces contributing to a full expression of one's reality (Butler, 1992).

Oral patterns and communication are predominant means for information sharing (Ho, 1987). The African American worldview is affected by a thought process characterized by a strong reliance on internal cues and reactions as a means of problem solving. Butler (1992) pointed out that there is a cultural respect for internal cues and "hunches" as a means for acquiring information and knowledge. Given the humanistic orientation of African Americans, this type of thought assists in social interaction and the ability to be empathetic (Butler, 1992). All of these components have strong implications in determining service delivery.

Barriers to Treatment

Barriers to treatment in the African American community vary from programs that impose white norms and expectations to service agencies being located in hard to access areas. Similar to the Hispanic community, many African Americans find themselves in pharmacological treatment programs rather than psychological treatment programs (Caetano, 1989). The focus on individual responsibility in substance abuse behaviors also acts as a barrier to effective treatment given the African American worldview, interactional styles, and humanistic orientation.

Other barriers that contribute to underuse of mental health services for the African American community include (1) the lack of a historical perspective on the development of the family and support systems within the African American community; (2) a lack of awareness and understanding of the unique characteristics of the value systems of African American families; and (3) communication barriers that hinder the development of trust between the African American client and the non-African therapist (Wilson, 1987). For more information, see Ho (1987), McAdoo (1988), and Sue and Sue (1990).

Prevention and Intervention

The key to prevention with African Americans is complex and yet practical if strategies are developed to meet individual, family, and community needs. By recognizing cultural values, social status, drug-use patterns, drug-related problems, and attitudes toward drugs in the African American community, programs can be implemented to meet community needs (Gary & Berry, 1985; Nobles, 1988).

Ecological factors have a strong effect on African American communities; they are important in fostering attitudes toward substance use. For instance, there are a large number of liquor stores in African American neighborhoods, located near schools, churches, and homes. This is not the case in predominately white neighborhoods (Austin, 1990). Watts and Wright (1985) call this "economic exploitation" (p. 2).

Globetti, Alsikafi, and Morse (1980) have pointed out that one major obstacle to program effectiveness is a lack of awareness of the seriousness of substance abuse issues in the community or a reluctance to admit it. This reluctance is a result of ambivalent attitudes within the community, particularly with alcohol.

Another factor affecting program development and implementation is the influence of racial consciousness on use. Gary and Berry (1985) found a strong correlation between those who were highly racially conscious (identifying with their African ancestry and U.S. experience) and attitudes of intolerance toward substance abuse. They concluded from this study that more consideration of the strong ethnic identity be applied to programs as an alternative to a strong emphasis on anti-drug tactics in substance abuse prevention programs.

Community programs can augment school-based programs to address needs in the family and community. Community-based programs are not programs offered in the community from the outside, but rather programs that involve community members, values, and perspectives from within the community.

HISPANICS

The term *Hispanic* was generated as a U.S. government catch phrase to conveniently classify different subgroups and subcultures of people who are of Cuban, Mexican, Puerto Rican, and South or Central American descent (Arbona, 1990; Nieves-Squires, 1991). While Hispanics do have much in common (language; religion; customs; and attitudes toward self, family, and community), the subgroups have considerable variation in ethnic origins, socioeconomic groups, dialects, immigration status, and histories (Casas & Vasquez, 1989; Chilman, 1993). The Census Bureau (U.S. Department of Commerce, 1991) reported 22.3 million Hispanics in the United States in 1990. This reflects a population increase of 65% since the 1980 census. This increase has been attributed to both immigration and high fertility rates. The census data do not reflect undocumented Hispanics who choose to "pass" due to fear of deportation, or for economic, political, or personal reasons (Goffman, 1963).

Booth, Castro, and Anglin (1990) noted that until the mid-1980s little information on substance abuse and Hispanics was available. What did exist failed to delineate differences among the various Hispanic subgroups. A generalization did emerge that Hispanics were more likely to use drugs than other groups. Later research (National Institute on Drug Abuse, 1987) indicated that although portions of the Hispanic community have been affected by serious drug problems, the Hispanic population as a whole is not more likely to use drugs than other groups. Many of the factors associated with substance abuse among other oppressed minority groups in the United States appear to operate for Hispanics as well (Booth, Castro, & Anglin, 1990).

Research has shown that Hispanics "suffer the full impact of the 'culture poverty' . . . low income, unemployment, underemployment, undereducation, poor housing, prejudice, discrimination, and cultural/linguistic barriers" (President's Commission on Mental Health, 1978, p. 905). In addition to the stress of the 'culture poverty' many Hispanics also experience acculturation stress. The intergenerational transition from one's culture of origin to the development of bicultural abilities places stress and strain on the individual and the family system (Ruiz & Casas, 1981).

Known as cultural shift, Mendoza and Martinez (1981) point out one pattern of acculturation whereby an individual substitutes one set of practices with alternative cultural characteristics. A dramatic point of stress in the acculturational process is a shift from a culture that values family unity and subordination of the individual to the welfare of the group to a highly individualistic culture predominant in U.S. society (Ho, 1987). If substance abuse is used to cope with stress, then levels of drug use will vary depending on the level of acculturation (Booth, Castro, & Anglin, 1990).

La Familia and Cultural Values

Discord and family disruption have been identified as an antecedent of substance use and abuse among Hispanic adolescents and young adults (Santisteban & Szapocznik, 1982). To gain insight into the Hispanic individual, investigation of "la familia" is paramount, because the family is the basis of Hispanic cultures. Often divided by generation, the immigrant's status tends to guide the adherence to the values and mores of one's culture of origin.

The acculturation process can produce tremendous amounts of stress for the individual and place dramatic strains on the family system. Those who have immigrated alone, leaving behind their extended family support system, face the potential of adjustment problems (De La Rosa, 1988; Glick & Moore, 1990).

Cultural Values

Hispanics underuse mental health services and tend to terminate therapy after one contact at a rate of more than 50 percent (Atkinson, Morten, & Sue, 1993; Rogler, Malgady, & Rodriguez, 1989). Sue and Sue (1990) have suggested that ineffective and inappropriate counseling approaches to the values held by this group are often reasons for early termination. Certain unifying cultural values distinguish Hispanics from the dominant culture (Ho, 1987). An increased awareness of the cultural concepts can foster a positive therapeutic experience for the Hispanic client.

Ho (1987) stated that the Hispanic family provides support, identity, and security for its members. The strong sense of obligation ensures that the family's needs as a unit supersede individual needs. Sue and Sue (1990) noted that children are expected to be obedient and are not generally consulted on family decisions, and adolescents are expected to take responsibility for younger siblings at an early age.

The Hispanic nuclear family is embedded in the extended family consisting of aunts, uncles, grandparents, cousins, godparents, and lifelong friends (Ho, 1992). During times of crisis the family is the first resource for advice before help is sought from others (Carillo, 1982). Due to this strong tie, Ho (1987) suggested the importance of enlisting the family in therapy.

The cultural value of personalism defines an individual's self-worth and dignity from inner qualities that give self-respect (Keefe, 1978). The Hispanic culture values the uniqueness of inner qualities that constitute personal dignity. This sense of self-respect, self-worth, and dignity in oneself and others demands showing and receiving proper respect (Ho, 1987). A therapist that conveys personalism develops trust and obligation with the Hispanic client.

Sex-role norms and hierarchy within the family unit continue to influence both Hispanic men and women; however, acculturation and urbanization appear to be affecting both of these standards (Booth, Castro, & Anglin, 1990). Traditionally, males are expected to be the strong and dominant provider while the female role is more nurturant, self-sacrificing, and submissive to the male (Mejia, 1983; Sue & Sue, 1990). Espin (1985) suggested that some Hispanic women are more modern in their views of education and work, but remain traditional in their personal relationships.

In addition to sex roles, a hierarchy of leadership and authority is related to gender and generation. The father's role is one of superior authority and the mother's role can be viewed as the center of the family and purveyor of culture. (Falicov, 1982). "Although the father is seen by himself and others as the family leader who has power, the culture also includes a strong sense of related parental responsibility" (Chilman, as cited in McAdoo, 1993, p. 153). Children are expected to obey their parents, and younger children are expected to obey older siblings who are role models (Chilman, 1993). Understanding the roles and hierarchy of each Hispanic family is vital in assisting with problem solving, renegotiation, and redefinition of power relationships (Ho, 1987).

Spiritual values and the importance of religion can be a strong influence on the behavior of Hispanics (Atkinson, Morten, & Sue, 1993). Spiritualism assumes an invisible world of good and evil spirits who influence behavior (Delgado, 1978). The spirits can protect or cause illness, so an individual is expected to do charitable deeds to be protected by the good spirits (Ho, 1987).

Catholicism is the primary religion for Hispanics. Acosta, Yamamoto, and Evans (1982) noted that traditional adherence to the religious values of enduring suffering and self-denial may prevent some Hispanics from seeking mental health treatment. Therapy can be augmented by enlisting other support systems, such as the church or folk healers.

Barriers to Treatment

Barriers to treatment for Hispanic groups include the disproportionate number of Hispanics enrolled in programs that emphasize pharmacological treatment rather than psychological treatment (Caetano, 1989). This barrier may be due to the economics of treatment costs or the lack of treatment programs to operate effectively across cultural milieus. The inability of service agencies to respond to the needs of Hispanics is the result of several factors.

First, cross-cultural counseling has just been recognized as a viable fourth force in the mental health field (Pedersen, 1991). The responsibility of this approach requires that mental health professionals be familiar with standard models of treatment in the field and that these models be analyzed as to how they may complement or belittle cultural beliefs and perspectives. These perspectives would include, for example, the view of alcoholism as a disease as well as the belief that an individual who abuses it is morally weak. The latter view is not consistent with the disease model of alcoholism; however, is a common perspective among Hispanics (Caetano, 1989).

Cultural perspectives such as this one have implications for service delivery at all levels. As an example, working with a self-referred Hispanic male who believes the above, the mental health worker may also need to help him work through the shame of being morally weak within a traditional concept of machismo. In addition, an understanding of the meaning of substance abuse behaviors and their social contexts may produce an awareness of how competing values cause stress and influence substance abuse coping responses (Galan, 1988).

Bilingual language ability and bicultural skills have been identified as essential elements in the provision of services to Hispanic groups, which, until the early 1980s, were vastly underrepresented in service delivery (Galan, 1988; De La Rosa, 1988; Glick & Moore, 1990). These factors have continued to affect program service delivery (McGlogen & Denniston, 1990). This problem speaks to the need for training programs to actively recruit and train Hispanics into the human services professions.

Immigrant legal status can also be a barrier if individuals have entered the country illegally. These individuals may not seek assistance due to fear of deportation. This group may be at particular risk for substance abuse, especially if they do not have well-developed support systems in place (De La Rosa, 1988; Pearson, 1990).

Research-based investigation into risk factors and conceptual models of alcohol and other drug use can also act as barriers when they are based on faulty assumptions. One example of this type of barrier can be found in research that was limited to a single model. This model paralleled an early drinking model developed for African Americans (by non-African researchers), which focused on heavy drinking and alcohol problems as a product of anomie or deprivation (Caetano, 1989). Caetano (1989, 1990) has argued that the issues concerning Hispanic drinking behaviors are more complex than earlier models would indicate. When considering Hispanic substance abuse behaviors together with the effect of ethnic minority status and stresses of recent immigration to the United States, the earlier models are not sufficient to explain substance abuse behaviors of Hispanics.

Current research findings provide a better perspective on substance use patterns among Hispanic populations. Contrary to popular myth, data on national drug use patterns indicated Anglos have the highest lifetime use of cigarettes, alcohol, hallucinogens, and stimulants, regardless of age (National Institute on Drug Abuse, 1989). Hispanic men were found to be more likely to use the drugs previously mentioned than Hispanic women. Data reveal sex differences in use and experimentation at age 35 with substance use among Hispanic populations. One hypothesis that may contribute to this difference of use in age and sex is that older cohorts (age 35 and above) were probably raised with stronger traditional norms discouraging drug use among women, while those younger than 35 appear to be experimenting and using at higher rates (National Institute on Drug Abuse, 1987). Other possible explanations for this may be level of acculturation, or the influence of peer pressure combined with stages of development for younger Hispanics.

This same study also revealed differences among subgroups of Hispanics. Among Hispanics, Puerto Ricans between the ages of 18 and 34 had the highest rates of lifetime drug use (Booth, Castro, & Anglin, 1990). Puerto Ricans reported greater use of cocaine than Anglos, African Americans, or any other Hispanic subgroup. From these differences it is hypothesized that subcultural experiences may be critical to substance use, and that socioeconomic status and level of urbanization may be causal factors related to abuse and lifetime prevalence (Booth, Castro, & Anglin, 1990). It is important to note that this study did not control for differences in SES or social class which have been implicated in affecting differences in survey research.

Other recent findings from the Hispanic Health and Nutrition Examination Survey reported by National Institute on Drug Abuse (1987) suggest that acculturation is important in assessing abuse patterns. Data from this study suggested that a higher level of acculturation is associated with greater lifetime rates of substance use. Further, women tended to have a lower use rate, except as noted earlier. Both of the aforementioned studies document that inhalant use is much lower among Hispanic populations than current stereotypes would suggest (National Institute on Drug Abuse, 1987, 1989).

Prevention and Intervention

With the dearth of research on treatment for Hispanics in general and even less known about long-term effects of intervention, the following recommendations are drawn from the literature and presented as a guide for the reader. Prevention and intervention with Hispanic groups needs to be culturally sensitive to the individual client's life circumstances, including one's level of acculturation, availability of natural support systems, and environmental conditions. In addition, mental health professionals working with Hispanic populations need to incorporate into the counseling process such cultural concepts as *confianza* (trust), *dignidad* (dignity), and *respeto* (respect); current time orientation, preference for action-oriented advice, and the belief that human beings are at the mercy of supernatural forces (De La Rosa, 1988; Sue & Sue, 1990).

Primary prevention programming can use characteristics of Hispanic communities such as strong family and extended family ties to support efforts aimed at adolescents and adults. Programming that addresses anticipated stressors or themes of conflict and that focus on strengths and skills for optimum functioning will enable individuals to combat potential negative effects of acculturational stressors. Peer pressure has been cited as a strong factor in substance abuse (McGlogan & Denniston, 1990). Community and school programming that focuses on leadership skills and problem solving can be helpful if they are continuous and provide consistent opportunities for youths to explore their own creativity.

CONCLUSION

Four themes emerge from the selected groups presented in this chapter. The first is the broad effect of stressors— environmental, social, and cultural—on, among, and within group interactions. This theme challenges us as mental health workers to expand our understanding of the interplay of populations outside the mainstream, with those who have full participation within the mainstream.

The second theme can be summed up as perception, which is influenced by culture. This theme requires investigation into cultural and environmental conditions as they relate to community perceptions of alcohol and other drug behaviors. The question that arises from this theme is how to mobilize a community against the detrimental affects of substance abuse behaviors, within a cultural relevant and meaningful approach?

The third theme speaks to acculturation and identity development. All the groups presented in this chapter, at some level, need to learn to cope with the development of bi-cultural skills. It is our position that the learning of bi-cultural skills and the appreciation of diversity is not only the responsibility of selected populations, but rather the necessary responsibility of us all. Finally, the fourth theme to emerge is the multiplicity in ways of knowing, which are influenced by society, culture, socioeconomic status, age, and cultural, social, and gender identity development.

All these themes speak to the need of mental health workers to challenge their perspective of the world. The challenge is to develop an awareness of how one perceives the culturally different client. In developing this awareness, counselors need to gain an understanding of the history and background of their clients to address the clients' issues within the context in which they are presented. By doing so they will not only serve their clients needs more fully, they will also empower them within the process.

REFERENCES

Acosta, F. X., Yamamoto, J., & Evans, L. A. (1982). *Effective psychotherapy for low income and minority patients.* New York: Plenum Press.

Arbona, C. (1990). Career counseling research and Hispanics: A review of the literature. *The Counseling Psychologist, 18*(2), 300-323.

Atkinson, D. R., Morten, G., & Sue, D. W. (1993). *Counseling American minorities: A cross-cultural*

perspective. Madison, WI: Brown and Benchmark.

Austin, G. A. (Ed.). (1990). *Substance abuse among black youth.* Madison, WI: Wisconsin Clearinghouse.

Austin, G. A., Prendergast, M. L., & Lee, H. (1990). *Substance abuse among Asian American youth.* Madison, WI: Wisconsin Clearinghouse.

Beauvais, F., & LaBoueff, S. (1985). Drug and alcohol abuse and intervention in American Indian communities. *International Journal of the Addictions, 20*(1), 139-171.

Billingsley, A. (1968). *Black families in white America.* Upper Saddle River, NJ: Prentice Hall.

Booth, M. W., Castro, F. G., & Anglin, M. D. (1990). What do we know about Hispanic substance abuse? A review of the literature. In R. Glick & J. Moore (Eds.), *Drugs in Hispanic communities,* (pp. 21-44). New Brunswick, NJ: Rutgers University Press.

Braroe, N. B. (1988). *Indian and white: Self-image and interaction in a Canadian Plains community.* Stanford, CA: Stanford University Press.

Brod, T. M. (1975). Alcoholism as a mental health problem of Native Americans. *Archives of General Psychology, 32,* 1385-1391.

Butler, J. P. (1992). Of kindred minds: The ties that bind. In M. A. Orland (Ed.). *Cultural competence for evaluators: A guide for alcohol and other drug abuse prevention practitioners working with ethnic/racial communities,* (pp. 23-54). Rockville, MD.: Office for Substance Abuse Prevention.

Caetano, R. (1990). Hispanic drinking in the U.S.: Thinking in new directions. *Journal of Addiction, 85,* 1231-1236.

Caetano, R. (1989). Concepts of alcoholism among whites, blacks, and Hispanic populations. *Journal of Studies on Alcohol, 50*(6), 580-582.

Carillo, C. (1982). Changing norms of Hispanic families. In E. E. Jones and S. J. Korchin (Eds.), *Minority mental health* (pp. 250-266). New York: Praeger.

Casas, J. M., & Vasquez, M. J. T. (1989). Counseling the Hispanic client: A theoretical and applied perspective. In P. B. Pedersen, J. G. Draguns, W. J. Lonner, & J. E. Trimble (Eds.), *Counseling across cultures.* University of Hawaii Press: Honolulu.

Chang, S. H. (1981, June). *Drug abuse preventions strategies for Asian American youth.* Center for Multicultural Awareness.

Chi, I., Lubben, J. E., & Kitano, H. H. L. (1989). Differences in drinking behavior among three Asian American groups. *Journal of Studies on Alcohol, 50,* 15-23.

Chilman, C. S. (1993). Hispanic families in the United States: Research perspectives. In H. P. McAdoo (Ed.), *Family ethnicity: Strength in diversity* (pp. 141–163). Newbury Park, CA: Sage.

Courtney, R. (1986). Islands of remorse: Amerindian education in contemporary world. *Curriculum Inquiry, 16*(1), 43-64.

De La Rosa, M. (1988, Summer). Natural support systems of Puerto Ricans: A key dimension for well-being. *Health and Social Work,* 181-190.

Delgado, G. (1978). *Steps to an ecology of mind.* New York: Ballantine.

Edwards, E. D., & Egbert-Edwards, M. (1990). American Indian adolescents: Combating problems of substance use and abuse through a community model. In A. R. Stiffman, & L. E. Davis (Eds.), *Ethnic issues in adolescent mental health,* (pp. 285-302). Newbury Park, CA: Sage.

Espin, O. M. (1985). Psychotherapy with Hispanic women. In P. Pedersen (Ed.), *Handbook of cross-cultural counseling and psychology.* Westport, CN: Greenwood Press.

Falicov, C. (1982). Mexican families. In M. McGoldrick, J. K. Pearce, & J. Giordano (Eds.), *Ethnicity and family therapy* (pp. 134-163). New York: Gardner.

Franklin, J. H. (1988). A historical note on black families. In H. P. McAdoo (Ed.), *Black families* (2nd ed.), (pp. 23-26). Newbury Park, CA: Sage.

Galan, F. (1988). Alcoholism prevention and Hispanic youth. *The Journal of Drug Issues, 18*(1), 49-58.

Gary, L. E., & Berry, G. L. (1985). Predicting attitudes toward substance abuse in a black community: Implications for prevention. *Community Mental Health Journal, 21*(1), 42–51.

Glick, R., & Moore, J. (1990). *Drugs in Hispanic communities.* New Brunswick, NJ: Rutgers University Press.

Globetti, G., Alsikafi, M., & Morse, R. (1980). Black female high school students and the use of beverage alcohol. *International Journal of the Addictions, 15*(2), 189-200.

Goffman, E. (1963). *Stigma: Notes on the management of a spoiled identity.* Upper Saddle River, NJ: Prentice Hall.

Guilmet, G. M., & Whited, D. (1987). Cultural lessons for clinical mental health practice: The Puyallup tribal community. *The Journal of the National Center of American Indian and Alaskan Native Mental Health Research, 1*(2), 32-49.

Gurnee, C. G., Vigil, D. E., Krill-Smith, S., & Crowely, T. J. (1990). Substance abuse among American Indians in an urban treatment program. *The Journal of the National Center of American Indian and Alaskan Native Mental Health Research, 3*(3), 17-27.

Ho, M. K. (1992). *Minority children and adolescents in therapy.* Newbury Park, CA: Sage.

Ho, M. K. (1987). *Family therapy with ethnic minorities.* Newbury Park, CA: Sage.

Ishisaka, H. A., Nguyen, Q. T., & Okimoto, J. T. (1985). The role in the mental health treatment of Indochinese refugees. In T. C. Owan (Ed.), *Southeast Asian mental health treatment, prevention services, training, and research.* Washington, DC: National Institute of Mental Health.

Keefe, S. E. (1978). Why Mexican Americans' underutilize mental health clinics: Facts and fallacy. In J. M. Casas & S. E. Keefe (Eds.), *Family and mental health in the Mexican American community* (pp. 91-108). Los Angeles: Spanish-Speaking Mental Health Research Center, University of California (Monograph No. 7).

Kinzie, J. D. (1985). Overview of clinical issues in the treatment of Southeast Asian refugees. In T. C. Owan (Ed.), *Southeast Asian mental health treatment, prevention services, training, and research* (pp. 113-135). Washington, DC: National Institute of Mental Health.

Kitano, H. H. L., Hatanaka, H., Yeung, W. T., & Sue, S. (1985). Japanese American drinking patterns, In L. A. Bennett & G. M. Ames (Eds.), *The American experience with alcohol: Contrasting cultural perspectives* (pp. 335-357). New York: Plenum Press.

LaFromboise, T. D., & Groff Low, K. (1989). American Indian children and adolescents. In J. T.

Gibbs & L. N. Huang (Eds.), *Children of color: Psychological interventions with minority youth,* (pp. 114-147). San Francisco: Jossey-Bass.

Lee, J. C., & Cynn, V. E. H. (1991). Issues in counseling 1.5 generation Korean Americans. In C. C. Lee and B. L. Richardson (Eds.), *Multicultural issues in counseling: New approaches to diversity* (pp. 127-140). Alexandria, VA: American Association for Counseling and Development.

Lee, C. C. & Richardson, B. L. (1991). *Multicultural issues in counseling: New approaches to diversity.* Alexandria, VA: American Association for Counseling and Development.

Lemert, E. (1982). Drinking among American Indians. In E. Gomberg, H. White, & J. Carpenter. (Eds.), *Alcohol, Science, and Society Revisited,* (pp. 80-95). Ann Arbor, MI: University of Michigan Press.

Lewis, R. G. (1982). Alcoholism and the Native American: A review of the literature, In *National Institute on alcohol and alcoholism, Alcohol and Health Monograph,* 4. Special Populations Issues. Washington DC: U.S. Government Printing Office.

Lorenzo, M. K., & Adler, D. A. (1984). Mental health services for Chinese in a community health center. *Social Casework, 65,* 600-610.

Loretto, G., Beauvais, F. & Oetting, E. R. (1988). The primary cost of drug abuse: What Indian youth pay for drugs. *The Journal of the National Center of American Indian and Alaskan Native Mental Health Research, 2*(1), 21-32.

Mail, P. D. (1989). American Indians, stress, and alcohol. *The Journal of the National Center of American Indian and Alaskan Native Mental Health Research, 3*(2), 7-26.

Manns, W. (1988). Supportive roles of signifigant others in black families. In H. P. McAdoo (Ed.), *Black families* (2nd ed.), (pp. 270-283). Newbury Park, CA: Sage.

May, P. A. (1988). The health status of Indian children: Problems and prevention in early life. *The Journal of the National Center of American Indian and Alaskan Native Mental Health Research Monograph, 1*(1), 244-289.

May, P. A. (1982). Substance abuse and American Indians: Prevalence and susceptibility. *International Journal of Addiction, 17,* 1185-1209.

May, P. A., Hymbaugh, K. A., Aase, M., & Samet, J. M. (1983). Epidemiology of fetal alcohol syndrome among American Indians of the southwest. *Social Biology, 30,* 374-387.

Mbiti, J. S. (1970). *African religions and philosophies.* Garden City, NY: Anchor Books.

McAdoo, H. P. (1993). *Family ethnicity: Strength in diversity.* Newbury Park, CA: Sage.

McAdoo, H. P. (1988). *Black families,* (2nd ed.). Newbury Park, NJ: Sage.

McGlogen, B. R., & Denniston, R. W. (1990). *Alcohol and other drug use among Hispanic youth.* OSAP Technical Report-4. Washington, DC: U.S. Department of Human Services.

Mejia, D. (1983). The development of Mexican-American children. In G. J. Powell, J. Yamamoto, A. Romero, & A. Morales (Eds.), *The psychosocial development of minority group children* (pp. 77-114). New York: Brunner/Mazel.

Mendoza, R. H., & Martinez, J. L. (1981). The measurement of acculturation. In A. Baron, Jr. (Ed.). *Explorations in Chicano psychology,* (pp. 71-82). New York: Praeger Publishers.

National Institute on Drug Abuse (1989). *National household survey on drug abuse: 1988 population estimates.* Rockville, MD: National Institute on Drug Abuse.

National Institute on Drug Abuse (1987). *Use of selected drugs among Hispanics: Mexican-Americans, Puerto Ricans, and Cuban Americans: Findings from the Hispanic health and nutrition examination survey.* Rockville, MD: Department of Health and Human Services.

Neligh, G. (1990). Mental health programs for American Indians: Their logic, structure and function. *The Journal of the National Center of American Indian and Alaskan Native Mental Health Research Monograph, 3*(3).

Nieves-Squires, S. (1991). Hispanic women: Making their presence on campus less tenuous. *Project on the Status and Education of Women.* Washington, DC: Association of American Colleges.

Nobles, W. W. (1988). African American family life: An instrument of culture. In H. P. McAdoo (Ed.), *Black families* (2nd ed.), (pp. 44-53). Newbury Park, CA: Sage.

Ogle, L. T., Alsalam, N., & Rogers, G. T. (1991). *The condition of education 1991* (Vol. 1). Elementary and secondary education. Washington DC: U.S. Government Printing Office.

Pearson, R. E. (1990). *Counseling and social support: Perspectives and Practice.* Newbury Park, CA: Sage.

Pedersen, P. B. (1991). Special Issue: Multiculturalism as a fourth force in counseling. *Journal of Counseling and Development, 70*(1), 4-251.

Peregoy, J. J. (1993). Transcultural counseling with American Indians and Alaskan Natives: Contemporary issues for consideration. In J. McFadden (Ed.), *Transcultural counseling: Bilateral and international perspectives,* (pp. 163-191). Alexandria, VA: American Counseling Association.

Phillips, M. R., & Inui, T. S. (1986). The interaction of mental illness, criminal behavior and culture: Native Alaskan mentally ill criminal offenders. *Culture, Medicine and Psychiatry, 20,* 461-482.

Plaiser, K. J. (1989). Fetal alcohol syndrome prevention in American Indian communities of Michigan's upper peninsula. *The Journal of the National Center of American Indian and Alaskan Native Mental Health Research, 3*(1), 16-33.

Prendergast, M., Austin, G., & Miranda, J. (1990). *Substance abuse among youth with disabilities.* Wisconsin Clearinghouse, University of Wisconsin-Madison.

President's Commission on Mental Health. (1978). *Report to the president* (Vol. 1). Washington, DC: Government Printing Office.

Robins, L. N., & Pryzbeck, T. R. (1985). Age of onset of drug use as a factor in drug use and other disorders. NIDA Research Monograph No. 56, U.S. DHHS Pub. No. 1415, (pp. 178-193). Washington DC: U.S. Government Printing Office.

Rogler, L. H., Malgady, R. G., & Rodriguez, O. (1989). *Hispanics and mental health: A framework for research.* Malabar, FL: Robert E. Krieger.

Ruiz, R. A., & Casas, J. M. (1981). Culturally relevant behavioristic counseling for Chicano college students. In P. B. Pedersen, J. G. Draguns, W. J. Lonner, & J. E. Trimble (Eds.), *Counseling across cultures* (2nd ed.) (pp. 181-202). Honolulu: University of Hawaii Press.

Santisteban, D., & Szapocznik, J. (1982). Substance abuse disorders among Hispanics: A focus on prevention. In R. M. Beceraa, M. Karno, & J. Escobar (Eds.), *Mental health and Hispanic Americans: Clinical perspectives,* (pp. 83-100). New York: Grune and Straton.

Sleeter, C. E., & Grant, C. A. (1993). *Making choices for multicultural education: Five approaches to race, class, and gender*. Upper Saddle River, NJ: Prentice Hall.

Snake, R., Hawkins, G., & LeBoueff, S. (1976). Report on alcohol and drug abuse, Task Force Eleven. *Final Report to the American Indian Policy Review Commission*. Washington, DC: U.S. Government Printing Office.

Solomon, B. (1976). *Black empowerment*. New York: Columbia University Press.

Staff (1991). Homicide among young black males-United States, 1978-1987. *The Journal of the American Medical Association, 265*(2), 183-184.

Sue, D., & Sue, D. W. (1991). Counseling strategies for Chinese Americans. In C. C. Lee & B. L. Richardson (Eds.), *Multicultural issues in counseling: New approaches to diversity,* (pp. 79-90). Alexandria, VA: American Association for Counseling and Development.

Sue, D. W., & Sue, D. (1990). *Counseling the culturally different: Theory and practice*. New York: John Wiley & Sons.

Sue, S., & Sue, D. W. (1971). Chinese American personality and mental health. *Amerasia Journal, 1*, 36-49.

Trimble, J. E., & Fleming, C. M. (1989). Providing counseling services for Native American Indians: Client, counselor, and community characteristics. In P. B. Pedersen, J. G. Draguns, W. J. Lonner, & J. E. Trimble (Eds.), *Counseling across cultures,* (pp. 127-134). Westport, CT: Greenwood Press.

Trimble, J. E., Padilla, A., & Bell, C. S. (1987). *Drug use among ethnic minorities*. Rockville, MD: National Institute on Drug Use.

Tung, T. M. (1985). Psychiatric care for southeast Asia: How different is different? In T. C. Owan (Ed.), *Southeast Asian mental health treatment, prevention services, training, and research*. Washington, DC: National Institute of Mental Health.

U.S. Bureau of Commerce (1992). *Statistical Abstract of the United States*. (112th ed.). Washington DC: U.S. Government Printing Office.

U.S. Department of Commerce. (1991, March 11). *Bureau of the Census News*, CB 91-100. Washington, DC: U.S. Department of Commerce.

U.S. Department of Commerce. (1992). *Census of population and housing characteristics-1990 summary*. Washington, DC: U.S Government Printing Office.

U.S. Department of Commerce (1991). *Statistical abstract of the United States 1991*. Washington, DC: U.S. Government Printing Office.

U.S. Department of Education (1992). *Digest of education statistics 1992*. Washington, DC: U.S. Government Printing Office.

Vallo, D., Frogg, W., Garcia, V., & Baker, G. (1980). *Indian in the Red*. U.S. Department of Health and Human Services. DHHS Pub. No. (ADM) 81-492.

Watts, T. D., & Wright, R. (1985). Some notes on black alcoholism prevention. *Journal of Alcohol and Drug Education, 30*(2), 1-3.

Wilson, G. T. (1987). Cognitive studies in alcoholism. *Journal of Consulting and Clinical Psychology, 55,* pp. 325–331.

Wong, H. Z. (1985). Training for mental health service providers to Southeast Asian refugees: Models, strategies, and curricula. In T. C. Owan (Ed.), *Southeast Asian mental health treatment, prevention services, training, and research*. Washington, DC: National Institute of Mental Health.

Maintaining Behavior Change: Relapse Prevention Strategies

Patricia Stevens Smith, Ph.D.

Individuals involved in recovery and the treatment of recovering individuals recognize that maintaining sobriety is perhaps the most difficult aspect of recovery. There is a high degree of consensus in the field that relapse is a common element in the recovery process (Annis, 1986). It is interesting to note, therefore, that relapse and relapse prevention have had little research and even less attention in most treatment programs until recently.

The meaning of *relapse* has changed over the years. Relapse was originally seen as the failure of an individual in recovery. According to Alcoholics Anonymous (AA), when individuals relapse, they revert to a pre-abstinence level of abuse or dependency and must begin the process of recovery from the beginning. As other concepts of both etiology and maintenance of dependency have developed, the view of relapse has also changed. Relapse is now viewed by many as a normal part of the recovery process and as a learning experience for the recovering individual.

Recovery is defined as not only the abstinence from mind-altering chemicals or nonproductive compulsive behaviors, but also changes in physical, psychological, social, familial, and spiritual areas of functioning. These changes are seen as a process and not as an event in the recovering individual's life. It is generally accepted that the dynamics that enable an individual to maintain sobriety are as different as the factors that initiate sobriety (Daley, 1988a). Just as there are differences in individuals in the treatment process, there are differences in individuals in the recovery process. The stage of recovery as well as unique individual differences both play a part in the process.

Some important factors in this process are (1) the length and severity of their abuse or dependency, (2) gender and ethnicity, (3) the perception of the problem, (4) the motivation to change, (5) the availability of support systems both professional and nonprofessional, and (6) the degree of damage in each aspect of the individual's life (Daley, 1988b). A recovery plan must take into account all these aspects of the individual. It would also be fair to say that recovery, as with all changes in an individual's life, is ultimately governed by the individual's drives and motivation to change. It is well established in psychotherapy that positive treatment outcome is highly correlated with the individual's motivation to participate in treatment, understanding of the treatment process, and desire for change (Cormier & Cormier, 1985). At times in substance abuse and dependency counseling, as in other areas of psychotherapy, the therapist or significant other's motivation for change may be greater than the individual's motivation for change (Marion & Coleman, 1991).

Relapse has many definitions. One definition is a breakdown or setback in a person's attempt to change or modify a target behavior (Marlatt, 1985a). Webster's *New Collegiate Dictionary* defines it as "a recurrence of symptoms of a disease after a period of improvement." A simple definition would be the return to substance use or to the dysfunctional pattern of compulsive behavior. Daley (1988a) gives two definitions of *relapse*. The first is the "event" of resumption of use and the second is the "process" whereby attitudes or behaviors are exhibited that indicate a likelihood of resumption of use. It is also true that these indicators vary from individual to individual and therefore may be difficult to recognize and identify.

A part of relapse to be considered is a *slip* or *lapse*—the initial return to use after a period of sobriety. It may be a single episode or it may lead to a relapse. A slip or lapse is usually temporary, as opposed to a relapse, which is considered a return to uncontrolled use. Although AA defines a slip as a failure in sobriety and indicates that the individual must begin the path to sobriety again, many mental health practitioners believe that a slip can be used to help the client (and the therapist) learn what the factors are that motivate the client to return to substance use. This information can be used to develop a plan to prevent other slips and a return to substance use.

DETERMINANTS OF RELAPSE

Although several models of relapse prevention will be discussed later in this chapter, it is of interest to note that all these models incorporate common elements that are precursors of renewed substance use. It is also important for the counselor to note that these different elements are overlapping and integrated. They represent every element of the client's life. Recovery, therefore, means a restructuring of one's entire life system.

Environmental

When clients are in treatment, either residential or intensive outpatient, they believe strongly that they can abstain from use. This belief is based in the comfort of the protected and supportive atmosphere of treatment. When clients return to their own environment, this protection and support are usually not as available. Feelings of self-efficacy and control are replaced by anxiety, insecurity, and doubt (Marlatt & Gordon, 1985).

High-risk situations—incidents, occurrences, or situations that threaten the client's control—increase the likelihood of a return to use. Examples of high-risk situations would be going to a party with old friends who still use, riding by the bar or crack house or dealer's house where the client previously purchased the substance, or frequenting locations where the client previously used substances.

When clients place themselves in these situations, they also put themselves in a negative emotional state. This state accounts for 35% of all relapses. Interpersonal conflict, which may also be high at this time as the client endeavors to decide which behavior to engage in, accounts for 16% of relapses. Social pressures account for 20% of relapses (Cummings, Gordon, & Marlatt, 1980). All three of these components— negative emotional state, interpersonal conflict, and social pressure—exist when a client is in a high-risk situation.

Negative emotional states refer to anger, anxiety, frustration, depression, or boredom. *Interpersonal conflict* refers to arguments or confrontation with family, friends, or significant others in the client's life. *Social pressure* occurs when the client is exposed to environmental or peer pressure to resume substance use (Lewis, Dana, & Blevins, 1994).

Behavioral

Clients who have few or no coping skills to respond to these high-risk situations are more likely to return to substance use. Several studies emphasize the importance of teaching clients alternative coping skills to deal with these situations (Hawkins, Catalano, & Wells, 1986; Marlatt, 1985a). It is also important to teach the client new decision making skills (Marlatt, 1985b). A sober lifestyle requires integration into "normal" family life, work, recreation, diet and exercise, stress management, and handling the desire to use drugs again. This is a daily endeavor which is stressful in and of itself. Abstinence does not mean an absence of problems in life. Learning to deal with stress and negative emotions in a healthful way is imperative to recovery.

Cognitive

Researchers have found a variety of cognitive variables that affect relapse. Clients' attitudes toward sobriety (Chalmers & Wallace, 1985), their perception of their ability to cope or self-efficacy (Annis, 1986; Annis & Davis, 1987), and their expectations of relapse (Annis & Davis, 1987). AA and Narcotics Anonymous (NA) refer to "stinking thinking" or the faulty thinking of substance abusers which can contribute to relapse. It may not be the actual thought or pattern of thinking but more how the abuser interprets or manages the thinking that determines the outcome (Marion & Coleman, 1991).

Affective

Negative as well as positive emotional states may lead to substance reuse. Depression and anxiety have been shown to be major determinants of relapse (Hatsukami, Pickens, & Svikis, 1981; Pickens, Hatsukami, Spicer, & Svikis, 1985). However, the research is unclear as to whether the depression and anxiety exist before the use resumes or is a product of the relapse.

The stress of everyday living changes can create negative emotions in the recovering person. Learning to handle these emotions positively can prevent relapse. For many clients, the purpose of using was to numb their feelings. So the first step in avoiding relapse needs to be learning how to recognize, label, and communicate feelings productively (Marion & Coleman, 1991). Relaxation techniques, assertiveness skills, and other coping skills will be important to reducing the risk of relapse.

Two strong emotions that must be dealt with in recovery are guilt and shame. *Guilt* is a consequence of the dependency process both for the addict and for the significant others in the addict's life. When the guilt becomes tied to "who I am" and not "what I did," it is known as *shame*. Dealing with the guilt and shame affects an individual's self-esteem through negative feedback. These feelings can become overwhelming in recovery and easily lead to relapse in an attempt to protect oneself from a confrontation with these feelings (Marion & Coleman, 1991).

Relational

The lack of a supportive family or social network has been highly correlated with a return to substance use (Zackon, McAuliffe, & Ch'ien, 1985; Daley, 1987; Hawkins & Fraser, 1987). Many times the primary significant other is also an active substance abuser. And, as noted earlier in this text, many of these individuals come from families with substance abuse problems that span generations. Lack of productive work or leisure-time activities has also been shown to be a determinant of relapse (Catalano, Howard, Hawkins, & Wells, 1988).

The family is the most significant relationship that is harmed in the process of abuse and dependency. Broken promises, hurts, isolation, and in many cases verbal, physical, or sexual abuse have been present. Taking responsibility for the behaviors and mending the relationships is a large part of recovery. The family must be engaged in the recovery process to minimize the possibility of relapse. As abusers become aware of the behaviors in which they engaged when using and move toward health, if the family is not engaged in this same process, the results could be devastating.

Work and leisure time are two other components that may create a problem in recovery. Many times the individual has lost a job or been demoted because of the substance abuse problem. Finding satisfying work is an important component to avoiding relapse. Leisure time for the substance abuser has previously meant time when the individual was either looking for drugs or alcohol, using the substance, or hiding the fact that they were using. Without these activities, recovering individuals find themselves with lots of time on their hands. Boredom, because of a lack of social support or activities, is a leading cause of relapse.

It is easy to see that recovery is a complex system. Every aspect of the individual's life has been affected by substance use. These aspects must now be changed, and change creates stress and anxiety. Stress and anxiety have previously been handled through the use of a substance. Without that means of coping, the individual is lost. It is apparent, then, that the learning of new skills is paramount in the recovery process.

Several models of relapse prevention have been developed through the years. The first model was Alcoholics Anonymous. This model has become the framework for a multitude of self-help/support groups including Narcotics Anonymous, Cocaine Anonymous, and Overeaters Anonymous. Many researchers have also developed models of relapse prevention. Along with the AA model of recovery, the cognitive-social learning strategy, a developmental model, and a psychoeducational model for maintaining sobriety will be discussed.

ALCOHOLICS ANONYMOUS MODEL

Alcoholics Anonymous was founded on June 10, 1935, the day when Dr. Robert H. Smith had his last drink. The groundwork for the organization had been laid earlier, however, when William G. Wilson, sought support to maintain his new-found sobriety. He made several calls and was told to talk with Dr. Smith. Dr. Smith was drinking at the time, and Wilson found himself reaching out to Dr. Smith with the message of his own sobriety. By the fourth year after its founding, there were about 100 members in the groups (Nace, 1987). These early members wrote about their struggle to maintain sobriety and Bill W. published these in the first edition of the book *Alcoholics Anonymous* in 1939. Included in this first edition of the "Big Book" were the Twelve Steps and Twelve Traditions of the organization. AA has developed into a fellowship of more than 94,000 groups in 114 countries with a total membership estimated at more than 1 million people. It is often said by AA members that "wherever you can find a liquor store, you can find an AA group."

The cornerstone of the AA model is the paradoxical belief that to gain control of one's life one must give up control to a Higher Power. Although God is mentioned in AA, members believe that one's Higher Power can be many things or beings. AA distinguishes between spirituality and religion, but believes that addiction is a spiritual disease as well as a physical one. By embracing spirituality, not a specific religious dogma, AA allows all individuals to embrace a Higher Power of their own choosing.

Fundamental in the AA philosophy is the belief that abstinence from substance use is not enough. Individuals must also be willing to make attitudinal and behavioral changes in their lifestyles. The AA model is designed to enable members to address every aspect of their life—physical, emotional, social, and spiritual—and to make positive changes in each of these areas (see Figure 9.1). Having made these changes, the individual will then reach out to others in an effort to offer assistance in recovering from a substance using lifestyle (Marion & Coleman, 1991).

AA considers five aspects of recovery as the most important in the program: (1) learning to give up control to gain control, (2) self-examination and discussion of this examination, (3) making amends, (4) participation in group meetings, and (5) daily reminders (Hoffman & Gressard, 1994). These factors work best when combined in a noncoercive atmosphere of participation, which is present in AA.

Giving Up Control to Gain Control

The first three steps of AA are about recognizing and acknowledging one's limitations. These steps require that individuals accept that their resources are not enough to solve life's problems. The third step requires that they give control of the problem to a "Higher Power." The paradox of giving up control to gain control is one of the

---

The Twelve Steps

1. We admitted we were powerless over alcohol—that our lives had become unmanageable.
2. Came to believe that a Power greater than ourselves could restore us to sanity.
3. Made a decision to turn our will and our lives over to the care of God *as we understood Him.*
4. Made a searching and fearless moral inventory of ourselves.
5. Admitted to God, to ourselves, and to another human being the exact nature of our wrongs.
6. Were entirely ready to have God remove all these defects of character.
7. Humbly ask Him to remove our shortcomings.
8. Made a list of all persons we had harmed, and became willing to make amends to them all.
9. Made direct amends to such people wherever possible, except when to do so would injure them or others.
10. Continued to take personal inventory and when we were wrong promptly admitted it.
11. Sought through prayer and meditation to improve our conscious contact with God *as we understood Him*, praying only for knowledge of His will for us and the power to carry that out.
12. Having had a spiritual awakening as the result of these steps, we tried to carry this message to alcoholics, and to practice these principles in all our affairs.

FIGURE 9.1   The Twelve Steps of Alcoholics Anonymous

Note: From *Alcoholics Anonymous* (pp. 59–60), 1976, New York: Alcoholics Anonymous World Services, Inc.

most difficult for the individual to understand (Hoffman & Gressard, 1994). It is the experience of AA members (and substance abuse counselors) that after the initial behavior change has been accomplished, individuals begin to feel they are in control of their behavior and do not need to continue with the meetings, meditations, and group support of AA. It is imperative for the counselor to watch for signs of over-confidence in the client that would indicate this belief. Statements like "I have this under control," or "I have this problem licked," or "I haven't had the urge to drink/use in weeks. I can cut down on meetings for a while," should trigger an immediate response from the alert counselor. When these comments are made in the early stages of recovery, the client should be reminded of the difficulty of behavior change maintenance and of the paradox of control.

Self-Examination

Self-examination is essential in recovery. Steps 4 through 7 are about self-assessment and include a series of change-oriented activities. They require that individuals do a "searching and fearless moral inventory" of their behavior. They then discuss this inventory with another trusted individual. Steps 8 and 9 direct individuals to make amends for injuries to others and Step 10 requires an on-going moral inventory. The consistent review of feelings and behaviors is imperative to sobriety. While using drugs, an individual represses and/or avoids feelings. Acknowledging and examining these feelings is an important part of "working the program" in AA.

Making Amends

Steps 8 and 9 are about making amends for their past behavior. Through this inventory and the process of making amends, the individual may work through the guilt and shame associated with past behaviors and to recognize the limits of personal responsibility (Doweiko, 1993). Making amends is a way to alleviate guilt associated with the negative effect of the addict's past behaviors with family, friends, and associates. Not dealing with these past behaviors can strain the individual's support system as well as become a component in returning to substance use. Accepting responsibility for one's behavior and the consequences of that behavior is a step in learning a healthy behavior patterns.

Steps 10 through 12 encourage building on the framework developed in the previous steps. Step 10 requires an ongoing inventory and admission of wrongdoing. Spirituality is the focus of Step 11, and the need to be involved with and help others is addressed in Step 12.

Group Participation

The fourth powerful component of AA is the group support provided by AA meetings. Anonymity is an integral element in AA, both to protect the identity of its membership and so that no one person becomes a spokesperson for the group

(Doweiko, 1993). AA sees a commitment to recovery as a commitment to or involvement in AA.

Individuals in AA are also supported by "sponsors." A sponsor is an AA member with a history of sobriety who has worked through the 12 steps and has a basic understanding of his or her own addiction. This individual is available 24 hours a day, seven days a week for the newly recovering individual. Sponsors serve a variety of purposes. They listen, provide support and confrontation, are the most common recipient of the "moral inventory" information, encourage AA attendance, and may even provide recreational activities. Sponsor also serve as spiritual guides.

The sponsor is interested in the individual's recovery but is not responsible for that recovery (McCrady & Irvine, 1989). In the AA philosophy, the responsibility for recovery rests with the individual. The role of the sponsor is often similar to that of a psychotherapist and, in fact, the sponsor may embody many of the same characteristics (Rogers, 1961).

Daily Reminders

The fifth necessary component in the AA recovery program is the constant awareness of the disease and the recovery principles. This awareness is facilitated through the use of daily reminders. AA has developed daily meditations, slogans, readings, and prayers to keep the individual focused on these principles. It is AA's belief that without these daily reminders it is easy to forget the necessary components of recovery and thereby to relapse. It is of particular importance for sobriety to remember the "truth" of Steps 1-3. These slogans offer practical advice to the recovering person such as "Take It Easy," "One Day At A Time," and "Let Go and Let God." AA also offers free literature to anyone on how to deal with the many life problems that are a part of the recovery process.

How Effective is AA?

AA is viewed by many professionals in the field as the single most important component to recovery. Yet critics of the program suggest caution. It is apparent that those people who join AA and remain members may not be a representative sample of the substance abusing population. The fact that these people remain members separates them from those who do not join or who join and do not remain active. Yet, it must also be commented that Jellinek's original work on the stages of alcoholism was drawn from the membership of AA (Doweiko, 1993).

There has also been criticism about the AA program from women's groups and minority groups who feel disenfranchised by AA. Many women believe AA perpetuates the powerlessness of women in Steps 1–3. A feminist version of the 12-Steps addresses this issue (Figure 9.2). Minority groups believe that AA serves the white middle class and does not address ethnic issues in its philosophy. It would appear that some research supports the theory that AA is most effective with "socially stable white males over 40 years of age, who are physically dependent on alcohol and prone to guilt, and who are the first born or only child" (Doweiko, 1993, p. 368). However, there is little evidence to support research and most believe that this is not reliable in predicting successful membership in AA (Ogborne & Glaser, 1985).

There is also some evidence to indicate that AA is not effective with individuals who are coerced into attendance. People who are sentenced to jail or to educational programs for driving under the influence appear to have better subsequent driving records than those who are court-ordered to attend AA. (Peele, Brodsky, & Arnold, 1991).

---

1. We acknowledge we were out of control with our addiction but have the power to take charge of our lives and stop being dependent on others for our self-esteem and security.

2. We came to believe that the Universe/Goddess/Great Spirit would awaken the healing wisdom within us if we opened ourselves to that power.

3. We declared ourselves willing to tune into our inner wisdom. To listen and act based upon these truths.

4. Made a searching and fearless inventory of how the culture has mired us down with guilt and shame, recognizing how hierarchy has harmed us, and how we have been complicit in harming ourselves—and only then look at how we have harmed others.

5. We examined our behavior and beliefs in the context of living in a hierarchical, male-dominated culture.

6. We shared with others the way we have been harmed, harmed ourselves and others, striving to forgive ourselves and to change our behavior.

7. We admitted to our talents, strengths, and accomplishments, agreeing not to hide these qualities to protect others' egos.

8. We became willing to let go of our shame, guilt, and other behavior that prevents us from taking control of our lives and loving ourselves.

9. We took steps to clear out all negative feelings between us and other people by sharing grievances in a respectful way and making amends when appropriate.

10. Continued to trust our reality and when we were right, promptly admitted it and refused to back down. We do not take responsibility for, analyze, or cover up the shortcomings of others.

11. Sought through meditation and inner awareness the ability to listen to our inward calling and gain the will and wisdom to follow it.

12. Having learned to care for and love ourselves as a result of these steps, we give to others out of choice and seek to practice these principles in all our affairs.

FIGURE 9.2   The Feminist Alternative to the Twelve Steps

Note: From *CoAcoAA Newsletter 4*(3), (pp. 2–3), Spring 1991.

The answer to effectiveness may be far too complex to answer by a simple study. Effectiveness research in the field of substance abuse, for AA or any recovery program, is limited. It might best serve the mental health practitioner to be aware of which individuals are best served by AA and which individuals might be better served through other approaches.

OTHER 12-STEP PROGRAMS

Using the AA model of recovery as a basis, several 12-step programs have developed. Narcotics Anonymous (NA), Cocaine Anonymous (CA), and Overeaters Anonymous (OA) are examples of these programs. All are based on the AA philosophy and use a variation of the Twelve Steps of AA. The difference in these groups is the scope of each group. NA, for example is all-inclusive with its definition of addiction. It includes any mood-changing, mind-altering substance. CA limits its membership to individuals who identify cocaine as their or drug of choice. And OA is directed toward individuals with compulsive eating habits.

Al-Anon, Alateen, and Narnon are examples of examples of support groups for families of substances users. Al-Anon and Narnon are for the family and friends of users. While the substance abuser is in AA or NA, families meet to share experiences and discuss problems. These groups apply the same 12 steps to their own lives.

Alateen, which began in 1957, is for teen-agers who live in alcoholic or drug-abusing families and for substance-using teen-agers. It also uses the 12-step model (see Figure 9.3). It was started to create an opportunity for teen-agers to come together to share experiences, learn about alcoholism and drug dependency, and to solve problems.

DEVELOPMENTAL MODEL OF RELAPSE PREVENTION

The developmental theorists integrate concepts of the disease model with a developmental model of recovery. Gorski and Miller (1982) developed a six-stage/nine-step model of recovery. This model is known as the CENAPS Model of Relapse Prevention (Gorski, 1989, 1990) and is based on the belief that substance abuse creates dysfunction at every level in an individual's life (Gorksi, 1990). It is, therefore, imperative in relapse prevention to focus on treatment at each of these levels.

This model is a relapse prevention planning model, which takes into consideration that relapse is a progression of behaviors that allows the substance use to be reactivated if intervention does not take place. Gorski and Miller (1982) view addiction as a chronic and progressive disease and advocate for change in all aspects of an individual's life for recovery to happen. Another aspect of this developmental model, which borrows from the AA model, is the belief that individuals must admit they

1. I am powerless over alcohol, drugs and other people's behavior, and my life got really messed up because of it.
2. I need help. I can't do it alone anymore.
3. I've made a decision to reach out for a Power greater than me to help out.
4. I wrote down all the things that bother me about myself and others, and all the things I like, too.
5. I shared these with someone I trust because I don't have to keep them secret anymore.
6. My Higher Power helps me with this, too.
7. The more I trust myself and my Higher Power, the more I learn to trust others.
8. I made a list of all the people I hurt and the ways I hurt myself. I can now forgive myself and others.
9. I talked with these people even if I was scared to because I knew that it would help me feel better about myself.
10. I keep on discovering more things about myself each day and if I hurt someone, I apologize.
11. When I am patient and pray, I get closer to my Higher Power, and that helps me to know myself better.
12. By using these steps, I've become a new person. I don't have to feel alone anymore, and I can help others.

FIGURE 9.3   Twelve Steps for Kids

Note: From *Kids' Power* (p. 61) by J. Moe and D. Pohlman, 1989, Deerfield Beach, FL: Health Communications, Inc.

have a problem and then abstain from substance use. Gorski and Miller believe this model works best for patients who have been in treatment and relapsed.

The six stages of the developmental model:

1. **Transition.**   The individual begins to experience more severe symptoms and dependency and recognizes the need for treatment and seeks it.
2. **Stabilization.**   This is the beginning stage of treatment, and may include detoxification. The individual is stabilized and immediate problems are solved to facilitate the termination of substance use.
3. **Early recovery.**   Clients become aware of how the use of substances has affected thinking and they begin to manage feelings without use.
4. **Middle recovery.**   A balanced lifestyle change begins.
5. **Late recovery.**   Clients have used the counseling process to understand core psychological issues that might create relapse potential.
6. **Maintenance.**   Maintenance is a lifelong process of sharpening coping skills to deal with life problems (Gorski, 1989).

Gorski and Miller (1982) and later Gorski (1990) developed nine steps or principles to facilitate relapse prevention. Skills are needed at each stage of recovery, and the role of the counselor is to help clients with each of these steps or principles:

1. The first step is to stabilize the client or help her or him develop a daily structure. This is a mechanism to solve immediate problems and to help the client begin to live without substance use.

2. The second principle is teaching the client continual self-assessment. This gives the client a way to understand previous relapse patterns and to intervene in those patterns.

3. Educational information is given concerning the disease and the biopsychosocial models of dependency.

4. The counselor helps the client identify the warning signs of an impending relapse.

5. After identification of warning signs, the counselor facilitates the client's ability to manage her or his own warning signs.

6. The client creates a set of activities to use when these warning signs appear, to avoid relapse.

7. The relapse dynamic is interrupted. Problems that are associated with the warning signs are discussed and resolved.

8. The counselor may have been working throughout this process with family and friends. At this point, significant others become involved in the relapse planning program.

9. This final step is a consistent follow-up for a minimum of two years and reinforcement by the counselor of the client's progress during this time.

Similar to the AA model, the developmental model is structured with the assumption that relapse problems and warning signs will change as the individual progresses through the stages of recovery. These changes will necessitate the re-working of these steps or principles with each developmental stage of recovery.

COGNITIVE-BEHAVIORAL/SOCIAL LEARNING MODEL

The cognitive-behavioral model (Cummings, Gordon, & Marlatt, 1980; Mackay & Marlatt, 1991; Marlatt, 1982, 1985c; Marlatt & Gordon, 1985) is based on social learning theory (Bandura, 1969). Social learning theory holds that substance use and abuse is a learned behavior in which use has been increased in frequency, duration, and intensity for psychological benefit (Lewis, Dana, & Blevins, 1994). In other words, use is associated with reinforcement, either immediate or delayed.

Social Learning Theories

Drive-reduction theory holds that internal tension creates a drive state. A chemical substance is used to reduce the drive. This use reduces tension, which is reinforcing to the individual. This reinforcement strengthens the substance use behavior. The substance will then be used more frequently in response to the need to reduce the drive.

Drive-reduction theory takes into account the individual's continued use in the face of negative effects from using. If the drive is intense, the immediate reinforcement—or drive-reduction effect—will overshadow the negative effects created by continued use (Hull, 1943; Thorndike, 1932).

Another social learning theory perspective examines the effect of environmental stressors on substance use. This theory asserts that substance use is a mechanism to reduce stress, learned through reinforcement and modeling. As substance use continues, the individual may use more frequently and at higher dosages to avoid withdrawal (Lewis, Dana, & Blevins, 1994).

The importance of self-efficacy must not be overlooked in any discussion of social learning theory (Bandura, 1969). Research substantiates the validity that low self-efficacy or perceived ability to cope with high-stress situations is correlated with a return to drinking behavior and smoking (Condiotte & Lichtenstein, 1981). Therefore, if high self-efficacy is positively correlated with abstinence, then a crucial element in relapse prevention would be the development of a strong sense of capacity to handle situations. Self-efficacy theory provides that "hands-on" practice handling situations of ever-increasing difficulty creates this sense of ability to handle situations. Certain criteria are important in these practice sessions, however, to increase confidence. According to Bandura (1978) these are:

1. The exposure to substance use is challenging to the client.
2. Only a moderate degree of effort is needed to experience success.
3. Little external aid is necessary.
4. The success was part of a pattern of improvement.
5. An increase in personal control is demonstrated.
6. The successful performance is relevant to the client's own life situations.

In relapse prevention planning it is important for clients and counselors to monitor situations in an ongoing manner. It is helpful for the client to record problem situations; behaviors, thoughts, and feelings immediately before and after the situation; and any means used to cope with the situation. This log will facilitate the client's awareness of any unique triggers to substance use and allow for the client and the counselor to plan for realistic situations in the client's life.

This planning also allows for anticipation of problem situations. The client should be encouraged to look at the days or week ahead and anticipate situations that might prompt a desire to return to substance use. With forewarning of possible difficulties, the counselor and client can successfully plan an appropriate relapse prevention technique for each situation.

A significant factor in self-efficacy theory is the rehearsal or practice of using methods before the difficulty is encountered. These practice sessions lead to increased perceived ability or self-efficacy on the part of the client. Whenever possible, practice within a therapy session or group can be used.

The client should not only plan intervention techniques to avoid a return to substance use but should also work with the counselor to determine how a slip will be handled in the most constructive manner possible. Plans for interrupting a relapse should also be considered. Support and intervention are imperative at these times not only to interrupt the lapse, but also to deal with any negative feelings the client may experience due to the return to substance use.

Reviewing with the client how behavior has changed is an important reinforcement technique. It encourages the client to continue improvement, and also allows the client to examine the substance use in a multidimensional way. Improvement in each aspect of the client's life can be discussed and reinforced (Annis & Davis, 1987).

COGNITIVE BEHAVIORAL MODEL

Marlatt and his colleagues have developed the most widely used cognitive behavioral model of relapse prevention. Marlatt bases this theory on the belief that "the goal of relapse prevention is to teach individuals who are trying to change their behavior how to anticipate and cope with the problem of relapse" (Marlatt & Gordon, 1985, p. 3). Although we will address the use of this model with substance abusers, the model appears to work with many compulsive or addictive behavior patterns. In any situation, it is most effective with individuals who are motivated to change their behavior and who have expressed a commitment to do so. Individuals who are changing due to external motivational influences, such as court-ordered clients, or clients responding to a work or marital crises, may not respond as well.

This relapse prevention model is based on three assumptions:

1. The etiology of addictive behaviors and the process of change "may be governed by different factors or learning principles."

2. "The process of changing a habit involves at least three separate stages"—commitment and motivation, implementation of change, and long-term maintenance of behavior change.

3. "The maintenance stage of behavior change accounts for the greatest proportion of variance associated with long-term treatment outcomes" (Marlatt & Gordon, 1985, p. 21).

A fourth assumption may be added to the list: Relapse may be viewed as a "transitional process . . . (or) . . . a fork in the road . . . with one path returning to the former problem level . . . and the other continuing in the direction of positive change" (pp. 32–33). In other words, in contrast to the AA model, relapse is not seen as a failure but as a learning tool for the individual. The slip is used as a means to assess the antecedents to the lapse and to formulate a more successful coping strategy for the future. One of the most important factors in determining whether the individual will return to substance use is the individual's perception of the slip. Does the client see this as a failure or as a way to learn and develop stronger skills? (Marlatt, 1985a)

This approach stresses the need for lifestyle change. Exercise, biofeedback, meditation, stress-management techniques, relaxation training, and cognitive restructuring are a few examples of these changes. Self-monitoring is also important. Clients must learn new coping skills to deal with high-risk situations. But, Marlatt (1985a) believes that new coping skills alone are not sufficient to maintain sobriety. He believes that positive addictions, and substitute indulgences are also necessary.

The cognitive-behavioral model assumes a collaborative relationship between the client and the therapist. Together they will identify, assess, and plan for situations that may prove problematic for the client. These situations can be interpersonal or intrapersonal and fall into three categories: (1) negative emotional states, (2) interpersonal conflict, and (3) social pressures (Cummings, Gordon, & Marlatt, 1980). For clients to become aware of these situations, daily self-monitoring is encouraged.

The next step for the client is to develop new coping skills for handling these situations without returning to substance use. Each client needs to learn, in cooperation with the therapist, a unique set of skills appropriate to the client's situation. New cognitive and behavioral skills can be learned. Behavioral skills include assertiveness training and alternative behaviors such as exercise or meditation. Cognitive restructuring, imagery, and self-talk might also be implemented.

A balanced lifestyle is emphasized throughout this model. Clients must learn to replace negative addictions with positive addictions such as aerobics, running, walking, relaxation, or other pleasurable activities. An equality between what one "should" do and what one "wants" to do is another aspect of a healthful lifestyle. Too many "shoulds" lead to a feeling of deprivation which could be an antecedent to relapse. All of these skills combined are designed to decrease the frequency of desire to return to substance use and to increase the client's overall coping capacity (Marlatt, 1985a). This model is flexible and manageable. Its success is based in the fact that it responds to the unique and individualized needs of clients.

THE CONCEPT OF RE-JOYMENT

Fred Zackon (1988) writes about the role of joy in the recovery process. Zackon makes the point that definitions of relapse have something in common: It is a "subdynamic of addiction . . . stimulated by conditioned drug-craving responses to internal and environmental cues or the result of inadequate preparation for stressful situations . . . such as social relationships . . . intensified by faulty thinking . . . and inadequate external intervention" (p. 68). Relapse prevention models also incorporate similar concepts and skills. Zackon states that the "various methods . . . proposed . . . to prevent these problems could usually coexist peaceably in the same program, likely with addictive value" (p. 68). Having made these two observations, Zackon then proposes that the question we forget to ask is, "What is the relationship between joylessness and relapse?" (p. 69).

In our diligent and caring quest to teach clients all the cognitive and behavioral skills necessary to stay clean and sober, we may be overlooking an intrinsically important aspect of recovery. Becoming clean and sober requires the substance abuser to give up a lifestyle that is "psychologically comfortable" and to enter unfamiliar territory. Abusers must leave friends who shared a value system and created a sense of community for them. Recovery requires that the person "abandon an entire universe of feelings for another" (p. 71).

The world of the substance abuser is one of high stakes and high risk. Adrenaline runs high. Risk-taking behavior is common. Entering a world of "mundane" pleasures creates boredom and joylessness. The recovering individual does not remember how to experience joy or enjoyment with everyday living. Many common social situations are uncomfortable. Addicts must allow for a lowering of their "pleasure threshold" (Zackon, 1988, p. 75). In other words, they must learn to enjoy more moderate stimulation than that experienced while using in everything from food to fun to sexual activity.

Also, early recovery means detoxification and withdrawal symptoms which may linger. It also means facing the pain of one's life both before, during, and after the drug use: Destroyed relationships, financial problems, legal problems, high expectations, physical pain, and the consistent—sometimes strong—drug cravings. This heavy burden of unhappiness drains energy and prolongs the lack of joy in the individual's life.

So it becomes incumbent upon the counselor to not overlook the relearning of pleasure in the recovery process. Relearning takes time, and counselors need to remember that it can be blocked by guilt and shame, or simply by lack of money to participate in activities. Counselors should also remember that many individuals began using "for want of pleasure in a mean world" (Zackon, 1988, p. 76), and that the world is still as mean as ever.

In relapse prevention models and programs, counselors should emphasize and systematically support "re-joyment." This may mean that they take the nontherapeutic role of "coach" in these activities. Aftercare groups, AA, NA, and other social support groups can provide much-needed activities for recovering individuals.

In summary, the determinants of relapse and the prevention models share commonalties. Relapse prevention skills, cognitive and behavioral, are important in creating a clean and sober lifestyle. However, simply put, the intentionality and joy with which the individual is living life may be a much more powerful deterrent to relapse than the so-called living skills taught in a conventional relapse prevention program.

REFERENCES

Annis, H. M. (1986). A relapse prevention model for treatment of alcoholics. In W. R. Miller & N. Heather (Eds.), *Treating addictive behaviors: Process of change* (pp. 407-421). New York: Plenum.

Annis, H. M., & Davis, C. (1987). Assessment of expectancies in alcoholic dependent clients. In G. A. Marlatt & D. Donovan (Eds.), *Assessment of addictive behaviors*. New York: Guilford.

Bandura, A. (1978). Reflections on self-efficacy. *Advance in Behavioral Research and Therapy, 1,* 237–269.

Bandura, A. (1969). *Principles of behavior modification*. New York: Holt, Rinehart, & Winston.

Catalano, R., Howard, M., Hawkins, J., & Wells, E. (1988). Relapse in the addictions: Rates, determinants, and promising prevention strategies. *1988 Surgeon General's Report on Health Consequence of Smoking*. Washington, DC: U.S. Government Printing Office.

Chalmers, D., & Wallace, J. (1985). Evaluation of patient progress. In Zimberg, Wallace, & Blume (Eds.), *Practical approaches to alcoholism psychotherapy*, (pp. 174–185). New York: Plenum.

Condiotte, M. M., & Lichtenstein, E. (1981). Self-efficacy and relapse in smoking cessation programs. *Journal of Consulting and Clinical Psychology, 49,* 648–658.

Cormier, W. H., & Cormier, L. S. (1985). *Interviewing strategies for helpers* (2nd ed.). Belmont, CA: Brooks/Cole.

Cummings, C., Gordon, J., & Marlatt, G. (1980). Relapse: Prevention and prediction. In W. Miller (Ed.), *Addictive behaviors: Treatment of alcoholism, drug abuse, smoking and obesity*, (pp. 62–74). New York: Pergamon.

Daley, D. C. (1988a). Five perspectives on relapse in chemical dependency. In D. C. Dale (Ed.), *Relapse: Conceptual, research and clinical perspectives* (pp. 3-26). New York: Haworth Press.

Daley, D. C. (1988b). *Surviving addiction: A guide for alcoholics, drug addicts and their families*. New York: Gardner Press.

Daley, D. C. (1987). Relapse prevention with substance abusers: Clinical issues and myths. *Social Work, 45*(2), 38-42.

Doweiko, H. F. (1993). *Concepts of chemical dependency* (2nd ed.). Pacific Grove, CA: Brooks/Cole.

Gorski, T. T. (1990). The CENAPS model of relapse prevention: Basic principles and procedures. *Journal of Psychoactive Drugs, 22,* 125-133.

Gorski, T. T. (1989). *Passages through recovery: An action plan for preventing relapse*. Center City, MN: Hazelden.

Gorski, T., & Miller, M. (1982). *Counseling for relapse prevention*. Independence, MI: Independence Press.

Hatsukami, D., Pickens, R., & Svikis, D. (1981). Post-treatment depressive symptoms and relapse to drug use in different age groups of an alcohol and other drug use population. *Drug and Alcohol Dependence, 8*(4), 271-177.

Hawkins, J. D., Catalano, R., & Wells, E. (1986). Measuring effects of a skills training intervention for drug abusers. *Journal of Consulting and Clinical Psychology, 54*(5), 661-664.

Hawkins, J. D., & Fraser, M. W. (1987). The social networks of drug abusers before and after treatment. *The International Journal of Addictions, 22*(4), 343-355.

Hoffman, F. J., & Gressard, C. F. (1994). Maintaining change in addictive behaviors. In J. A. Lewis (Ed.), *Addictions: Concepts and strategies for treatment* (pp. 143-160). Gaithersburg, MD: Aspen Publishers.

Hull, C. (1943). *Principles of behavior*. New York: Appleton-Century-Croft.

Lewis, J. A., Dana, R., & Blevins, G. A. (1994). *Substance abuse counseling: An individualized approach* (2nd ed). Pacific Grove, CA: Brooks/Cole.

Mackey, P. W., & Marlatt, G. A. (1991). Maintaining sobriety: Stopping is starting. *International Journal of Addictions, 25,* 1257–1276.

Marion, T. R., & Coleman, K. (1991). Recovery issues and treatment resources. In D. C. Daley & M. S. Raskin (Eds.), *Treating the chemically dependent and their families* (pp. 100-127). Newbury Park: Sage.

Marlatt, G. A. (1982). Relapse prevention: A self-control program for the treatment of addictive behaviors. In R. B. Stuart (Ed.), *Adherence, compliance, and generalization in behavioral medicine* (329–378). New York: Brunner/Mazel.

Marlatt, G. A. (1985a). Relapse prevention: Theoretical rationale and overview of the model. In G. A. Marlatt & J. R. Gordon (Eds.), *Relapse prevention: Maintenance strategies in the treatment of addictive behavior* (pp. 104-105). New York: Guilford.

Marlatt, G. A. (1985b). Lifestyle modification. In G. A. Marlatt & J. Gordon (Eds.), *Relapse prevention: A self-control strategy for the maintenance of behavior change* (pp. 280-350). New York: Guilford.

Marlatt, G. A. (1985c). Cognitive features in the relapse process. In G. A. Marlatt & J. R. Gordon (Eds.), *Relapse prevention: Maintenance strategies in the treatment of addictive behaviors* (128–200). New York: Guilford Press.

Marlatt, G. A., & Gordon, J. (Eds.). (1985). *Relapse prevention: A self-control strategy for the maintenance of behavior change*. New York: Guilford.

McCrady, B. S., & Irvine, S. (1989). Self-help groups. In R. K. Hester & W. R. Miller (Eds.), *Handbook of alcoholism treatment approaches*. New York: Pergamon Press.

Nace, E. P. (1987). *The treatment of alcoholism*. New York: Brunner/Mazel.

Ogborne, A. C., & Glaser, F. B. (1985). Evaluating Alcoholics Anonymous. In T. Bratter & G. C. Forrest (Eds.), *Alcoholism and substance abuse: Strategies for clinical intervention*. New York: The Free Press.

Peele, S., Brodsky, A., & Arnold, M. (1991). *The truth about addiction and recovery*. New York: Simon & Schuster.

Pickens, R., Hatsukami, D., Spicer, L., & Svikis, D. (1985). Relapse by alcohol abusers. *Alcoholism: Clinical and experimental research, 9*(3), 244-247.

Rogers, C. R. (1961). *On becoming a person*. Boston: Houghton Mifflin.

Thorndike, E. (1932). *The fundamentals of learning*. New York: Teachers College Press.

Zackon, F. N. (1988). Relapse and "re-joyment": Observations and reflections. In D. C. Daley (Ed.), *Relapse: Conceptual, research and clinical perspectives* (pp. 67-78). New York: Haworth Press.

Zackon, F., McAuliffe, W., & Ch'ien, J. (1985). Addict aftercare: Recovery training and self-help. DHHS Pub. No. (ADM). 85-1341. Rockville, MD: NIDA.

Research and Contemporary Issues

Robert L. Smith, Ph.D.

T here is a need and demand for a greater emphasis on research in substance abuse treatment, specifically concerning the efficacy of treatment programs. This chapter examines the major problems that have prevented concise, well-focused research in treating substance abuse, followed by a summary of what is known about the effectiveness of many current treatment models. The second section of this chapter examines contemporary issues in the field of substance abuse counseling and treatment, many of which are related to research concerns that demand further investigation and professional discussion.

RESEARCH

Problems with Substance Abuse Research

Research attempts in substance abuse treatment have produced a limited number of studies that can be replicated and clinically applied. Despite an ongoing interest and a concern for "what works" in the field, few definitive answers to this widespread phenomenon have evolved. There are several reasons for the dearth of well-designed, clearly stated studies on substance abuse treatment. Foremost is the fact that substance abuse is usually not attributed to a single cause, or even a small number of events. Why one abuses a substance can be affected by social, psychological, cultural, and biological variables. The degree to which each of these factors influence and eventually affect the long-term use of substances defies quantification.

Treatment methods for substance abuse are also wide ranging. Too often they are limited to the therapist's specific training or experience. Treatment centers or agencies can also obscure comparative scientific studies by advocating only theoretical stances previously used and perpetuated by administrative policy. Treatment centers that use multidimensional approaches with their clients are often unable to determine what specific treatment modalities are responsible for producing change (The Walden House Day Treatment Program, 1995). For example, many substance abuse clients participate in several concurrent programs such as cognitive therapy, family systems therapy, AA groups, education seminars, and peer consultation groups. When successful, the combination of these treatment modalities can be seen as a major change agent. What specific treatment modalities are the most significant to the change process is rarely studied.

Additional concerns in treatment research include the lack of standardized measures to gather information about substance abuse clients. Methods of obtaining the health history of clients vary widely, and are often germane to a particular center or agency, therefore producing independent sets of nonstandardized data. Comparative analyses in these cases are impossible. There is also minimal consistency in the use of standardized instruments to measure change as a result of treatment. Because of this, comparing outcome research findings in substance abuse treatment is often not possible.

Alcoholism Outcome Research

There is significantly more research into the effects of treatment on alcohol abuse compared with other drugs. Also, alcohol treatment programs have yielded better results compared with other drug abuse treatment programs. Hester (1994) provided an overview of outcome research on alcoholism according to the following groupings: no evidence of effectiveness, insufficient evidence of effectiveness, indeterminate evidence of effectiveness, fair evidence of effectiveness, and good evidence of effectiveness. Hester reviewed studies that included control or comparison groups. Summarized findings from 250 studies follow:

No Evidence of Effectiveness

Treatment programs in this group that have no evidence of effectiveness include the following. This list reflects a review of control group studies only.

- Anti-anxiety medications
- Cognitive therapy
- Confrontational interventions
- Educational lectures/films
- Electrical aversion therapies

- General counseling
- Group therapies
- Insight-oriented psychotherapy
- Nausea-aversion therapies
- Residential milieu therapies

It should be made clear that effectiveness in the previous review is based on whether controlled or comparison groups were used. Therefore, a special note concerning general counseling and group therapy deserves mention. Often in treatment, general counseling and group therapies are defined in global terms, hence not rendering themselves to research possibilities. Therefore, one should not conclude general ineffectiveness of these treatment models based on the criteria used by the investigator.

Insufficient Evidence of Effectiveness

The following treatments have a minimal number of studies that fit Hester's criteria for scientific rigor. Treatment programs in this group that have insufficient evidence of effectiveness include the following:

- Alcoholics Anonymous
- Minnesota model of residential treatment
- Halfway houses
- Acupuncture
- Calcium carbide (an antidipsotropic medication not available in the United States)

A special notation needs to be made concerning the AA model of treatment, which lacks controlled studies. Like many other treatment models, AA can identify a significant number of individuals that will attest to its effectiveness in dealing with alcohol abuse. Research on the AA model is presented later in this chapter.

Indeterminate Evidence of Effectiveness

A minimal number of controlled or comparison studies have been located using the following treatments, making it difficult to determine their effectiveness:

- Nonbehavior marital therapy
- Hypnosis
- Lithium

The structural and strategic theoretical approaches are included in the list of nonbehavioral marital therapies studied.

Fair Evidence of Effectiveness

Hester (1994) found four or more controlled studies that reasonably supported the following treatment modalities, indicating a fair level of effectiveness with alcohol abuse:

- Antidepressant medication
- Behavior contracting
- Covert sensitization
- Oral and implant disulfiram

Good Evidence of Effectiveness

The following treatment models have produced enough control studies to report good evidence of effectiveness according to Hester (1994):

- Behavioral marital therapy
- Brief interventions
- Community reinforcement approach (CRA)
- Self-control training
- Social skills training
- Stress management

Behavioral marital therapy includes increasing the frequency of positive reinforcements given in a relationship. Both conjoint therapy and couples therapy use communication skill building and problem solving reflecting a behavioral approach producing significant results. Manuals describing this approach are available (McCrady, 1982; O'Farrel & Cowles, 1989; O'Farrell, 1986; O'Farrell & Cutter, 1984). Many of the other approaches listed in this category are also behavioral in nature.

The brief intervention model in the previous list includes "FRAMES" elements (Miller & Rollnick, 1991):

Feedback regarding a patient's drinking that is individualized and objective
Responsibility placed on the patient for deciding what to do regarding drinking
Clear **A**dvice to change
A **M**enu of interventions and options for change, including a willingness to negotiate the goals of change
An **E**mpathic style of counseling
Self-efficacy

Outcome research on methadone maintenance programs, outpatient programs, and residential programs are examined below. Results are often reported in terms of degrees of improvement over time and the extent to which clients relapse.

Methadone Maintenance Outcome Research

Methadone maintenance (MM) programs, specifically designed for narcotic analgesic dependence, have been widely discussed and reviewed. Used mainly for the treatment of heroin addiction, the foundation of the methadone maintenance program is that all narcotic analgesics can be substituted for one another. The use of methadone in this regard has been extensive due to minimal clinical side effects (Gerstein & Harwood, 1992).

Early research on the methadone maintenance programs (Dole, Robinson & Orraga, 1969) found that most patients using this approach would remain in treatment when compared with others experiencing outpatient psychotherapy, and that patients' behavior in the community drastically improved. In addition, early findings showed a decrease in criminal behavior as well as a decline in the use of other drugs. A well-designed study in Sweden (Gunne & Grombladh, 1984) revealed significant findings on the use of methadone with 34 heroin-dependent individuals. In this study, 17 individuals were randomly assigned to MM, and a second 17 were given outpatient nonmethadone treatment. A two-year follow-up revealed that 71% of the MM patients were doing well, compared with 6% from the control group. A five-year follow-up found 13 methadone patients remaining in treatment and not using heroin. For the control group, 9 patients subsequently entered MM, with 8 not using heroin. Of the 8 control patients not applying for MM, 5 were reported dead of an overdose of drugs, 2 were in prison and 1 was drug free. Other studies in which MM was used either in public or private settings (due to the closure of many clinics) have produced similar results (Anglin, Speckart, & Booth, 1989; McGlothlin & Anglin, 1981).

An issue raised in relation to effectiveness of methadone treatment involves clinic policies and counselor characteristics. Programs committed to low average doses of methadone for patients due to a clinic philosophy or influence from state regulators, have revealed lower retention rates and greater drug use by patients. It has been documented that higher dose levels of methadone are significantly more successful than lower ones in controlling drug consumption during treatment (Hargreaves, 1983). The dose level of methadone has been shown to be the most discriminate factor in predicting success as determined by drug use. Gerstein and Harwood (1992) also report that programs with high illicit drug consumption used low methadone dosage. It was also found that these programs had high rates of staff turnover along with poor relationships between staff and patients. These factors may be considered additional reasons for lower levels of effectiveness.

Cocaine Studies

Only recently has research on the treatment of substances outside of alcohol begun to appear. Of the illicit drugs, cocaine has been of greatest concern, because it was the only illicit substance whose use had significantly increased through the mid-1980s. Few cocaine treatment programs have been studied, even though cocaine use has been acknowledged as widespread. In addition, the pharmacological, behavioral, and environmental factors related to cocaine present special problems of treatment and the study of treatment attempts.

Randomized clinical studies on psychotherapeutic approaches used with cocaine abusers are rare. One study, however, did examine psychotherapeutic treatments for cocaine abuse (Carroll et al., 1994). In this investigation, 42 ambulatory cocaine abusers were randomly assigned to (1) a relapse prevention (RP) group, using a cognitive behavioral approach, or (2) an interpersonal psychotherapy (IPT) group, using a short-term psychodynamic approach. The drop-out rate was high for each group following a 12-week treatment, but it was significantly higher for the IPT group (62%), compared with the RP group (33%). Abstinence was significantly higher for the high-severity subjects in the RP group, compared with the IPT group. The high attrition rate of this study revealed at least some success with cocaine abusers who are treated psychotherapeutically with better results using a cognitive-behavioral approach adapted for cocaine abusers.

Other studies have used or modified Washton's (1989) program design for the treatment of cocaine and crack addiction, with an emphasis on structure, intensity, and frequency. This usually has meant a highly structured outpatient regimen combining individual, group, and family counseling; education; urine testing; and self-help (Washton & Stone-Washton, 1991). Studies indicate that employed cocaine and crack addicts can be treated successfully in inpatient or outpatient programs that are followed by intensive aftercare treatment emphasizing relapse prevention (Washton, 1989). In addition, intensive outpatient treatment can be a cost-effective alternative to inpatient care. Results reported by Washton (1989) showed a 77% abstinence rate for inpatient clients and a 74% abstinence rate for outpatient clients at the end of treatment. In a 6-to-24-month follow-up, 68% of the outpatients and 64% of the inpatients were abstinent. Washton's recommendation and findings on treating cocaine abusers is supported by Kang et al. (1991), who also reported a need for an intensive level of outpatient contact or residential treatment followed by aftercare with patients trying to sustain abstinence. In a related study examining cocaine as well as opiate and alcohol treatment, McLellan et al. (1994) found that the same factors predict outcomes of cocaine treatment as in opiate and alcohol treatment. In all cases, the more severe the drug abuse at the beginning of treatment, the higher the relapse rate found in follow-up. Better social adjustment at follow-up was predicated by fewer employment, mental, and family problems.

Outpatient Programs Research

As early as 1956, outpatient (day treatment) programs have been used to address alcohol-related problems (Fox & Lowe, 1967). Outpatient programs are wide ranging in duration and treatment methods. They range from a one-session assessment followed by a referral, to three-to-six-month programs including weekly psychotherapy, to one-to-two-year programs with psychotherapy combined with other treatment activities. Because of this wide variance in outpatient programs, it has been difficult to study treatment effectiveness. However, research conducted by the Drug Abuse Reporting Program (DARP) and the Treatment Outcome Prospective Study (TOPS) enables one to make some general conclusions concerning outpatient programs (Hubbard, Marsden, & Rachal, 1989; Sells 1974; Simpson, Savage, & Lloyd, 1979).

One conclusion is that the longer patients remain in outpatient treatment, the better the outcome (Gerstein & Harwood, 1994). Patients staying in treatment fewer than 90 days showed negligible improvement, compared with those who stayed in longer than 90 days. The TOPS study suggests that the critical retention threshold for patients is six months (Hubbard, Marsden, & Rachal, 1989). Patients involved in outpatient program activities longer than six months significantly improved in drug abstinence and quality of life.

A few descriptive reports of full-day outpatient treatment programs are available (Alterman & McLellan, 1993). There is some evidence of the effectiveness of full-day treatment programs that include counseling, group therapy, psycho-education, vocational training, and other helping services (Alterman, O'Brien, & Droba, 1993; Feigelman, Hymany, Amann, & Feigelman, 1990). Recent findings suggest that such programs can be used effectively as a precursor to residential treatment, and that some clients can be treated effectively in day treatment alone (Guydish, Werdegar, Chan, Nebelkopf, & Acampora, 1994). Six-month follow-ups show that clients who enter full-day outpatient treatment with severe alcohol and other related substance abuse problems and remain for at least two weeks report significantly fewer substance abuse, legal, and psychiatric problems, and increased levels of social support. These programs have multiple components and include structure, daily contact, intensive therapeutic contact (individual and group), and psycho-educational services.

Controlled studies of the effectiveness of different therapies have been limited. However, individual therapy and group therapy as treatment modalities with alcoholic individuals have been studied (Solomon, 1982). This study reported better success with group therapy than with individual outpatient therapy used by itself. Woody, Luborsky, & McLellan (1983) revealed an effectiveness of individual therapy alone when working with opium-addicted patients. The use of addiction counseling as described in the Solomon study focused less on identifying and changing intrapsychic processes and more on managing and changing current problems of addiction. The individual treatment concentrated on the addict's problems and addictive supporting behaviors. Treatment is concrete and specific, with less of an indirect and intrapsychic focus than in psychotherapy. However, because of the high level of comorbidity between substance use disorders and a wide range of psychiatric symptoms as characterized by DSM IV (depression, dysthymia, and anxiety disorders), it is believed that clients can gain from approaches that combine psychotherapy and addictions counseling. Washton (1989) advocates such a treatment consisting of structured abstinence-oriented activities, drug education, family involvement, 12-step participation, group therapy, and individual psychotherapy. In Washton's program, drug-focused counseling and psychotherapy are often provided by the same professional.

Specific psychotherapeutic techniques used in outpatient programs have been adopted to deal with addiction problems (Khantzian, 1985, 1987; Levin, 1987). Supportive expressive psychotherapy (psychoanalytic therapy), interpersonal psychotherapy (psychoanalytic therapy), cognitive treatment (cognitive therapy), behavioral therapy, and family systems therapy have all been used alone or in combinations with addicted patients. Only in the past two decades have the above approaches been subject to scientific investigation of their efficacy with substance abusing patients. According to Carroll et al. (1994); LaRosa, Lipsius, & LaRosa (1974); Resnick, Washton, Stone-Washton(1981); Woody, Luborsky, & McLellan (1983) there is enough evidence to support psychotherapy as an effective treatment model for substance abuse in outpatient programs.

These studies suggest that certain conditions need to be met for positive outcomes. Examples include a need for greater structure and more frequent visits than traditional psychotherapy and a more general use of a pharmacological treatment modalities. Individual psychotherapy has been found to be more effective when combined with other outpatient treatment services. Traditional psychotherapeutic methods, as expected, also seem to be more effective with patients experiencing clinical problems along with addictions. Currently, research has not found any one psychotherapeutic treatment method in outpatient treatment programs to be superior to any other forms of treatment.

Inpatient Programs

Inpatient programs for substance abuse are highly structured, intensive, and expensive. For years, the typical patient was described as 40 years old, white, and alcohol dependent. Programs have changed to a large degree by including patients with varied drug problems and multiple substance abuse issues, and a large number of adolescents. Inpatient treatment has been referred to as the Minnesota model, 28-day, 12-step, or Hazelden-type treatment (Gerstein, 1994)

Inpatient programs for treating alcohol abuse have been more successful than programs treating other drugs or multiple substances. The Care Unit study (Comprehensive Care Corporation, as cited in Gerstein & Harwood, 1994) sampled 1,000 adult patients with at least a 5-day stay. Follow-up studies found 61% classified as recovering. The recovery rate of users of illicit drugs was 10% lower than that of alcohol abuse patients (Gerstein, 1994). Hazelden studies also indicated better results with alcohol abuse problems, compared with abstinence rates of other drug users (Gilmore, 1985; Laundergan, 1982). Inpatient treatment programs for cocaine abuse have been limited. One study reported effects of an inpatient cocaine treatment program compared with outpatient and no treatment (Rawson, Obert, McEann, & Mann, 1985). It can be concluded that inpatient programs are fairly effective in treating alcoholism, but have not been adequately evaluated as to their effectiveness with other drug use.

EFFECTIVENESS OF SPECIFIC PROGRAMS

A number of studies examining the efficacy of specific substance abuse programs deserve mention. Certain programs have been reported as successful, either alone or along with other treatment modalities. Treatment programs discussed in this section include the 12-step, Alcoholics Anonymous approach, individual outpatient counseling programs, group counseling programs, family therapy, and multidimensional programs.

12-Step Programs

In 1992, there were 94,000 Alcoholics Anonymous groups, 22,000 Narcotics Anonymous groups, more than 32,000 Al-Anon groups, and thousands more related groups across the country. Because of widespread availability, 12-step programs are considered by many the best hope in stopping the continued growth of substance abuse. Nace (1987) found that 70% of those who stayed sober for one year while attending AA meetings remained sober at the end of the second year, while 90% of those who stayed sober at the end of the second year remained sober at the end of their third year.

However, Ogborne & Glaser (1985), in a review of AA research studies, concluded that AA was effective only with certain populations: white males older than 40 who were physically dependent on alcohol and who possessed certain characteristics. In addition, Hester (1994) challenged the effectiveness of mandatory attendance programs such as AA and NA. After studying 600 AA and NA programs, Hester found insufficient evidence demonstrating their overall effectiveness, despite indications that relapse was significantly affected. Yet, Emerick, Tonigan, Montgomery, & Little (1993) suggest that AA and NA meetings are effective since relapse is more likely to occur when clients do not participate in AA meetings.

Early studies designed to evaluate AA groups and their effectiveness were burdened with scientific design problems. Most did not include control groups, for example. However, these findings, despite their limitations, have generally shown positive results (Leach & Norris, 1977; Madsen 1974; Bebbington, 1976). Leach (1973) reported four studies involving AA treatment in London, Finland, the United States, and Canada. The results of studies in the United States and Canada reported that 38% of the sample of 11,355 were abstinent from one to five years. Madsen (1974) compared AA treatment with other approaches in California. Through the use of questionnaires in an ethnographic study, conclusions were that AA showed outstanding gains when compared with a variety of other treatment modalities.

A number of current studies, and even a meta-analysis have examined the effectiveness of AA with substance abuse clients (Emerick, Tonigan, Montgomery, & Little, 1993; Institute of Medicine, 1990). Findings are still mixed due to several uncontrolled variables: an inability to use control groups, questions of mandatory versus voluntary participation, and the wide variance among AA meetings conducted across the country. Positive findings (Emerick, Tonigan, Montgomery, & Little, 1993) correlate AA attendance and participation with positive outcomes. The meta-analysis of AA studies found that individuals most likely to affiliate with AA had a history of (1) using external supports to stop drinking, (2) losing control of drinking and behavior when drinking, (3) consuming a high quantity of alcohol, (4) expressing distress about their drinking, (5) being obsessively/compulsively involved with alcohol, (6) believing that drinking enhances mental functioning, and (7) engaging in religious/spiritual activities (Montgomery, Miller, & Tonigan, 1995).

Recent studies have began to examine the efficacy of AA before and after treatment. Emerick, Tonigan, Montgomery, & Little (1993) found participation in AA before treatment not to be a significant factor when predicting treatment outcome. However, AA attendance during or after treatment was found to be positively associated with successful outcomes (Emerick, 1989; Emerick, Tonigan, Montgomery, & Little, 1993). Montgomery, Miller, & Tonigan (1995), supported in part by grants from the National Institute on Alcohol Abuse and Alcoholism, studied whether AA involvement would predict treatment outcome. Their findings, supported by previous research (Emerick, Tonigan, Montgomery, & Little, 1993), suggested that it is active participation in the AA process, rather than mere attendance at AA meetings, that predicts more favorable outcomes after treatment. These findings are also consistent with discussions centered on mandated versus voluntary AA meetings. When attendance is voluntary, and when such members actively participate in AA meetings, there is strong evidence of successful outcomes. One has to wonder whether the same axiom holds true for other treatment modalities used with substance abuse clients.

The above studies point to the powerful force of AA, despite on-going questions concerning AA's effectiveness (Doweiko, 1990). One suggestion for future AA research is that meetings need to be more closely examined. Researchers should look at aspects of AA believed to be effective, for whom, and under what conditions. This direction of research can be most promising, recognizing existing evidence indicating both the value and overall effectiveness of AA and NA programs and their underlying concepts. For now, there seems to be a consensus concerning the value of AA as an important, often necessary, adjunct to other treatment modalities (Gallegos, Lubin, & Bowers, 1992; McLellan, O'Brien, & Metzger, 1992; Zweben, 1987; Bloise & Holder, 1991; Hoffman & Miller, 1992).

Individual Counseling Programs

Individual counseling programs remain a viable option for many addicted patients. The outpatient counseling model offers the individual a chance to live at home, and in most cases continue working. There is a belief that for many patients, individual outpatient drug addiction counseling is as effective as inpatient chemically dependent programs (Doweiko, 1990). Individual counseling approaches for drug use are viewed as heterogeneous in nature (Institute of Medicine, 1990), and often serve clients with less severe drug-related problems.

The goals of individual outpatient substance abuse counseling programs include (1) abstinence from alcohol and other drugs, (2) stabilization of marriage and family, (3) stabilization of employment, (4) improved physical and emotional health, (5) legal problem resolution, and (6) spiritual strengthening (Lewis, Piercy, Sprenkle, & Trepper, 1991).

Thousands of clients who used drug abuse counseling programs were studied through the Treatment Outcome Prospective Study (TOPS) funded by the Research Triangle Institute. Results indicated that individual counseling programs were effective in two areas: (1) reducing drug use and (2) improving employment. Due to a low rate of retention in these programs, however, the TOPS findings have been questioned. Yet, the Drug Abuse Reporting Program (DARP), conducted by the Institute for Behavior Research at Texas Christian University, supported many of the TOPS findings. Conclusions drawn from this research indicated that individual counseling approaches in outpatient drug abuse programs were generally effective. But there also was a call for clearer descriptions of specific counseling interventions and individual treatment modalities used (Woody, Mercer, & Luborsky, 1994).

Findings from the Institute of Medicine (1990), concluded there exists only a minimum amount of research pointing to effective individual counseling interventions used with drug abusing clients. Findings by the Institute include:

1. Among young problem drinkers, 50% to 60% of men and 70% of women experience improvement without formal treatment.
2. For middle-age drinkers in trouble with alcohol, the rate of improvement without formal treatment is 30% to 40% for men and 30% for women.
3. In older drinkers the rate for improvement without formal treatment are about 60% to 80% for men and 50% to 60% for women.

Additional conclusions were that the wise health care provider will seek to activate or enhance "naturally" occurring factors that facilitate the remission of alcohol problems (Institute of Medicine, 1990)

A number of earlier studies attempted to examine individual therapeutic techniques used with substance abuse clients and their families. These techniques included (1) behavior therapy (Lesser, 1976; Ulmer, 1977), (2) reality therapy (Schuster, 1978–1979), (3) autogenic training (Roszell & Chaney, 1982), and (4) counseling in general (Weiner, 1975; Schilit & Gomberg, 1991). Evidence concerning effectiveness of these approaches has been inconclusive. There is, therefore, a need for controlled studies examining the effects of individual counseling programs compared with controlled populations not undergoing treatment.

Group Counseling Programs

Interpersonal relationships and social interactions are major factors affecting substance abuse clients. Because of this, the group counseling process has been historically considered one of the most viable approaches to use with substance abusers—

either alone or in conjunction with other treatment methods. Group programs help clients alter distorted concepts of self, learn from others, regain hope, and reduce isolation. (Vannicelli, 1982). Despite the advantages of using group counseling approaches with substance abusing clients, these programs have been sparsely researched. Hester & Miller (1989), after reviewing studies on the efficacy of group counseling programs with substance abuse clients, concluded that measurable effective outcomes have yet to be consistently demonstrated.

Yet the general view has been that group therapy programs are effective with adolescent substance abusers (Agazarian & Peters, 1991) Others such as Khantzian (1986) identified group therapy as the most commonly used psychotherapy technique for the treatment of alcohol problems.

Fram (1990) stated that the use of groups made up exclusively of substance abusing clients will maximize treatment efforts. Fram further indicated that the use of the small-group treatment method with substance abusers was so effective that most drug rehabilitation centers now use it as the core of their program. Stein and Friedman (1971) stated that group psychotherapy is, in most instances, the treatment of choice for the psychological problems of alcoholism, and they estimate that 60% to 70% of patients in group psychotherapy improve, versus 20% to 40% of patients receiving only individual psychotherapy.

Others have also endorsed the effectiveness of group work with substance abuse issues, including approaches such as gestalt, psychodrama, transactional analysis, and aversion therapy groups (Doroff, 1977; Fox, 1962). Despite such endorsements, a review of the literature reveals few well-controlled studies measuring the effects of group psychotherapy with substance abusers.

Yalom (1974) offers a basic explanation—although not a scientific investigation—of why groups are effective. Lawson (1994) reviewed Yalom's curative factors of groups in relation to chemically dependent clients and supports Yalom's curative factor premise.

In summary, research is needed to scientifically support these concepts. It is hoped that research will catch up to theory concerning the effectiveness of group therapy with addicted clients.

Family Therapy

Family therapy has been seen as a promising treatment approach for substance abusers (Kaufmann, 1979). Family therapy treatment is an active process that may include substance abusers and their spouses, substance abusers and their family of origin, or substance abusers and their children. On certain occasions, three generations may be involved in the treatment process. When therapy includes family members, research has shown that its effect can be significant, particularly with alcoholic patients (Liepman, Nirenberg, & Begiw, 1989).

In controlled studies where family therapy was used with substance abusers, Stanton and Todd (1982) reported it to be superior compared with certain individual approaches used alone. Hendricks (1971), found that narcotics addicts receiving family therapy treatment were significantly more likely to remain in treatment than those who did not participate in family treatment.

Todd and Selekman (1991) found that when family therapy was used with substance abuse cases, individuals tended to stay longer in treatment and maintain sobriety for longer periods of time. McCrady (1986) also found that alcoholic abusing clients were more likely to stay in treatment, remain abstinent, and maintain marital satisfaction when marital therapy was part of their treatment.

The number of family members involved in substance abuse treatment seems to affect the outcome of substance abuse counseling in a positive direction. Additional studies found a family therapy intervention model with adolescents to be significantly more effective in reducing adolescent drug use than a straight family education intervention (Lewis, Piercy, Sprenkle, & Trepper, 1991). In a study funded by the National Institute on Drug Abuse, Joanning, Quinn, Thomas, & Mullen (1992) examined the effectiveness of Family System Drug Education (FSDE) with adolescent drug abusers. Family Systems Drug Education therapy was seen as an effective approach in reducing adolescent drug abuse. As indicated previously, some data from recent projects demonstrated that family therapy can be effective with substance abusers, when used in conjunction with other treatment modalities. However, there remains a call for more research on how effective family therapy approaches alone are with substance abuse clients (Lawson, 1994).

Multidimensional Programs

Research in substance abuse counseling often fails to identify specific treatment methods, approaches, or techniques that produce change with identified drug abuse problems. Most substance abuse treatment programs currently favor a multidimensional approach when dealing with addictions. Multidimensional or multimodality treatment approaches include detoxification, individual counseling, group counseling, family therapy, in-patient treatment, education, and so on. Multidimensional models are becoming more widely used by both outpatient and inpatient programs. They have been recommended as the treatment models of choice to counteract addictions (Lewis, Dana, & Blevins, 1994; Doweiko, 1990). Research studies demonstrating treatment combinations that might work best as a multidimensional model are nonexistent. However, some generalizations can be made, such as combining AA and NA programs with individual counseling and family therapy modalities. Which treatment modalities work with which addiction problems needs to be researched.

SUMMARY OF EFFECTIVENESS OF PROGRAMS

A certain amount of evidence suggests that substance abuse treatments can be effective in reducing substance use and in bringing about improvements in the areas of employment, criminal activity, social adjustment, and health care (Anglin & Hser, 1990; Ball & Ross, 1991; Institute of Medicine, 1990; McLellan et al., 1994). Yet success has been mixed with outcome studies identifying large numbers of clients who broke the law or were re-admitted for additional care. Results of these studies have led researchers to investigate pre-treatment variables that might predict outcome of substance abuse treatment. Variables being studied (McLellan et al., 1994) include severity of dependence, family and social supports, psychiatric symptoms, and personality type. This is a difficult process, compounded by differences in the substances being studied and by variances in treatment.

Both inpatient and outpatient programs have reported success in dealing with alcohol abuse and cocaine abuse patients. As a result, some clear guidelines and program recommendations for treatment have evolved (Washton, 1990). There have been reports that individual counseling and group counseling, when used alone, are at times effective with substance abuse clients. However there are only a few studies of this nature, and most treatment programs combine these modalities with other methods of treatment. More information is being obtained on the successful use of AA programs, particularly as related to mandated versus voluntary attendance. Level of participation, rather than simply the number of meetings attended, is a significant variable in predicting abstinence. There seem to be enough studies available examining the treatment of cocaine abuse and other illicit drugs to conduct meta-analysis research in these areas similar to studies by Emerick, Tonigan, Montgomery, & Little (1993) on alcohol abuse.

CONTEMPORARY ISSUES

Many of the contemporary issues involving substance abuse counseling center on research: Research about "what works" with specific problems, substance abuse etiology, predictability of substance abuse, adolescent substance abuse, gender differences, and programs for minorities. Several of these areas are mentioned briefly in this section in an attempt to stimulate discussion, additional reading, and further research.

The Disease Concept of Alcoholism: Still Questions

Most physicians, counselors, and psychologists view alcoholism according to the disease model. Alcoholism is seen as a disease with treatment emphasizing total abstinence. This concept has been challenged by the decision of the Supreme Court in Traynor v. Turnage (1988). The court ruled against a plaintiff who was seeking an extension of education benefits due to alcohol abuse. The client's condition was argued to be a disease that prevented the plaintiff from using educational benefits granted by the military. The court ruled against the plaintiff in this case stating that consumption of alcohol is not regarded as totally involuntary. Soon after, many professionals thought this ruling would affect the widely held belief in the disease model of substance abuse. However, this has not been the case.

Today, the full endorsement of the disease model is being challenged by many therapists, treatment centers, and social scientists. A number of counselors and treatment centers have begun to advocate gradual reductions of alcohol consumption by their clients and some use a "safe amount" of drinking as part of their treatment. A commonly accepted view is the conceptualization of alcoholism and substance abuse along a continuum from nonproblematic to highly problematic (Lewis, Dana, & Blevins, 1994). Treatment stresses working with clients in terms of where they are on the continuum, and does not assume progression according to the disease model. It is predicted that treatment approaches and ideas will continue to be examined and implemented, and that they will often not align with a particular set of beliefs as the disease model of alcohol abuse.

Defining Abuse Within the Context of Diagnosis

The debate continues as to the definition of *abuse* when discussing the use of substances. While the term *substance* can generally be agreed upon as a drug of abuse, a medication, or a toxin (DSM IV), the term *abuse* seems to be defined more as to the degree of use and often as part of a value or belief system. Despite the development of more specific criteria identifying substance abuse, as per the DSM IV, questions of labeling and definition persist. Should someone who takes a substance that leads to a physically hazardous situation, be labeled a substance abuser, or should the context in which this occurred be considered? In cases where several psychosocial factors lead to the use of a substance and create impairment or distress, should the substance abuse classification take preference, or should commingling factors enter into the diagnosis? Is it possible that systemic factors lead to the use of the substance, indicating that they should be given first priority?

Is one drinking episode followed by social or employment problems enough to be classified as substance abuse, or is a lengthier history needed? It is believed that such classifications or labels need to be continually discussed so they are not aligned with a preconceived belief and value system surrounding substance in general.

Substance abuse definitions are complicated by dual diagnosis, or comorbidity, issues. This creates an additional challenge to the practitioner. For years it has been known that psychiatric symptomology is often manifested by individuals addicted to various substances. In many cases, substance abuse disorders are linked to affecting disorders (Mayfield, 1985), sociopathy (Kay, 1985), schizophrenia (Alterman, 1985), depression (Hesselbrock, Meyer, & Keener, 1985), and so on. Questions of diagnosis and treatment under these conditions become extremely complex.

Determining Treatment Goals

Related to the definition of abuse is the issue of determining proper treatment goals. Treatment goals in the substance abuse field vary greatly. For example, the question of moderate "acceptable" drinking versus complete sobriety continues to be discussed. Advantages of the sobriety model have been advocated by AA, clinics, hospitals, and supporters of the disease model. Others believe that some individuals can learn to control their drinking and operate at more moderate levels of alcohol consumption (Lewis, Dana, & Blevins, 1994). This controversy is negated by a lack of data from nontreated problem drinkers who generally recover through what has been called *spontaneous recovery*. Many have raised the question of whether abstinence is a realistic goal.

Other issues have surfaced over treatment goals with drugs such as cocaine, heroin, and marijuana. Less documentation is available showing permanent or long-term abstinence with patients using these drugs. Research has also shown high levels of relapse. Goals of treatment are therefore being revisited in relation to the substance being treated and relapse predictability. Many therapists and treatment facilities have begun to re-examine the treatment process and keep statistics on relapse. Relapse is seen by many as a part of the therapeutic process, with complete withdrawal from substance use viewed as unrealistic for certain clients. These concepts are disturbing for many, including funding agencies and legislators. Government agencies and practicing professionals have to wrestle with indefinite solutions and change that is difficult. Unfortunately the etiology of drug abuse and its complications are multifaceted, perhaps demanding diversity of treatment and intermittent goal setting.

Gender Issues and the Use of Drugs

Studies have shown major differences between men and women who are treated for alcohol and drug abuse. George (1990) states that compared with women, male alcoholics:

- Take their first drink at a younger age.
- Participate in more morning drinking.
- Have more extensive histories of delirium tremors.
- Have more blackouts.
- More frequently lose jobs and friends due to drinking.
- Have more school problems.
- Have more alcohol-related arrests.
- Have fewer suicide attempts.

George (1990) further cites work by Horn and Wanberg (1973) stating that women who abuse alcohol:

- Begin to drink later in life.
- Drink more often at home alone.

- Have shorter drinking binges.
- Often use alcohol in an attempt to improve job performance.
- Are less gregarious drinkers.
- Are more often solitary drinkers.
- More often perceive their alcoholism as becoming worse.

Despite these findings, treatment differences according to gender are seldom discussed and often not implemented. Research conducted on alcohol abuse and drug abuse treatment have excluded large samples of women. Traditional stereotypes of men and women alcoholics persist with views of a male drunk as one who is accepted and often seen as humorous, while the female alcoholic or drug user is disdained, exhibiting behavior that is unacceptable or disgraceful.

Gender in terms of the therapist-client relationship is a related issue. Some findings show that same-gender therapists and clients work best. Issues also have been raised about gender bias. Sensitivity to the client's gender and research on the role of gender in therapy around substance abuse is long overdue.

Training and Background of Substance Abuse Counselors

The question of who is best qualified to work with substance abuse issues continues to be debated. Many agencies are split in terms of background, experience, and training needed for one to effectively work in the field. For years a large segment of substance abuse helpers believed that to be an effective counselor, one must be a recovering substance abuser who had gone through the substance abusing process and treatment. Having gone through this process, one would be accepted by clients with a similar problem. The belief is that personal experience provides counselors with the understanding of recovery and the insight into the life experiences of the addict.

As the field of substance abuse counseling has evolved, others have advocated the professional training "education" approach to preparing substance abuse counselors, emphasizing formal training, including clinical work with drug users. Often a masters degree in counseling, social work, or psychology is obtained, with an emphasis in substance abuse counseling and a clinical supervised internship.

George (1990) suggests that substance abuse counselors have certain minimum skills and knowledge to maximize the therapeutic effect on clients. Such individuals would possess a working knowledge of chemical dependency. A knowledge base for substance abuse counselors has been developed by the International Association for Addictions and Offenders Counselors (IAAOC). These standards have been implemented as Specialty Certification Standards for Substance Abuse Counselors with the National Board for Certified Counselors (NBCC). Under this substance abuse specialty, individuals qualify by completing a masters degree with designated coursework and experiences in substance abuse counseling. The Master Addiction Counselor (MAC) certification developed jointly by the National Association of Alcoholism and Drug Abuse Counselors (NAADAC) and NBCC is considered by some to be the most widely regarded certification in the field (Cahillane, 1996). Other existing boards, such as the National Board of Addiction Examiners, offer certification at the baccalaureate, masters, and doctoral levels, as well as a skill-based level.

Parallel to certification has been the evolution of masters-level training programs with specialties in substance abuse counseling. An example of one of the first full-fledged masters degrees in substance abuse counseling was started at Northeast Louisiana University (Locke, 1992), offering students a degree in substance abuse counseling. East Carolina University and Penn State University offer similar programs.

Despite differences of opinion as to how one enters the field of substance abuse counseling, either through direct experience as a recovered alcohol or drug user, or through formal training, most would agree that continued training and experience are necessary in this field. With multiple-diagnosis cases, the need for family treatment, use of medication, and so on, substance abuse counselors will need to continually update their skills and knowledge base.

Ethical Issues and Substance Abuse Counseling

The area of substance abuse counseling has recently developed more complete codes of ethics helpful to counselors working with a variety of drug abusing clients. Despite such codes, developed by the National Association of Alcoholism and Drug Abuse Counselors and the International Association for Addictions and Offenders Counselors, all potential ethical dilemmas cannot be covered by a set of predetermined standards. Of particular relevance with substance abuse cases is the issue of confidentiality, especially concerning drug use, lapses in alcohol abstinence, or drug supplying. The counselor is caught among the client, the referring agency, the client's workplace, the employee assistance program, and the client's family network. When and under what circumstances confidentiality should be breached needs to be carefully thought out and clearly articulated to the clients and their families.

As multidimensional approaches are more frequently implemented, numerous problems will evolve about the sharing of information. How much information is shared from individual counseling sessions, family sessions, and from other client experiences? Under what circumstances and according to what conditions does one share professional information with others who are working with or close to the client? Each incident is considered case by case, with a decision of what to do based on (1) what is best for the client, (2) the policies of the agency, and (3) how it fits with the rule of no harm to self and others. Until further precedent is established examining a wide range of cases, counselors will be left with making decisions based on their personal experiences and their best judgment.

Burnout

The mental health profession has a history of high levels of burnout. Lack of clear results, case overload, unrealistic expectations, minimal agency support, and funding reductions are some of the reasons. Many counselors are unable to remove themselves from the job and establish the necessary distance from their clients. Often they are unable to detach from the problems and pain expressed by their clients. A feeling of helplessness is present with difficult cases.

Substance abuse counselors seem to be more prone to experience these situations and are therefore more susceptible to burnout (George, 1990). Counselors who work with court-mandated cases may be particularly vulnerable. There is often a sense of loss of control, particularly in treatment centers that seem chaotic as clients begin treatment only to terminate in the first few weeks. There is little time for consultation with peers and often few opportunities to support or seek support from others. Caseloads in many clinics are exhausting. Mortality rates of severe drug cases are high, and each death from a drug overdose takes it toll on the counselor.

There also is a high level of turnover in substance abuse treatment clinics. Many professionals start out as substance abuse counselors and than move to other positions in the counseling profession where more clear-cut results can be seen, and where the caseloads might be more reasonable.

Suggestions for preventing burnout of substance abuse counselors include (1) maintaining an appropriate workload, (2) leaving one's work at the office, (3) setting boundaries with clients and staff, (4) developing and maintaining an independent personal life away from the job, and (5) attending conferences and workshops that provide opportunities for both skill building and sharing with colleagues (George, 1990).

Burnout will continue to be an issue with substance abuse counselors as cases become more complex. As this occurs, the suggestions to cope and prevent burnout will take on greater relevance.

Ethnic Minorities and Substance Abuse

Special attention is needed in the area of ethnic minorities and the use of substances, as noted previously in this text. Although the general health of Americans has improved over the last two decades, many minorities have not experienced these improvements. Most of the minorities continue to have higher death rates from chronic diseases and lower life expectancies compared with white populations (Schilit & Gomberg, 1991). There have been few studies and very little written on the treatment of ethnic minority drug and alcohol abusers. Despite this, there is a belief that culture-specific treatment programs need to be explored to meet the needs of varied ethnic groups.

Some suggestions include building on the role of the church with African American or Hispanic substance abusers. For many ethnic minorities, the church—rather than AA—is seen as a place to share problems outside of the family. Spanish-speaking substance abuse counselors who are culturally sensitive to ethnic minority issues need to be sought for treatment centers.

Limited information has been published about the alcohol and drug use of Asian and Pacific American populations. It is known that a stigma is placed on substance abuse in this group, causing them to be overlooked in the research. In comparison, American Indians and the use of substances, particularly alcohol, have received much attention. It has been reported that alcohol contributes to 4 of the 10 leading causes of death for American Indians (Heath, 1989). At the same time, studies reveal that alcohol treatment programs for American Indians have yielded poor results (Walker, Benjamin, Kwlahan, & Walker, 1989).

Continued study is needed concerning ethnic minority groups and related issues of substance abuse and treatment. Attention first needs to be devoted to methods of encouraging minority groups to seek treatment. An examination of the best methods of treatment, sensitive to cultural differences, can than be studied.

Other Areas of Study

A number of additional issues could have been included in this chapter as related to substance abuse counseling. Of particular concern is the treatment of substance abuse with adolescent populations, briefly discussed in this text. Other issues, such as drugs and violence, and substance abuse treatment related to managed care, will need to be more fully examined in the future. However, it is the evolution of these issues and thoughtful responses to them that make substance abuse counseling a challenging and exciting professional area.

REFERENCES

Agazarian, S., & Peters, R. (1991). *The visible and invisible group.* London: Routledge & Kegan Paul.

Alterman, A. I. (1985). Substance abuse in psychiatric patients: Etiological, development and treatment considerations. In A. I. Alterman (Ed.), *Substance abuse and psychopathology* (pp. 121–136). New York: Plenum.

Alterman, A. I., O'Brien, C. P., & Droba, M. (1993). Day hospital vs. inpatient rehabilitation of cocaine abusers: An interim report. In F. M. Tims & C. G. Luekenfeld (Eds.), *Cocaine treatment: Research and clinical perspectives* (pp. 150-162). NIDA Research Monograph 135 (NIH Publication No. 93-3639)

Alterman, A. I., & McLellan, A. T. (1993). Inpatient and day hospital treatment services for cocaine and alcohol dependance. *Journal of Substance Abuse Treatment, 10,* 269-275.

Anglin, M. D., Speckart, G. S., & Booth M. W., et al. (1989). Consequences and costs of shutting off methadone. *Addictive Behavior, 14,* 307–326

Anglin, M. D., & Hser, Y. (1990). Legal coercion and drug abuse treatment. In J. Inciardi (Ed.), *Handbook on drug control in the United States* (pp. 235–247). Westport, CT: Greenwood Press.

Ball, J. C., & Ross, A. (1991). *The effectiveness of methadone maintenance treatment.* New York: Springer-Verlag.

Bebbington, P. E. (1976). The efficacy of Alcoholics Anonymous: The elusiveness of hard data. *British Journal of Psychiatry, 128,* 572–580.

Bloise, J. O., & Holder, H. D. (1991). Utilization of medical care by treated alcoholics: Longitudinal patterns by age, gender, and type of care. *Journal of Substance Abuse, 3*(1), 13–27.

Cahillane, B. (1996, July 1). Certification information. *International Association for Addictions and Offender Counselors*.

Carroll, K. M., Rounsaville, B. J., Nich, C., Gordon, L. T., Wirtz, P. W., & Gawin, F. (1994). One year follow-up of psychotherapy and pharmacotherapy for cocaine dependence. *Archives of General Psychiatry, 51,* 989-997.

Dole, V. P., Robinson, J. W., & Orraga, J., et al (1969). Methadone treatment of randomly selected criminal addicts. *New England Journal of Medicine, 280,* 1372-1375.

Doroff, D. R. (1977). Group psychotherapy in alcoholism. In B. Kissin & H. Begleiter (Eds.), *The biology of alcoholism: Treatment and rehabilitation of the chronic alcoholic* (Vol. 5). New York: Plenum.

Doweiko, H. (1990). *Concepts of chemical dependency*. Pacific Grove, CA: Brooks/Cole.

Emerick, C. D. (1989). Alcoholics anonymous: Membership characteristics and effectiveness as treatment. In M. Galaner (Ed.), *Recent developments in alcoholism, Vol. 7: Treatment research* (pp. 37-53). New York: Plenum Press.

Emerick, C. D., Tonigan, J. S., Montgomery, H. A., & Little, L. (1993). Alcoholics Anonymous: What is currently known? In B. S. McCrady & W. R. Miller (Eds.), *Research on Alcoholics Anonymous: Opportunities and alternatives*. Piscataway, NJ: Rutgers Center of Alcohol Studies.

Feigelman, W., Hymany, M. M., Amann, K., & Feigelman, B. (1990). Correlates of persisting drug use among former youth multiple drug abuse patients. *Journal of Psychoactive Drugs, 22,* 634-641.

Fox, R. (1962). Group psychotherapy with alcoholics. *International Journal of Group Psychotherapy, 12,* 56-63.

Fox, V., & Lowe, G. D. (1967). Day-hospital treatment of the alcoholic patient. *Quarterly Journal of Studies on Alcohol, 29,* 634-641.

Fram, D. H. (1990). Group methods in the treatment of substance abusers. *Psychiatric Annals, 20*(7), 385-388

Gallegos, K. V., Lubin, B. H., & Bowers, C. (1992). Relapse and recovery: Five to ten year follow-up study of chemically dependent physicians—The Georgia experience, *MMJ, 41*(4), 284-318.

George, R. L. (1990). *Counseling the chemically dependent: Theory and practice*. Englewood Cliffs, NJ: Prentice Hall.

Gerstein, D. R. (1994). Outcome research. In M. Galanter & H. D. Kleber (Eds.), *Textbook of substance abuse treatment* (45-64). Washington, DC: American Psychiatric Press, Inc.

Gerstein, D. R., & Harwood, H. J. (Eds.). (1992). *Treating drug problems* (Vol. 2). Washington, DC: National Academy Press.

Gilmore, K. M. (1985). Hazelden primary residential treatment program: Profile and patient outcome. Center City, MN: Hazelden Educational Materials.

Gunne, L., & Grombladh, L. (1984). The Swedish methadone maintenance program. In G. Serban (Ed.), *The social and medical aspects of drug abuse* (pp. 205-213). Jamaica, NY: Spectrum Publications.

Guydish, J., Werdegar, D., Chan, M., Nebelkopf, E., & Acampora, A. (1994). Challenges in developing a drug abuse day treatment program. In B. Fletcher, J. Inciardi, & A. Horton (Eds.), *Drug abuse treatment: The implementation of innovative approaches* (pp. 195-207). Westport, CT: Greenwood Press.

Hargreaves, W. A. (1983). Methadone dose and duration for methadone treatment. In J. R. Cooper, F. Altman, B. S. Brown, et al (Eds.), *Research on the treatment of narcotic addiction: State of the art*. NIDA Treatment Research Monograph (pp. 19-79) (DHHS Publication No. ADM 83-1281).

Heath, D. B. (1989). American Indians and alcohol: Epidemiological and sociocultural relevance. In D. L. Spiegler, D. A. Tate, S. S. Aitken, & C. M. Christian (Eds.), *Alcohol use among U.S. ethnic minorities* (NIAAA Research Monograph No. 18, pp. 207-222) Washington, DC: Government Printing Office.

Hendricks W. J. (1971). Use of multifamily counseling groups in treatment of male narcotic addicts. *International Journal of Group Psychotherapy, 21,* 34-90.

Hesselbrock, M., Meyer, R., & Keener, J. (1985). Psychopathology in hospitalized alcoholics. *Archives of General Psychiatry, 42,* 1050–1055.

Hester, R. K., & Miller, W. R. (1989). Self-control training. In R. K. Hester & W. R. Miller (Eds.), *Handbook of Alcoholism Treatment Approaches: Effective Alternatives* (pp. 141–150). Elmsford, NY: Pergamon.

Hester, R. K. (1994). Outcome research: Alcoholism, in *Textbook of Substance Abuse Treatment,* Washington, DC: American Psychiatric Press.

Hoffman, N. C., & Miller, N. S. (1992). Treatment outcomes for abstinence-based programs. *Psychiatric Annals, 22.*

Horn, J. L., & Wanberg, K. (1973). *Females are different: On the diagnosis of alcoholism in women.* Proceedings of the First Annual Alcoholism Conference of the National Institute on Alcohol Abuse and Alcoholism. Washington, DC: U.S. Government Printing Office.

Hubbard, R. L., Marsden, M. E., Rachal, J. V., et al (1989). Drug abuse treatment: A national study of effectiveness. Chapel Hill, NC: The University of North Carolina Press.

Institute of Medicine. (1990). Prevention and Treatment of Alcohol Problems: Research Opportunities. Washington, DC: National Academy Press.

Joanning, H., Quinn, W., Thomas, F., & Mullen, R. (1992). Treating adolescent drug abuse: A comparison of family systems therapy group therapy, and family drug education. *Journal of Marital and Family Therapy, 18*(2).

Kang, S., Kleinman, P. H., Woody, G. E., Millman, R. B., Todd, T. C., Kemp, J., & Lipton, D. S. (1991). Outcomes for cocaine abusers after once-a-week psychosocial therapy. *American Journal of Psychiatry, 148*(5), 630-635.

Kaufmann, E. (1979). The application of the basic principles of family therapy to the treatment of drug and alcohol abusers. In E. Kaufmann & P. Kaufmann (Eds.), *Family therapy of drug and alcohol abuse.* New York: Gardner Press.

Kay, D. C. (1985). Substance abuse in psychopathic states and sociopathic individuals. In A. 1. Altennan (Ed.), *Substance abuse and psychopathology* (pp. 910–920). New York: Plenum.

Khantzian, E. J. (1987). A clinical perspective of the cause—consequence controversy in alcohol and addictive suffering. *Journal of the American Academy of Psychoanalysis, 15,* 521-537.

Khantzian, E. F. (1985). The self-medication hypothesis of addictive disorders: Focus on heroin and cocaine dependency. *American Journal of Psychiatry, 142,* 1259-1264.

LaRosa, J. C., Lipsius, J. H., LaRosa, J. H. (1974). Experience with a combination of group therapy and methadone maintenance in the treatment of heroin addiction. *International Journal of Addiction, 9,* 605–617.

Laundergan, J. C. (1982). *Easy does it! Alcoholism treatment outcomes: Hazelden and the Minnesota model.* Center City, MN: Hazelden Educational Materials.

Lawson, A. (1994). Family therapy and addictions. In J. Lewis (Ed.), *Addictions: Concepts and strategies for treatment.* Gailhersburg, MD: Aspen Publication.

Leach, B. (1973). Does AA really work? In P. G. Bourne & R. Fox (Eds.), *Alcoholism: Progress in research and treatment* (pp. 245-284). New York: Academic Press.

Leach, B., & Norris, J. L. (1977). Factors in the development of Alcoholics Anonymous (AA). In B. Kissiw & H. Beglerter (Eds.), *The biology of alcoholism: treatment and rehabilitation of the chronic alcoholic* (Vol. 5) (pp. 441–543). New York: Plenum Press.

Lesser, E. (1976). Behavior therapy with a narcotics user: A case report: Ten-year follow-up. *Behavior Research and Therapy, 14*(5), 381.

Levin, J. P. (1987). *Treatment of alcoholism and other addictions: A self-psychology approach.* Northwall, NJ: Jason-Aronson.

Lewis, J. A., Dana, R. Q., & Blevins, G. A. (1994). *Substance abuse counseling: An individual approach* (2nd ed.). Pacific Grove, CA: Brooks/Cole.

Lewis, R. A., Piercy, F. P., Sprenkle, D. H., & Trepper, T. S. (1991). The Purclue brief family therapy model for adolescent substance abusers. In T. Todd & M. Selekman (Eds.), *Family therapy approaches with substance abusers* (pp. 29–48). Needham Heights, MA: Allyn & Bacon.

Liepman, M. R., Nirenberg, T. D., Begiw, A. M. (1989). Evaluation of a program designed to help families and significant others to motivate resistant alcoholics into recovery. *American Journal of Drug and Alcohol Abuse, 15,* 209-221.

Locke, D. W., (1992, July). Personal conversation.

Madsen, W. (1974). The American alcoholic. Springfield, IL: Charles C. Thomas.

Mayfield, D. (1985). Substance abuse in the affective disorders. In A. I. Alterman (Ed.), *Substance abuse and psychopathology* (pp. 69-90). New York: Plenum.

McCrady, B. S. (1982). Conjoint behavioral treatment of an alcoholic and his spouse. In W. M. Hay & P. E. Nathan (Eds.), *Clinical case studies in the behavior treatment of alcoholism* (pp. 127-156). New York: Plenum.

McCrady, B. S. (1986). The family in the change process. In W. R. Miller & N. H. Heather (Eds.), *Treating addictive behaviors: Processes of change* (pp. 305–318). New York: Plenum.

McGlothlin, W. H., & Anglin, M. D. (1981). Shutting off methadone: Costs and benefits. *Archives of General Psychiatry, 38,* 885–892.

McLellan, A. T., Alterman, A. I., Metzger, D. S., Grissom, G. R., Woody, G. E., Luborsky, L., & O'Brien, C. P. (1994). Similarity of outcome predictors across opiate, cocaine, and alcohol treatments: Role of treatment services. *Journal of Consulting and Clinical Psychology, 62*(6), 1141–1158.

McLellan, A. T., O'Brien, C. P., Metzger, D. et al (1992). How effective is substance abuse treatment—compared to what? In C. P. Brien & J. J. Jaffe (Eds.), *Addictive States,* pp. 231–251. New York: Raven Press, Ltd.

Miller, W. R., Rollnick, S. (1991). *Motivational interviewing.* New York: Guilford.

Montgomery, H. A., Miller, W. R., & Tonigan, J. S. (1995). Does Alcoholics Anonymous involvement predict treatment outcomes? *Journal of Substance Abuse Treatment, 12*(4), 241-246.

Nace, E. P. (1987). *The treatment of alcoholism.* New York: Brunner/Mazel.

O'Farrel, T. J. (1986). Marital therapy in the treatment of alcoholism. In N. S. Jacobson & A. S. Gurman (Eds.), *Clinical Handbook of Marital Therapy* (pp. 513–535). New York: Guilford.

O'Farrel, T. J., & Cowles, K. S. (1989). Behavioral marital therapy. In R. K. Hester & W. R. Miller (Eds.), *Handbook of Alcoholism Treatment* (pp. 183-205). Elmsford, NY: Pergamon.

O'Farrel, T. J., & Cutter, H. S. G. (1984). Behavioral marital therapy couples groups for male alcoholics and their wives. *Journal of Substance Abuse Treatment, 1,* 191-204.

Ogborne, A. C., & Glaser, F. B. (1985). Evaluating Alcoholics Anonymous. In T. E. Bratter and G. G. Forrest (Eds.), *Alcoholism and substance abuse: Strategies for clinical intervention.* New York: The Free Press.

Rawson, R. A., Obert, J. L., McEann, M. J., & Mann, A. J. (1985). Cocaine treatment outcome: Cocaine use following inpatient, outpatient, and no treatment. In L. S. Harris (Ed.), *Problems of drug dependence.* Proceedings of the 47th Annual Scientific Meeting, The Committee on Problems of Drug Dependence, Inc. National Institute on Drug Abuse Research Monograph 67. DHHS Pub. No. (ADM) 86-1448. Washington, DC: U.S. Government Printing Office.

Resnick, R. B., Washton, A. M., Stone-Washton, W., et al. (1981). Psychotherapy and naltresone in opioid dependence. In L. S. Harry (Ed.), *Problems of drug dependence,* National Institute on Drug Abuse Research Monograph 67. DHHS Pub. No. (ADM) 86-1448. Washington, DC: U.S. Government Printing Office.

Roszell, D. K., & Chaney, E. F. (1982). Autogenic training in a drug abuse program. *International Journal of the Addictions, 17*(8), 1337-1350.

Schilit, R., & Gomberg, E. S. (1991). *Drugs and behavior.* Newbury Park, CA: Sage.

Schuster, R. (1978–1979). Evaluation of a reality therapy stratification system in a residential drug rehabilitation center. *Drug Forum, 7*(1), 59–67.

Sells, S. B. (Ed.). (1974). *Studies of the effectiveness of treatments for drug abuse, Vol. 1, evaluation of treatments.* Cambridge, MA: Ballinger Publishing Company.

Simpson, D. D., Savage, L. J., Lloyd, M. R. (1979). Follow-up evaluation of treatment of drug abuse during 1969 to 1972. *Archives of General Psychiatry, 36,* 772–780.

Solomon, S. D. (1982). Individual versus group therapy: Current status in the treatment of alcoholism. *Advances in Alcohol and Substance Abuse, 2,* 69–86.

Stanton, M. D., & Todd, T. C. (1982). *The family therapy of drug abuse and addiction.* New York: Guilford.

Stein, A., & Friedman, E. (1971). Group therapy with alcoholics. In H. I. Kaplan & B. J. Sadock (Eds.), *Comprehensive Group Psychotherapy.* Baltimore, MD: Williams & Wilks.

Steinglass, P. (1987). *The alcoholic family.* New York: Basic Books.

The biology of alcoholism: Treatment and rehabilitation of the chronic alcoholic (Vol. 5). New York: Plenum.

Todd, T. C., & Selekman, M. (1991). Family therapy with adolescent substance abusers. Needham Heights, MA: Allyn & Bacon. Traynor v. Turnage. (1988). 99 LED 2nd 618.

Ulmer, R. A. (1977). Behavior therapy: A promising drug abuse treatment and research approach of choice. *International Journal of the Addictions, 12*(6), 777–784.

Vannicelli, M. (1982). Group psychotherapy with alcoholics. *Journal of Studies of Alcoholism, 43,* 17-37.

The Walden House Day Treatment Program. (1995). A day treatment program in a therapeutic community setting: Six-month outcomes. *Journal of Substance Abuse Treatment, 12*(6), 441-447.

Walker, R. D., Benjamin, G. A., Kwlahan, D., & Walker, P. S. (1989). American Indian alcohol misuse and treatment outcome. In D. L. Spiegler, D. A. Tate, S. S. Aitken, & C. M. Christian (Eds.), Alcohol use among U.S. ethnic minorities (NIAAA Research Monograph No. 18, pp. 301-311). Washington, DC: Government Printing Office.

Washton, A. M., & Stone-Washton, N. S. (1991). *Step zero: Getting to recovery.* Center City, MN: Hazelden Educational Materials.

Washton, A. M. (1989). *Cocaine addiction: Treatment, recovery, and relapse prevention.* New York, W. W. Norton.

Washton, A. M. (1990). Cocaine recovery workbooks. Center City, MN: Hazelden Education Materials.

Weiner, H. (1975). Methadone counseling: A social work challenge. *Journal of Psychedelic Drugs, 7*(4), 381–387.

Woody, G. E., Luborsky, L., McLellan, A. T., et al. (1983). Psychotherapy for opiate addicts: Does it help? *Arch Gen Psychiatry, 40,* 639—648.

Woody, G. E., Mercer, D., & Luborsky, L. (1994). Individual Psychotherapy. In M. Galanter & H. D. Kleber (Eds.), *Textbook of substance abuse treatment.* Washington, DC: American Psychiatric Press, Inc.

Yalom, I. D. (1994). *The theory and practice of group psychotherapy.* New York: Basic Books.

Yalom, I. D. (1974). Group psychotherapy and alcoholism. *New York Academy of Science, 233,* 85–103.

Zweben, J. E. (1987). Recovery-oriented psychotherapy: Facilitating the use of 12-step programs. *Journal of Psychoactive Drugs, 19,* 243–251.

Index